The Chinese Peasant Economy

Harvard East Asian Series 47

The East Asian Research Center at Harvard University administers research projects designed to further scholarly understanding of China, Japan, Korea, Vietnam, and adjacent areas.

The Chinese Peasant Economy

AGRICULTURAL DEVELOPMENT IN HOPEI
AND SHANTUNG, 1890–1949

Ramon H. Myers

Harvard University Press, 1970
Cambridge, Massachusetts

Distributed in Great Britain by Oxford University Press, London

Preparation of this volume has been aided by a grant from
the Ford Foundation

Library of Congress Catalog Card Number 79–115189

SBN 674–12451–0

Printed in the United States of America

This book is affectionately dedicated to the scholars of the Third Unit (unit for research of old customs), North China Economic Research Branch of the South Manchurian Railway Company.

Andō Shizumasa
Hatada Takeshi
Hayakawa Tamotsu
Honda Etsurō
Konuma Tadashi
Liu Chün-jen
Murata Kyūichi
Niida Noboru
Sano Riichi
Shiomi Kingarō
Suginohara Shunichi (team leader)
Sugiura Kanichi
Yamamoto Akira

Acknowledgments

In paying tribute to those who were involved in this study, I think it is useful to describe exactly how the present study came to be written. In June of 1964 my family and I left Hong Kong for Australia. I had accepted a three year Research Fellowship in the Department of Economics of the Research School of Pacific Studies of the Australian National University. Australia may appear to some as an unlikely location for the study of Chinese economic history, but I want to convince these skeptics this is not the case. I found Canberra an ideal location for research: calm, isolated from turmoil, and with able minds pursuing new knowledge. In short, I had happily stumbled upon a stimulating institution committed to the aim of supporting good scholarship.

My initial plan was to write some essays on salient problems of modern Chinese economic history. Contemporary China was difficult to study. How was it possible to measure any sort of economic change for such a brief period and understand its significance without first determining some suitable benchmarks for the pre-1949 period? Furthermore, how could the impact of new economic policy be properly assessed without understanding how this traditional economy had responded to outside influences after the mid-nineteenth century?

After outlining some topics for research related to the 1880–1949 period and submitting these for departmental consideration, I commenced the first essay, a historical study of a north China village. Previous Chinese village studies had been descriptive pieces for a single point of time. I hoped to show how one village had evolved since the late nineteenth century by using information obtained from Japanese village surveys in Hopei between 1939 and 1943. After completing the first draft, I began to realize the enormous importance of these village materials. I had only skimmed them most superficially. They contained enough information to write four or five studies showing village change over time. Why not relate village change to the development of north China for the same period? The problem now became analytical and more challenging. It would be necessary to combine the micro-analysis of villages with the macro-analysis of regional development. The nexus between expanding urban centers and the village economy would have to be identified and examined. Here was a topic suitable for a monograph. I abandoned the essays and began again.

Further research, however, was only possible if more materials dealing with north China could be collected and examined. Thanks to my department chairman Professor Heinz Arndt and the director of the Research School of Pacific Studies, Sir John Crawford, I received financial support for six months of travel to Taiwan, Japan, and the United States to visit such libraries as Tōyō Bunko and Tōyō Bunka Kenkyūjo in Tokyo and the libraries of the University of California (Berkeley) and Stanford University. Upon returning to Canberra I spent the remainder of 1965 writing the first draft. When problems of method arose, my colleague David M. B. Butt never hesitated to drop his work and give me encouragement and advice. Mr. Butt later read two drafts of the manuscript and continually prodded me to revise and clarify the text. I was also assisted by my research assistant Mrs. Mary Vere Jones who compiled the tables in the statistical appendix relating to the thorny problem of Chinese crop statistics.

The manuscript's first draft was sent to scholars in Taiwan, Hong Kong, Japan, United States, and England. By mid-1966 useful critical comments had been received from such scholars as Ch'uan Han-sheng of New Asia College, Muramatsu Yūji of Hitotsubashi University, G. William Skinner of Stanford University, Dwight Perkins of Harvard University, C. K. Yang of the University of Pittsburgh, and Niida Noboru who was then in London.

A. V. Chayanov's *Peasant Farm Organization* had just been translated and published.* This study convinced me that the peasant economies of Russia and China had much in common during the first quarter of this century. I decided to revise the manuscript drastically and develop a new section that would treat family farm organization. The sections relating to family farm cycle and the use of land, labor, and capital by the peasant farm were inspired by Chayanov's study. My debt to him is enormous.

By the fall of 1966 a second draft had been completed. Meanwhile, a new project had begun to take form in the department. Dr. R. Shand was organizing colleagues to contribute to a study of Asian agricultural development. I was asked to write an essay on Taiwan agricultural history, and for this purpose the department again generously financed a two month field trip to Japan and Taiwan in October and November of 1966. This trip gave me the opportunity to collect additional materials for the north China study and meet with a group of Japanese scholars at the Tōyō Bunka Kenkyūjo of Tokyo University. Thanks to Professor Banno Masataka of Tokyo Metropolitan University and Professor Fukushima Masao of Tokyo University a seminar was organized to discuss the first draft of my manuscript. Several of the scholars who participated actually had taken part in the 1939–1943 north China village surveys. This proved to be a most fruitful meeting, and I left Japan convinced that I had not misinterpreted these village documentary materials.

In passing I must mention my long friendship and correspondence with Professor Amano Motonosuke. Professor Amano needs no introduction to China specialists. His many publications on Chinese farm economy and

* Daniel Thorner, Basile Kerblay, R. E. F. Smith, eds., *A. V. Chayanov on the Theory of Peasant Economy* (Homewood, Ill.: Richard D. Irwin, Inc., 1966).

rural technology and his life-long association with the South Manchurian Railway Company have established him as one of the world's leading authorities on the Chinese peasant economy. Our correspondence began in 1963 and still continues. Whenever I was confronted with some difficulty of interpreting a measurement unit or textual reference, Professor Amano soon supplied me with the necessary information. He also loaned me from his personal library books which are unavailable in the archives and on occasion sent me various essays pertinent to my research. His wise advice and continual encouragement have been a constant inspiration for me.

In early 1967 I set about finishing the second major draft. I was ably helped in this chore by my new research assistant Mrs. Moira Salter. Special thanks are also in order for Mrs. Heather Harding, departmental secretary, for constructing charts and for the Cartography Unit of the Department of Geography for maps.

In the summer of 1967 I was invited by the East Asian Research Center to spend an academic year at Harvard University. My research fellowship was nearly terminated, and after nearly four years abroad my family and I returned to the United States. The manuscript was circulated among scholars of the East Asian Research Center, and I sent a copy to Professor A. B. Lewis, an agricultural economist, then attached to the Agricultural Development Council, New York. Professors Ezra Vogel, Dwight Perkins, and Ardron B. Lewis read the entire manuscript and gave me much constructive advice for further revision. In December I submitted the final, revised draft to the East Asian Research Center. I am grateful to the Center for sponsoring this publication. The staff of the Center assisted me in putting the notes and bibliography in proper order and Miss Daisy Kwoh of Yale University helped me compile the glossary.

Every scholar owes a special, unpayable debt to his family, and in this case the efforts and sacrifice of my wife deserve some comment. She assisted me in matters of translation, and even more important, endured without complaint the difficulties and uncertainties that are bound to arise during a long period abroad. It was her suggestion that I dedicate this work to the team of Japanese scholars whose field work made this study possible.

Coral Gables, Florida, 1969 R.M.

Contents

Tables

APPENDIX TABLES

Figures

Maps

I. The Problem

MEASUREMENT UNITS

Capacity measure

1 sheng	= 1 pint
10 sheng	= 1 tou
1 tou	= 1 peck
10 tou	= 1 shih
1 shih	= 100 catties weight

Weight

1 catty	= 1.3 lb or 0.6 kilograms
100 catties	= 1 picul or 0.6 quintal
1 picul	= 133.3 lb.

Square measure

1 mow	= 0.15 acre or 0.06 hectare
1 kuan mow	= 0.45 acre or 0.18 hectare

Currency value

1 yuan	= $0.29 (1937)
1 fen	= U.S. $0.0029 (1937)

Introduction

It was not until the eighteenth and nineteenth centuries that agriculture in Europe became more efficient and could support a larger nonfarming population than at any previous time. This revolution, for this is the only appropriate term to describe this new development, still has not spread to other parts of the world. In today's underdeveloped countries three quarters or more of the population still labor and live under poor and servile conditions reminiscent of our European ancestors during the Middle Ages.

China is one of the oldest agricultural countries of the world. Although its political and economic history differs considerably from other Asian and Western countries, the conditions under which its peasantry have farmed the land are similar to those in many agrarian societies. A study of traditional Chinese agriculture is useful and relevant to the present for four reasons.

An important concept used widely today by social scientists is that of a dual economy consisting of an advanced and a backward sector characterized by different production functions, factor endowments, and rates of population expansion. Some economic growth models postulate that, under conditions of rapid rural population growth and the spread of capital intensive production methods in the urban centers, the advance sector fails to influence favorably the backward sector and agriculture stagnates.[1] A study of Chinese agriculture can test the validity of growth models using the dual economy concept.

The rise of communism in the twentieth century has occurred primarily in rural societies. Is it likely to be repeated only in countries with a large peasant population? The emergence of Communist power in twentieth-century China was essentially a peasant movement led and manipulated by an urban intellectual elite. Knowledge about village society and economy can increase our understanding of why and how communism originated in the countryside and not in the cities.

The proposition that a large, poor farming population constitutes a major obstacle to the modernization of a backward country is frequently used to explain China's alleged retarded economic development. Only recently have we learned that manufacturing industries grew very rapidly, yet the economy did not experience a major transformation. One argument advanced to explain this phenomenon is that the agricultural sector "was not only lagging behind in the process of economic growth and modernization; it must also have been a very serious limiting factor, acting as a brake on economic transformation." [2] If true, it would be interesting to know precisely why and how the agrarian economy responded so slowly to the growth of cities and industry.

Finally, the study of Chinese traditional agriculture is justifiably interesting in itself. Before 1949, approximately seven or eight out of every ten people lived by farming. Agriculture was not only the main industry, it was the mainstay of the economy. Yet its historical development remains obscure and relatively unknown. The study of Asian peasant economies is still in its pioneering phase. Some excellent work has been done on Japanese agricultural history, but we are still very poorly informed about the recent rural histories of China, India, and countries of Southeast Asia.

The principal reason I chose to study the North China provinces of Hopei and Shantung was the existence of a unique collection of relatively unused historical materials.[3] Between 1939 and 1943 a series of rural surveys were made by Japanese researchers of the South Manchurian Railway Company research unit in Peking of villages in Hopei and Shantung. These efforts led to the collection of an enormous quantity of unprocessed materials about economic and social conditions and political administration in the north China countryside. These field reports and other historical materials related to these two provinces form the factual basis of this study.

The regional approach has merit in another respect. In the light of China's great size and topographical diversity, it is premature to study the entire country at this stage of our knowledge. Considerable documentary evidence exists for other regions. Once these are examined in detail, it may be possible to formulate propositions which can be compared to the findings of this study. If such comparisons show similar results, we will be in the possession of some well-tested theories which are valid and relevant to all of Chinese agriculture. If regional comparisons show different results, further research will be needed to refine our propositions.

The period 1890–1949 was critical in modern Chinese economic history because the country was opened to foreign trade and Western influences. A commercial and industrial enclave developed, but the historical relationship between this enclave sector and agriculture remains obscure and complex. My aim is to clarify and explain some of the interactions between these sectors.

My original plan was to use a quantitative approach to measure how extensively agriculture had been influenced by the enclave sector. I believed this could be demonstrated because there existed a large quantity of crop statistics for each county. My approach was to show zones of commercialization by maps which spatially identified how and where urban development had influenced rural land values, wages, and crop production. This approach eventually had to be abandoned because of insufficient price data.

Another approach had to be found. The problem was to find some method by which village survey data could be used to show regional agricultural development. I decided to present first a detailed, historical account of several villages for which evidence existed to determine whether any patterns of village economic organization and development existed. Once this was done, it became possible to shift to a more technical discussion of how peasants in this region organized farming. Most of the available village survey literature contains information on how peasant households used their labor, income, and land. This evidence was used to show how peasants allocated labor between farming and nonfarm work, invested in farming or nonfarm activities, and used their land for growing cash or subsistence crops. This analytic discussion established the basis for examining other developments taking place in this region: population growth, expansion of exports, import of food, the growth of cities. Through an analysis of household economic decision making together with a study of the broad economic changes taking place, an understanding of how the enclave and rural economies interacted and developed can be gained.

The final section further extends the analysis to show the many-sided relationships between villages and the market town and treaty port economy. The key question here is whether or not merchants, landlords, moneylenders, and local officials made it unnecessarily difficult for farmers to make a living from the land. Was there a mechanism by which these wealthy classes exploited the peasantry, and if so, can the degree of exploitation be measured? Is it possible to theorize convincingly that these socioeconomic classes obstructed rural development because of the particular type of relationship they had with villages? Which of these groups played a key role in influencing technological change, rural capital accumulation, and management of the land? Answers to these questions will show something of the commercial nexus binding villages to market towns and how the countryside was influenced by the growth of the enclave sector.

Much research and theorizing about the Chinese rural economy was done in the 1920s and 1930s, and our present views and explanations of what happened in agriculture can be traced to these two decades of research and writing. Therefore, I have made an inventory of this literature and attempted to classify various theories into two rough categories. The reader is urged to keep these in mind as we move through the village studies, a discussion of the economic organization of this family farm economy, and an analysis of the relationships between villages and the enclave sector of the economy. In this way traditional explanations are tested against the empirical findings of numerous village survey reports.

Despite Nationalist government attempts to unify and systematize measurement units in the early 1930s, these reforms made little headway at the county level because war intervened and interrupted the efforts of local officials to introduce the new standardized units in rural markets. In reality, units of weights and measures differed greatly between counties and between market towns of the same county. For example, within Wei county of Shantung the square measurement unit used to measure land, the *kung*, differed as much as 40 per cent between villages.[4] In Hopei the difference in land measure unit, the *mow*, was as large as 55 per cent for some districts. Even larger differences were recorded for capacity units to meas-

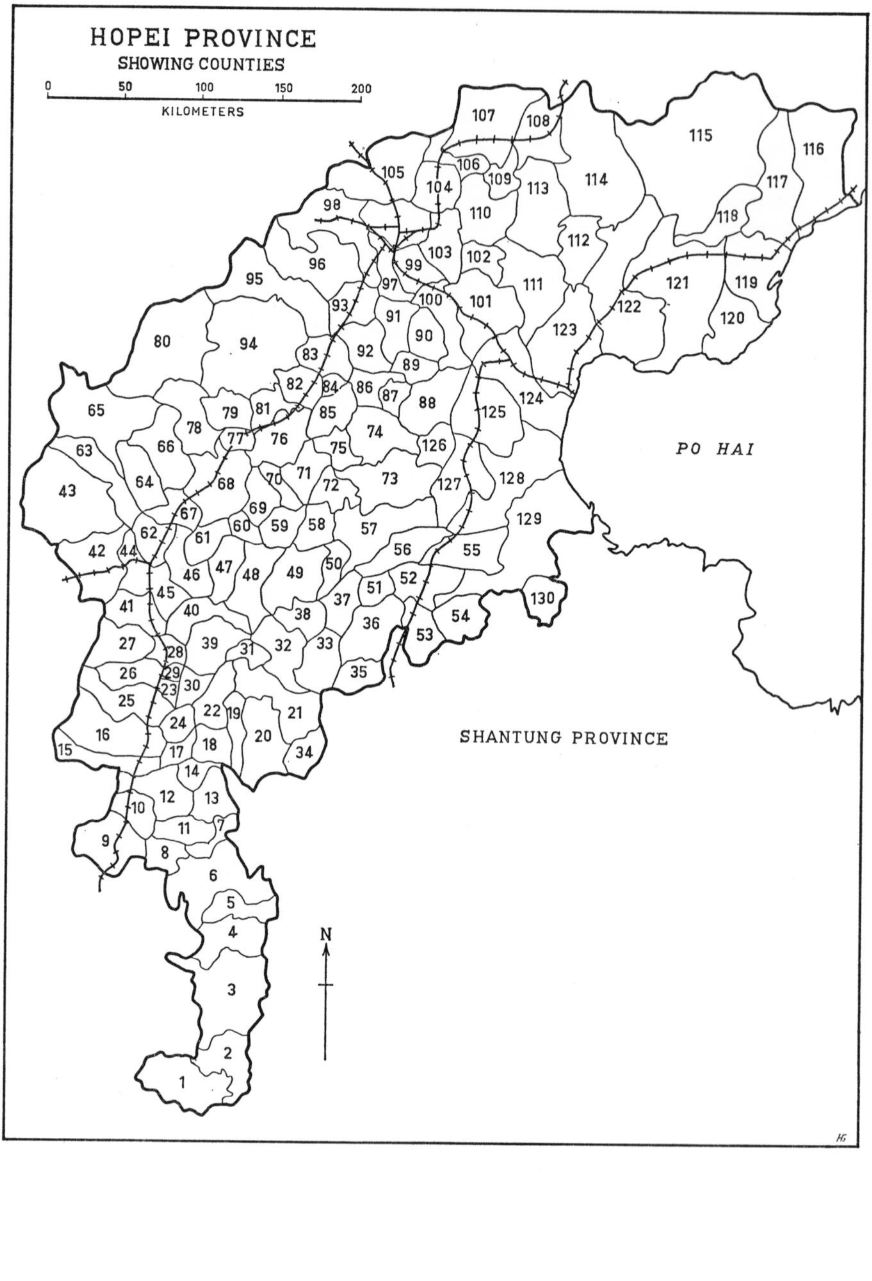
HOPEI PROVINCE
SHOWING COUNTIES
0 50 100 150 200
KILOMETERS
PO HAI
SHANTUNG PROVINCE
N

Map 1. Counties of Hopei Province

1. Ch'ang-yuan
2. Tung-ming
3. Pu-yang
4. Ch'ing-feng
5. Nan-lo
6. Ta-ming
7. Kuang-p'ing
8. Ch'eng-an
9. Tzu
10. Han-tan
11. Fei-hsiang
12. Yung-nien
13. Chu-chou
14. Chi-che
15. Sha-ho
16. Hsing-t'ai
17. Nan-ho
18. P'ing-hsiang
19. Kuang-tsung
20. Wei
21. Nan-kung
22. Chu-lu
23. Yao-shan
24. Jen
25. Nei-ch'iu
26. Lin-ch'eng
27. Ts'an-huang
28. Kao-i
29. Pai-hsiang
30. Lung-p'ing
31. Hsin-ho
32. Chih
33. Tsao-chiang
34. Ch'ing-ho
35. Ku-ch'eng
36. Ching
37. Wu-i
38. Heng-shui
39. Ning-chin
40. Chao
41. Yuang-shih
42. Ching-hsing
43. P'ing-shan
44. Huo-lu
45. Luan-ch'eng
46. Kao-ch'eng
47. Chin
48. Shu-lu
49. Shen
50. Wu-chiang
51. Fou-ch'eng
52. Tung-kuang
53. Wu-chiao
54. Ning-chin
55. Nan-p'i
56. Chiao-ho
57. Hsien
58. Jao-yang
59. An-p'ing
60. Shen-che
61. Wu-chi
62. Cheng-ting
63. Ling-shou
64. Hsing-t'ang
65. Fou-p'ing
66. Chu-yang
67. Hsin-lo
68. Ting
69. An-kuo
70. Po-yeh
71. Li
72. Su-ning
73. Ho-chien
74. Jen-ch'iu
75. Kao-yang
76. Ch'ing-yuan
77. Wang-tu
78. T'ang
79. Wan
80. Lai-yuan
81. Man-ch'eng
82. Hsü-shui
83. Ting-hsing
84. Jung-ch'eng
85. An-hsin
86. Hsiung
87. Hsin-chen
88. Wen-an
89. Pa
90. Yung-ch'ing
91. Ku-an
92. Hsin-ch'eng
93. Cho
94. I
95. Lai-shui
96. Fang-shan
97. Liang-hsiang
98. Wan-p'ing
99. Ta-hsing
100. An-tz'u
101. Wu-ch'ing
102. Hsiang-ho
103. T'ung
104. Shun-i
105. Ch'ang-p'ing
106. Huai-jou
107. Mi-yun
108. Hsing-lung
109. Ping-ku
110. San-ho
111. Pao-chih
112. Yu-t'ien
113. Su
114. Tsun-hua
115. Ch'ien-an
116. Lin-yü
117. Fu-ning
118. Lu-lung
119. Ch'ang-li
120. Lo-ting
121. Luan
122. Feng-jun
123. Ning-ho
124. T'ien-chin
125. Ch'ing-hai
126. Ta-ch'eng
127. Ch'ing
128. Ts'ang
129. Yen-shan
130. Ching-yun

ure grain. In Shantung, examples can be found where within a county the capacity unit, the *tou,* differed as much as one and two hundred per cent between market towns. The references to weights and measures in this study are not based on converting local measurement units with the well-known standardized units. The chart for measurement units used in this study only provides a very rough approximation to similar units used in market towns.

Geographical Conditions of Hopei and Shantung

In 1931 the combined populations of Hopei and Shantung totalled 55 million and exceeded that of the United Kingdom and Japan, which had populations of 49 and 50 millions respectively.[5] These two provinces contained a population equivalent to that of a large country, so that their study involves the examination of a rural economy of incredibly large size.

Hopei and Shantung fall between latitudes 32° and 40° and constitute most of the area John Lossing Buck refers to as the "wheat-kaoliang region." [6] The principal food crops were wheat, sorghum,[7] corn, and millet, followed by a variety of summer crops like the potato, peanut, cotton, soy bean, and vegetables. Wheat was the main winter crop. The growing season, less than 180 days, was short. Corn, millet, and sorghum were planted in early April, just when the harvest of winter wheat commenced. Cotton, peanuts, potatoes, and vegetables were planted soon after. These crops were intensively irrigated and weeded during the summer months, and their harvesting took place at various intervals beginning in late August and ending in mid-October. One of the major difficulties confronting farmers was the variability of rainfall.

North China has always been "that part of China-proper with the most frequent drought, the greatest mean annual rainfall variability, and the lowest average annual rainfall." [8] The central Asian steppes lost heat by radiation and cooled during the winter. High pressure mounted and cold, dry winds blew southwesterly throughout the winter making it impossible for anything except winter wheat and oil-seed crops to be grown. The opposite was true in the summer when central Asia heated and warm air expanded forming a low pressure area causing winds to be drawn from the Pacific ocean to blow northwesterly over China. These moist summer winds blew for only about four and a half months. The concentration of rainfall in the summer months, because of the contrast between deserts and ocean, was one cause of the high flood percentage in the summer.[9] If insufficient moist air was blown across the north China plain, rain did not fall during July and August, precisely when rainfall was most urgently needed. If a late summer rain followed a drought, the grain shoots were usually swept away by flood waters, which could not be absorbed rapidly by the caked soil.

The water supply problem would normally not have been serious if the major rivers originating in the T'ai Hang mountain range bordering the high north China plateau of Shansi, Kansu, and Mongolia did not carry tremendous quantities of silt to the gulf of Po Hai. The accumulation of silt at the lower reaches of these rivers in Honan, Hopei, and Shantung made it necessary to dike them. William Lockhard in the mid-nineteenth century wrote that the deposit of sand in the Yellow river bed had "caused a gradual elevation of the whole of the water-way, until the stream passed through the Empire at an elevation of several feet above the surrounding country, giving rise to frequent inundations from the breaking of the banks or bunds, erected on the river-bank which alone restrained the stream to its bed." [10] The Yellow river emerged from northern Honan, cut across the Grand Canal in Shantung, and flowed northeast to the Po Hai gulf. The Grand Canal extended from northern Kiangsu to Tientsin and flowed through western Shantung along the Hopei boundary line. Heavy summer rains often crushed the frail barriers erected by the peasants, and water gushed through inundating hundreds of square miles of cultivated land.[11]

The silt that accumulated on the bottom of the north China rivers made them too shallow to accommodate large ships. Although these rivers were long, their narrowness made navigation by any vessel difficult except along short stretches at their lower reaches. Before the war, there were numerous plans to build dams to control these rivers, but very few were constructed to form lakes and reservoirs to enable these rivers to irrigate the surrounding countryside.[12]

Soil conditions were also poor because "rainfall was insufficient to leach out most of the lime so that the soil was alkaline." [13] Large quantities of fertilizers were needed to make this soil yield a good crop. Native fertilizers barely contained enough of the appropriate chemicals to give the soil the nutrients it required. Tests conducted by the Litsun experimental station in Shantung in 1930 showed that chemical fertilizers contained more than double the amount of nitrogen contained in the compost placed on the fields,[14] and this was precisely the chemical needed most to raise yields. In many parts of Hopei and Shantung great quantities of carbonate of soda precipitated out on the soil giving it the appearance of a light snow fall. In the late nineteenth century an American consulate official in Tientsin wrote that the soil "was so saturated with it in many parts of this province as to render it useless for cultivation; and during some seasons of the year it rises to the surface of the ground, giving the country the appearance of being covered with snow." [15] A major reason for the great stretches of poor quality soil was poor drainage. The water table was uniformly close to the surface, rarely deeper than ten feet and normally within six feet. Wells were easily constructed, but in low, flat areas which frequently flooded and remained under water for long periods the water drained slowly. It was difficult "to pump water out of the substratum faster than it could come in,

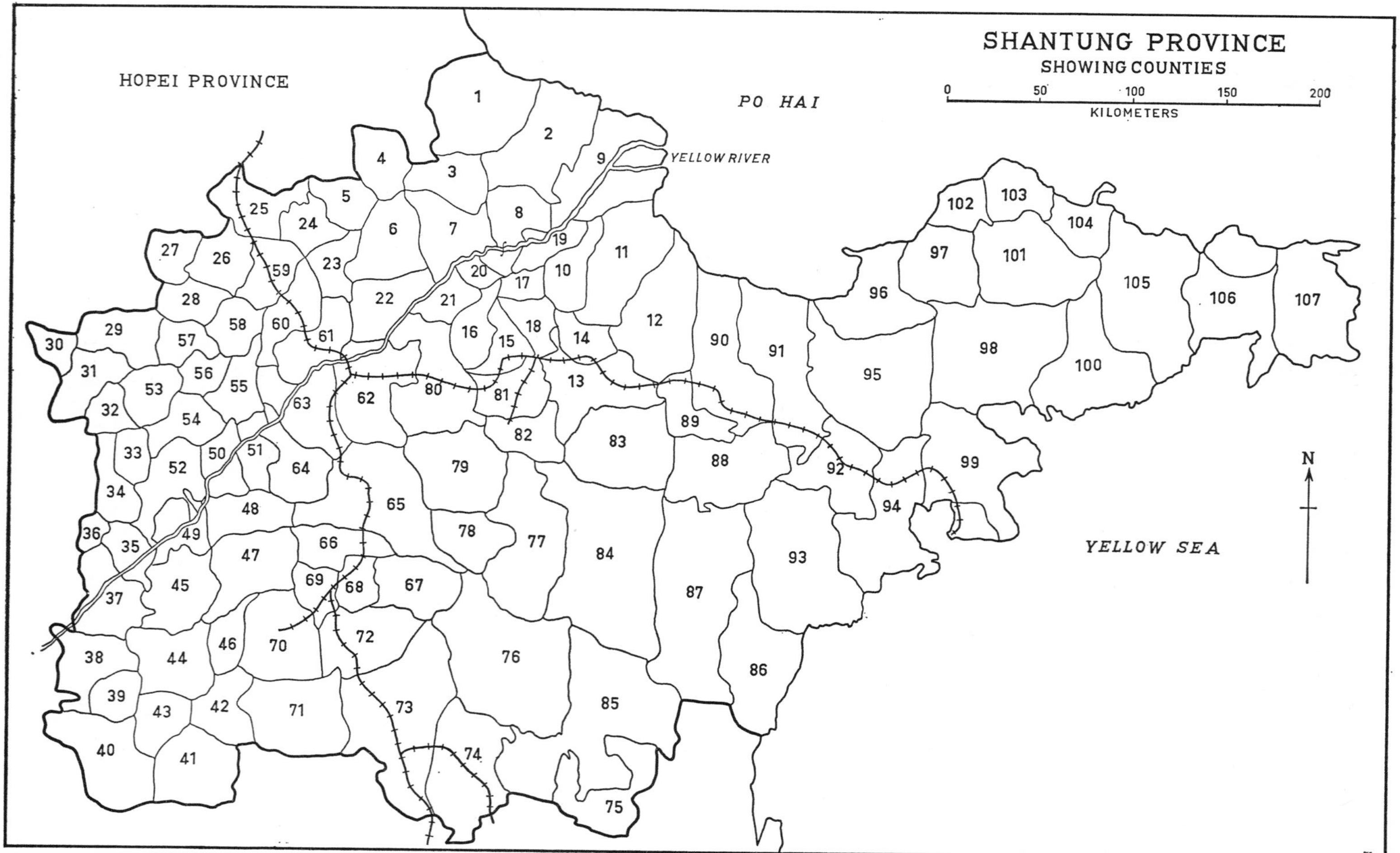
SHANTUNG PROVINCE
SHOWING COUNTIES
0 50 100 150 200
KILOMETERS
HOPEI PROVINCE
PO HAI
YELLOW RIVER
YELLOW SEA
N
1
2
3
4
5
6
7
8
9
10
11
12
13
14
15
16
17
18
19
20
21
22
23
24
25
26
27
28
29
30
31
32
33
34
35
36
37
38
39
40
41
42
43
44
45
46
47
48
49
50
51
52
53
54
55
56
57
58
59
60
61
62
63
64
65
66
67
68
69
70
71
72
73
74
75
76
77
78
79
80
81
82
83
84
85
86
87
88
89
90
91
92
93
94
95
96
97
98
99
100
101
102
103
104
105
106
107

Map 2. Counties of Shantung Province

1. Wu-ti
2. Chan-hua
3. Yang-hsin
4. Lo-ling
5. Te-p'ing
6. Shang-ho
7. Hui-min
8. Pin
9. Li-chin
10. Po-hsing
11. Kuang-jao
12. Shou-kuang
13. I-tu
14. Lin-tzu
15. Ch'ang-shan
16. Tsou-p'ing
17. Kao-yuan
18. Huan-t'ai
19. P'u-t'ai
20. Ch'ing-ch'eng
21. Ch'i-tung
22. Chi-yang
23. Lin-i
24. Ling
25. Te
26. En
27. Wu-ch'eng
28. Hsia-chin
29. Lin-ch'ing
30. Ch'iu
31. Kuan-t'ao
32. Kuan
33. Hsin
34. Chao-ch'eng
35. Fan
36. Kuan-ch'eng
37. Pu
38. Ho-che
39. Ting-t'ao
40. Ts'ao
41. Tan
42. Chin-hsiang
43. Cheng-wu
44. Chü-yeh
45. Yun-ch'eng
46. Chia-hsiang
47. Wen-shang
48. Tung-p'ing
49. Shou-chang
50. Tung-o
51. P'ing-yin
52. Yang-ku
53. T'ang-i
54. Liao-ch'eng
55. Shih-p'ing
56. Pa-p'ing
57. Ch'ing-p'ing
58. Kao-t'ang
59. P'ing-yuan
60. Yü-ch'eng
61. Ch'i-ho
62. Li-ch'eng
63. Ch'ang-ch'ing
64. Fei-ch'eng
65. T'ai-an
66. Ning-yang
67. Ssu-shui
68. Ch'ü-fu
69. Tzu-yang
70. Chi-ning
71. Yu-t'ai
72. Tsou
73. Teng
74. I
75. T'an-ch'eng
76. Fei
77. Meng-yin
78. Hsin-t'ai
79. Lai-wu
80. Ch'ang-ch'iu
81. Tzu-ch'uan
82. Po-shan
83. Lin-ch'ü
84. I-shui
85. Lin-i
86. Jih-chao
87. Chü
88. An-ch'iu
89. Ch'ang-lo
90. Wei
91. Ch'ang-i
92. Kao-mi
93. Chu-ch'eng
94. Chiao
95. P'ing-tu
96. I
97. Chao-yuan
98. Lai-yang
99. Chi-mei
100. Hai-yang
101. Ch'i-hsia
102. Huang
103. P'eng-lai
104. Fu-shan
105. Mou-p'ing
106. Wen-teng
107. Jung-ch'eng

thus accomplishing a lowering of the water table throughout the region of pumping." [16]

Hopei province contained 130 counties during the Republican period and had only one major port, Tientsin, to link the hinterland to foreign markets. Peking and Tientsin were the largest provincial cities although a number of medium-sized cities had rapidly mushroomed after railroads were built in the 1890s. The counties and railway lines are shown on Map 1.

Shantung province, extending into the Gulf of Po Hai, was a peninsula at lower elevation and contained 107 counties and two major railway lines. In the northeast the topography was hilly and the soil poor. In the west the land was flat, merely an extension of the Hopei plain, and very fertile because of deposits of rich loess soil over the countryside when flooding occurred. Numerous rivers emerged from the mountains of T'ai, Lu, and I in south-central Shantung and flowed north to the Po Hai gulf, and like the rivers of Hopei, they provided little irrigation or transportation for the surrounding countryside. The large port of Tsingtao provided an outlet for the export of crops such as cotton, tobacco, and peanuts. Map 2 shows the counties and railway lines.

Although farmers were at the mercy of the elements, their environmental conditions were not any more severe than in other grain producing regions of the world. The potential for elevating crop yield was enormous. Success depended greatly upon effective control of rivers during flood season and stabilizing the water supply by constructing more wells and reservoirs to catch rainfall. As long as additional technological improvements such as new seed varieties, pesticides, and chemical fertilizers were not introduced, however, such unfavorable geographical circumstances as the short growing season, erratic rainfall, and highly alkaline soils continued to be insuperable obstacles, which the peasants found difficult to overcome.

2. *Theories of China's Agrarian Problem*

Few writers concerned themselves with agriculture in China before 1920 and little of a scholarly kind was written about the peasantry.[1] Westerners traveling in rural areas commented only on the differences between Chinese and Western farming methods. They were more critical of the management of enterprise and the organization of commerce than they were of farming conditions in the interior. In 1878, the *North China Herald* expressed the opinion of many when it said, "We have many times in these columns alluded to the real actuating cause of most of the stagnation and distress in China, namely the grasping policy of the official class, which seeks to monopolize in its own hands all the profits from industry and trade." [2]

Although high officials in late nineteenth-century China agreed that "the greatest rewards in society must go to agriculture," [3] they were more concerned about raising tax revenue, many believing that the rural economy was healthy but that corruption reduced tax funds available to the government.[4] Ch'ing officials were too preoccupied with Western penetration of the Chinese interior and internal politics to consider the advantages of introducing Western technology to the agricultural sector.[5]

The 1920s and 1930s, however, were decades of intellectual ferment and energetic scholarly study. Revolutionaries and scholars became aware of disparities between the countryside and cities and focused their attention on the shortage of food production, the inequality of land distribution, and the plight of the peasants. In 1924 Sun Yat-sen declared, "The chief problem in the min-shen (livelihood) principle is the food problem." [6] In 1927 Mao Tse-tung, recognizing the peasantry as a source of untapped energy, urged party colleagues to realize that "The rise of the present peasant movement is a collosal event." [7] In 1935 Fang Hsien-t'ing of the Nankai Research Institute in Tientsin counted 102 monographs and 251 periodicals published between 1920 and 1935 dealing with the land problem. Of these, 90 per cent of the monographs appeared after 1927 and 87 per cent of the periodicals after 1933.[8]

Why was an interest in agriculture not prompted until after 1927? The answer is that China, although by now having many of the characteristics of a modern society, was in a transitional stage of development.[9] The rapid growth of urban population — over 4 and 5 per cent per annum after 1870 for the six largest cities — resulted from a large influx from towns and villages.[10] The increased number of schools, the emergence of newspapers, and the rise of a new urban intelligentsia that accompanied this urban expansion meant that new views and questions received widespread hearing. As more people traveled, as communications and transport improved, and as contact with foreigners became more frequent, those living in the cities were conscious of the widening gap between themselves and the villagers.

The Problem

In late 1931 economic depression struck at China's most vulnerable quarters: agriculture and handicraft. The decline of farm prices, the increased cost of credit, and the widespread bankruptcy of businesses and banks caused intolerable rural suffering. In the past, great famines, such as that which swept through north China in the mid 1870s, had received little comment and had sparked little interest in rural suffering, but now agricultural depression intensified the depression in urban commerce and industry. None could miss the distress signals from the countryside in the form of mounting indebtedness, increased land sales, and the rising number of landless peasants. Now, for the first time, the consequences of poor village harvests and the attempts of peasant associations to force landlords to reduce rents were described vividly in newspapers and served as the theme for short stories and novels.[11] The greater interdependency between villages and cities made urban dwellers acutely aware that cities were small islands of modernization in a sea of rural backwardness. This awareness prompted scholars, revolutionaries, and officials to take a closer look at the peasantry and to consider their problems seriously. Each group felt that, unless some way was found to reform agriculture, China could never be independent and strong and would fail to realize its potential for economic development.

A Taxonomy of Theories on the Agrarian Problem

Two main types of explanation of the backwardness of Chinese agriculture and peasant poverty can be found in the literature before World War II. The first is what I will call the distribution theory, and the second, the eclectic theory. This nomenclature does not do justice to the rich material presented by some writers. I make this dichotomy simply to separate and isolate for discussion two major theoretical approaches to the agrarian problem.

The distribution theory is that such a large portion of income was taken from the peasants in rents, high interest charges, taxes, and unfair terms of price exchange that they were left with little surplus to improve or enlarge their farms and raise their living standards. Landlords, merchants, small industrialists, usurers, and officials made up the social classes with the wealth and power to protect themselves by law and exploit the peasantry in a variety of ways. As these classes became richer, they used their wealth to accumulate more land and were thus able to exact a greater share of what the peasantry produced. Land ownership became more unequal, and a greater share of the agricultural surplus went to large landholders than to peasants. As population increased and the hegemony of landlord-merchant-moneylender-official classes took a larger share of the surplus as tribute, less was reinvested by peasants to raise yields and production. Agricultural technology and farming methods remained frozen at their traditional levels, and the peasantry became poorer.

The eclectic theory is that peasants were poor not only because a large proportion of their income was siphoned away by taxes, high rents, and the like, but also because production was depressed in the first place. This was due to improperly organized farms, poor transport, inadequate government support, and insufficient quantities of basic inputs to elevate yields. Because of the many interrelated factors, these writers regarded the problem as enormously complex, and they failed to present a unified theory to show which relationships were significant between the many elements. Their contribution was one of listing the major factors only.

Ch'en Han-seng

Ch'en Han-seng was a leading proponent of the distribution theory. As research fellow of the National Research Institute of Social Sciences in the Academia Sinica, Ch'en wrote several studies on the agrarian problem in the 1930s. These were distributed widely by the Institute of Pacific Relations and have become minor classics. Ch'en relied on village and county surveys to provide information on the distribution of land ownerships.[12] From this information Ch'en asserted that, in the early 1930s, the class of peasants with little or no land had become larger, and that Chinese agriculture was moving toward polarization as more peasants lost land that reverted to a powerful class of landlords.

The crux of the agricultural problem was peasant land hunger. Though random factors like famine, war, and banditry accounted for some losses of land, it was mainly the exploitive behavior of the landlord class which was responsible for the poverty of peasants and loss of their land. No pure and simple landlord class existed, and absentee landlords were numerous. The merchant, small industrialist, or official might also be a landlord. The village administration was "simply permeated by the omnipotent influence of the landlord" [13] and the tax, police, judicial, and educational systems were built by the power of this class. Landlords squeezed taxes, rents, and high interest charges from peasants, leaving them with little surplus as a cushion against adverse seasons or banditry.

Most of Ch'en's data are for the years 1928–1933, and though these data confirm much of what he asserts, the question remains whether he is, in fact, discussing a trend or a phase of a cycle. It could also be argued that agriculture between 1928–1933 was affected more by natural disasters, internal war, and the world depression. Ch'en's analysis is really a point of time analysis and does not take into account historical evidence. When he asserts that the peasantry had become poorer in recent years[14] he is, in effect, making inferences from limited data covering only two years.

Other scholars used the same framework as Ch'en's,[15] but they contended that the landlord and gentry classes allied themselves with imperialist groups of traders, bankers, and industrialists to become "cat's paws for the imperialists who controlled China's agricultural products and exploited the large masses of village laborers." [16] Cities did not develop as nodal centers stimulating progressive change in villages, because "imperialism did not permit the free development of capitalist agricultural development." [17] Industrial capital penetrated the village and through unequal price exchange drew wealth from the countryside to the cities leaving the villages poor. Even though peasants switched to growing industrial crops to prevent a deterioration of their living standards, they were unable to improve their lot. This was the conclusion reached by Ch'en Han-seng in his study of tobacco production in 127 villages in Shantung, Honan, and Anhwei provinces.[18]

American seed tobacco was introduced in 1913, and by 1934 it had caught on so rapidly that its cultivated area exceeded that of local tobacco. In some counties three fifths of the peasants grew this crop. Those with less land tended to adopt it sooner because higher prices enabled them to purchase food. Foreign and native tobacco companies gradually developed a tobacco-leaf purchasing system, but foreign companies with their huge financial resources grew more rapidly and came to purchase most of the raw tobacco marketed and to dominate the domestic cigarette market.

Ch'en claimed that when peasants marketed their tobacco they were dependent upon one buyer and were too ignorant of the weighing, grading, pricing, and paying procedures to obtain a fair price for their crop.[19] Tobacco production costs were three to five times higher than for other crops, and growing tobacco required much more labor and fertilizer than for grain crops. Peasants had to pay higher rents on land to grow tobacco, and interest rates were high for the credit they borrowed to buy fertilizer. As a result the peasants were caught in a cost-price squeeze which left them with little income to buy land. Many lost their land and became landless peasants or emigrated.[20] The penetration of industrial capital into the rural economy merely speeded up the process already at work creating a landless peasantry, and the introduction of cash crops left the peasants worse off than they were before.

Ch'en's data and argument are defective in two ways. First, his data for production costs only covered two years and do not show producers' profits over a long run. Second, high costs of production such as high land rents, interest rates, and fertilizer costs on tobacco land can also be interpreted to mean the peasant anticipated and earned a high income. Ch'en did not compare tobacco profits with that of other crops nor did he explain why so many peasants abandoned conventional crops to grow tobacco.

Ch'en's solution to the agrarian problem was not carefully spelled out in his writings, but he made inferences of the policy he would endorse. These were reforms to equalize land holdings and lower rents and interest rates. He was a firm believer in the view that China had to become independent of foreign control before the peasantry could acquire the bargaining power to gain fair prices for their crops.

L. Magyar

L. Magyar was a Russian economist on Borodin's team advising the Kuomintang between 1923 and 1925. From discussions with revolutionaries and scholars and a study of government agricultural statistics and rural survey reports, he wrote a study of Chinese agriculture, which appeared in Russian in 1931 and was later translated into Chinese and Japanese.[21]

Magyar's study is a remarkable blend of keen observation, common sense, and a rigorous framework akin to that of Ch'en Han-seng. Yet it is a neglected work and would certainly have ranked with the classics on Chinese agriculture had it been translated into English. Magyar relied greatly on the data supplied by the Agricultural-Commerce Bureau (the Nung shang pu), the Decennial Customs Reports, the Chinese Economic Monthly, and the village surveys of Wagner, Kulp, Volk, and Buck. He was aware of the limitations of government data because "they had been collected for the purpose of obtaining revenue," but he did not hesitate to use it whenever he thought it could strengthen his argument.

Although Magyar was impressed by the large number of people the impoverished soil could support, he believed the land was unlikely to produce more for three reasons. First, water control on rivers had broken down and village irrigation systems were in decline.[22] Second, cash crops were being grown more extensively, and land needed more fertilizer. But this input was scarce because peasants had to pay higher taxes, interest rates, and rents; furthermore, income from handicrafts had declined.[23] Third, whatever the reasons, animal husbandry and livestock supply had never been developed to the extent that the soil could benefit from more animal fertilizer and better soil preparation. In recent years the livestock supply had even been reduced because of wanton slaughter.

Magyar recognized that improved communications and transportation had evolved, handicraft industries had been stimulated through foreign trade, and more cash crops were being processed and exported, but he did not see how these developments could reverse the long-run trend of soil deterioration and stagnation in farm production. The major obstacle blocking agricultural progress was a social class structure responsible for the unequal distribution of land ownership.

Magyar believed that social class relationships determined the ownership of land and how it was used. He classified peasants into groups of rich, middle, and poor according to the amount of land they owned. From village data, Magyar observed certain characteristics of land use and farming, which he regarded as part of a process that had been taking place for some time.[24] On farms larger than 20 mow, peasants owned more livestock, but these farms accounted for only a small fraction of the total. For farms with less than 20 mow, more man-hours of labor had to be expended to compensate for the scarcity of livestock. On farms under 10 mow, the peasants' income was so little, that additional income had to be obtained from nonfarm activities. Wealthy peasants had better opportunities to provide for their families, but the majority of households having little land appeared to constitute an increasing share of the peasantry. More households were entering this group constantly because of the heavy exactions taken from them by landlords, moneylenders, officials, and merchants. At the same time the rural economy was characterized by overpopulation, a poverty-stricken peasantry, and a farming system based strictly on century-old techniques.

Magyar held out little hope for the success of the Kuomintang's proposed agrarian reform legislation of lowering tenant rents, extending tenant leases, and giving tenants the right to buy the land they rented.[25] These problems were too deeply rooted in socioeconomic institutions such as the land tenure system. Drastic surgery was required to eliminate the institutions which prevented the peasants from raising their living standards. This could best be done by creating soviets comprised of poor peasants and tenants with the power to expropriate landlord land and abolish the landowning system. He looked favorably upon the efforts of peasant associations in Kwangtung to do these very things as the correct solution to China's agrarian problem.[26]

Fei Hsiao-tung

Fei Hsiao-tung, an anthropologist well known for his field studies and illuminating essays on social structure, saw the agrarian problem as one of social and economic disintegration brought about by a breakdown of the traditional political and economic order. Fei contended that an equilibrium existed prior to 1840 between the countryside and the ruling elite, which rested upon a particular political and economic arrangement.

Standing between monarch and peasantry was a scholar-gentry class responsible for upholding tradition and supplying officials to administer the country. The scholar-gentry endeavored "to put forward a set of ethical principles which should restrict the forces of political power." [27] Although this class exercised no power, it possessed social prestige and special privileges, which it retained by promoting and justifying a social division of labor acceptable to the peasantry and legitimate to the monarch. This class instructed the peasants to labor and obey their rulers. It adopted a conservative policy of upholding the status quo and provided an effective political stabilizer for society for nearly two millennia.[28]

Theories of China's Agrarian Problem

By the turn of the twentieth century the scholar-gentry found it needed more income to live in the treaty ports. Many sought entry into the bureaucracy and resorted to corrupt practices to earn the necessary income, while others co-operated with compradors, warlords, and even bandits to extract more income from the peasantry. The cities attracted the energetic and talented, who fled the villages and market towns for city life.[29] This left a leadership vacuum in the countryside, quickly filled by local bullies eager to wring what they could from the little the peasants possessed.

Rural industry had always provided peasants with additional income by which a minimum standard of decent living had been maintained.[30] Fei concluded from his village studies that the peasantry had produced enough to support their families as long as they had some means of employment to supplement their farm income. This balance had been upset when lower priced, higher quality imports began to displace handicraft goods from local markets. With traditional handicraft industries in ruins, rural unemployment rose and purchasing power declined. Without access to additional income the majority of peasants with plots less than 10 mow could barely live.[31]

Although Fei did not adhere to the concept of unequal land distribution as the motive force causing a decline in peasant income, he believed that taxes, rents, and interest charges in the rural economy had to be reduced. A "lightening of the farmer's burden constituted the first pre-requisite in the task of rural reconstruction." [32] Fei opposed the idea of combining plots to make large farms because the rural population was already huge and land was scarce. Progress was only possible after peasants had accumulated some capital, and this could best be done through small cooperatives to buy raw materials and market goods. With these foundations "the large masses of the farming population [could begin] to start saving, and to invest in their own production enterprises," which, in turn, would create the demand for large-scale manufacturing to develop.[33]

The state could assist by enacting laws to lower peasant rents, by taxing landlords more heavily and using these funds to modernize transport and improve rural infrastructure, and by providing credit at lower interest.[34] By transferring income from the landlord class to the state, the first step toward solving the agrarian problem would have been taken.

John Lossing Buck

The field studies of John Lossing Buck produced considerable statistical evidence, which is still regarded as very trustworthy. Between 1922 and 1924 Buck conducted his first pilot rural survey using Chinese students to examine 2,866 farms in seventeen counties of seven provinces in north and east central China.[35] His second survey, undertaken between 1929 and 1933, covered 16,786 farms in twenty-two provinces.[36] The purpose of the latter survey was to examine land use and its determinates for different parts of the country rather than to study "the so-called agrarian situation, which may be thought of in terms of the political, economic, and social relationships between the farmers and other classes of society." [37]

After 1945 Buck began to write directly about China's agrarian problem and how it could be solved.[38] The problem was how to raise income and output in agriculture. Both depended on the proper combination of land, labor, capital, and technology and an efficient organization of farming. Peasant agriculture was backward for many reasons: land was improperly used; farms were too small; peasants had insufficient capital and limited access to new technology; there was little control over nature; primitive transport increased marketing costs. Chinese farming was characterized by an unusually large amount of intense labor utilization because of the shortage of capital. Yet the return on investment in farms was as low as 2 or 3 per cent per annum, and this hardly induced the wealthy to invest in agriculture. The long-run trend of substituting labor for scarce capital had to be reversed, more capital and technical skill had to be given to the peasants, and the pathetically low rate of profit raised.

Buck placed little faith on land reform as a solution to the agrarian problem: "Redivision of land, one of Sun Yat-sen's basic principles, would not change the man-land ratio but would, on the contrary, decrease the size of farms, reduce their economic efficiency and depress the standard of living." [39] The program of collective farming was still untested and must be considered too risky to introduce. The system of private farming could be improved greatly with the assistance of specific, low-cost government policies. Government could provide more credit at lower terms, improve marketing channels, establish extension service, correct abuses in the landlord-tenant system through legislation, register and measure land for land tax reform, and guarantee the peasantry better water control.[40] As for the seriousness of the land hunger problem, Buck believed the evils of the land tenure system had been greatly exaggerated. His data had led him to conclude that not more than 1 to 4 per cent of the total credit extended to farmers came from landlords. Nor was the number of tenants large because "over one-half of the farmers were owners, less than one-fourth were part owners and less than one-fourth were tenants." [41]

The policy measures required to transform agriculture naturally took time to introduce and carry through before their full impact could be felt. Buck believed that if these policies had a fair chance, China, in fairly short order, could feed its population and supply her industries with the necessary raw materials. But for this program to be implemented successfully, China needed a government which inspired the people and had its full confidence.

Richard Henry Tawney

In 1931 J. B. Condliffe of the Institute of Pacific Relations invited Richard Henry Tawney to visit various research institutes in China. The outcome of this short trip was a long memorandum presented at the Conference of Institute of Pacific Relations held in Shanghai in the same year and later published under the title *Land and Labour in China.* With little knowledge of Chinese history and contemporary conditions, Tawney yet managed to come to grips with the basic problems plaguing China. His essay presents no new statistics or information but the clarity of his analysis and his sure grasp of the complexity of the Chinese economy make this an outstanding study for its period. "The problems presented by the economic conditions of rural life in China are of two principal types. There are those, in the first place, which spring from natural or inherited disadvantages, such as poverty or exhaustion of soil, a deficient or irregular rainfall, the destruction of forests, rivers liable to flood, the physical limitations of the cultivable area and the immense number of human beings, which, as a result of past history, that area must support. There are those, in the second place, which have their source in defects of economic organisation or in social habits: the absence, for example, of a tolerable system of communications, the miseries inflicted by civil disorder, primitive methods of cultivation, the exploitation of the peasantry by dealers and money-lenders, the unsatisfactory character of land tenure in parts of the country, and the tyranny of a tradition which gives an artificial stimulus to the increase of a population already excessive." [42]

A host of forces converged, interacting along the way, to produce in circular, causal, and cumulative fashion a type and level of economic activity which resembles conditions of the Middle Ages. Tawney makes no attempt to disentangle this web of forces or factors or assign more weight to one category than the other, but he has raised many fascinating questions which still await research: what specific institutions caused land fragmentation and the trend toward small plots? How monopolistic or competitive were rural markets and what power did the middleman have over prices and production? What were the institutions that retarded technical improvement of agriculture? Why did animal husbandry fail to develop?

Tawney believed that the land tenure system was "a smaller evil than the inability of the farmer to get the best price for his produce, and his exploitation by the money lender." [43] He also argued that high transport costs severely limited the market and prevented the peasant from receiving a higher share of his crop price. Tawney listed a number of variables that undoubtedly influenced the size of the peasant's income. The task of sorting and specifying which are key variables and the sequence in which they operate remains to be done.

Tawney proposed no radical reform of free-hold farming but hoped a number of ventures would be started. Legal reforms were required to end abuses in the land tenure system. The state had to build an infrastructure of schools, roads, dams, and extension services for agriculture. Farmers could best help themselves by forming cooperatives to purchase materials and sell their crops.

In the final analysis, however, a successful solution of the agrarian problem could only be achieved in the context of broad industrialization, which shifted people out of agriculture.

Wilhelm Wagner

Wagner was a German agricultural economist who in 1911 went to Tsingtao to teach in a German-Chinese Middle School. He later worked at the Litsun Agricultural Experimental Station in Shantung where he continued his studies of agriculture both past and present. Wagner's *Die chinesische Landwirtschaft,* published in 1926, was a detailed study of the Chinese rural economy based on personal field work and many years of first-hand observation and reading.[44] Like Magyar's study, it made little impression on Western scholars, but it was inevitably translated into Japanese.

Wagner's account is in the best tradition of German scholarship. It begins with a ponderous and detailed discussion of the physical-geographical conditions of different regions. There is no historical analysis of why regional farming differences emerged. Wagner correctly sees that land tenure customs differed even within a single province. He attributed the tendency for farms to fragment and become smaller to the inheritance custom of dividing land equally among the sons.[45]

Poor transport and a shortage of fertilizer had made it impossible to raise output very high. Wagner believed that China was squandering valuable resources by exporting soy bean cake instead of using it to make fertilizer. He calculated that between 1911 and 1913 the quantity of soy bean cake exported was equivalent to the loss of 33,920 tons of nitrogen, 6,784 tons of potash, and 6,784 tons of phosphorous, which, if it had been processed to make chemical fertilizer, would have increased farm output greatly.[46]

From limited household budget data collected for three different sized farms, a large farm of 42 mow, a medium farm of 20 mow, and a small farm of 14 mow, Wagner showed that taxes were exceedingly heavy, tenant rents too high, and that for peasants with less than 15 mow an outside source of income was necessary.[47] A variety of historical conditions and institutions combined and interacted to make farm income very low. With the heavy burden farmers were compelled to pay, it was little wonder they had no surplus at the end of the year to make improvements. Wagner firmly believed that better technology, more fertilizer, and proper water control could turn the tide in the peasants' favor. Though he advocated no clear, systematic agrarian policy, his detailed remarks about rural conditions suggest that both a technical revolution and institutional reform were necessary prerequisites for modernizing agriculture.

Conclusion

There are many difficulties in classifying theories defining and explaining the prewar agrarian problem: it is necessary to distinguish between theories that rely upon only a few studies and those based upon wider coverage; it is necessary to sort out theories explaining long-run trends as opposed to those dealing with a problem at a single moment in time; finally, it is necessary to separate theories concerning only resource allocation and scarcity from those explaining comprehensively why scarcities existed at all.

The distributionist group relied much more on individual, specific studies and scraps of data to support their case than did the eclectics, who concentrated on presenting an enormous quantity of factual information. It is worth noting too that the distributionists, although differing in their emphasis, believed that the peasantry's lot had decidedly deteriorated since the mid-nineteenth century. The eclectics were more cautious in asserting this and less historical in their study of agriculture. The distributionists used the term "decline," which is vague and defies quantification. Their basic concern was to detect the mechanism by which the events they were describing could be explained. Their framework was broadly conceived in terms of social classes and institutions such as the land tenure system. The eclectics were more interested in noting the kinds of scarcities that existed in the rural economy and what might be done to remedy the problem.

Though the eclectics presented a wealth of factual information, the view of change in rural China as perceived by the distributionists seems to be held by many even today.[48] A summary of this view would probably be as follows.

Three major developments were taking place in the nineteenth century and continued on into the twentieth. There was persistent population expansion, which led to rural overcrowding and an increase in landless peasants. There was increased neglect of the rural economic infrastructure, the transport, irrigation, and flood control systems, through corrupt and inept bureaucratic management. And there was the existence of a landlord class which rack-rented the peasantry and tried to accumulate more land for itself. These developments interacted to produce rather alarming consequences for the rural economy. Land ownership distribution became more unequal, pressure on peasants to migrate became more intense, and the landless peasants became an almost inexhaustible source of manpower for bandits and warlord armies.

By the end of the nineteenth century three new developments began to take place and slowly impinged on the rural economy. First, the import of manufactured goods ruined many handicraft producers and forced peasants to sell their land. Second, the export of agricultural staples came under the control of powerful native and foreign traders, who through credit and price control were able to exploit smaller traders and peasant producers. Third, the establishment of Western enterprise in the treaty ports through special exemptions made it impossible for Chinese entrepreneurs to compete on an equal footing. In the treaty ports, the Western enclave sector grew at the expense of Chinese enterprises, and in the economy proper, the treaty ports grew at the expense of the rural hinterland. The economy was gradually being twisted in such a way that the cities, rather than stimulating the growth of the more backward countryside, merely exploited the village economy.[49] Instead of agricultural development, there was decline. Peasant living standards became more depressed, and the prospects for reform and a technological revolution in the countryside became more bleak. The rural economy merely reproduced itself in its own image.

This paradigm explains why the internal market was weak, the level of savings low, the rate of return on agricultural investment low, capital accumulation slow, and farm production at low levels. As a hypothesis, it explains a great deal of modern China's economic history, but it must be tested before it can be accepted as a standard, valid interpretation of China's recent economic development.

II. The North China Village

3. *Japanese Village Studies in North China*

The following studies of four villages is based upon a vast store of material resulting from half a century of serious and vigorous efforts by the Japanese to understand the institutions and customs governing Chinese society. These studies are based on surveys undertaken between 1939 and 1943 by Japanese researchers of the South Manchurian Railway Company.[1]

Japanese interest in Chinese rural conditions began in 1898 when General Kodama Gentarō and Gotō Shimpei were formulating a colonial policy in Formosa to develop its resources to serve Japan's long-range imperial interests. Gotō Shimpei, one of the most brilliant and dynamic bureaucrats of the late Meiji official administration, believed that before major reforms could be introduced a thorough study of social and economic institutions was necessary in order to anticipate their impact upon a traditional society and to minimize the costs and difficulties of colonial rule. Gotō asked Dr. Okamatsu Santarō, a professor of civil law at Kyoto Imperial University, to organize a group of scholars to study Formosan social and economic institutions. Their findings provided useful information for Gotō in introducing several key reforms which made later Japanese administration of the island an outstanding success.[2]

In 1907 Gotō was made the first president of the South Manchurian Railway Company. He again invited Dr. Okamatsu to examine rural customs in Liaotung and districts along the railway line in south Manchuria. These results were subsequently published in nine volumes between 1913 and 1915,[3] and like the Formosan studies they contained information on a wide range of institutions and customs relating to agriculture and commerce.[4] Unlike the Formosan studies, however, their results were never used to formulate Japanese colonial policy in south Manchuria because Gotō and his successors were unable to reach agreement with the military and civil administration on the long-run goals and strategies Japan should adopt in administering her south Manchurian interests. Okamatsu's work inspired further field research in Manchuria, and later the South Manchurian Railway Company's research office in north China, the Mantetsu chōsabu, continued this tradition.[5]

The Genesis of the Chūgoku nōson kankō chōsa *or the Survey of Chinese Village Customs*

In the fall of 1938 several Japanese research organizations, quite independently of one another, began to formulate ambitious programs for the economic and political study of mainland China. The North China Economic Research Office of the Mantetsu chōsabu considered cooperating with the Shanghai General Affairs Office on a ten-year plan of research "to shed light on Chinese society in order that its legal and economic system be revamped and a comprehensive plan formulated for Japan to follow with respect to her China policy." [6] In Tokyo the Tōa kenkyūjo (East Asian Research Office) and the Association for Promoting Learning in Japan proposed a study of land tenure systems in Shantung, Hopei, and Inner Mongolia, to be followed with field studies of commercial customs and organizations in Kiangsu and Chekiang.

The North China Economic Research Office worked out an arrangement with the Tōa kenkyūjo whereby both agreed to merge their financial resources, combine their research, and settle upon a division of labor between them. The research was to be organized by the Sixth Investigation Committee in the Tōa kenkyūjo under the chairmanship of Dr. Yamada Saburō. Dr. Yamada assigned to Professor Suehiro Itsutarō, a distinguished law professor at Tokyo Imperial University, the task of leading a group to survey rural customs in north China and asked Professor Tanaka Kotarō to assemble a team to examine commerce and credit in central China.[7]

A ten-year research plan with a budget outlay of 5.5 million yen was drawn up, and both groups were to be given a full-time staff of 14 scholars. Specified topics were to be studied each year, and the expenditures required to complete each phase of research were estimated.[8] Suehiro received permission to begin a north China rural study, and he instructed Dr. Suginohara Shunichi, head of the North China Economic Research Office in Peking, to select a staff, formulate a research plan, and decide upon the areas for field study.[9] Suginohara picked a team of half a dozen scholars trained in Oriental history and culture, and the group immediately began to plan their research.

In December 1941 the Sixth Investigation Office published a preliminary report on the north China rural survey with a leading article by Suehiro on methodology.[10] This is a remarkable essay, appearing as it did in wartime Japan in an atmosphere of strict censorship and control, by a member of an academic community generally given to Marxist theory. The essay is also interesting because it gives some hint as to how these rural surveys were conceived and their purpose.

Suehiro's essay begins by summarizing the approach set forth by Jules Henri Poincaré in "La Science et l'hypothèse" and then suggests how this method can be applied to the social sciences. Before studying a problem the researcher must conceptualize a hypothesis to explain the expected results of his research. The hypothesis should not limit the researcher to gather specific facts but should guide him to select and organize his data in a way which will either confirm or disprove the hypothesis. If the hypothesis cannot explain the results, it is modified or replaced by a new one, and further investigation is made. The researcher must explain the irregularities in his original results, repeatedly revise the original hypothesis, and continue his investigations until a satisfactory proposition is found. Suehiro wanted to formulate hypotheses and test them in the survey work being done in north China.

In a later memorandum Suehiro stated the purpose of the rural surveys and how they were to be organized and conducted. He considered the surveys as a means to examine the basic institutions determining the way of life of the peasantry so that this type of society could be better understood. "The purpose of this survey is to investigate legal practices and customs in Chinese society. However, I want to make it clear that it is not to collect reference materials for law and administrative purposes as was the survey of traditional customs carried out in Taiwan. Moreover, if one asks what is the ultimate purpose of these investigations, we may say that they are to observe the institutional setting within which the Chinese people live their lives. Our objective must be to record the essential characteristics of this society by portraying as vividly as possible its customs and practices." [11]

Suehiro urged that "standard villages be selected in zones" which showed uniform characteristics.[12] If unusual circumstances prevailed between villages within such a zone, different institutions and customs might be explained by the comparative approach. Finally, a research outline was to be drawn up to conduct research just as an engineer first constructs a blueprint to build a structure. "If we cannot make an outline and a plan of research, the research cannot be done. If we are successful and our research progresses, it is natural that we will find it necessary to re-examine our outline, revise it and modify it in various ways. Our research will move along on the basis of subsequent revisions of the outline, and when we consider it necessary to modify it still further we will do so." [13]

Suehiro's plan was to have the north China group formulate a research outline, select the villages for study, carry out the field research, and then assemble the data for the Tōa kenkyūjo in Tokyo. The Tokyo group's task was to examine this raw data and select relevant information for writing analytic studies of the north China rural society and economy. Field surveys were discontinued in 1943 before the Tokyo group had sufficient time to evaluate the raw data and write these studies. Apparently, these studies were to set forth propositions that could be tested by further village field work. Because of the time element, no suitable hypotheses were ever formulated, except in a study of land tenure, written by Isoda Susumu, which elicited Suehiro's approval and praise. Suehiro undoubtedly intended to repeat rural surveys to check on the analytic studies of the Tokyo group, and for this reason, this collection of materials must be regarded as the product of an early phase of research.

Suehiro had little personal contact with Suginohara's Peking research team, and as events turned out he never took part in field research. Suginohara seems, however, to have unswervingly adopted his mentor's methodological suggestions, and the field surveys from beginning to end bear the stamp of his resolute guidance.

Suginohara's main problem was to integrate the different skills and interests of his staff to study a village and show how village organizations, social institutions and customs, and economic activity were interrelated. In line with the research outline suggested by Suehiro, each researcher was assigned a topic according to his special interests, experience, and abilities

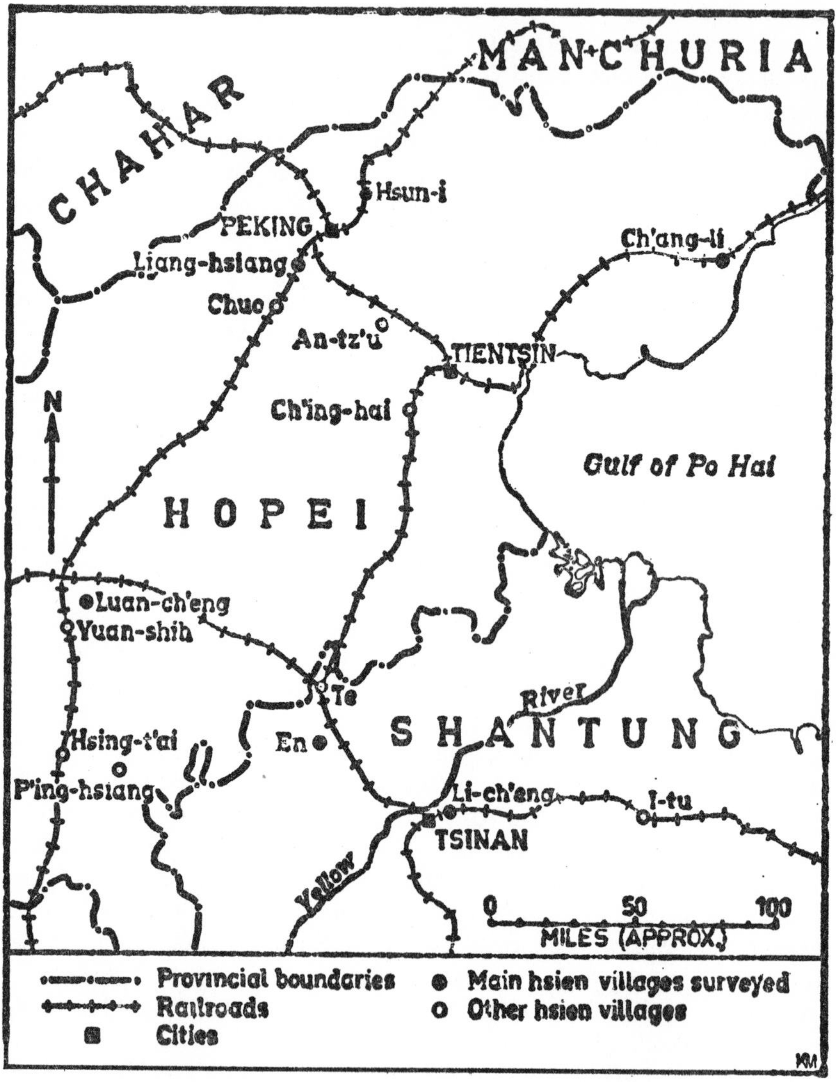

Map 3. Hopei and Shantung and main hsien villages surveyed.

and was asked to submit a detailed outline to guide this selection of facts and their arrangement in logical order.[14] Suginohara's contention was that each team member had to participate in formulating the team's research outline. "In order to undertake scientific investigation, each researcher who has a particular subject must strive on his own to make up a clear plan of research and then follow up with a suitable research outline of how he intends to carry out this plan. If the basic plan of research and the outline are not of his choosing, the team member will be unable to carry on scientific work. At the time I assumed responsibility for this survey there was neither a basic research plan nor outline of how to conduct group research." [15] Members of the team frequently discussed their outlines with Suginohara, and group meetings were held periodically where ideas were freely exchanged and outlines criticized. All outlines were combined to make a single team outline consisting of ten topics: general village conditions, family membership, land ownership, tenants, land transfers, commodity exchange, village credit, water utilization, taxes, and county administration. This outline was circulated among members of the Mantetsu chōsabu where it was severely criticized.[16] The team weathered the storm, and Suehiro at Tōa kenkyūjo was satisfied. On that note actual field work commenced.

The Team's Field Research

In Map 3 are shown the counties where individual villages were surveyed. In Figure 1 are set forth the date of village surveys, their locations, and the topics studied.

Chinese guerilla activity made it unsafe for Japanese to venture far into the countryside, and for this reason the villages were selected close to railway lines and county seats. The selection of counties, however, was probably dictated by the crops grown. For example, Sha-ching village in Shun-i county north of Peking lay in the wheat-kaoliang area; Hou chia ying in Ch'ang-li of northeast Hopei and Wu-tien village in Liang-hsiang south of Peking were perhaps selected to give a broader coverage of the wheat-kaoling-producing areas of northern Hopei. Ssu pei ch'ai in Luan-ch'eng county of central Hopei lay in the cotton-producing area. Ling shui kuo in Li-ch'eng county of central Shantung produced mainly wet rice, and Hou hsia chai in En county of northwest Shantung produced peanuts.

Members of the Japanese research team spoke little Chinese and interpreters were employed to converse with villagers. In the fall of 1940, teams of four Japanese, accompanied by interpreters, visited the villages of Sha-ching, Ssu pei ch'ai, and Ling shui kuo.

The team visiting Sha-ching village was based in the county seat, Shun-i, and on this occasion most of the data collected from county officials concerned general conditions in the county. One or two members of the re-

Fig. 1. Dates of village surveys, locations, names of researchers, and topics investigated.

Volume number of *CN*	Province, hsien, and village	Survey number 1 Nov.–Dec. 1940	Survey number 2 Feb.–March 1941	Survey number 3 May–June 1941	Survey number 4 Oct.–Dec. 1941	Survey number 5 Feb.–March 1942	Survey number 6 May–June 1942	Survey number 7 Oct.–Nov. 1942	1943 and after
I	*Hopei* Shun-i hsien, Sha-ching village	Family (Honda) Village – (Hatada)	Family (Niida) Family (Hayakawa) Village (Hatada)		General conditions (Yamamoto)	Village (Hatada) General conditions (Suginohara)	Family (Niida)	Village (Hatada)	Village (Hatada) Nov. 1943
II	*Hopei* Shun-i hsien, Sha-ching village	Taxes (Konuma) Water (Honda) Exchange (Honda) Tenancy (Yamamoto) Credit (Hatada)	Taxes & Water (Sugiura) Exchange (Hayakawa) Exchange (Hatada and Andō) Tenancy (Sano) Tenancy (Yamamoto) Taxes (Honda) Taxes (Konuma) Taxes (Shiomi) Credit (Andō)			Credit (Andō) Taxes (Shiomi) Tenancy (Honda) 17 Household Statistical Survey in Sha-ching village (Andō)			Tenancy (Honda) Aug. 1944

III	*Hopei* Luan-ch'eng hsien, Ssu pei ch'ai village	Taxes (Sugiura) Water (Sugiura) Exchange (Andō) Tenancy (Sano) Taxes (Shiomi) Family (Sano, Andō) Village (Sugiura)		Tenancy (Yamamoto) Taxes (Konuma) Taxes (Honda)	Exchange (Sugiura) Tenancy (Honda) Tenancy (Sano) Taxes (Shiomi) Credit (Andō) Family (Hayakawa) Village (Hatada)	Family (Hayakawa) Family (Niida) Taxes (Konuma) General Conditions (Suginohara) Tenancy (Sano) Exchange (Sugiura)			
IV	*Shantung* Li-ch'eng hsien, Ling shui kou village	Exchange (Hayakawa) Tenancy (Hayakawa) Taxes (Murata, Liu) Water (Murata, Liu) Credit (Murata, Liu) Family (Niida, Hayakawa) Village (Murata, Liu)		Credit (Andō) Family (Niida)	Exchange (Sugiura) Tenancy (Sano) Tenancy (Honda) Taxes (Shiomi) Taxes (Konuma) Family (Hayakawa) Village (Yamamoto) Village (Hatada)	Conditions in Lu chia chuang village (Hatada, Niida, Honda, Shiomi, Andō)	En hsien Hou hsia chai village Family (Niida) Village (Yamamoto) Exchange (Sugiura) Credit (Sugiura) Taxes (Honda) Tenancy (Honda)		

Fig. 1 (Continued)

Volume number of *CN*	Province, hsien, and village	Survey number 1 Nov.–Dec. 1940	Survey number 2 Feb.–March 1941	Survey number 3 May–June 1941	Survey number 4 Oct.–Dec. 1941	Survey number 5 Feb.–March 1942	Survey number 6 May–June 1942	Survey number 7 Oct.–Nov. 1942	1943 and after
V	*Hopei* Ch'ang-li hsien, Hou chia ying village						Village (Suginohara) Family (Andō) Credit (Andō) Exchange (Konuma) Taxes (Yamamoto) Water (Yamamoto)	Family (Suginohara) Village (Hatada) Credit (Andō) Taxes (Konuma) Family (Hayakawa) Exchange (Sugiura) Tenancy (Honda) Family (Niida)	
VI	*Hopei* Liang-hsiang hsien, Wu-tien village						Village (Hatada) Credit (Hayakawa, Sano) Family (Sano, Hayakawa) Taxes (Shiomi) Exchange (Shiomi) Tenancy (Sano) Conditions in Ching-hai	Family (Suginohara) Credit (Andō) Taxes (Konuma) Family (Hayakawa) Exchange (Sugiura) Tenancy (Honda)	

							hsien (Hatada, Shiomi, Sano, Suginohara, Hayakawa)	Family (Niida)	
VII	Other areas covering general conditions, water, and source materials		Materials regarding the area of Shun-i (Sugiura)	Ching-shan Railroad in Hopei (Andō & Liu). Tientsin—Pukow Railroad line (Niida) Shansi T'ung-pu and Tung-lu. Railroad lines. (Shiomi, Yamamoto, Hopei, Yuan-shih hsien; Shantung, Te hsien and I-tu and Tsingtao areas (Sano, Sugiura).	Materials regarding taxes in Li-Ch'eng (Konuma) Material regarding taxes in Shun-i (Konuma)		Water in Hsing-t'ai hsien (Yamamoto) Water in Chuo-hsien (Yamamoto) Materials regarding Hsing-t'ai hsien (Yamamoto)	Water (T'ien-chin hsien (Yamamoto) Water (Nan-ho, jen, Hsing-t'ai and P'ing-hsiang hsiens (Yamamoto) Water (Hsing-t'ai hsien (Yamamoto)	Conditions of An-tz'u hsien (Niida, Sugiura).

Source: *CN*, VI, 8–9.

Field researchers: Niida Noboru, Hatada Takashi, Konuma Tadashi, Andō Shizumasa, Suginohara Shunichi, Yamamoto Akira, Shiomi Kingarō, Murata Kyūichi, Sano Riichi, Honda Etsurō, Hayakawa Tamotsu, Sugiura Kanichi, and Liu Chün-jen.

search team visited Sha-ching to interview peasants,[17] but these interviews only covered general village conditions, and it was not until later surveys that villagers were questioned in more detail.

The teams surveying the other two villages were less concerned with county conditions. Japanese military authorities and civil advisers to the puppet government were consulted initially, but the teams soon moved on to the villages. Interviews were first conducted with the village headman on general village affairs, and then peasants were questioned individually on such subjects as land tenure, the transfer of land, and the family.

Despite the rigorous preparation of the interview schedules, there was room for flexibility and an unusual or unexpected reply could and did open new avenues of inquiry. Informants were reimbursed in cash, with an additional bonus of tobacco or cloth for the village headman and for those peasants who had been particularly cooperative.

At the end of the first survey, the research teams returned to Peking where a conference was held to thrash out problems and review progress, and it is interesting that the basic interview schedule was abandoned for later surveys. The information gathered on this occasion was transferred to cards, and small booklets containing the results were distributed to the Mantetsu chōsabu's offices in Dairen and Peking and to the Sixth Investigation Committee office in Tokyo. The Tokyo staff evaluated the data, which, together with that from later surveys, formed the basis for four studies of tenancy, credit, land transfers, and taxation, but these studies merely classified the data still further.[18]

The second survey was conducted in early 1941 and all teams converged this time on Sha-ching, as it was now believed that this village of seventy households representing the typical north China village. It is not at all certain how the interviews were conducted without the aid of a schedule, but some team members later reported that their previous field experience had enabled them to probe deeper into uncharted areas and that they merely needed to improvise on the spot by asking whatever questions made sense or were prompted by informants' replies.[19]

As a result of the second survey, many members declared that their original preconceptions of village society would have to be discarded. For example, few absentee landlords were discovered and the role this class played in village affairs was now thought to be negligible and village leadership to be something more fluid than hitherto imagined. Many researchers were no longer sure how such concepts as "semi-feudal" could be applied to this rural society. These frank admissions pointed clearly to the fact that many of the popular beliefs and opinions regarding the relationships of Chinese society did not square with the facts and that the methods used by these researchers were producing a great deal of new and interesting information.

The third survey was also conducted in 1941 after the spring planting, and this time the research teams split up to visit Ssu pei ch'ai, Ling shui kou, and several counties along the railway lines in Hopei and Shansi. A fourth survey, covering the same villages, followed in December of this year, and a fifth early in 1942, once again was made of Sha-ching village. On this occasion, a thorough survey of a small sample of seventeen households was undertaken to determine sources of income, the amount of income in cash and kind, and the nature of household expenditure.

The military situation in north China began to deteriorate, and this restricted future field research, only two brief visits to these same counties being conducted in the second half of 1942.

Except for visits to Sha-ching, all further field work was canceled in 1943. Sha-ching was visited several times in 1943 and 1944, but in March 1944 the project was officially discontinued. The survey results were published in 123 pamphlets and sent to Tokyo.[20] The team disbanded, some members returning to the Dairen office of the Mantetsu chōsabu while others remained in Peking working on special assignments until the end of the war.

In the 1950s former members of the north China group under the guidance and inspiration of Niida Noboru published the contents of the original 123 pamphlets in six large volumes. So concluded one of the most ambitious attempts ever made before the revolution to study the Chinese rural economy. There is a vast mass of primary material collected on strictly Baconian principles and not yet thoroughly explored. It is from this source that the materials used in the next four chapters have been taken.

The Method of Writing Village Studies from the Chūgoku nōson kankō chōsa

Obviously the prior question must be asked whether this material, such as it is, is a true report. It was collected via interpreters and might be distrusted for that reason alone. It was collected by citizens of a conquering power, by foreigners whose compatriots had committed aggression of the most naked kind. I have proceeded in the faith — and in the last resort it can be no more than faith — that, despite this, the material is veracious. It seems to be internally consistent. There is no doubt that the scholars collecting it were true scholars, concerned only with the truth and guided at every step by strict canons of scientific method. The real problem is whether the peasants told the truth. Their characteristic tolerance (and long experience) of alien powers suggests that they probably did; nor is it inconceivable to suppose that they could understand that these particular investigators were not the usual servants of the invading army; and the consistency of the evidence they gave suggests this — they could scarcely have planned a consistent set of lies even if they had a devious interest in doing so.

The method used by the Japanese research workers — that of the personal interview — has provided us not only with information about rural conditions in the early nineteen forties but also with a historical perspective of change in village society. Peasants were questioned on the functioning of village organizations over the last twenty or fifty years, and it is possible to construct a picture of the types of organization that emerged during this period, how long they existed, and how they changed. Though human memory may dim and historical facts become distorted because they are viewed and interpreted subjectively, these village surveys provide us with a record, possibly somewhat prismatic, of rural society for over half a century. No other material exists which can enable us to observe village change over such a long period.

It is precisely because these surveys provide us with a picture of rural change since 1890 that they are so valuable. It is thus possible to compare conditions in the countryside for different periods, particularly the periods before and after 1937. Although a score or more Japanese scholars have used these materials to study various facets of village life,[21] they have not been used by anyone so far to construct an account of how the village economy was organized, how it functioned and changed over time.

The raw materials contained in the six volumes are presented geographically and chronologically. The names of research workers and informants are listed, and each investigator's question and each informant's reply are listed. The reader opening these volumes for the first time is immediately bewildered by the prolixity of material and the lack of any relationship between topics. He is likely to wander in a maze and understand little of the significance of the material until he has firmly understood how the research was conceived, organized, and carried out. Perhaps it is for this reason that no scholar has yet attempted to write a comprehensive study of any single village with these materials.

The four villages Sha-ching, Ssu pei ch'ai, Ling shui kou, and Hou hsia chia were chosen because (1) more household data were available; (2) these villages were surveyed before peasants became hostile to the Japanese researchers; (3) these villages specialized in different crops, were located in different sections of the provinces, and were similar distances from county seats.

The village was regarded as the unit of production and exchange subject to change due to the activity of its households and the behavior of merchants, landlords, and officials living in market towns. The village land, labor, capital, and technology determined the level and diversity of output and the extent to which villages were able to earn a livelihood from farming or from nonfarming activities. These factors of production are examined to determine what change occurred in them, either singly or together. Village groups influencing the organization of farming were, to some extent, the product of economic change taking place within the village. When the origins and growth of key groups are examined in some detail, the extent of village change in this period can be measured. Village leaders and their role in village economic affairs are also examined. Finally, the fiscal relationship between village and county administration between 1900 and 1940 is analyzed.

I selected the relevant information from the interviews which best illuminated these points and organized it around this broad framework. Information was easy to obtain because of extensive repetition throughout many interviews, and it is this very repetition which makes our story more convincing and accurate. When different interviews relating to transfer and renting of land, marketing of crops, and credit facilities were compared, it was possible to discuss the regularities in peasant economic behavior, the similarity in economic organization and institutions between villages, and the long-run trends in each village. Where information from different informants conflicted, it was compared with other informants' replies. Only in a few instances were such contradictions unresolved.

There is no dearth of village studies of rural China, but what has been conspicuously lacking in these studies is a sense of history. The village studies of the 1920s and 1930s were single-dimensional with respect to time and give no clue as to what factors were constant or had changed. The 1939–1943 village surveys were far superior to any yet undertaken because they produced such an enormous quantity of raw data pertaining to conditions both past and present. If these materials are exhaustively mined and properly interpreted, the results should deepen our understanding of what took place in rural China from the late nineteenth century to the mid-twentieth century.

4. Shun-i County: Sha-ching Village

Shun-i, a small rural county measuring nine miles east to west and seven miles north to south, lay about 25 miles north of Peking on the Peking-Ku pei k'ou railroad line. Between 1884 and 1931 the county's population rose from 84,000 to 165,000 people, and by 1937 the population stood at 179,000. Refugees and Japanese troops increased the number to 225,535 in 1940.[1] The county contained over 500 large villages connected by cart paths and was divided into eight administrative districts with the main office in the county seat. Shun-i produced and exported corn, wheat, sorghum, vegetables, and beans. Five small markets served the county seat, which was the main grain collection center. These markets were located in towns having small handicraft establishments producing flour, tobacco, brooms, rush mats, bean curd, and wood carvings, and each employed around five workers. There had not been any significant change in the output proportions and type of farm and handicraft products between 1900 and 1940.[2]

The county's principal river, the White river, had flooded its banks every five years since 1877.[3] The soil was highly alkaline and sandy, and there were many swampy areas. The county was poorer than most because it lacked industry, mining, and cotton, and land prices were much lower than in neighboring Wu-ch'ing, Juh-wu, Su, Feng-jun, and Luan counties.[4]

Sha-ching village lay a half mile west of the county seat near two villages. It had been settled by immigrants from Hung-t'ung county of Shansi during the late Ming period when civil war raged in the north. The village received its name (sand and wells) because of the sandy soil deposited by the nearby Hsiao-chung river and its numerous wells.

In 1895, the village population was 191,280 in 1912, 340 in 1931, and 394 in 1941.[5] The annual rate of population growth was 1.5 per cent, about the same as for Shun-i county. In 1940, there were 5.6 persons per household.[6] Thirty per cent of the village population was under fifteen years of age, 63 per cent between sixteen and sixty-five, and 7 per cent over sixty-five years of age.[7] The dependency ratio of 37 per cent was high but slightly lower than that of many underdeveloped countries today. Although we do not know how this demographic profile changed after 1890, it is quite likely that the same average number of persons per household existed then as in 1940.

The land around Sha-ching was also sandy and highly alkaline, and extensive leaching of the soil had not occurred. Wells provided some water for irrigating the fields, but rainfall, which varied greatly from year to year, was the chief water supply. Droughts were frequent between January and May and, if prolonged, the spring wheat harvest was ruined.[8] The Hsiao-chung river, one of the county's many small creeks, frequently flooded the village and damaged many homes. In 1894–95 a great flood had completely ruined the food crops and brought near famine conditions; many villagers had had to eat bark and grass, but no one had moved away. Locust attacks were rare, but in 1924 a horde had devoured the entire crop. In the summer of 1931 violent hail storms had ruined the harvest. Villagers never knew when a disaster threatened, yet with few resources the peasants had survived a major calamity every ten years and their numbers increased.

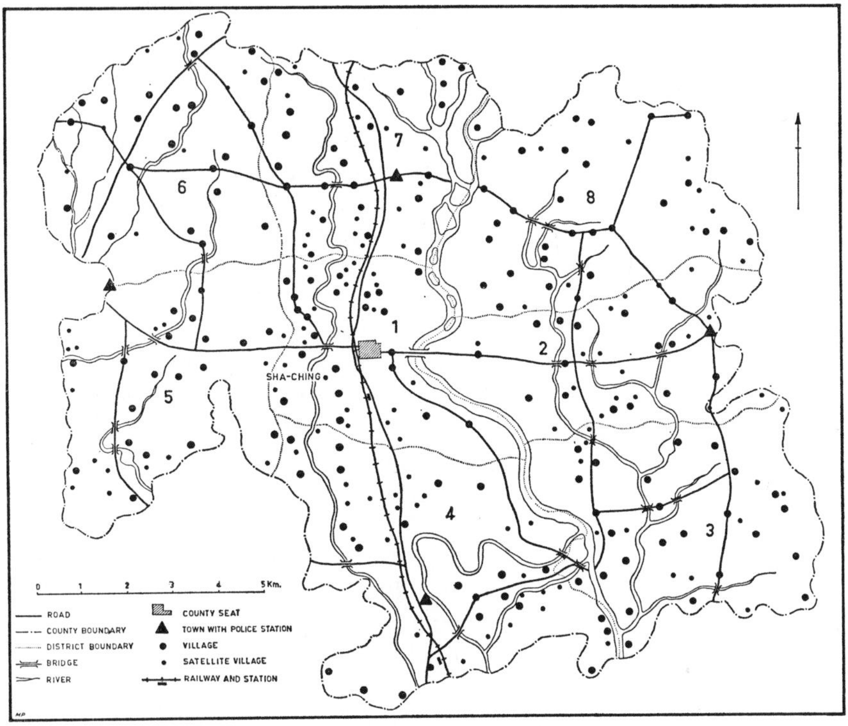

Map 4. Shun-i county, February 1941.

Since 1917 all arable village land had been farmed. Sha-ching had a cultivated area of 1,140 mow; a small patch of woods covered 12 mow; 25 mow was occupied by graves; and the village proper took another 70 mow. The average household owned 14 mow or a little over 2 acres.

Wheat, sorghum, corn, and spiked millet were the main crops. On one occasion, tobacco was tried but was found to be too hard on the soil. Each household had a small garden plot, but the main fields were parceled out in different parts of the village, and the peasant had to walk a great distance to his land each day.

In September, winter wheat was planted on three fifths of the village land, and the remainder lay fallow until the spring when sorghum, corn, and millet were sown.[9] Sorghum was planted in late February and early March, and when the first sprouts emerged all hands came to the fields to weed and ridge the new sprouts. While wheat was being harvested, grain had to be planted. The cereals were harvested after August. Each year wheat and other grain crops were rotated on the land, and this cycle had been repeated every year since the nineteenth century and probably even before.

Figures do not exist to show the change in long-run output of the village, but villagers reported they could recall no increase in yield and output over the past half century. Because of the inferior land, yields of corn, sorghum, wheat, and soy beans were lower than those reported by Buck in his survey of fourteen Hopei localities.[10]

Land was allocated to different crops on the basis of the income they earned. Because wheat prices were 30 to 40 per cent higher than that of millet and sorghum, four to five times as much land was devoted to wheat.[11] Sorghum prices exceeded corn prices, and the cultivated area for sorghum was roughly twice that for corn. Sorghum and corn were the main food crops, and though peasants preferred to eat wheat, they marketed it for cash. The peasants estimated that they sold about 40 per cent of what they produced, the remainder being retained for seeds and food.[12]

Between 1911 and 1921 grain prices as expressed in copper cash were fairly stable, but during the 1920s they rose substantially, declined slightly between 1929 and 1931 and slowly rose thereafter to accelerate upwards sharply after 1938.[13] For the early period, harvests had been good, but in 1921–22 the north China famine had sent prices rocketing and political instability thereafter kept prices up. Grain prices tumbled during the worldwide depression years, but after the outbreak of war in 1937 prices began their upward rise again. Except for several two- or three-year intervals, the peasants had only experienced various rises in price between 1911 and 1940.

Rising commodity and land prices affected peasant livelihood in various ways. Peasants enjoyed favorable terms of trade because grain prices advanced more rapidly than those of kerosene, matches, or cotton cloth. After 1937 the terms of trade became unfavorable as these consumer goods prices increased more rapidly than grain prices because the supply declined. Chou Shu-tang, former village headman, commented on the price increase after 1937 as follows.

Chou: At first, there were no major changes in village life. Then prices continued to rise and living became more difficult. Many sold their land, the reason being not to pay taxes but simply to live.

Question: What is now the household's biggest expense?

Shun-i County: Sha-ching Village

Chou: Taxes are not heavier, but clothing is the biggest expense.

Question: Is this because your crop prices are not rising as rapidly as the prices of other commodities?

Chou: Those who are very poor must buy their goods from other people. The poorer one is, the poorer he becomes.

Question: Which is better? When prices are stable or taxes are stable?

Chou: If both are stable that is fine. But as for which is better, it is best that commodity prices be stable.

Question: Has there been any tendency to produce for one's own needs because of the higher prices at which you must now buy?

Chou: This tendency has occurred, and we now produce for our own needs such things as clothes, hats, shoes, and other items.

Question: Does this not mean there is more nonfarm employment and side-work?

Chou: There seems to be no suitable side-work in our village, and there are now more who leave the village to work elsewhere.[14]

Although land prices rose steadily, there is little evidence that they increased more rapidly relative to other commodity prices. Steadily rising land prices enabled peasants to redeem more easily land they mortgaged. If a peasant mortgaged several mow of land for credit, he could redeem this land after five or ten years either by selling a very small plot of land whose price had risen or by mortgaging a smaller parcel. The peasants benefitted from moderately rising commodity prices, but the post 1938 inflation definitely made for hardship in Sha-ching.

Land

The distribution of land was very unequal, with 60 per cent of the households owning only 14 per cent of the land and 15 per cent owning 52 per cent. In Figure 2, I have compared land distribution in Sha-ching with that of Wu-tien, Ssu pei ch'ai, and Hou hsia chai villages. Inequality of land distribution was great in all villages but was most unequal in Sha-ching.

At the turn of the century the village had one large landlord, but in 1940 no farm owned enough land to be considered a landlord household. The five top-ranking households who owned most land before 1900 were not the same large landholders in 1941. In the nineteenth century four or five households owned as much as 200 or more mow of land, but in 1941 there was only one household owning slightly more than 100 mow. In 1941 each

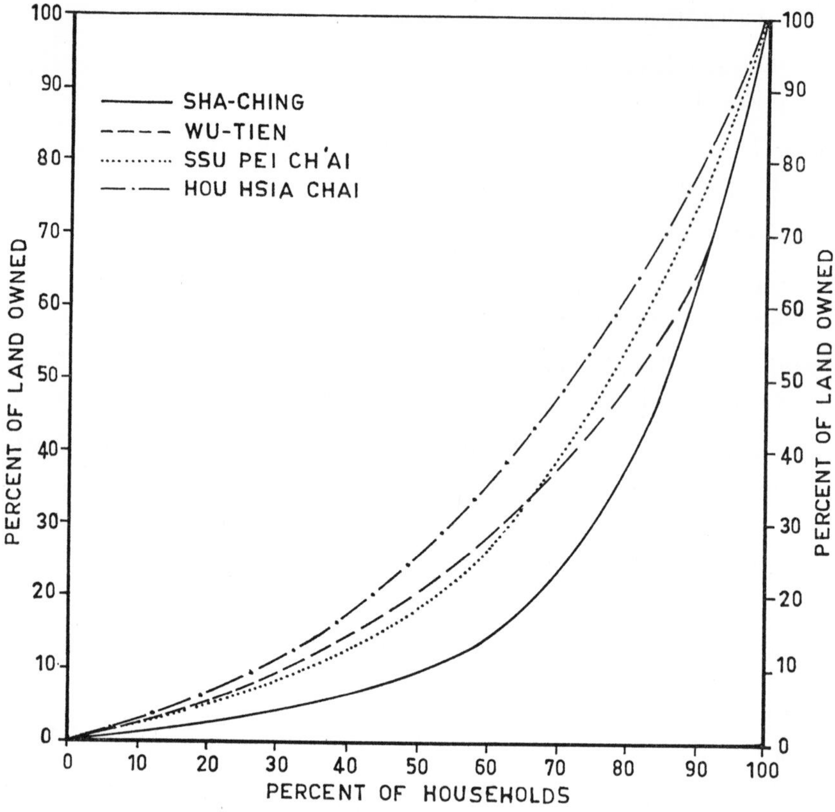

Fig. 2 Lorenz curve showing land distribution in Sha-ching, Wu-tien, Ssu pei ch'ai, and Hou hsia chai villages, 1941.

Sources: Sha-ching, I, 67; Ssu pei ch'ai village of Hopei (III), p. 5; Hou hsia chai village of Shantung (IV), p. 10; Wu-tien village of Hopei (V), p. 6.

household was asked what changes in landownership had occurred between 1911 and 1941. According to the replies, some households gained land, others lost land, nearly half reported no change, and another portion simply did not know. Because large landholdings disappeared, we must infer from this limited data that the average size of a household farm became smaller; more households, making up the majority of villagers owned small farms; and a few households had managed to increase the size of their farm slightly. There was no indication that more land had accumulated in the hands of fewer households, nor had land distribution changed very much, if at all, during this thirty-year period.

Shun-i County: Sha-ching Village

Table 1. Changes in land ownership, 1911–1941.

Land ownership since 1911	Number of households reporting in 1941	Per cent of households
Change in ownership		
Reported no change	29	40
Unknown	20	27
Reported loss of land	11	15
Reported gain of land	13	18
Total	73	100
		Amount (mow)
Distribution of ownership		
Land owned by Sha-ching peasants outside the village in 1941		460
Land in Sha-ching owned by peasants of other villages in 1941		515
Land lost (sold) by Sha-ching villagers in recent years		55

Source: CN, II, 1–24.

Capital

The organization of farming would not have been seriously affected if there had been technological change and households had accumulated more farm capital. Sha-ching's agricultural technology scarcely changed over this half century, and with the exception of a new corn seed that became available in Shun-i in the early 1920s, new crops had not been introduced.[15] Seeds for planting were selected from previous harvests as was the traditional practice, and chemical fertilizers were still not used.

Question: Has anyone in this village been able to introduce new crops?

Answer: It is impossible to introduce upland rice because of the water shortage.

Question: Has there not been anyone who attempted to grow some new crop?

Answer: No one. The crops are the same today as they were in former times.

Question: There have been announcements of new fertilizers in this area. Has anyone purchased these for trial use?

Answer: No one has purchased anything like this. The land is too poor, and further, one must spend quite a lot of money to do this.

Question: Didn't the Hsin min hui sponsor the use of fertilizers?

Answer: No one from that organization came to this village, and we have heard no reports of this sort of thing.

Question: Didn't the railroad station authorities sponsor fertilizers in Ai-huo village?

Answer: No.[16]

Human and animal excrement was the sole fertilizer and was mixed with dirt to produce a compost to be taken to the fields in early spring. Animal excrement came mainly from pigs; five pigs produced enough fertilizer for 30 mow, but a family of five people produced enough only for 8 mow. One villager traveled to Peking every August to sell his crop for human waste, which he then resold to the other villagers in Sha-ching. With this one exception, night soil was not purchased outside the village.

The stock of village capital had not increased to the extent that it was possible to observe a larger amount of capital per farm household. Transfers of capital goods had taken place between peasants, and as new households were formed, they managed to purchase some capital, so that capital stock per farmstead probably remained the same. In 1941 the village owned one cow, two horses, two mules, and twenty-five donkeys, and there was only one bicycle and eleven carts. The chief farming instruments were earth-turning instruments (ploughs, hoes, rakes), weeding tools, and harvesting implements (brooms, sickles, rakes, and rollers).[17] Tools became difficult to buy and replace after 1940 because of the scarcity of materials. The basic farm tools, consisting of different hoes, rakes, and brooms, were the same as those used during the Ming and Ch'ing periods. Carts were expensive and their price rose greatly after 1940.[18] In the late 1920s, at the peak of the civil war, police had come to the village and requisitioned horses, mules, and carts, and in 1937 this had occurred again, causing a 10 per cent decline in livestock.

Families owning less than 10 mow usually did not own a draft animal to plough the land and haul manure and grain. These peasants used a system of buying and sharing mules and carts between themselves called *ta-t'ao*.

Question: What is *ta-t'ao?*

Answer: When there are two families which are poor and have no mules, *ta-t'ao* is used. Both agree to cooperate and buy the mule together. But this practice is not confined just to mules. They will also co-operate to prepare the ground for planting, or when agricultural workers are to be employed, both will pool their money to hire the necessary labor.

Question: How is this done in the case of buying a mule?

Answer: Suppose the mule cost $100.00. Each will contribute $50.00, and one will use the mule for three days and the other will use it for three days.[19]

The usual case was for two households to buy and share capital goods, but sometimes three families shared their wealth. About 40 per cent of the households acquired and shared capital in this way.[20] Such families bore the same surname or were good friends and neighbors.[21] *Ta-t'ao* was practised most frequently during the sowing and harvesting seasons, but in some instances it involved two families jointly renting land and farming it together.

Land Tenure

According to the village elders, twenty new households appeared in the village after 1912, an increase due to dividing land among the male sons. The number of peasants owning and cultivating land remained the same, but as village land became scarce, their percentage of total households declined from 60 to 44 per cent. The number of households formerly leasing some land declined slightly too, probably because as the size of the farm became smaller they needed to farm all their land in order to survive. The biggest change came for those peasants who did not have enough land and had to rent a few extra mow. Their number increased greatly during the 1920s, but remained constant after 1931. The changes in tenant and cultivator status are shown in Table 2.

Table 2 is only as accurate as villagers' recollections of the past, and for this reason error is likely. Some discrepancies are immediately detected when Table 2 is compared with household data from a village survey in 1941. This survey showed that only one household completely rented the land it farmed, and the number of owner-cultivator tenants was 24, slightly below the figure in Table 2.[22] Ten households survived solely on their farm income, six depended completely on nonfarm income, and six derived their income from wages and what they produced on rented land. Fifty-three households, 78 per cent of all village households, supplemented their farm income by working outside the village.

These data suggest that the village found it increasingly difficult to depend solely on farming. As population doubled and new households formed, land fragmented, the size of the farm declined, and land became scarcer. More peasants either had to rent land from other peasants or work outside the village. But as farms became smaller in size, there was a limit to the amount of land wealthier peasants could lease to poorer peasants.

Table 2. Changes in tenant and cultivator status in Sha-ching, 1912–1940.

Year	Number of households	Owner cultivator	Owner cultivator-tenant	Tenant[a]	Huo-chung[b]
1912	50	30	10–12	8–10	1–2
1916	56–57	36	10	10	1–2
1921	60	38	11	11	0
1926	63–64	28	24	7–8	0
1931	65–66	28	30	7–8	0
1936	67–68	29	30	7–8	1
1937	67–68	29	30	7–8	1
1938	67–68	29	30	7–8	1
1939	68–69	30	30	7–8	3
1940	70	31	30	7–8	3

Source: CN, II, 72.

[a] Tenants possessed no land of their own. Their decline in 1926 is said to have been caused by an abrupt rise in tenant rents brought about by flood conditions and rising food and land prices.

[b] The *Huo-chung* group consisted of tenants cooperating with owner cultivators to farm land on a share basis; rent was paid in kind by the tenant after the harvest.

When money wage rates rose rapidly in the late 1930s, it became more attractive for peasants to work outside the village for short periods rather than rent inferior land where the return was exceedingly low. Even in the late nineteenth century, some peasants worked outside the village for short periods, and many households rented land from other households. This was because land distribution was still very unequal, and some households possessed plots too small to support their numbers. But fifty years later, in the late 1930s, farming was more difficult because households simply did not have enough land to support themselves.

The land tenure system must be considered as a system to equalize land use by informal agreement. It functioned to enable peasants with little land to farm more and those who could not farm their land efficiently to earn income by leasing it. Because a peasant's farm consisted of many small plots haphazardly located about the village, he found it advantageous to rent a nearby plot from another who found it too difficult or inconvenient to farm. In many instances this meant poorer peasants rented inferior land, and the wealthier peasants farmed their superior land more efficiently.

Land was rented and leased only after the harvest. A peasant wanting to rent land sought a prospective landlord or relied on a friend to act as a go-between to do this for him.[23] When someone was found, both parties discussed the terms of rent: amount of land to be rented, amount of rent per mow to be paid in cash, and the period of tenancy. The go-between typically arranged the terms of rent, paid the landlord the cash rent in advance, and received a small commission for his trouble from the tenant. If tenant and landlord privately met and discussed these matters, they did not enter the terms of agreement in a rent book or sign a rent contract. The landlord paid the land tax on the leased land, but the tenant paid fees on the land to the village crop-watching association.

The terms landlord and tenant are misnomers suggesting a commercial relationship that in reality did not exist. The two parties never met throughout the year to discuss how the land was to be used or developed and what rent would be refunded if the tenant used fertilizer to improve the land. The landowner did not supply any capital nor did he make any provision to reduce the rent if the tenant decided to improve the land.

Social relationships between the two were exceedingly informal. The landlord held no special status which necessitated the tenant presenting gifts or addressing him in dignified language as was the case between tenant and landlord in Tokugawa and modern-day Japan. Any disputes arising between these two parties were resolved by them alone, and rarely was the village headman consulted to arbitrate. Cases of this sort were never taken to the county seat for adjudication.

The period of lease usually lasted only one or two years. One reason for this was that peasants regarded their land as a form of near-money. Peasants invariably mortgaged and sold land or used it as a security to obtain a loan.[24] Only in the rare cases of leasing garden land for growing vegetables were contracts drawn up for as long as five or six years.[25]

There was still another land tenure arrangement although in 1940 only two out of ten households practiced it. This was called *huo-chung* where landlord and tenant agreed to share the harvest in kind, on terms agreed upon before the spring wheat was sown.[26] Even in the nineteenth century peasants paid rent in cash. When several poor harvests occurred, peasants shifted to the *huo-chung* system as a guarantee they would have grain. After 1912 more households had shifted to the cash rent system. It should not be understood that peasants marketed more of their crops in 1941 than in 1890, or that there had occurred some discrete leap toward using more money for household expenditures.

The strong preference for money rents might have arisen because more peasants urgently needed cash. If peasants had less land to mortgage or sell and prices were steadily rising, their demand for cash would be greater than under circumstances where the opposite held true. On the other hand, when the village was beset by two or three years of very poor harvest, it was to the peasants' advantage to have grain on hand, for often grain could not be purchased in the local markets or its price was extremely high. Peasants had the choice of renting additional land or working elsewhere. As more chose to work outside, the bargaining power of those renting might have improved to the extent that they could insist on paying rents in cash.

It was to their advantage to pay the money rent in advance and earn more in the subsequent year after farm prices had risen.

Whatever the correct explanation for this change in rent payments, it would seem that paying cash rents benefitted both landlord and tenant. During periods of bad harvest, however, the landlord could insist that rents be prepaid in kind. Households leasing land had barely enough capital to farm their own land, and they could not assist their tenants to develop the land. This land tenure system also had to accommodate a credit system whereby peasants considered their land as near-money, to be used for security, mortgaged, or sold when cash was needed. Land tenure can only be properly understood in the light of the actual farming conditions and the land inheritance system.

In 1928, the local government organized an agricultural association but did not attempt to organize the tenants, reduce their rents, or send representatives to the village.[27] The organization existed only on paper, and officials did nothing to improve farming conditions throughout the county.

Labor

The peasants referred to those working away from their land as short-term laborers, *tuan-kung,* and long-term laborers, *ch'ang-kung.*[28] Most of Sha-ching's peasants either worked for short periods on the plots of wealthier peasants or went to the county seat's labor market and offered themselves for short-term work. Such jobs included making incense sticks, carving buffalo horns, baking rice cakes, watching crops in other villages, selling old clothes, making rice jelly, candy, and noodles, manufacturing straw mats, hauling goods by cart, and serving as clerks in stores. Each fall seventeen households sent a worker to Peking to work in several shops that produced a special kind of cake for Buddha's birthday.

A few peasants worked as long-term laborers, and they came from the very poor families. Such a family might send a daughter to work as a servant in another household for six months or more. Only the wealthy peasants employed long-term workers on a servant basis. The long-run changes in short-term and long-term laborers are shown in Table 3.

In the early Republican period more long-term workers and fewer short-term workers were employed. Most of these laborers resided outside Sha-ching. In the mid 1920s a change took place when the number of long-term workers declined and that of short-term laborers increased. One explanation for this is that the wage differential between the long- and short-term worker widened during the 1930s, and more peasants could earn higher money wages by working for short periods. Another reason is that there were fewer wealthier peasants able to employ these workers.

Between March and May and late August and October all male hands were needed in the fields to prepare the ground, plant seeds, weed, irrigate,

Table 3. Change in status of farm workers, 1912–1940.

		Short-term workers	
Year	Long-term workers	Within Sha-ching	Outside Sha-ching
1912	10[a]	7–8	4–5
1916	6–7[a]	7–8	1–2
	3–4		
1921	10	10	0
1926	6–7	20	0
1931	5–6	15–16	0
1936	3–4	13–14	0
1937	3–4	10	0
1938	3–4	10	0
1939	3–4	10	1
1940	3–4	15–16	2

Source: CN, II, 87.
[a] Number of laborers from outside Sha-ching.

and harvest. Simple hand tools were used, and as large implements and draft animals were few or totally lacking, more labor was required for these activities than was usually the case in the advanced rural communities producing grain crops. From data on the availability of laborers according to their age, I have calculated that in a household averaging 5.6 people, the labor free for field work was 1.3.[29] Marginal labor requirements rose rapidly on farms larger than 5 mow.[30] Therefore, on plots of 20 mow or more, 4 or 5 workers had to be hired during the spring and fall harvest. The land in Sha-ching was so distributed that 60 per cent of the households owned 14 per cent of the land, which means that 42 households probably had plots smaller than 6 or 7 mow. In these cases household labor was sufficient to farm the land. But for the dozen households with farms of 40 mow or more, as many as 8 or 9 laborers had to be employed during the busy season. Labor, like land, was distributed unequally. Peasants solved this problem by privately employing other peasants for a cash wage.

Credit

Each of the five periodic markets in Shun-i opened on different days to enable merchants and peddlers to move from market to market and give villagers an opportunity to market several times a week.[31] Sha-ching's peasants sold their wheat, sorghum, and millet in June and October, and only two households had sufficient reserves to enable them to store their grain and sell later. Before 1900, the county shipped its grain to Peking, but afterwards merchants shipped more grain to Tientsin because it brought higher prices.

The peasants often obtained credit from the shops in Shun-i during the spring when their cash was scarce, and they urgently needed food, cloth, or kerosene. These loans were repaid after the next harvest at an interest charge of 2 to 3 per cent per month. No interest was charged on loans less than 100 yuan. When prices rose the peasant repaid his loan according to the value of the goods he had obtained on credit, but when prices fell he paid the original loan.[32]

Peasants borrowed money in the event of sickness, a poor harvest, weddings, and funerals. Small sums were obtained from close friends or relatives and repaid quickly without interest. Large sums of 100 yuan or more were borrowed from merchants or wealthy families in Shun-i by the method called *chih-ti chieh-ch'ien*. The majority of peasants borrowed in this way.[33] The borrower looked for a go-between and financial guarantor called a *pao-chung-jen,*[34] who was a reputable, honest man and who knew who had money and was willing to lend. When the go-between located a lender, he brought both parties together to discuss the terms of the loan. Once the amount of loan was agreed, the borrower offered a piece of land, usually valued at half the loan, as security in the event he was unable to repay. The interest rate was 2 to 3 per cent per month, and loan and interest charges had to be repaid within a year, usually right after the harvest. No document was drawn up and signed. The borrower continued to use his land as he saw fit, but if he failed to repay on time, the land had to be sold or offered as a mortgage to repay the lender.

Mortgaging land, the custom of *tien,*[35] was described by the peasants in the following way.

Question: What is *tien?*

Answer: There are two types: *tien-fang,* mortgaging a house, and *tien-ti,* mortgaging land. The more common type of *tien* is when a household urgently needs money, and mortgages some of its land which is valued say at $1,000.00. The cash received as loan would come to about $400.00. No interest is paid on this sum. When the money is later repaid, the land is redeemed.

Question: Aside from cases of house and land mortgages, are there other examples such as for farm tools, livestock, etc.?

Answer: None.

Question: For example, is there any case where livestock is mortgaged and not returned until the original loan is repaid?

Answer: There is no example of this type in this area.

Shun-i County: Sha-ching Village

Question: Is it possible to mortgage land of middle grade value? [36]

Answer: Any kind of land can be mortgaged. Naturally, better grade land can be mortgaged for a higher amount of loan.[37]

Again the go-between, who also served as financial guarantor for the borrower, brought borrower and lender together to discuss the amount of land to be mortgaged, the land's present worth, and the size of the loan. The land was valued according to prevailing prices and the expected harvest, and some fraction of that value, usually around two thirds, was then agreed upon as the loan.[38] The peasant mortgaging the land did not pay interest because the party receiving the mortgaged land had the right to use it until the loan was repaid. The period of mortgage was usually three to five years, but there were cases when the period was longer. If the loan was not repaid, the peasant could not redeem his land.

During the late Ch'ing period when villagers had more land, the mortgage period was only one to three years. The practice of *tien* had been extremely common at that time, and peasants redeemed their land quickly. In the early 1930s there were fewer cases of mortgaging land and the mortgage period was longer, because the peasants had less land to mortgage and redeeming land had become more difficult.

All land in Sha-ching was private land and could be freely sold, so that if mortgaging land proved insufficient to obtain the desired amount of money the land was sold. The household head sold the land after the harvest and, again, he used a go-between to find a buyer to arrange the terms of sale.[39] Once a buyer was found, a deed was drawn up and signed by the seller, the go-between, and the buyer. The deed was taken to the county tax collecting office of that district and a deed tax was paid by the buyer. Henceforth, the new owner paid all taxes or levies on the land.[40] The middleman received a small commission from the seller. There is no evidence that land sales in Sha-ching had increased in recent years.[41]

Land was the key asset used to obtain credit. In this rural economy where loanable funds were scarce and formal credit institutions did not exist, security for the lender could only be provided through a third party or middleman who guaranteed that the borrower could repay the loan. In this way peasants minimized the possibility of defaulting on repayment of loans.

Peasant Incomes and Savings

Peasants never kept tidy accounts of their income and expenditure. This is not to say they were not interested in increasing their income for they used their land for crops which commanded the highest price and carefully allocated labor between farming and working outside the village to earn whichever income was greatest.[42]

The Japanese collected good household budget data from seventeen households for 1941, which deserve some analysis.[43] They selected a household sample and a cross-section of tenants and owner-cultivators large enough to represent the village. Determining household consumption and production was most difficult, and their first problem was to establish consistent categories by which households could be measured and compared.

They solved the problem by using a unit called adult equivalents. Individuals between 12 and 60 years of age were counted as 1.0 adult equivalent; between 8 and 11 years and above 61 counted as 0.8 adult equivalent; children between 3 and 7 years were 0.5 and those under 2 as 0. A household was scored according to its adult equivalents.

The next task was to determine a standard food unit for different crops to measure household consumption. It was decided to make six *tou* of wheat and millet of grain and seven *tou* of sorghum equivalent to 1 *shih* of grain. It was then estimated that 1.0 adult equivalent should consume at least 3 *shih* of grain per year. With these units the annual household consumption requirements were obtained for seventeen households. The amount of farm output produced by each household was also calculated and stand-

Table 4. Grain production and consumption for 17 households in 1941 (10 tou = 1 shih)

	Annual grain production		Annual grain consumption		Deficit or surplus	
Family	shih	tou	shih	tou	shih	tou
Yang Che	15	1	10	5	+ 4	6
Shih Chen-wang	15	6	12	0	+ 3	6
Tu Hsiang	4	3	19	8	−15	5
Li Juh-yuan	36	2	40	5	− 4	3
Chang Ch'eng	11	2	16	2	− 5	0
Chao Ting-k'uei	18	8	24	0	− 5	2
Ching Te-fu	11	2	10	5	− 7	0
Tu Shou-t'ien	9	3	19	5	−10	2
Chang Shou-hou	12	0	19	5	− 7	5
Chang Lin-yung	18	9	12	0	− 6	9
Li Shu-lin	5	3	14	4	− 9	1
Fu Chu	7	7	11	4	− 3	3
Li Hsiu-fang	14	3	17	7	− 3	4
Chang Yung-jen	12	3	30	6	−18	3
Tsung Wen-ch'i	1	0	13	5	−12	5
Chang Shou-jen	8	2	12	0	− 3	8
Yang Jun	7	6	14	4	− 6	8

Source: CN, II, 270–291.

arized according to the above food units. It was then possible to compare household production with consumption to determine whether a food surplus or deficit existed. I have constructed Table 4 from this seventeen-household survey data.

Only twelve per cent of the sample (2 households) produced enough grain to meet their annual consumption needs. The remainder had to purchase grain with income earned from marketing vegetables, working outside the village, or borrowing.

In Table 5 income and outlays for these seventeen households are presented. When aggregate expenditures are compared with income, there is a large deficit amounting to 13 per cent of total household income. We do not know to what extent this deficit fluctuated or disappeared in years when the harvest was exceptionally good.

We also note that sales of farm products were enough for the food purchased by households but not enough to cover total outlays. Therefore, income from nonfarming activities was crucial to each household budget if there was not enough land. Nearly one fourth of total income came from nonfarm employment, and this should be regarded as the amount of village income earned from nonfarming activities.

From household income, 90 per cent was spent for food, clothing, and other essentials. After taxes, rents, and debt repayments, there was nothing left for the peasants to buy farm capital. This is why the village capital stock had not increased greatly, and households shared capital between themselves. Sha-ching, of course, was an extremely poor village, and not all villages were as poor.[44] But the fact remains that since the late nineteenth century Sha-ching depended more and more on nonfarm income.

Land Inheritance

The eldest, able-bodied male was the family head or *hu-chang*.[45] He arranged the farm work, controlled family income, and decided when to divide the land or sell it. There were many kinship groups in the village carrying the same surname and related by blood.[46] Households of the same kinship group gathered to celebrate a wedding or funeral, but each group was too small and weak to organize large activities and assist its members. If a household wanted to borrow money or mortgage or sell land, it first approached someone within its kinship group and then sought out other villagers. These groups did not keep genealogical records or emphasize clan functions. They appeared to be vestiges of more powerful kinship groups of former times. The family was the basic decision-making unit in the village.

The periodic division of household wealth, *fen-chia* or *fen-chü*, strongly influenced the size, use, and distribution of land and in turn governed the economic and social status of a household.[47] This division of all household

Table 5. Household budget data for a sample of 17 households of Sha-ching village, August 1942 (in yuan).

	A	B		C		D	E	F
Family name	Total household income	Income from farm sales		Nonfarm income		Quantity of output consumed (value)	Quantity of output marketed for consumption (value)	Total household expenditures
		Amount	Per cent	Amount	Per cent			
Li Juh-yuan	2,084	1,884	90.4	200	9.6	1,303	581	1,983
Li Hsiu-fang	962	867	90.1	95	9.9	540	327	1,045
Tsung Wen-ch'i	405	25	6.2	380	93.8	25	0	455.8
Chang Shou-hou	745	535	71.8	210	28.2	300	235	715
Shih Chen-wang	570	570	100.0	0	0	430	140	815
Li Shu-lin	417	192	46.0	225	54.0	192	0	417
Chang Cheng-jen	1,208	1,138	94.2	70	5.8	388	750	1,276
Tu Shou-t'ien	802	532	66.3	270	33.7	394	138	928
Tu Hsiang	742	542	73.0	100	27.0	256	286	945
Ching Te-fu	924	664	71.9	260	28.1	408	256	1,055
Yang Tze	980	935	95.9	45	4.1	599	336	1,042
Yang Jun	542	245	45.2	297	54.8	245	0	1,057
Chang Ch'eng	683	443	64.8	240	35.2	443	0	708
Chao Ting-k'uei	1,399	1,199	85.7	200	14.3	708	491	1,439
Fu Chü	587	337	57.4	250	42.6	205	132	559
Chang Shou-jen	563	283	50.3	280	49.7	283	0	1,233
Chang Lin-yung	676	676	100.0	0	0	551	125	759
Total	14,289	11,069	77.5	3,220	22.5	7,271	3,798	16,431.8

	G	H	I	J	K	L	m (G − D)	n (A − F)
Family name	Necessary food consumption (value)	Fuel and clothing expense	Capital, labor, fertilizers, etc., expense	Taxes	Tenant rents	Other expenses, e.g., funeral, marriage, interest	Deficit of consumption	Surplus or deficit of budget
Li Juh-yuan	1,303	100	300	130	0	150	0	+ 101
Li Hsiu-fang	540	20	54	121	60	200	0	− 83
Tsung Wen-ch'i	250	65	0	0.8	120	20	− 225	− 50.8
Chang Shou-hou	487	55	0	20	88	65	− 187	+ 30
Shih Chen-wang	430	100	135	90	0	60	0	+ 155
Li Shu-lin	332	30	25	0	0	30	− 140	0
Chang Cheng-jen	820	160	65	81	0	150	− 432	− 68
Tu Shou-t'ien	514	120	5	38	96	155	− 120	− 186
Tu Hsiang	411	100	100	34	100	200	− 155	− 203
Ching Te-fu	577	100	68	155	0	155	− 169	+ 14
Yang Tze	599	100	165	78	0	100	0	+ 53
Yang Jun	505	210	20	42	0	280	− 260	+ 515
Chang Ch'eng	550	50	0	33	49	75	− 7	− 74
Chao Ting-k'uei	708	150	80	41	260	200	0	− 40
Fu Chü	325	20	0	14	160	40	− 125	+ 28
Chang Shou-jen	378	110	280	65	50	350	− 95	− 670
Chang Lin-yung	551	50	0	58	0	101	0	+ 55
Total	9,280	1,540	1,297	1,000.8	983	2,331	−1,909	−1,454

Source: CN, II; 270–291.

land was to be made equally among the male heirs. The *hu-chang* did not insist that the land be kept intact within the family. It is not clear why this was so, although the reason for dividing the household land seems clear enough. Dividing the land equally among the male heirs guaranteed a livelihood to their families and ensured continuation of this family line. But this practice also reduced the size of family farm and prevented wealth from accumulating in a family after two or three generations; on the other hand, it increased social and economic mobility in the village. As a result of land being periodically redistributed among different households, some families acquired land and improved their fortune, but for most, their plots became fragmented, and several small farms formed in the place of one.

Table 6. Frequency of division of household land in Sha-ching, late nineteenth century–1941.

Type of case	Number	Per cent
Household division reported		
Before 1890	3	4.2
1890–1909	10	13.9
1910–1919	3	4.2
1920–1929	12	16.7
1930–1941	30	27.8
Cases reported as unknown	15	20.8
No household division reported	9	12.4
Total	82	100.0

Source: *CN*, I, appendix.

I have constructed Table 6 from information obtained by a household survey in 1941. A count was made of all replies to the question of whether or not the household had divided land. The results were arranged according to time periods, and the unknown cases and reports of no household division were calculated as percentages of the total number of household replies.

The undulating character of these household divisions is of interest. In the 1930s there were more cases of dividing the land than in the past. Peasants stated that fewer households had enough land to divide equally among the sons, and it should be divided while households still possessed a little land.

Question: Has there been a tendency toward more or less division of households in Sha-ching in recent years?

Answer: Recently, it has become much greater. This is particularly true when the parents die.

Shun-i County: Sha-ching Village

Question: What is the cause of this new tendency?

Answer: The reason is that it is best to distribute something for everybody before conditions worsen and nothing remains. When family conditions deteriorate, dividing the household wealth must be done quickly or else soon there is nothing left to divide.

Question: How many households have divided their property this year?

Answer: Two. In the Liu household there was Liu Fu, the eldest son, Liu Chen, the second son, and Liu Hsiang, the youngest. Liu Chen has left and the other sons live together with their mother. There was also the Li family consisting of Li Shu-lin, the eldest son, Li Hsiang-lin, the next eldest, then Li Chung-lin, the youngest. Li Hsiang-lin left first, and now the eldest son lives with his other brother. The household split up in March of this year.[48]

The decision to divide the family property was usually associated with friction and tension between sons and father or quarrels between brothers and their wives, which became so serious it was necessary for separate households to be established.[49] A witness was called in by the *hu-chang* and long discussions were held on how the property was to be divided. Once an agreement was reached, a certificate was drawn up to indicate the amounts each male was to receive.[50] The document, signed by a witness, the *hu-chang,* and each son, was retained by the *hu-chang* and duplicates were given to each son. This act did not mean immediate departure of the sons, but it did mean new work schedules and different household budgeting. Eventually separation took place.

Village Leadership and Organizations

Village leadership was embodied in a headman, his assistant and a council of nine peasants. Before 1900, the duties of the headman had been to arbitrate village disputes and to deal, on behalf of the village, with local county officials.[51] In these matters he was supported by his assistant, who also acted as his deputy in his absence and was the convenor of the village council, a body which appeared to fulfill only an advisory capacity.

The roles of headman, assistant, and members of the council were filled by influential peasants from the landowning class. Table 7 gives the relevant data on land ownership, age, and household size for all but the headman in 1941. The position of headman was filled by a member of one of the leading village clans and he achieved this status by election — by oral vote until 1930 and thereafter by ballot. Headmen were drawn from one of three dominant village groups: the Li, Chang, and Yang clans. Between 1901 and 1922, four headmen had come from the Li clan; between 1922

Table 7. Age, household size, and amount of land owned and managed by Sha-ching's council members, 1941.

Name	Land received from father (mow)	Land owned (mow)	Total land managed (mow)	Age	Number of persons
Chao Ting-k'uei	20	14	34	38	10
Li Jun-yuan	16	76	76	65	17
Chang Yung-jen	20	46.2	57.2[a]	64	13
Yang Che	35	35	35	37	5
Yang Cheng	35	40	40	42	5
Yang Jun	110	110	11[b]	37	5
Li Hsiu-fang	?	49.5	54.5	24	9
Yang Yuan	30	40	40	44	5
Chang Ch'eng	?	16	23	54	7
Tu Hsiang	?	11.5	18.5	57	10

Source: CN, I, 124, and appendix.
[a] Eleven mow of mortgaged land was added.
[b] Land was leased to other households.

and 1940, the Chang and Yang clans had supplied headmen.[52] These men served for no longer than six years at a time, but a headman could hold the job for as long as he wished, provided villagers were content with his performance. Leadership, therefore, was flexible and based on popular support; a peasant continuing in this role had to meet his responsibilities satisfactorily.

The average age of this elite group was 46; their families numbered more than the village household average; and their average landholdings were 34 mow. Council members were among the largest landholders in the village and most of the members owned or managed more land than they had inherited. This indicates they were successful, hardworking peasants who had increased their landholdings — a major achievement in the village during this period.

Prior to 1900, few village matters demanded the attention of the headman and his council. Village society was loosely knit, and few village organizations had been established. The headman settled land disputes, and on the rare occasion when a county tax office demanded a village levy, the council met to assess the proportion to be paid by each villager owning land.[53]

Around 1900 the local government ordered all villages to establish crop watching associations or *ch'ing-miao-hui*.[54] The local authorities were trying to increase taxes, and they believed this could be done by preventing crop theft. The peasants could then harvest more and pay higher taxes.[55] As it turned out this organization gave villages a unique means to raise revenue to pay higher taxes. After 1900 periodic levies or *t'an-k'uan* became numerous, and their revenue gradually began to exceed even that of the land tax.

Prior to 1900 villagers hired peasants with little land to watch their crop during the summer months.[56] This was done on an individual basis, and the crop watcher received fees from peasants whose land he guarded. When the crop watching association was organized, the village council supervised its activities and employed several crop watchers each summer and early fall to patrol a prescribed area of the village and drive away thieves. The council decided the fee to be levied for each mow of land, and this fee was paid twice a year by every household which farmed land. Formerly the council assessed only landowners, but now, through the crop watching association, they assessed all who used the land. The association became the organization by which the council raised revenue when the village had an important expenditure to make. These funds were used to finance the village school, to pay for repairs and upkeep of the village temple, to compensate households who sent a peasant to fulfill Sha-ching's corvee labor quota, and to pay the periodic tax levy.[57] When these levies became more frequent and heavier and the association's funds were insufficient, the council met and assessed a certain fee per mow for all peasants who farmed land within the zone guarded by the crop watching association irrespective of whether they owned or rented the land. At the same time crop watching fees were gradually increased, and between 1937 and 1941 they rose rapidly from 15 *ch'ien* to 60 *ch'ien* per mow.[58]

Prior to the establishment of the crop watching association, a village boundary had not really existed in any formal sense.[59] Numerous disputes broke out between peasants in different villages over rights to use the land, and the absence of any fixed boundary made it difficult to determine and define villagers' land rights and peasants' obligations to their village. Several customs were widely practised which further support the view that the village as a fixed and corporate entity did not exist.[60] There was the system of *k'ai-yeh-tzu,* whereby the council fixed a specific time when villagers and outsiders could freely enter the sorghum fields and pick the leaves.[61] There were two reasons for the adoption of this system. First, picking the leaves hastened the crop's fruition so it could be harvested in the early fall. Second, the council considered the practice a means of discouraging pilfering and theft later on. There were other such customs, such as permitting villagers and outsiders to gather the leavings on the field after the harvest, to collect stalks and refuse in the fields during the winter, and to graze livestock on fields not in use.[62] After increased tax pressure was brought to bear upon villages, the crop watching association became the institution delimiting the area which a village could call its own. The crop watching boundary became synonomous with the village boundary.

The headman and council were also responsible for supervising the *pao-chia* system, which was established in 1938 by order of the county government. Ten households were combined to form a *chia,* and the 6 *chia* heads in Sha-ching concurrently served on the village council.[63] These 6 *chia* formed a *pao,* whose chief was the village headman. The local government used this organization to collect census data, report the movements of villagers, and mobilize the village for self-defense. By grouping households into *chia,* the council found it easier to decide which households would take up night patrol in the village during the summer and fall. A monthly schedule was drawn up on the basis of the amount of land each household owned: households with 5 mow supplied a guard for one night each month, and those with 10 mow provided a guard for two nights of every month.[64]

The headman also supervised the village primary school, which accepted children from nearby Wang hsien ssu village.[65] The school was supported by crop watching association fees from Sha-ching and Wang hsien ssu. Children were taught sections of the classics and fine arts; technical subjects on farming, history, mathematics, and geography were not taught. Families eagerly sent their sons, but not their daughters. Students never graduated but gradually ceased to attend school as work in the fields demanded more time. Newspapers and magazines did not circulate in the village, and only a few peasants understood the more simple characters on wall posters or legal documents.

In 1928 a new road linked Shun-i to Peking, but repairs frequently had to be made to keep the road open and the villages were often asked to supply labor for this purpose. After 1937 villages were also requested to supply labor to guard the railroad lines and construct fortifications. The village headman was instructed to supply a certain number of workers for a short period at no cost to the county.[66] The headman and council worked out a rotation system whereby each household supplied one or more male laborers according to the amount of land owned. Members of the council served their work days like other villagers, but they received a small payment from the crop watching association.

It is clear that formal organizations only emerged in Sha-ching after 1900, and their creation was in response to local officials demanding increased taxes and corvee labor and trying to regulate village life. The village met these demands through its leadership, which managed to create certain organizations and allocate tax and corvee burden on an equitable basis to placate the local authorities and maintain village harmony and peace.

Village and County Finance

The local government's main purposes were to keep the peace, maintain communications, and collect taxes. A large police and militia had

Table 8. Comparison by different categories of Shun-i county's budget expenditure and revenue, 1931–1940.

Expenditure and revenue	Per cent of total expenditure and revenue	
Type of expenditure	*1931*	*1940*
Direct administrative costs (police and judiciary)	67	93
Education	24	7
Construction and loans to villages	8	0
Tax collection	2	?
Total	100	100
Components of revenue	*1931*	*1940*
Land tax and surcharge on land tax	31	9
Extraordinary levies (*t'an-k'uan*)	37	49
On peasants	30	36
On merchants	7	13
Slaughter and market excise taxes	12	21
Other incomes and taxes	0	21
Total 67,000 yuan	100	204,778 yuan 100

Source: Data for 1931, *Shun-i hsien-chih*, 6:2 (1933); for 1940, *CN*, II, 327.

been created to achieve these ends, and this meant more tax revenue was needed to pay their salaries. The Shun-i local government had not undertaken a land tax reform until 1938. In that year officials attempted to check the amount of cultivated land and revise the land tax records, but the survey was never completed. The county authorities were forced to increase revenue through the traditional tax system.

The fiscal relationship between the county administration and Shun-i's villages can be seen in the great increase in revenues and expenditures which took place between 1931 and 1940. (See Table 8.)

Expenditures and revenues rose roughly three-fold in the nine year period between the times when the Nationalist government administered Shun-i and the Japanese military established their control after 1937. Administrative, police, and militia costs increased greatly and were paid by increased periodic levies on the peasants and merchants, the *t'an-k'uan*. In 1931, three fifths of county expenditure went for administration and police stations as against nine tenths in 1940. The outlays for education and economic development were drastically reduced during the period of Japanese occupation. Although the land tax was not increased, other levies were increased greatly, and in 1940 they accounted for half of the county's revenue as opposed to only one third of total revenue in 1931. In the 1890s the major source of county revenue, roughly 90 per cent, came from the land tax, and nearly all outlays went for official salaries.[67] By 1928 the situation had changed: the share of land tax revenue had fallen and that of *t'an-k'uan* greatly increased. This trend continued thereafter.

In the late Ch'ing period Shun-i had six departments called *hu-fang*. These were staffed by sixteen lower-ranking officials, called *shu-chi*, responsible for collecting the land tax.[68] The office of *shu-chi* was hereditary and remained within the same kinship group.[69] Their salary was a fixed per cent of the land tax and so fluctuated each year unless supplemented by bribes. The *shu-chi* were assisted by two groups of tax collecting agents: the *pao-cheng*, who worked at the district level and were paid by the district, and the *ti-fang*, who worked at the village level and were paid by the villagers.[70] Their function was to see that delinquent taxes were paid and that peasants paid their tax on time. The six tax collecting departments kept tax records called *hung-pu*, which showed the amount of land taxed and the taxpayer allegedly owning the land.[71] When land changed hands, the buyer was supposed to report the transaction to the tax department holding records of the land and to pay a fee called the *kuo-ko*, which was a small percentage of the purchase value.[72] After this fee was paid, the *shu-chi* entered the new landowner's name in place of the old taxpayer in the tax records. Peasants paid their land tax each year to the tax department nearest their village, and these taxes were then forwarded to the county tax office in Shun-i. The land tax had been slightly increased during the 1920s by the levy of a fixed surcharge, but the peasants had not regarded this as greatly burdensome.[73] The tax they dreaded most was the *t'an-k'uan* or periodic levy.

The official in charge of the Shun-i tax office outlined the *t'an-k'uan* system as follows.

Question: What is the tax called *t'an-k'uan?*

Answer: For example, in budgeting the county's revenue and outlays for a given year, if there is insufficient revenue, the burden falls on the peasants and merchants. This is called *t'an-k'uan*. *T'an* means to equalize, and *k'uan* means a quantity of money. The amount of money to eliminate the deficit is apportioned one third to merchants and two thirds to peasants.

Question: Taking the merchants as a group, how is their levy share divided equally between each merchant?

Answer: At first the burden is apportioned to each town in the county. For Shun-i the share is 30 per cent, and for the towns of Yan k'o chuang, Wu lan shan, Li sui chen, and Li chia kao it is 35 per cent,

25 per cent, 8 per cent, and 2 per cent respectively. In each case the burden is apportioned to the merchant association of that city. I do not know the exact amount each merchant pays, because the tax office has nothing to do with the way each city association divides the quota among its members.

Question: In the case where there is a deficit of 1,000 yuan, how much of this would fall on the peasants and how much on the merchants?

Answer: Peasants would pay 700 and the burden would be apportioned to each of the 8 districts. All 8 districts would be assessed equally. Each district would apportion a share to each village, but the amount paid by each village would not necessarily be the same. I do not know the exact share each village pays.[74]

As prices gradually climbed and administrative costs rose, it became increasingly expensive for the local government to maintain the size of the county defense corps, police, and local government personnel. Inflation seems to have been the main reason why the *t'an-k'uan* became more frequent and burdensome in the late 1930s. In 1940 Sha-ching paid 4 levies compared with one levy per year in the early 1930s. The police were primarily responsible for collecting the *t'an-k'uan*. Each district police station ordered all village headmen to report and discuss the allocation of the levy among the villages.[75] Each village was allotted a share of the district quota, and the headmen returned to their villages to confer with the village councils on how much to assess each household. As already mentioned, villagers were assessed on the basis of the amount of land they farmed, which was prescribed by the crop watching association. When the peasants were informed of the new fees they brought their money forward to the headman, who gave it to the police when they came to collect. Merchant associations in each market town were notified of their quotas in a similar manner, and each association then discussed how to divide the levy quota equitably among its members.[76] Each merchant then paid the stipulated amount at an agreed time. In 1931 four fifths of the *t'an-k'uan* burden fell on the peasants and merchants paid the remainder, but in 1940 the share paid by merchants had increased to one third the amount of the county *t'an-k'uan*.

It is not precisely clear when police stations (*fen-so*) were established in each of Shun-i's eight administrative districts. It is quite likely they date from the 1920s.[77] These police stations were supposed to keep the peace, assist the local government in matters of rural administration, and make sure that villages paid their taxes. The budget outlays for these police stations increased greatly during the 1930s, and it appears that if funds were insufficient, as was most often the case, the *fen-so* collected the revenue they needed by *t'an-k'uan*. These police stations became an integral part of the local government and played a very important role in the tax collection system.

The next large item of tax revenue consisted of a variety of taxes called *ya-tsa-shui,* which were excise taxes levied on nearly all commodities exchanged in the county's market towns.[78] Several persons were selected in the principal market towns and made responsible for collecting these revenues and forwarding them to the county tax office. One such important tax was the surcharge levied when farm animals and fowl were slaughtered, called the *t'u-tsai-shui.*[79] In each market one person was designated to collect these fees, which depended on the number of animals slaughtered and their type. The introduction of these new taxes after 1911 was made possible only by extensive tax farming. Private individuals appointed by the local government to collect these taxes were allowed a fixed percentage of the revenue as their salary.

5. Luan-ch'eng County: Ssu Pei Ch'ai Village

Luan-ch'eng county, located on the south central Hopei plain a few miles east of the Peking-Hankow railway and about 30 miles south of the large city of Shihmen, had always had easy access to large markets. In the nineteenth century the main road linking northern Hopei to the south passed through this county and not far to the east lay the Grand Canal. After the railroad was built, the nearby city of Shihmen quickly became a large grain and cotton transshipment center.[1]

Luan-ch'eng, like its neighbors Ning-p'u and Chao counties, had specialized in cotton since the Ming period. Although in 1910–1911, more land was devoted to cultivating millet, a rise in cotton prices resulted in a shift to cotton, so that by 1930 cotton occupied 70 per cent of the cultivated area, and Luan-ch'eng ranked sixth in Hopei for area under cotton and quantity produced.

From 1937 onwards war disrupted urban industry and marketing, and consumer goods and food prices rose rapidly. When agricultural output data of 1942 are compared with those of 1930 (Table 9), they show that land under cotton was reduced and greater attention was being given to food production. A possible discrepancy is the 5 per cent rise in cotton output taking place when cultivated area declined 21 per cent. Assuming the statistics to be correct, such an increase can only be explained by more efficient irrigation and more intensive cultivation of the land and a bumper harvest. Total cultivated area had declined while population continued to increase in the early 1940s.[2] Even the irrigated area of farm land declined.

Land distribution in the county was very unequal with 64 per cent of households owning less than 50 mow farms.[3] This meant that two thirds of the peasantry had farms fewer than 8 acres per household. There were a dozen well-known, powerful, absentee landlords with 500 and 600 mow living in the county seat and other large cities and leasing their land to tenant peasants. Below this group were numerous, smaller absentee landlords with several hundred mow or less living in the county seat and market towns where they owned property, financed the operation of stores, wine shops, and cotton brokers, and loaned money.

The county's population in 1840 was 85,000, by 1933 it numbered 97,000 and by 1942 it had risen to 121,000.[4] This sharp increase could well be due to the turmoil caused by the war, when large groups of urban refugees moved through the countryside and the populations of many counties were abnormally swollen.

The villagers of Ssu pei ch'ai came originally from Hung-t'ung county in Shansi during the late Ming and early Ch'ing periods.[5] The village was first

Table 9. Change in number of households, cultivated land, and output for Luan-ch'eng, 1930–1942.

Population and crop change	1930		1942 (January)	
Rural change in county				
Total number of households	17,700		22,043	
Total cultivated area	491,000 mow		418,184 mow	
Total irrigated area	396,000 mow		349,739 mow	
Total non-irrigated area	95,000 mow		68,445 mow	
Cultivated area of American cotton seed	68,000 mow		28,000 mow	
Cultivated area of native cotton seed	170,000 mow		160,000 mow	
Individual crop change	Area (mow)	Output (catties)	Area (mow)	Output (catties)
Wheat	103,000	21,049,000	–	12,726,000
Sorghum	17,000	2,476,000	12,000	2,116,881
Cotton	238,000	8,579,000	188,000	8,979,700
Potato	12,000		16,000	
Vegetables	3,000		7,000	
Soybeans	17,500		78,000	

Sources: For 1930 see Tōa kenkyūjo, *Shina nōgyō kiso tōkei shiryō* (Tokyo, 1940), I, 15, for data on households and p. 41 for data on land cultivation. For 1942 see *CN*, III, 15.

named Ch'ai, but as population increased, two more villages formed in the vicinity with the same name. Peasants distinguished between them by naming each according to the compass points. The first village lay to the north, near a temple, hence the characters for temple and north were combined to give the village its name, Ssu pei ch'ai.

The village was located about 2 miles north of the county seat and had a total land area of 2,000 mow. By 1928, the village contained 125 households with around 680 people, and by 1942 the households had increased to 140 with 719 people.[6] Map 5 shows the village's location with respect to two large rivers, the county seat, and the railroad.

Agricultural output had fluctuated sharply from year to year because of erratic rainfall and frequent droughts. Wells were used for irrigation and drinking water, but they were expensive to construct, costing somewhere around 300 yuan in 1940 if taken to a depth of 20 or 30 feet. The annual income for a wealthy peasant with 40 mow of land was about 600 yuan, and three quarters of this was normally spent on consumption.[7] The majority of peasants owned land and earned income considerably less

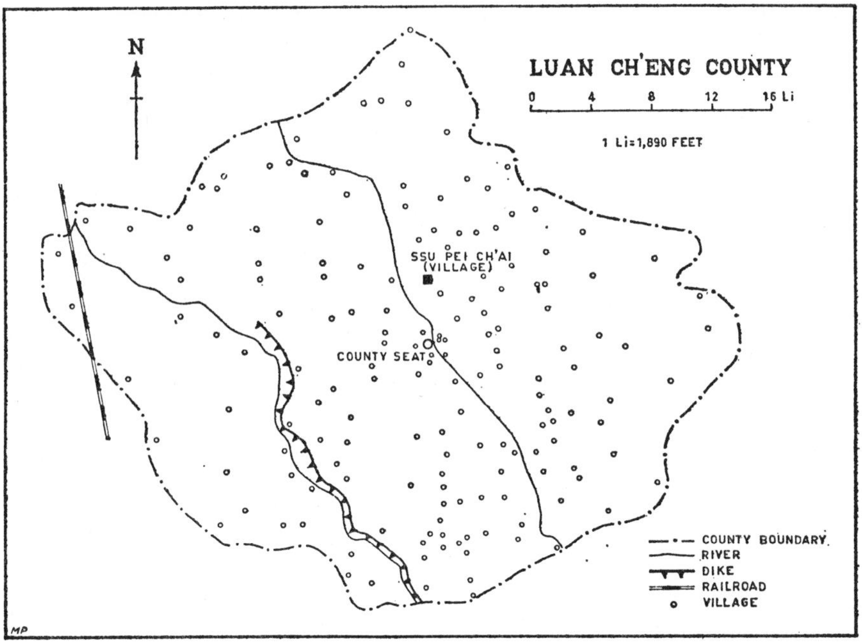

Map 5.

than this and poverty limited the number of wells in the village. There were 42 for irrigation and 12 for drinking water; an average well supplied water for 20 mow of land and, therefore, only 840 mow could be irrigated, leaving about 1,200 mow of land without a dependable water supply.[8]

It was exceedingly difficult to obtain large loans for constructing wells, and the village had recently been very lucky to obtain credit from the Hsin min hui, an association established by the Japanese, to build several wells.[9] Once constructed, a well needed to be repaired at least once every 10 years or it became unusable. Households had no system of renting water or sharing wells. Peasants with wells simply shared their water with friends and neighbors. The village depended mainly on rainfall, and when drought occurred, all village wells quickly ran dry so that no household could control the supply of water through its well.

It usually rained in the late spring and early summer. If rainfall was light during the spring sowing months, the villagers could expect to harvest only half their normal crop. If rain did not fall between January and June, as often was the case, drought usually ruined the cotton and grain harvests. On the other hand, if heavy rain fell in June, the cotton and grain crops were washed away. In the summer of 1917, six days of heavy rain caused flood and complete destruction of the harvest; later that year officials had to import food from Shansi. In 1921, a dry season between January and July caused drought and ruined the year's harvest. In the spring of 1928, severe hailstorms wrecked the cotton crop and injured many peasants, and in 1931 and 1932, pests attacked and ruined the cotton crop.

Land

In the spring, cotton was planted in a given area, and beans, vegetables, and certain medicine crops were planted between the rows and on the remaining land. These crops were harvested in late August and September. The land used to grow cotton was then turned to wheat, which was harvested in the following spring. At spring time, cotton was planted in another section, and that land which had cultivated cotton and wheat was used to grow millet or beans. In the subsequent year cotton was again grown in its former area, and this cycle was repeated.[10] This was the system of two harvests every three years, and this crop rotation system had been used ever since the Sung and Yuan periods.

Land Tenure

Ssu pei ch'ai is a fascinating example of how owner-cultivators became tenants and absentee landlords came to control village land. The data in

Table 10. Distribution of land according to occupancy in Ssu pei ch'ai, 1941.

Type of occupancy	Amount (mow)	Per cent
Owner-cultivated	682.2	32
Tenant-farmed	1,392.2	68
Total	2,074.4	100
Mortgaged to outsiders	599.3	95
Mortgaged to villagers	28.0	5
Total	627.3	100
Tenant farm leased by outsiders	1,325.9	91
Tenant farm leased by villagers	66.1	9
Total	1,392.0	200
Mortgaged to outsiders and worked as tenant land	599.3	46
Owned by outsiders	726.6	54
Total	1,325.9	100
Village land owned by outsiders	1,325.9	67
Outside land owned by villagers	682.2	33
Total	2,008.1	100

Source: CN, III, 5.

Luan-ch'eng County: Ssu Pei Ch'ai Village

Table 10 show the amount of owner-cultivator and tenant land in 1941 and the amount of land villagers and outsiders owned.

As a result of poor harvests during the 1920s and early 1930s, many villagers had been forced to borrow from the wealthy in the county seat.[11] This meant mortgaging land, and if the loans were not repaid within five years the land was sold. As a consequence of poor harvests and this type of credit system, about two thirds of the village land had shifted into the hands of outsiders, but nearly one half of this land was mortgaged and could still be redeemed. Yet, allowing for the fact they could redeem all their land, roughly one half of the village land would still have been owned by outsiders. A large amount of land had simply been sold because households had been desperate for cash.

The land mortgaged to obtain credit was still used by the original owners provided they paid rent. If the peasant had to sell his land, the new absentee owner continued to rent the land to someone else in the village. Few villagers mortgaged land to other villagers because none had sufficient cash to lend. Few leased land to other villagers because they needed to farm all their available land to earn a living.

The example of Ssu pei ch'ai must not be used to infer that landlords had generally increased their power and number in Luan-ch'eng. Such examples have often been cited to prove such a trend was taking place throughout China. The fact is that the large landlords of this county had decreased in number and owned less land than in former times. Before 1920 there were more than a score of landlords owning over 500 mow, but by 1940 only a dozen were in this category. Landlords with 500 mow and less had become wealthy by lending money and accepting land as security from the borrower. When the borrower defaulted on his loan, the moneylender acquired the land and then leased it, using the rent to pay taxes and manage his small business in the market towns.[12] The fourteen largest absentee landlords who owned and held mortgaged land in Ssu pei ch'ai are presented in Table 11 according to their main business, amount of village land owned, type of rent contract with tenant, and length of tenant lease. Only one landlord actually farmed land; the others were in business or in the county administration. Those holding mortgaged land permitted their debtors to use the land and pay a fixed amount of rent. Leases varied from very short term to 10 years or more, but most were fixed according to when the mortgaged land would be redeemed. Only a small amount of rents returned to the village in new credit. These absentee owners made no provision in their rent contracts to assist their tenants to develop their land nor did they care how the land was used.

Thirty-eight households or 36 per cent of total households farmed plots of more than 20 mow, a little less than half the number of households farmed less than 10 mow, and nearly 20 per cent or 25 households did not cultivate any land.[13]

Table 11. Amount of land, type of rental contract, period of lease, and main business of fourteen landlords in Ssu pei ch'ai.

Landlord's name and residence	Amount of land (mow)	Type of rent contract	Length of tenant lease (in years)	Main business
Wang Tsan-chou, Pei kuan	390	Tenant and tenant-mortgaged (fixed rent)	1–14	Money lending
Wang Lo-yao, Pei kuan	244	Tenant and tenant-mortgaged (fixed rent)	1–10	Coffin making
Wang Lo-k'uei, Pei kuan	89	Tenant and tenant-mortgaged (fixed rent)	4–20	Grain dealer
Wang Lien-kuei, Pei kuan (son of Wang Lo-k'uei)	27	Tenant and tenant-mortgaged (fixed rent)	4–6	
Wang Tien-kuei, Pei kuan (son of Wang Lo-k'uei)	9	Tenant-mortgaged (fixed rent)	1	Grain dealer
Wang Lien-tzu, Pei kuan	27	Tenant-mortgaged (fixed rent)	2	Farmer
Li Kuan-cheng, Pei Kuan	77	Tenant and tenant-mortgaged (fixed rent)	3–10	Landlord
Lin Feng-hsi, Hsi kuan	30	Tenant (fixed rent)	1	Wine shop
Chang Heh-tan, Hsi kuan (Deceased, survived by family)	30	Tenant (fixed rent)	1	
Li Lo-keng, Hsi Chieh (deceased, survived by two sons)	52	Tenant (fixed rent)	5–15	Wine shop
Li Chu-t'ing, county seat	40	Tenant (fixed rent)	15–20	Wine shop
Li P'ei-tzu, Hsi chieh	32	Tenant (fixed rent)	12	County official
? ? County seat	62 (incomplete)	Tenant and tenant-mortgaged (fixed rent)	1–8	
Ssu pei ch'ai, (? name)	59	Tenant and tenant-mortgaged (fixed rent)	1–8	?

Source: *CN*, III, 177–186.

Luan-ch'eng County: Ssu Pei Ch'ai Village

There were two rent-paying systems. The first was *shao-chung-ti,* in which a fixed percentage of the harvest was paid in kind by the tenant irrespective of change in harvest.[14] The more common method of paying rent, practiced by 8 out of the 10 rent-paying peasants, was *pao-chung-ti,* in which a fixed amount of the harvest was paid in kind in spite of any change in harvest.[15] The latter method of rent payment was used by landlords leasing their mortgaged land. After 1911 the peasants had switched from the *shao-ti* to the *pao-chung-ti* system because it benefitted both landlord and tenant to do so.[16] When the largest absentee landlord leasing land in Ssu pei ch'ai, Wang Tsan-chou, was questioned on when this took place, he replied as follows:

Question: Is it not true that in former times most of the land you leased was on the basis of tenants paying a fixed percentage of the harvest as rent?

Answer: In the early Republican period roughly 80 per cent of the land I leased was on that basis.

Question: When was it that land was leased on the basis of tenants paying their rent as a fixed amount of the harvest?

Answer: This occurred recently.

Question: Was it after the time bad weather caused a spate of poor harvests?

Answer: Not necessarily. The peasants and I recognized the mutual gain to be derived by fixing the rent in this way, and so more and more land came to be leased and rented on this basis.[17]

There are two possible explanations of the shift in rent from a proportion of the harvest to a fixed share. First, cotton prices rose rapidly after 1911, and a fixed share paid in rent left an increasing surplus for the peasant's own use. Second, there were many poor harvests after 1917, and this system guaranteed landlords their rent would be paid in full and on time.

Landlords adamantly refused to grant reduction unless all the crop was lost. In the case of any individual in financial distress, the landlord considered it out of the question to reduce rent. The absentee landlord, Lin Feng-hsi, undoubtedly spoke for his social class when he said: "There are no obligations between myself and the villagers of Ch'ai. I have no obligation to them except to receive my rents in kind or money as determined by our original rent contract." [18] This was the attitude of all absentee landlords toward their tenants. They merely leased the land which they had received through money lending and expected the tenants to supply their own capital. They neither instructed the peasants on how to improve farming nor encouraged them to adopt new techniques.[19]

On the rare occasion when a villager mortgaged land to another villager, the recipient farmed the land himself. Because most peasants had mortgaged land to moneylenders, they were permitted to farm the land as long as they paid rent. Absentee landlords had the right to lease the land to someone else, but this rarely happened.[20] Custom dictated that the recipient of the mortgaged land permit the debtor the agreed-upon time to redeem his land and rent it at the same time. Such land was only leased to another peasant as a means to punish a tenant who had tried to pay his rent with poor quality cotton or millet or had not paid his rent on time.[21]

The system favored the debtor during periods of rising prices. In the late 1930s prices rose rapidly and peasants could mortgage or sell additional plots, smaller in size, to repay debt and redeem a large amount of land.[22] Many peasants attempted to do this in 1940 and 1941, and it had created considerable ill feeling between landlord and tenants. The reason was that in 1937 and 1938, poor harvests caused by weather and fighting had made it impossible for many tenants to pay their full rent. In fact these rents had never been paid in subsequent years, and landlords refused to return mortgaged land even when the debt was repaid unless these back rents were paid. The tenants argued that it was impossible to pay these rents under the conditions that had existed in those years, and they demanded the land be returned to them. No landlord was willing to depart from convention on this score and treat his tenant with compassion for fear of losing face within his social class.[23] The outcome of this dispute was never observed by the Japanese. It is quite possible that tenant resistance and hostility to absentee landlords mounted after the appearance of Communist guerrillas in the village sometime in 1940. This example affords a clear illustration of how rancor between peasants and absentee landlords intensified over matters of paying back rents.

Capital

The peasants produced most of their fertilizer and only bought a small quantity of human waste from the county seat.[24] Livestock waste products, especially from pigs, was the main fertilizer, and this was mixed with dirt and stored in the open for a month or so before being applied to the fields. The capital owned by the peasants consisted of carts, ploughs, spinning wheels, looms, water wheels, mules, and donkeys. Only a few peasants possessed the full range of existing capital. There is little evidence that village capital stock fluctuated violently because of theft and loss or large purchases. Peasants with only a few hand tools but no draft animals borrowed from their friends or relatives on an arrangement similar to the *ta-t'ao* system in Sha-ching.

Labor

The peasants were idle in late fall and early winter, but in February the men took the mules to the fields, drew water from the wells, and irrigated the land where cotton was to be sown.[25] March signaled the beginning of the busy season. Cotton and millet had to be planted, and in April when their shoots emerged, they had to be weeded and thinned. Wheat also had to be harvested, and the demand for labor was so great, even women came to the fields to help the men. The grain, once separated from the stalks, was stored in the open fields. After the crop was harvested, it was then taken to the market and sold. Weeding of cotton and millet continued through May and June, only to be interrupted, briefly, by the planting of vegetables. The youth cared for these, while the men worked the fields. In August cotton was harvested, and wheat was planted the following month. Again, women came to the fields to help the men pick cotton as all hands were needed to ensure harvesting the complete crop. In October potatoes and cabbages were harvested and stored. The men now turned to making fertilizer compost, and in December and January they began to prepare the ground for spring sowing.

Growing cotton required much more labor for irrigating, fertilizing, and weeding than did growing grain, and labor could be used more regularly throughout the year, giving households few idle periods. In 1931 American cotton seeds began to appear in the markets, and two years later 2 out of every 10 mow of land growing cotton used these seeds. It required even more labor to make these seeds yield their expected harvest. In 1939 a cotton improvement association was established, and by 1940, 3 out of every 10 mow grew these seeds. In 1941 the association sent an instructor to each village to teach one peasant better methods of production with the expectation that he, in turn, would pass the information along to others.[26] By this time, the peasants had already begun to cut back cotton cultivation in favor of growing food. This belated attempt by the local government to introduce new techniques to increase production indicates the potential gain that peasants could have derived from an efficient and inspired group of administrators. Progress could have been achieved, and from all appearances, the peasants were responsive to the advice offered by outsiders. This was the only attempt during the previous fifty years to change the traditional farming pattern of this area.

In Ssu pei ch'ai, one able-bodied male was sufficient for the majority of households farming less than 10 mow, but peasants with larger farms had to hire workers during the spring and fall. These peasants were hired from within the village and paid a wage according to the seasonal wage rate. The wages for these short-term farmhands rose after January to a peak in June, dropped slightly in July, and then rose to a year's high in

August and September when the demand for field work became most intense.[27] The village supply of labor was enough to satisfy demand and the fields were properly tended and the harvest collected. But the sudden rise in wages during the spring and late summer months indicates that the village was short of labor.

Households with less than 5 mow or owning no land sent their farm-hands to work for other peasants or to the market towns to find odd jobs.[28] After the harvest 20 villagers were known to work as long-term laborers in the market towns of the county;[29] others went to Shihmen or more distant places to push carts, clerk in shops, or work as servants for police and county officials.[30] Some peasants worked as peddlers by going to the county seat to purchase goods and then traveling to other market towns to sell them. They could earn enough to live each day and yet save one or two yuan.[31] A few peasants cooperated to buy cotton from other villagers, and then divided the profits between them.

Strangely enough, after 1937, fewer peasants worked outside the village,[32] because war had drawn many villagers to the armed forces as soldiers or carters. Land transfers became more numerous because of inflation and uncertainty. As a result many peasants found themselves in the unusual situation of having more land to farm than before the war.

There is no historical evidence to show that as the size of farms dwindled, more peasants had to find work outside Ssu pei ch'ai. During the Ch'ing period many worked on other farms or sought jobs in market towns. Land distribution was already very unequal, and a class of peasants with very little land existed. Perhaps acute land scarcity had not driven more peasants to seek outside work, as in Sha-ching's case, because Ssu pei ch'ai specialized in cotton, which was a high income-earning crop. Although many peasants mortgaged their land and farmed it as tenants, the cash from cotton was nearly sufficient to see a family through for the year. If a household was short of cash, money wages could be earned by a few weeks work outside the village, but this was not an important source of peasant income.

Numerous households had divided their land and new households had formed with farms more fragmented than before; yet the population growth of this village and others like it in Luan-ch'eng seems to have been very slow. Demographic change varied greatly in north China. For this reason population pressure on the land had not become so severe in Ssu pei ch'ai as to force all peasants to find employment off the farm. However, there is every reason to believe that it would only be a matter of time before population growth would compel a greater percentage of households to depend on income from non-agricultural employment.

Credit

The methods for obtaining credit were similar to those in Sha-ching. Small sums were borrowed from friends and repaid quickly free of interest. Larger sums had to be obtained from moneylenders in market towns. Grain shops granted loans, but most peasants preferred to borrow from private moneylenders because interest was lower.[33] The peasant usually borrowed in the spring when he was short of the cash needed to buy grain until the fall harvest.[34] If a peasant borrowed 100 yuan in April, he was expected to repay 110 yuan in early September, which meant a monthly interest rate of about 2 per cent. These small loans had to be arranged through a middleman who introduced lender to borrower and arranged the terms of loan. The borrower made out a certificate showing the amount and value of land he offered as security. The majority of peasants borrowed in this way,[35] and they arranged to repay such loans within six months.[36]

If an amount of 400 or 600 yuan was borrowed, the peasant was forced to mortgage land. The value of the land to be mortgaged was calculated as a percentage of the current selling price of the land. The amount of land necessary to repay the loan was then calculated, and when both parties agreed, a mortgage contract was signed with the middleman serving as witness. If the lender lived outside the village, he preferred to allow the borrower to use the land and pay a fixed rent in kind.[37] The peasant could redeem his land in 2 or 3 years if he had paid his yearly rents. No mortgaged land was transferred to another party until the redemption period had passed.

Finally, land could be sold to obtain cash. The peasant only did this if he had exhausted the above methods and still needed cash. Since the poor harvests of the early 1930s many villagers had sold their land. One peasant remarked that "before and after 1937, land had only been sold to outsiders, and no one had been able to buy land from outsiders because everyone was so poor." [38] The seller first had the land surveyed to determine its size and value. Then a deed of sale was drawn up and a transfer deed's tax paid.[39] Again, a middleman brought buyer and seller together, assisted in the settlement of terms of sale, and served as a witness in making the transfer deed. If the seller had sufficient bargaining power to set a price, the buyer either agreed or rejected it.[40] In the past fifty years, several peasants had become specialists in surveying land, and they were always asked to provide this service for a small fee.[41] When the transfer deed was signed, it had to be endorsed by the village headman, who noted any change of land ownership in his records of village land holdings. The buyer paid the deed tax to the headman, who sent it and a copy of the deed to the county tax office.

There is little indication that county land sales increased before 1938. The volume of land sales and mortgages certainly fluctuated with the harvest, but the evidence is too scanty to suggest that a trend existed. Between 1938 and 1940 there were scarcely any land sales, because the wealthy had fled from the area, and few were willing to buy land.[42] After 1940 peace was restored, and land sales again increased because the price of land rose rapidly. Peasants in debt were able to redeem mortgaged land very easily by selling only a small plot.

The following examples are randomly selected from interviews to show what conditions forced villagers to sell their land. Ho Lao-k'ai mortgaged some land in 1927, and when prices declined in subsequent years, he had not saved enough to redeem his land. Conditions in his household became worse, and he decided to sell his mortgaged land.[43] Ho Ehr-ni mortgaged land to the absentee landlord Wang Lien-kuei. When his son married, there was not enough cash to finance his wedding. The mortgaged land was then sold to the landlord Wang Tsan-chou for cash. Ho Mao-tan was extremely poor, and he had to borrow to buy grain. He mortgaged a few mow of land, but later he was unable to redeem it and had to sell. Ho Lao-p'ei had to support his aged mother, wife, and children, and he had no grown sons to help him work in the fields. When his wife died, he borrowed money for her funeral, and to repay this loan he sold some of the land he previously mortgaged to the landlord Wang Lien-kuei. Chang Lo-ch'ing, whose eldest son in 1924 wanted to set up a restaurant in the county seat, borrowed a large sum of money from the landlord Lin Feng-hsi.[44] The venture was a failure, and he could not repay the loan. In December of 1930 Chang mortgaged 48 mow of land valued at 1,750 yuan to Lin Feng-hsi. He had five years to repay the loan and redeem the land. Five years later Chang was still unable to repay the loan. Thus, he became a tenant on his own land, paid a fixed amount of rent in kind per mow after each harvest, and his son helped him farm the land. In 1941 Chang had still not repaid the loan, but he was hopeful the rising price of land would enable him to sell a small portion of his mortgaged 48 mow to redeem the rest. Landlord Lin declared Chang could only do this if he paid the rents which had been in arrears for five years. Chang was wealthy compared to other villagers, but he too had mortgaged land to obtain credit.

This credit system enabled households to buy the goods they needed. The supply of loanable funds was held by a small group living in the market towns, who acquired land in lieu of loan repayments. They were unable to manage this land and see to its improvement.

Marketing

Luan-ch'eng contained six market towns, and the large market in the county seat served Ssu pei ch'ai and 80 other villages.[45] Peasants visited the rural market nearest their village on the prescribed market day to buy food, cloth, and fuel. On such days 50 to 60 villagers from Ssu pei ch'ai departed for market to mingle with 700 to 800 peasants from other villages.

The most important commodity the peasants marketed was cotton. Before setting out for market, the headman designated several peasants to collect a fee made up by a 1 per cent assessment of the selling price of all cotton sold to pay the village's market stall tax. After the tax was paid, any remainder went to reimburse the peasant tax collectors. These peasants also had to calculate price and be on speaking terms with the cotton brokers in the market in order to collect this tax.[46] When the villagers assembled at their stall, they commenced bargaining with the cotton brokers who circulated throughout the market. The day's cotton price was determined by haggling and bargaining. The cotton brokers had to compete vigorously with one another for they only possessed a small amount of working capital and their profit margin was determined by prevailing prices and the prices at which they expected to sell to the wholesalers of Shihmen.[47] These small brokers ginned, packaged, and shipped their cotton to these wholesalers, who in turn shipped the cotton to spinning mills in Tientsin.

The cotton brokers in the county seat market used ginning machines purchased thirty years before from Japan; the machines ginned about 100 catties per day. Before these machines were introduced, the traditional wooden, hand-operated gin, producing only 15 catties a day, was used. These brokers obtained some credit for working capital from native banks in Shihmen, and during the early fall about 30,000 to 50,000 yuan was transferred by these native banks to the county seat to enable brokers to buy cotton.[48] Many brokers also obtained advances from the large wholesalers. On the demand side, cotton brokers alone did not have sufficient market power to determine the price of cotton; they were too numerous and merely served as middlemen between the peasants and large wholesalers.

On the supply side, absentee landlords also sold cotton to the market, but their percentage of the total supply marketed probably was very small. They naturally preferred to sell long after the harvest when cotton prices resumed their rise. Ssu pei ch'ai was an extreme case of landlords controlling a large share of village output, possibly a third to a half of the village crop entering their hands as rent. This was not the case in other villages. Cotton prices were high during the winter months and low during the harvest period. Because landlords retained their cotton and sold during the early spring, their speculative action prevented prices at harvest time from being depressed still lower and prices in early spring from rising higher. Their earnings became savings to lend to the peasants.

After the harvest the peasants repaid debts, bought cloth and fuel, and stocked up on grain for the coming year. The volume of trading was very high at this time, and a considerable flow of funds from villages to market towns took place. In the spring, villages tended to incur debts with the market towns, and a flow of loanable funds to the villages took place. In this seasonal flow of goods and cash, individual peasants, moneylenders, and merchants gained or lost depending upon their business acumen and luck. The commodity and credit markets were organized on the basis of highly competitive bidding between many buyers and a fairly large number of suppliers. In the short run prices and interest rates rose and fell because of the harvest fluctuation. A good harvest meant lower prices and interest rates, with the opposite holding true when the harvest was poor.

In Chapter 9, I will show that agricultural commodities and consumer goods' prices rose together and quite rapidly after 1911. As long as the market in which peasants sold and purchased their commodities was fairly competitive on both the demand and supply side, rural prices were mainly determined by demand from the treaty ports, subject only to the character of the harvest. Interest rates had not changed over the previous fifty years, but after 1938 inflation caused them to rise abruptly. The stability of long-run rural interest rates merely suggests the supply and demand for loanable funds adjusted correspondingly with little lag, and that income distribution remained fairly constant so that the property-owning class in the market towns provided the bulk of loanable funds. Considerable specialization of cotton production had already taken place quite early in the Ch'ing period, and the peasants depended as much on marketing a high percentage of what they produced then as they did after 1911. Few basic changes in the production and marketing structure of this county worthy of comment seem to have taken place.

The relationship between market towns and villages consisted of claims to land by villagers and moneylenders changing over time because of the harvest and trend in farm prices. In Ssu pei ch'ai's case, a continued price rise made it easier for peasants to redeem their mortgaged land. Price decline was disastrous; households quickly spent more than they earned, and they had to mortgage land to do this. The rural credit system, the fluctuation of the harvest, and the trend of farm prices were the three basic factors explaining why the amount of tenant land varied from one village to another.

Land Inheritance

Villagers gave their loyalty, affection, and support to the family, not the clan or the village. The family linked the individual to his ancestors and encouraged the sons to acquire land and bring prestige to the family name. The task of keeping the family intact fell to the household head, whose authority in deciding family affairs was enormous. He controlled the household finances and received the money earned by his sons working outside the village. He went to the market and enjoyed the rare opportunity of socializing with other peasants. All his wisdom, experience, and foresight were required to plan production so as to ensure that the household would have sufficient income to buy food for the coming year. His major aim was to accumulate wealth for the household in order to bring prestige to the family name and provide security for the family. The method of dividing the land equally among the male heirs was regarded by the family head as a means of ensuring that all sons would have an opportunity to live on the land. Opportunities to leave agriculture were few, and the safest way of guaranteeing that the family unit would be preserved through each generation was to enable each son to start farming on his own with part of the family land.

According to a survey completed in the spring of 1942 only 39 of the 140 households had not divided their wealth between the sons, and of this number 19 households had no land and were so poor that dividing the wealth was out of the question. The remainder consisted of newly formed households, offshoots of older families which had already divided their land. The majority of households had divided their land at least once, in some instances twice, within a forty year period. Table 12 shows the

Table 12. Frequency of division of household land in Ssu pei ch'ai, late nineteenth century–1942.

Type of case	Number	Percent
Household division reported		
Before 1890	11	7.3
1890–1909	26	17.3
1910–1919	7	4.7
1920–1929	23	15.3
1930–1941	30	20.0
Cases reported as unknown	13	8.7
No household division reported	40	26.7
Total	150	100.0

Source: CN, III, appendix.

frequency of household division according to ten year periods and is based upon household replies to the 1942 survey.

Every twenty years a large number of households divided and new households formed. During the 1920s and 1930s there is some indication that the rate of household division had increased. The reasons for dividing land were the same as in Sha-ching: tensions led to disputes between family members and had to be resolved by separation of the quarrelling factions. A middleman from the same lineage group was called in to arrange the matter, and with his help a document was drawn up stating how the land

and property would be divided.[49] When the household head died, a small portion of land called *yang-lao-ti* was set aside to support his widow and pay her funeral expenses.[50] The widow could take turns living with each son while one son farmed the *yang-lao-ti* land. Dividing the land did not mean abrupt changes in the family, for members might continue to live together for some time. When a new home was constructed, the son and his wife departed. The custom of marrying the sons at an early age of between 15 and 18 years of age meant that a son's wife came to live in the same household just as he was arriving at adulthood. Under these circumstances it was very easy for disputes to arise between sons or sons and their father, which led to demands for greater independence from their parents.

The villages in Luan-ch'eng county contained many lineage groups, but usually one or two with the same family surnames dominated in village affairs by virtue of their number and wealth. In Ssu pei ch'ai there were 53 families with the surname Ho (read also as Hao or Shih), 23 with the surname Liu, 23 with Hsu, 19 with Chao, 9 with Chang, 8 with Wang, 4 with Li, one with Kuo, one with Yu, and one with Tung.[51] In some villages all households had one surname.[52] The Ho clan had migrated from Hung-t'ung about 500 years earlier to find new land. This lineage group consisted of five family groups with their respective household heads.[53] Clan members met for weddings, funerals, New Year's festivals, and for divisions of household property. The Ho clan was the only village clan that had kept a genealogy book to record its descendants, but the book was discontinued for unknown reasons. Despite the size and solidarity of this clan, these five household groups had never assembled together at one time. Families rendered assistance to one another, shared capital, and helped construct new homes, but that was the extent of cooperation. Although vestiges of clan organization remained in Ssu pei ch'ai, this social unit was extremely weak and played no important function in the village.

Village Leadership and Organization

Before 1938 a four or five man committee called the *tung-shih* decided village affairs and selected a village headman.[54] This group consisted of prominent villagers who owned land and could read and write. Village leadership changed little over this period except that the council expanded to include additional members. This expansion occurred in 1938 when the *pao-chia* system was established and 14 *chia* were formed. The head of each *chia* was made responsible for recording population change, organizing village defense and night patrol, allocating the tax levy burden, and deciding which household would send a person for the village corvee labor quota.[55] These *chia* heads also made up the village council and cooperated with the village headman to manage village administration.

Luan-ch'eng County: Ssu Pei Ch'ai Village

In 1930 the village headman was elected by household ballots. He was helped by an assistant and the *tung-shih,* and after 1938, the leaders of the 14 *chia.* The village headman had to have sufficient land to be able to devote his attention to village affairs. He also had to arbitrate village quarrels and deal effectively with county officials. Much of his time was taken up in village matters, and his only remuneration was to collect a 1 per cent fee on the value of land sales, of which a part was his wage and a portion went to pay the land transfer deed's tax.[56] The assistant had to be a person of trust and ability to take over in the headman's absence.[57]

After 1920 the headman's duties had increased, and village organizations had multiplied.[58] Until 1940 crop watching was conducted on an independent basis by peasants guarding their own fields or paying wages in kind to others to watch the fields for them.[59] In 1940 a formal crop-watching organization called *k'an-ch'ing* was established; it consisted of ten people patrolling the fields and gardens during the summer and fall nights. These night guards were not paid, and the association did not collect any money. The village headman decided on a rotation system, in which different villagers took their turn each night until the crops were harvested.[60] Some villagers continued to watch their fields or hire guards privately.

In the late Ch'ing period the village council selected several peasants to manage the village granary or *chi-ku-hui.*[61] This group was responsible for each household paying one *sheng* of millet per mow of land a year which was collected and stored in the granary.[62] The scheme was that in poor harvest years peasants could borrow grain by merely signing a statement of the amount they wished to borrow and when they would return the grain. In 1917 the county government ordered all villages to organize granaries. Many villages refused to do so and evaded carrying out the order by bribing officials or deceiving them. In Ssu pei ch'ai the granary system was continued, and in the mid-1920s it provided many peasants with enough grain to tide them over until the next harvest. In 1936 the granary system was discontinued, and its disappearance may be attributed to the fact that collecting grain contributions was more difficult because fewer peasants owned their land; and peasants renting land were unable or unwilling to contribute. Furthermore, increased taxes may have made it difficult for peasants to continue to support this organization.

In 1928 a quasi *pao-chia* system was created with five households making a *lin* and 5 *lin* or 25 households making one *lu.* There were 5 *lu* heads, which made up the old council of *tung-shih.*[63] In the spring of 1938 this system was replaced by the *pao-chia* system. Villages in Luan-ch'eng containing over 160 households had two *pao* heads, but Ssu pei ch'ai had only one, who served concurrently as leader of the self-defense corps and village headman.[64] After 1928 a village self-defense corps was organized, consisting of 10 men who patrolled the village every night in the fall and winter.[65] In 1939 a new self-defense corps was created upon orders from the county seat, and all men between 20 and 40 years of age were organized into 4 groups of 40 men and instructed in matters of village defense. Their duties consisted of policing and patrolling the village.[66]

After 1938 many villages in Luan-ch'eng were ordered to supply labor for digging trenches and repairing roads.[67] Ssu pei ch'ai was fortunate to escape this burden,[68] but villages located near strategic sites which the Japanese military wished to protect had to contribute considerable labor for building trenches. These trenches, usually 4 meters deep and 5 meters wide, often stretched 20 miles and occupied an area of about 200 acres. They were constructed to keep guerrillas from attacking towns and garrisons. The peasants whose land was used in this manner were not paid by the county government. When workers were needed, villages in that locality were requested to provide a certain number of laborers and to appear at a designated place and time.

The most troublesome task for the headman was to collect the periodic levy or *t'an-k'uan* and pay the county tax office. *T'an-k'uan* had been collected during the Ch'ing period, but only on rare occasions. After 1920 these levies became frequent, and by the 1930s they became a conventional tax. The county government levied the *t'an-k'uan* when it urgently needed more revenue. The amount was distributed to each county district, which was in turn apportioned to each village on an ability to pay basis. It was the village headman's duty to apportion each household a share of the village levy and collect it. The village council used the method of assessing each household according to the amount of land it used: an owner cultivator paid a certain rate per mow; tenants paid on the basis of the same fee per mow for one out of every five mow they rented; tenants farming their mortgaged land paid on the basis of the same fee of one out of every three mow.[69] Outsiders who used land in Ssu pei ch'ai paid the village the same rate, but tenants who farmed this land did not have to pay. Ssu pei ch'ai's peasants using land in other villages paid this levy according to the fees set in those villages.

In 1940 the village headman Ho Kuo-liang reported that 10 levies had been paid in the village. Each levy usually amounted to 40 or 50 yuan, so that the total *t'an-k'uan* paid by the village came to nearly 500 yuan.[70] Before 1937 the village *t'an-k'uan* was much smaller. When Ho was notified of the amount of *t'an-kuan* the village had to pay at the prescribed time, he convened the council to decide how much to assess each household. Once the amounts were decided and announced to all villagers through the *chia* heads, a time was designated for each household to pay through its *chia* head the amount owing. Ho did not like this job, for every new *t'an-k'uan* meant an increase in assessments, and it exhausted his time, effort, and patience to persuade the villagers they had no alternative but to pay.

The conclusion to be drawn from this brief description of taxes is that the tax burden on Ssu pei ch'ai only became severe during the 1920s and after 1938. Aside from the village granary, the *pao-chia,* crop-watching association, and village defense units were established by order from the county government. The local government first began to press for closer administrative links with villagers after 1928, but only after 1938 do we observe these being created in Ssu pei ch'ai. These organizations actually gave the leadership elite a means of managing village affairs more efficiently.

The village was wealthy enough to pay taxes without recourse to a crop-watching association for the collection of funds, and fees were assessed only from those who owned land. Before 1938 there is little indication that the village had many formal organizations. Ssu pei ch'ai did not have a village boundary, and there were no formal rules in document form to clarify the legal rights and obligations of the village.[71] This is not to argue that villagers never possessed a sense of belonging to their village and were unable to organize associations and manage their affairs. Ssu pei ch'ai, like Sha-ching, is characterized by the fact that only after 1900 were organizations being created to give villagers an opportunity to promote economic development if they so desired. Does this suggest that historically, villages were amorphous social and economic units without substance? For an unspecified period, yes. But during the early stages of a new dynasty, like the Ch'ing in the late seventeenth century, the bureaucracy might have been very successful in controlling villages. Later, bureaucratic control may have weakened and conditions like those observed in Sha-ching and Ssu pei ch'ai may have become widespread.

Village and County Finance

The county government consisted of a general affairs office, a finance department, an education department, and a public safety department.[72] Within the finance department was a special bureau to collect the land tax in May and December and the *t'an-k'uan.*[73] The county contained five districts, each with a police office staffed with about 100 men and a contingent of military police totalling 180 men, making for a public security force of 1,500 for the county.[74] The police were responsible for collecting the *t'an-k'uan* and mobilizing village labor for construction work. They had direct contact with the villages and frequently ordered headmen to report and discuss matters of taxation, defense, and corvee labor;[75] by 1928 they had become the strong right arm of the county government.

The tax structure underwent considerable change after 1870. In the late Ch'ing period about 95 per cent of county revenue came from the land tax revenue; a large amount of county revenue was forwarded to the provincial finance office. But in 1940, 90 per cent was retained, of which nearly half went to support the public security forces. Table 13 shows the sources of tax revenue on a percentage basis and the allocations of expenditure for the county.

Table 13. Tax revenue and expenditure for Luan-ch'eng county, 1940.

Revenue	Per cent	Expenditure	Per cent
T'an-k'uan	49	Public security forces	45
Land tax and surcharges	24	Administration expenditure	23
Commodity excise taxes	14	Transfer to provincial finance office	10
Former year's surplus, fines, and sales of public assets	23	Other expenses	22
	100		100
Total	252,649 yuan	Total	211,789 yuan

Source: *CN*, III, 459–470.

The tax burden fell squarely upon the peasantry. The land tax had not been increased since 1900 except for small surcharges added to the original amount of tax per mow. The surcharges, once collected, were used by the county government for financing the police, county schools, and defense when planned budget outlays proved insufficient for these activities.[76] The county land was not divided into three grades for tax purposes but a flat tax rate per mow was levied. A householder paid this tax, according to the amount of land he owned, in March and October at the county tax office.[77]

The tax collecting bureau, the *ching-cheng-ch'u,* kept records of all village land, based on information supplied by village headmen, who reported what land transactions took place during a year.[78] From these records officials were able to see which villages paid their taxes and which did not.[79] The land tax was not reduced in the event of a poor harvest.[80] In the case of a bad harvest, the county tax office did not collect the land tax, but in the subsequent year several *t'an-k'uan* levies followed, which usually collected more than enough revenue to offset the previous year's loss of land tax.

There existed a group of quasi-official tax collectors referred to as *ti-fang,* selected from within each village to ensure that villagers paid their taxes.[81] The *ti-fang* were not formally appointed by the tax office, and their position appears to have been hereditary.[82] They did not receive any fixed salary but lived on fees and bribes; they often served as middlemen to arbitrate disputes between peasants. If a peasant failed to pay his land tax, he was visited by the *ti-fang,* who urged him to pay or often applied physical persuasion to make him pay. The *ti-fang* earned money in other ways. When a tenant became ill and could not pay his rent, he might hire the *ti-fang* to loudly denounce the landlord and to solicit public support for reducing his rent. In former times many *ti-fang* had held their posts for long periods, but by 1940 there was only one *ti-fang* residing in the county seat and he had served in this capacity for 20 years. In recent years, as police became more efficient in persuading villages to pay taxes, the *ti-fang*'s role became unimportant and they merely performed minor duties for the headman and assisted him to collect the *t'an-k'uan*.[83] Some also assisted the police and served as runners between the district police stations and the villages.

The *t'an-k'uan* was collected in the same way as in Shun-i county. The police allocated the levy burden among villages on the basis of their ability to pay. The headmen and council then assessed all peasants cultivating the land and set different rates for tenants farming their mortgaged land and tenants renting land.

In April of 1940, the county government ordered a land survey to measure the amount of land owned and cultivated so that the land tax could be adjusted accordingly.[84] This was done on the urging of the Japanese occupation government. Eight officials were sent to each district to confer with village headmen for several months to learn the actual amount of village land. However, these officials did not live in the villages or take the trouble to survey village land. The survey was a failure because it did not produce sufficient evidence to justify a reform of the land tax system, and the tax structure remained intact until the end of the war.

Commodity turnover taxes were paid by brokers and merchants to the tax office. These taxes were levied on cotton, grain, vegetables, and poultry and increased periodically. The county merchant association did not have to pay the *t'an-k'uan*. This association consisted of 755 merchants representing all retailing and wholesaling activities.[85] Merchants involved in the cotton trade had only to pay a tax on cotton and a brokers' tax called *ya-tsa-shui*.[86]

Villages were also expected to deliver cart loads of grass for the livestock and horses kept by the county's public security forces. Cart loads of brush wood were also ordered for fuel. Village headmen were requested to have their villages supply these deliveries, usually without compensation.

After 1928 local officials exerted greater control over the villages and increased the pressure to supply more tax revenue, labor power, and resources. The county budget was not used as a device to promote economic development but to maintain the bureaucratic structure, effectively collect taxes, and keep the peace. The villages had to make more tax payments and supply labor for construction projects. New organizations had to be created so that these burdens were equitably allocated among the villagers on an ability to pay basis. These changes were accompanied by the persistent application of traditional technology and use of age-old farming methods and organizations.

6. *Li-ch'eng County: Ling Shui Kou Village*

Village surveys in Li-ch'eng and En counties of Shantung were conducted after 1941 under difficult circumstances, which made it impossible to collect abundant data to show how county conditions had changed after 1938.[1] It is possible, however, to comment generally on how conditions had changed after 1910.

Li-ch'eng county was located east of Chinan on the Chinan-Tsingtao railway line. The 1924 county gazetteer reports the population to have been 385,000, but the national agricultural survey results published in 1933 show a population slightly over 700,000.[2] It is difficult to say which figures are correct, but it is more likely the 1924 report understated the true number.

Li-ch'eng was a densely populated rural county without industry and specializing in grain production. In 1910–11 the main crops grown ranked by size of cultivated area were sorghum, beans, wheat, and millet, but in 1930 the order was reversed to wheat, millet, beans, and sorghum.[3] Li-ch'eng ranked forty-first in wheat area in Shantung, but twenty-fifth in total wheat output.[4] Wheat yields were higher than other counties because fertilizer was purchased from Chinan, the land was better irrigated, and the soil more fertile.

As seen in Map 6 Ling shui kou village was located several miles northwest of the county seat not far from the Yellow river. In previous years frequent flooding of the area had made the soil very sandy and loamy. The land was flat and marshy and was suitable for rice cultivation.

The village had borne the name Ling shui kou for the past 70 years, but the villagers could not explain how the name originated.[5] This area of Shantung was settled around 1500 by families with the surname Li from Hopei who hoped to find land and a better life. The county seat and two large market towns were within convenient walking distance to the village. Chinan city, only 12 miles away, could be reached after a four hour walk. In the late 1920s a road had been constructed through the village to connect with Chinan. This road was serviced by bus, but villagers preferred to walk because it was cheaper. A half dozen peasants even owned bicycles. The county seat had telephone and telegraph services with Chinan and a post office. Li-ch'eng possessed more modern facilities than did Shun-i and Luan-ch'eng.

Land

The village occupied an area about a half mile long and a quarter mile wide with farm land totaling 4,200 mow. The village was without a fixed

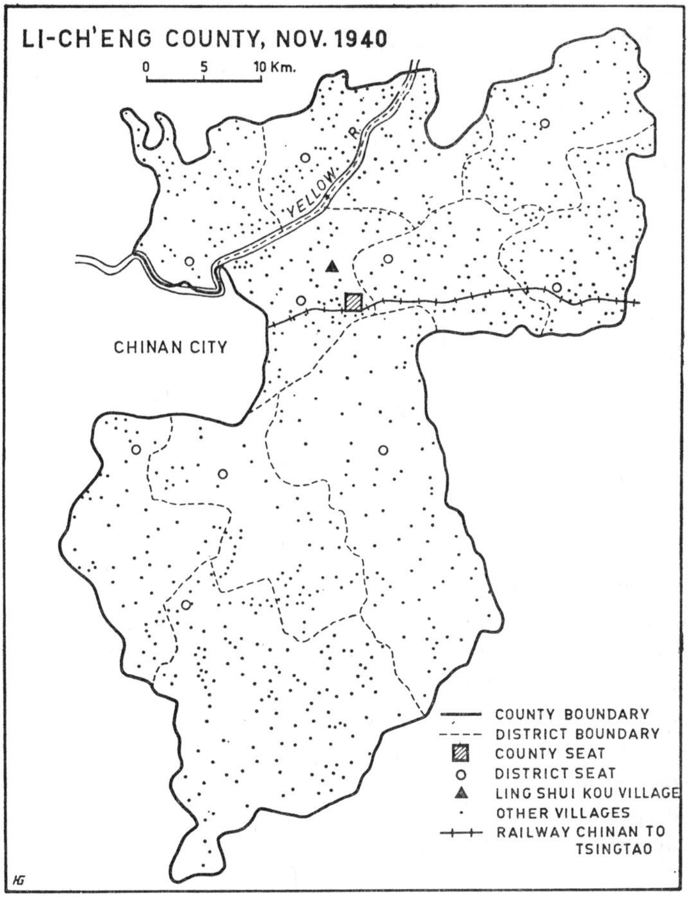

Map 6.

boundary line, and land was always changing from one village to another.[6] In 1928 Ling shui kou contained around 350 households, and in 1941 the number had increased to 360 with a population of 1,800 people.[7] The village headman reported that in 1941 the population had barely increased over the previous decade. Between 1911 and 1941 the village had lost roughly 500 mow through land sales to other villages and wealthy individuals living in Chinan.[8] Grain and vegetables were grown on 3,500 mow with the remainder devoted to rice. Crop yields in 1941 were considerably lower than yields registered for the county in 1931.[9] The village soil was very alkaline, and in the spring after long periods without rain, winds blew away much of the loose top soil exposing a white powdery, alkaline substance, which gave the land the appearance of just having had a light snow fall.

The village had three harvests every two years. After grain and vegetables were harvested in September, wheat was planted on the same land. The winter wheat was harvested in April or May and rice, millet, sorghum, and beans were then planted in place of the wheat. After these crops were harvested, the land was left fallow until the next year's spring sowing. Millet and sorghum were the main food crops. Wheat and rice were marketed; some wheat was retained for festivals, but the entire rice crop was sold.

Most peasants owned their land, but the size of farms ranged from as small as 1 mow to over 100 mow. Three fifths of the households owned 10 mow or less. This land was not sufficient for the majority of peasants to live by farming alone, and they had to earn extra income if they did not want to incur debt in the spring. About three hundred households needed additional non-farm income,[10] so that only 60 had enough land to produce for household needs. Land distribution was also very unequal,[11] but the majority of peasants were able to live in the village rather comfortably because they easily found employment in the market towns and Chinan.

Capital

Fertilizer consisted of bean cake or dirt mixed with pig and human waste and made into compost piles, which were allowed to ferment for several months before being taken to the fields in the winter. The principal tools were simply wooden ploughs, hoes, sickles, rollers, and carts.[12] There were a few wells, but these were expensive to construct and maintain, and the greater part of the land depended upon rainfall.[13] The wells were used intensively in late spring if rain had not fallen, but these soon dried up. When a spring drought threatened, the headman assessed all landowners a small fee to make small sacrifices to the local rain god.[14]

Labor

Peasants with less than 10 mow managed their farms without difficulty during the busy sowing and harvesting periods, but for those with 20 mow or larger, more labor was required than the household could supply. As long as villagers could remember, there had been designated places where people could hire a peasant for several days' work. These labor markets, where short-term labor could be hired, were located near temples and in market towns. One such market was near the village temple of Yang chia tun, several miles from Ling shui kou, where peasants gathered as early as 2:00 A.M. to be hired by those needing farm hands in the rice or grain fields. Another labor marketplace was in the nearby market town of Wang she jen, where peasants could find several days' work in the market town.

Women and children never went to these labor marketplaces to hire themselves out. In the peasant household all sons who could work went to these markets to seek employment, and no distinction was made between the eldest or youngest son working out of the village.[15] Because the land was to be divided equally between the sons, the eldest was not favored as would have been the case if the inheritance custom dictated the land revert to him. The sons gave their wages to the household head, who pooled it with the income earned from the harvest.[16]

Many villagers went to Chinan to work for a few months during the slack farming periods. A half dozen worked in a cement factory, a score worked as clerks in shops, and an unknown number worked as common coolie workers pulling carts.[17] After 1938 larger numbers of peasants departed for Manchuria to find work. In 1940 it was reported that 3,000 from Li-ch'eng had gone there to work in the Fushun mines, build roads, and construct railroads.[18]

There were 17 peasants from other villages employed in Ling shui kou in 1940 on a year-to-year basis as long-term workers.[19] One wealthy household hired three, another two, and the remainder were scattered about the village. Only three villagers worked outside as long-term workers, which shows that the village's living standard was higher than that of Sha-ching and Ssu pei ch'ai. A peasant desiring long-term employment had to have a friend serve as go-between to introduce him to an employer.[20] The go-between was not paid for this service but merely provided the introduction and personal reference.

A long-term laborer usually commenced employment in a household after the harvest. He cared for the livestock and assisted in the fields. He lived with the livestock, but his meals were the same as the household's. He was expected to provide his own bedding and clothes, but he was given tobacco and matches and was paid at the end of the year.[21] He received a month off to visit his home, and if he lived nearby, he was permitted several days holiday each month. If he worked hard and proved dependable, the family treated him as an equal but never permitted him to join the family when it discussed household affairs. The long-term worker was a servant and laborer. There were several classes of these workers depending upon their age and ability.[22] A top hand, hard-working and experienced, earned as much as 120 yuan a year in 1940; a second-class worker earned between 40 and 80 yuan, and elderly peasants earned only 20 to 60 yuan.[23] These wages were approximately double those paid in 1931.

There were various forms of side work by which peasants supplemented their farm income. A number of craftsmen, farming on a part-time basis, worked in the village: ten made tools in a small iron workshop; another dozen worked in a small ceramic shop.[24] Three households managed small shops selling paper, matches, and oil, purchased in Chinan. Their capital was small, and they earned just enough to get by.

The main village handicraft industry was making straw braids.[25] The straw was obtained from the rice harvest. One household gathered the straw and worked it to make braid. Another fifty households specialized in making containers to ship the straw braid to market. The remaining households produced straw braid during the winter months, and several peasants marketed the braid in Chinan. This division of labor was based upon the abilities of different households to perform special tasks. One village had purchased a straw braid making machine, but Ling shui kou's peasants feared that if they purchased such a machine too much braid would be produced and prices reduced.

The peasants produced their cloth from yarn purchased in the market towns. In former times they had spun their yarn, but when machine-made yarn became abundant and cheap after 1900 they purchased it instead. After 1938 yarn had become so expensive that most households had to reduce their weaving of cloth.[26]

Households pooled their tools, livestock, and labor during the busy farming seasons in an arrangement called *ho-chü*.[27] A household head with land but no capital sought out another peasant who possessed a tool or animal.[28] The two arranged to share the tools and livestock and assist each other in the fields. Households owning between 10 and 15 mow were the usual partners in this arrangement. There were only a few cases of such cooperation along lineage group lines, the majority being between friends and neighbors. These periods of cooperation lasted two or three years, and in some cases as long as 10 years. There were 80 to 90 cases of household cooperation reported in the village.[29] This custom was widely practiced in central Shantung and seems to have existed for over a century or more.

Land Tenure

Although the land tenure system was akin to that of Sha-ching and functioned mainly to equalize the use of land, the amount of tenant held land in the county villages was extremely small, and only a small percentage of farmers were tenants.

Ten absentee landlords holding land in Ling shui kou lived in Chinan, but they owned very little land — the owner of the largest amount held only 22 mow — and were primarily engaged in commerce.[30] There were several cases where land had been inherited by these landlords, but it was mainly acquired through moneylending.[31]

In the villages of Li-ch'eng, peasants with too much land or plots too far away to manage properly leased land to peasants owning less than 2 or 3 mow.[32] In Ling shui kou there were only 10 to 20 households renting land.[33] A peasant wishing to lease land would ask a friend or relative to act as middleman to find a prospective tenant and assist in arranging the terms of contract. Once the amount of land, rent, and type of payment were agreed upon, a rent agreement was drawn up and signed by tenant, landowner, and middleman.[34]

Li-ch'eng County: Ling Shui Kou Village

There were two types of rent systems. The first was called *fen-chung,* in which the harvest was divided on a share basis between landlord and tenant.[35] These shares were fixed irrespective of harvest fluctuation. The second system was called *tsu-ti;* a fixed amount of rent per mow of land was paid in kind after the harvest. This amount differed according to the type of crop.[36] The *fen-chung* arrangement was used for poor land, and tenants received only 20 to 30 per cent of the harvest.[37] The *tsu-ti* rent system, used on better quality land, assured tenant and landlord of a better yield, but as crop yields varied greatly throughout the village, *tsu-ti* rents naturally differed from plot to plot. Between 1911 and 1938 *tsu-ti* rents seemed to have remained constant,[38] but after 1938 they began to rise. Both rent systems had co-existed for as long as villagers remembered, and there seem to have been few households shifting from one system to the other.

The tenant did not receive any assistance from the landlord, and the relationship between the landlord and tenant was impersonal once they had decided the rent agreement. The period of lease usually lasted only 3 to 5 years.[39] Landowners continually leased land to one tenant and then another. Rent deposits were not demanded.[40] Rent payments were canceled only if the harvest was completely lost. The landlord did not offer capital or advice on how to farm or improve the land. He could sell the land under lease after the harvest, even though the original contract had a year or more to run.[41] Tenants were without rights and had only one obligation: to pay the rent on time. The landowner paid the land tax.

Credit

The demand for credit fluctuated from year to year because of harvest variations,[42] and even during the farming year credit fluctuated on a cyclical basis. Before the spring sowing, peasants borrowed small sums on a short term basis and repaid these loans after the fall harvest. The peasants usually borrowed from 30 to 50 yuan for weddings and funerals or to buy livestock, tools, and fertilizers, but occasionally larger sums of 200 yuan were borrowed.[43] Small sums of 20 yuan were obtained from friends and repaid within a few months. A sum of 50 yuan, usually about one sixth to one fifth a peasant's annual income, was obtained from wealthier villagers.[44] The usual procedure of borrowing, and 8 to 9 out of every 10 peasants borrowed in this way before they mortgaged their land,[45] was as follows.

The borrower sought out a friend or relative to introduce him to a lender. Land was pledged as security, and the terms of the loan were decided without recourse to a written document. Loans of small size did not carry interest, but for a large loan a document was drawn up stating the amount of interest, the collateral offered, and the period for debt repayment.[46] The interest charge was between 1 and 3 per cent per month, and before 1937 these rates had remained fairly constant. Only after 1937 did they begin to rise rapidly, and by 1941 they were 5 and 6 per cent.[47]

Peasants did not know how much land in Ling shui kou was mortgaged, but it was believed that the amount of mortgaged land varied each year depending upon farm prices and the harvest.[48] If a household needed a rather large sum of money, land was mortgaged; when the loan was repaid, the land was redeemed by the original owner. A middleman arranged the terms of mortgage. A mortgage contract or *tien-ch'i* was drawn up stating the amount of land, its mortgage value, and the period to repay the loan, but sometimes the mortgage period was extended to permit the borrower more time to repay the loan. Both parties, including the middleman, signed this document, and the transaction was concluded.[49] The recipient of the mortgaged land used it as he saw fit until the loan was repaid. In Ling shui kou several peasants continued to farm the land they mortgaged as tenants.

A holder of mortgaged land could transfer it to another.[50] Just as one's land was regarded as near-money, so too was mortgaged land. For example, if a third peasant offered a higher price than the original mortgaged value, the holder of mortgaged land could dispose of the land and realize a capital gain on the original loan transaction. This was done, however, only after a long period in which it became obvious to the mortgaged landholder that the borrower would not repay his loan. However, if the original borrower redeemed his land, the difference was repaid by the first mortgage holder, who had to make some arrangement to return the land to the original owner. Such cases were extremely rare, and usually occurred if a peasant holding mortgaged land suddenly found himself in need of cash. Where cash was scarce and land was regarded as near-money, claims to land were used to acquire cash. Taxes or *t'an-k'uan* on mortgaged land were paid by the original owners.[51] The mortgage period was usually 3 to 4 years, but sometimes as long as 6 or 10 years.[52]

Land that could not be redeemed was sold.[53] Land sales tended to rise after bad harvests. If a household owned considerable land which it could not farm, it sometimes sold 5 or 10 mow to pay for a funeral or wedding. Peasants in great need of cash also sold what little land they possessed.

The method of transferring land had not changed during the Ch'ing period; in spite of Chinan's great growth as an inland entrepot center, the arrangements for transferring land remained the same. A peasant wishing to sell land sought out a middleman who knew how to handle these transactions. The peasant informed him of the reason for wanting to sell, and a document was drawn up indicating the amount of land and its present value.[54] The middleman, with this document, now looked for an interested buyer.

Once a buyer was found, negotiations commenced on the selling price. When this was agreed upon, someone was called in to survey the amount of land to be sold. There were five or six peasants reputed to be skilful in surveying land, an art they had acquired from their fathers.[55] After the land was surveyed, a second document was drawn up indicating the amount of land, size, and location. This was the *pai-ch'i* and was signed by seller, surveyor, and middleman, who were then invited to eat at the home of the peasant selling the land.[56] This document became the basis for drawing up a final land deed called the *shih-ch'i,* which indicated the amount of land and its value. This document was also signed by buyer, seller, and middleman.[57] An enclosure was added to this document stating the fee the buyer paid to the seller when the transfer was concluded.[58] The buyer took the document to the local tax office and paid the land deed tax. The transaction was recorded and a red stamp was affixed to the deed indicating the legality of transfer and payment of deed tax. Henceforth the new owner paid all taxes on the land.

I have discussed in great length the complexity of this credit system and the role played by the middleman in it. In a society where individuals were without protection of property, using a third party to introduce, arrange, mediate, and guarantee was instrumental for minimizing risk and ensuring that transactions would be conducted honestly and agreements obeyed. Of course, this method did not provide 100 per cent protection against fraud and cheating, but it provided a minimum of safety whereby exchange and the transfer of funds could take place with reasonable security.

Finally, there was the credit association established by the peasants themselves called *ch'ien-hui.* In this village there were eight small loan associations composed of about a dozen peasants, who deposited small amounts at regular intervals in the association's safekeeping.[59] Each depositor could borrow the full amount of deposits and repay the sum without interest. The right to borrow was granted on a revolving basis, and each peasant took his turn. The three village shops could not extend credit because their working capital was too small.

No large inflow or outflow of credit and loan repayment characterized Ling shui kou. This was a large, wealthy village, and virtually all borrowing was done between the villagers themselves. Only in rare instances did a peasant go to Chinan to borrow more than 200 yuan from a moneylender. The credit arrangements in Ling shui kou had existed as long as villagers could remember.[60] The village had suffered neither poor harvests nor any ill effects of war. The number of tenant farmers had not increased nor had more peasants incurred debt.[61] The village was without moneylenders, and when peasants had extra cash they immediately purchased land.

Marketing

There were five markets to which the villagers went to buy and sell; these opened on alternate days so that the peasants could always market.[62]

Farm products flowed from the village to the markets on a seasonal basis even though the peasants visited the market towns several times each month to purchase necessities. Certain markets specialized in soybean cakes and livestock, but generally all the markets handled everything normally exchanged in the countryside. The peasants marketed their wheat in May, their vegetables in August, and their rice and grain in September. During the late fall and early winter they took straw, grass, and ducks to market.[63] The merchants of Chinan came to Li-ch'eng's markets to buy grain and vegetables to sell to city shops or directly to consumers. Prices were uniform throughout the country's market towns,[64] because so many city buyers were purchasing for a fairly standard market.

Small native banks or pawnshops did not operate in these market towns, but several did business in Chinan. Moneylenders could be found in every market town. There appears to have been very little flow of credit from Chinan to nearby rural market towns, whereas market towns definitely provided credit to villages. Merchants paid for goods on the spot, and peasants, too, spent their credit quickly for consumer goods.

Land Inheritance

The custom of *fen-chia* influenced the use and distribution of land, but two supplementary practices also increased the successive fragmentation of family plots. These practices were not confined to this area but were typical of north China. When the family property was divided equally among the sons, a portion was set aside for supporting the aged parents. This was the custom of *yang-lao-ti.*[65] If the household head had died and only his widow survived, land amounting to 2 or 5 mow, and sometimes as much as 10 mow, was so provided. This land could be leased to other peasants, but the rent was used to support the aged parent. This land was not to be mortgaged or sold until both parents died, and only then was it to be sold to pay for funeral expenses. Any remaining land was divided between the sons. If the land was not leased while the parents lived, one of the sons farmed it and divided the produce between the sons caring for the aged couple.

With one exception, the household head handled all land transactions and managed the land. When a son married, his wife sometimes brought a small sum of money with her called *ssu-fang-ti,* which was used to buy land.[66] After this land was purchased, it was not turned over to the family head, but son and wife rented it and collected income. They could not farm the land themselves as long as they continued to live with their parents.

There were only a few households in Ling shui kou which had not divided the land for a period of five or six generations.[67] Periodically, a number of villagers would make use of *fen-chia,* and in a fairly short period of time new households would arise in the village, and the land was further divided into smaller plots. Because village land had not changed in size since 1910, periodic division of land must have reduced the size of farms. The family head was strongly motivated to acquire as much land as he could during his life time. The more land he could leave his sons, the greater the assurance that his descendants would venerate him. It was natural for the family head to resist any pressure to divide the land so that the household could prosper that much more. As long as the household had land, its members were secure and other villagers held that family in high esteem. But this effort was often self-defeating. Eventually, the family grew so large it was difficult for the household head to mediate and keep personal relationships harmonious. When tension and friction became intolerable careful preparations were made to divide the land. A friend or relative was called in to assist in drawing up the documents necessary for dividing all property between the sons.

Village Leadership and Organizations

During the nineteenth century the village was without a headman. The village was divided into eight sections, each with a leader called the *shou-shih.*[68] The *shou-shih* made up the village council, which paid the land tax and arbitrated quarrels between villagers. The council did not manage any village organizations. Sometime after 1900 the village began to choose a headman, and the *shou-shih* — wealthy peasants owning between 20 and 80 mow — continued to assist the headman to collect the land tax, allocate the *t'an-k'uan,* and mediate between quarreling villagers. In 1928, the county government ordered that 25 households be grouped to form a *lu* and elect a leader.[69] Fourteen *lu* were founded at this time, and each *lu* head had the same responsibilities as the former *shou-shih.* They received no salary for their efforts, but they conferred and advised the headman and transmitted council decisions to all households in each *lu.* In 1939 the county government ordered that the *pao-chia* system replace the *lu-lin* system. Ten households were organized into a *chia* and a leader elected. Ten *chia* formed one *pao,* and the *chia* heads cast ballots to elect a *pao* head.[70] The *chia* heads carried out the orders of the headman, assisted him in taking the village census, allocated the burden of the *t'an-k'uan,* selected labor for road repair, and settled quarrels among households. They did not receive a salary and served for indefinite periods.

Table 14 has been compiled from data on village council members. These data show the amount of land each owned, how land ownership changed over time, and the degree of social mobility within the village elite.

The most important change since the late Ch'ing period was the decline in wealth of council members. Between 1900–1925 and 1928–1939 the average size farm of a council member declined from 52 to 28 mow. The number of council members increased until the *pao-chia* system was estab-

Table 14. Former village council members and amount of land they owned.

Village organizational system and council members	Amount of land (mow)
Shou-shih during the late nineteenth century (without headman)	
Li Hsiang-ling	–
Li Yu-chung	–
Li Feng-ming	–
Jen Fu-tseng	–
Yang Lao-tseng	–
Yang I-sheng	–
Wang Li-t'ing	–
Shou-shih with village headman until 1925	
Li Hsiang-ling	80
Li Feng-kuei	20
Li Feng-chieh	70
Li Wen-han	50
Yang Li-teh	30
Jen Teh-hsien	50
Wang Wei-hsi	40
Yang Han-ch'ing	80
Lu-lin, 1928–39	
Jen Fu-tseng	40
Li Yung-hsiang	26
Li Hsi-yeh	40
Li Hsing-chang	40
Li Feng-pei	18
Li Chang-hai	8
Li Feng-k'un	20
Yang Li-chien	10
Li Chung-p'u	20
Wang Ch'i-kuei	60
Hsieh Chang-tseng	18
Chang Tseng-hsi	35
Tu T'ing-nien	20 and more
Cheng Chen-sheng	6
Pao-chia after 1939	
Li Feng-k'un	–
Chang Tseng-hsi	–
Liu Hsi-ch'e	–
Jen Fu-yu	27

Source: CN, IV, 25.

lished in 1939. Before 1925 the smallest farm owned by a council member was 20 mow, but after 1928 it was only 16 mow. After 1930 few village leaders had the size of farm which characterized the wealthy *shou-shih* of the nineteenth century.

Between 1928 and 1940 only one peasant served as village headman.[71] Tu Feng-shan was not a wealthy peasant and only owned a few mow of land which he worked with the help of his brother, his 16 year old son, and wife. His main source of income was several hundred ducks. Tu seems to have been a very capable man, extremely patient and wise in handling people. Tu and his brother had not found it necessary to divide their land. His ability to judge fairly, find solutions acceptable to all concerned when disputes arose, and achieve compromise among divided groups explains why he was held in high esteem by the villagers and had retained the post of headman for so long.

It was difficult for Tu to hold this post without receiving a formal salary. For that reason he was given a small sum each year from the four *pao* heads as a token of their respect and gratitude for his services. In addition, he received 100 yuan from village revenue to cover his expenses to attend meetings at the county seat. Headman Tu's outstanding leadership qualities rather than the amount of land he owned enabled him to win the confidence of the villagers and decide village affairs.

Table 14 shows that leaders with the same surname predominated, but this is to be expected in a village where the majority of households have the same surname. What is surprising is to find that other households produced village leaders. Furthermore, village leaders changed, and new personalities bearing different surnames appear in each period. Only one peasant who served as *shou-shih* before 1925 appears in the *lu-lin* system after 1925. Between 1928 and 1939 only two peasants served in both the *lu-lin* and *pao-chia* systems. A particular family or clan did not dominate the village leadership over this fifty year period.

Clan influence in this village was also weak. Some clans possessed burial grounds, but they neither collected fees nor possessed wealth. Clan members gathered only for weddings, funerals, or when land was divided between the sons. Household heads did not confer first with the tutelar clan head before making an important decision. The family constituted the basic village unit.

The village headman had an assistant called the *ti-fang* or *ti-pao*.[72] The *ti-pao* received his pay from village revenue, and he served as liaison between the village headman and the county tax officials responsible for recording changes in land ownership. The *ti-pao* informed the tax office of the amount of land tax revenue it could expect to collect from villages. He also notified households of tax payments, performed a variety of odd jobs, and carried messages for the village headman.

The headman, Tu Feng-shan, had been elected by ballots cast by households owning land, paying land tax, and giving the *t'an-k'uan.*[73] This excluded the village poor, long-term workers, and tenants from having any voice in village government. The headman did not serve for any fixed period, and he remained at the job only as long as villagers tacitly approved his behavior. Tu Feng-shan was unable to read or write, but he was outstanding at dealing with officials and mediating between villagers. More important, he had the ability to get things done.

Just as village leadership became formal and characterized by a more elaborate organizational structure after 1928, so too did various organizations begin to appear. In 1920 the local government ordered villages to establish an organization for protecting crops and reducing crop loss in the fields.[74] This decision came at the precise time the county administration attempted to increase taxes. Prior to this time, crop watching in Ling shui kou had been organized on a private basis with peasants hiring others or watching the crops themselves during the summer months. The new system was called *k'an-p'o* and differed slightly from the *k'an-ch'ing* system of other districts.[75] *K'an-ch'ing* involved watching crops from planting time to harvest; *k'an-p'o* meant the crops were watched at regular intervals: that is, for 2 weeks in April when the wheat was harvested and 3 or 4 weeks in late August and early September when grain and rice were harvested. The village hired 8 peasants to guard each section of the village. They had to be residents of Ling shui kou to qualify for the job and be available for work during the crop watching period. Thus, crop watchers were poor peasants with little land. Several had held this job for 4 or 5 years and one for 20 years. Households whose crop they guarded were assessed a certain amount of grain according to the amount of land they owned, and after the harvest this grain was paid to the crop watcher.

It is not clear when the village leaders made a more vigorous effort to collect revenue, but it probably began after 1911 when *t'an-k'uan* levies became more frequent. Village revenue was not collected on a fixed, regular basis[76] but when funds were needed; the headman and council met to decide the amount each landowner would pay.[77] All households were then notified, and the fees were brought forward at the designated time. This revenue paid not only the *t'an-k'uan* levy, but expenses of the village headman, the village school, and temple.

It became increasingly difficult for the headman and council to collect the *t'an-k'uan,* because of the problem of apportioning the burden fairly on the basis of each household's ability to pay. The average annual *t'an-k'uan* paid by the village before 1937 was around 4,000 yuan,[78] but after the Japanese military occupied the area, the *t'an-k'uan* increased. By 1940 the village paid 12,000 yuan a year, and the fees ran from 15 *ch'ien* to 1 yuan 60 *ch'ien* per mow. In that year the *t'an-k'uan* was four times the amount of land tax paid. The village would be visited each year, depending upon the number of *t'an-k'uan,* by police or county officials requesting the levy be paid. The headman and council conferred on the assessment of each landowner. Any household owning land in another village paid the levy fee to that village.[79] Tenants did not have to pay land tax or *t'an-k'uan.*[80]

Another burden which became routine and irksome for the peasants was the conscription of peasant labor, without pay, to repair railroads and dig trenches. When county officials ordered a certain amount of labor to be supplied by villages, police instructed the headman of the county districts to meet to decide how much each village would contribute. The headman then conferred with his council on how to select peasants to fill the village quota. In Ling shui kou a household sent one laborer for every 3 mow of land it owned, and he was required to work one out of every 10 days that villagers were conscripted. However, a household could hire another peasant to replace the appointee. The headman assembled the workers and led them to the designated place to work. The usual village quota was 3 to 4 workers, but there were instances when several scores of peasants were recruited. Ling shui kou was one of four villages making a *hsiang* that embraced 995 households, and on one occasion this *hsiang* had to provide 300 men for one week's work without pay.[81]

Several para-military organizations were established in the village after 1938 by order of the county government. Youths between 12 and 25 were organized into an association called the *shao-nien-t'uan* to guard the railroad.[82] A village self-defense corps, called the *tzu-wei-t'uan,* was organized from young men between the ages of 18 and 25. This group never drilled or practiced together and merely served on a standby basis. In 1939 a night patrol called *ta-keng* was established to guard the harvested crops; the *ta-keng* consisted of men selected according to the amount of land owned by a household.[83] A household owning 5 mow was required to furnish one able-bodied man for an 8 hour night guard every 10 days.[84] A family could hire another peasant as substitute if sickness or absence prevented someone from performing his duty. The village had 8 groups to patrol each village section and watch for fires, thieves, and bandits. Each group was made up of 10 men, with 5 patrolling while the others slept; only large sticks were carried by the peasants.

Ling shui kou also cooperated with several other villages in 1928 to form a mutual self-defense unit called the *lien-chuang-hui* to defend the village against banditry.[85] Remnants of warlord armies were raiding villages for food, and the Nationalist government still had not restored order at the county level. The *lien-chuang-hui* was disbanded in 1937 when *ta-keng* were established in each village.

In 1913 an elementary school was established;[86] it was later expanded to accommodate students for high-school-level study. The village financed and supervised the school's operation and selected a principal, who was assisted by three teachers and a servant. The teachers were from the same village but each had received higher education in Chinan. Students paid for their books and paper, but teacher salaries and other expenses came from the village revenue fund. Girls were excluded, and the total student body was about 150 boys. Literacy was fairly high in this village, as 8 or 9 out of every 10 could write his own name,[87] and about one third could read a newspaper. The school received the Hsin min pao paper, and peasants came to the school to read it.

Since 1911 the county administration steadily increased its authority over villages in order to collect more taxes. Pressure from local government to tax was not matched by a willingness to develop the county's resources and promote economic development, but this pressure did produce a distinct response by the villages to organize and devise their own means of raising revenue. During the Ch'ing period the pressure from the local bureaucracy to raise revenue was not severe, and the variety of organizations that came to characterize villages after 1928 is not found in the late nineteenth century.

Village and County Finance

Since 1911 the county government had tried to extend its authority through the district level and *hsiang* to the village, and finally through the *lin-lu* and *pao-chia* systems to the household. In 1911 eight districts were created within the county. In the early 1920s, numerous *hsiang*, comprising a dozen-odd villages, were established. In 1928 the *lin-lu* system was organized, and in 1939 this was scrapped and replaced by the *pao-chia* system. Meanwhile, the county police force was increased in number, and after 1930 a county militia defense corps was created. These new organizations naturally required financing, and this meant introducing new taxes.

The county official in charge of Li-ch'eng was assisted by an office of propaganda and information, an office of education, a bureau for economic construction, and the county finance office.[88] The bureau for economic construction was responsible for communications and agricultural development. After 1928 it supervised the construction of new roads and telegraph lines, and the office of education also made considerable progress in creating new schools and developing existing institutions. These two bodies had insufficient time to make a progressive impact on the village economy, because after 1937 they either ceased to function or their resources were subverted by the county puppet government to aid the Japanese military forces.

The county police force consisted of 60 men organized into four groups, each with a leader. They worked closely with the finance office to ensure that taxes were collected.[89] The county defense militia guarded the railroad, patrolled road checkpoints, and stood by for any emergency. The county tax-collecting office, the *cheng-shou-ch'u,* collected the land transfer deed tax, the land tax, and miscellaneous excise taxes on commodities exchanged in the market towns.[90] By 1940, the county's administrative bodies were functioning only to extract more taxes from the peasants, supply labor for the Japanese military, and maintain order.

The administrative machinery to collect the land tax had not changed basically since the Ch'ing period. Collecting the land tax entailed recording all private land, identifying the landowner, noting the size of his land, and recording all transfers of land ownership. In each county district there existed an office called the *tsung-fang* occupied by a minor official responsible for recording village land of that district. These offices were under the *cheng-shou-ch'u,* and each officer was called a *li-shu.* Li-ch'eng county had 105 such *li-shu,* with one *li-shu* serving between 2 to 10 villages.[91] The *li-shu* for Ling shui kou lived in the county seat; he was a young man, a graduate of a high school, and able to read and write. His salary was 300 yuan a year plus extras in the form of "thank-you" money from villages.[92] The *li-shu* recorded the changes in land ownership in the villages under his authority, and each year he submitted to the tax office the amount of land tax the office could expect to collect from his area. This information was given to the police when households and villages were slow in paying their taxes, and they quickly visited the village in question. Such an event represented an extra burden for the villagers, for the official had to be feasted and given the assurance the taxes would quickly be sent. Households paid their land tax three times a year at offices called *kuei.* In 1930 there were 10 such offices in Li-ch'eng. During the Ch'ing period the clerks working in these offices held their position on a hereditary basis, but the position could be transferred to another by sale.[93]

The *li-shu* served as accounting and recording officials for collecting the land tax, but they were also responsible for collecting the tax on land transfer deeds. The first deed tax was called the *kuo-po* and was paid by the buyer to the *tsung-fang* clerk when he registered his land purchase. The other, called the *shui-ch'i,* was paid by the buyer at the county tax office to register ownership of the land. The registration of land sales originated during the reign of the Emperor K'ang-hsi in the early Ch'ing period, and it was regarded by the administration as a means of conferring ownership of the land to the new landowner.[94] After 1911, the local governments, by order of the provincial finance office, insisted that land transfer deeds be registered at the county tax office and a deed tax paid.[95] This law did not clarify and systematize the land tax cadastres but was passed merely to capture more tax revenue for the local government.

The original land tax schedules had not been increased, but surcharges had been added so that by 1940 the rate of tax came to 4 yuan for every 13 mow or roughly 1.5 *sheng* of grain per mow.[96] This was not a heavy burden for the peasants to pay until the local government sought other means to raise taxes. While keeping the old land tax collection machinery intact, it began levying the *t'an-k'uan* and a series of turnover taxes on commodities exchanged in market towns. These turnover taxes were called *pao-shui* and consisted of excise taxes on grain, slaughter tax on fowl and pigs, and a tax on livestock. They were collected from the merchants by an official who was sent to make the rounds of each market town.[97] This official had 16 clerks assisting him in the market town of Wang she jen to collect these taxes monthly.[98] The tax on slaughtering livestock came to 2 per cent of the price of the animal,[99] and the slaughterhouses paid their fees directly to these clerks.[100] A merchant association existed in the county seat, but it had not been taxed as yet. Perhaps the reason for this was that the association had only recently been formed and, because many members owned land in villages and paid the *t'an-k'uan* levy to these villages, the authorities regarded their tax contribution to be quite sufficient.

There are few budget data for Li-ch'eng which can be assembled to show county finance as for Shun-i and Luang-ch'eng, but the picture that emerges from the available evidence is quite similar. In 1940, the largest source of tax revenue was the *t'an-k'uan*. The biggest expenditure, roughly 41 per cent in 1940, was for the military police, county defense, and county police.[101] Official salaries and administrative costs came to only 15 per cent; construction costs for communications came to 21 per cent; and an unusually large sum, about 23 per cent, was still being spent on education. The proportion of budget outlays for administrative salaries and overhead seems to have remained fairly constant throughout the 1930s.[102]

7. *En County: Hou Hsia Chai Village*

En county was situated in northwest Shantung near Hopei on the flat, drab central plain of north China. Eastward lay the Tientsin-Pukow railroad and westward on the Hopei-Shantung boundary line ran the old imperial grand canal, which flooded frequently and required extensive repairs of the dikes. The soil was sandy, alkaline and poor for crops except peanuts. Nine out of every ten households were in villages.[1] The cultivated area was larger than that of Li-ch'eng county, but peasants still owned very small farms.

Nearly 60 per cent of the rural households owned between 30 to 50 mow, 14 per cent farmed plots of less than 10 mow,[2] and only 4 per cent rented land.[3] According to the 1910 Ch'ing government crop survey, the crops in En county ranked by size of cultivated area were sorghum, soybeans, millet, wheat, corn, and a little cotton. By 1930 the crop ranking was wheat, sorghum, millet, peanuts, corn, soybeans, and some cotton.[4] Cotton was grown on only 77,000 mow in 1930 as compared to the 180,000 mow devoted to peanuts. En county ranked seventh in Shantung for area of peanuts cultivated. Within twenty years households had shifted cultivation to specialize in wheat and peanuts as cash crops. The county contained six administrative districts, several roads, and a number of market towns. These towns contained small mills for processing peanuts and ginning cotton. Wheat, peanut oil, and ginned cotton were shipped by rail to Tientsin or Chinan.

The village of Hou hsia chai was located several miles southwest of the county seat. Map 7 shows the density of villages and the county's proximity to the grand canal. Hou hsia chai was first established as a military settlement or *t'un,* but as migrants from Shansi settled the area in the early fifteenth century, it became a village.[5] In 1911, about 100 households lived in the village, and by 1941 this number had increased to 130. If we assume an average household contained five people, the rate of population increase over this 30 year period would be about 1 per cent per annum.[6] Villagers reported that in 1911 the village owned more land than in 1941 because in recent years some land had been sold to neighboring villages.[7] Natural disasters possibly accounted for frequent distress sales and the decline in villagers' land. In 1933 insects invaded the fields, and the peasants had to dig trenches to prevent them from devouring the crop. In 1937 a huge flood ruined the crop. In 1940, another insect invasion nearly destroyed the cotton harvest, and in 1941 violent hail storms lashed the region.

Land

The villagers remarked that their soil was poorer than that of nearby villages. Out of a total of 3,100 village mow, 400 mow was too poor to farm. Heavy rains in early summer flooded the low, flat land, covering it with

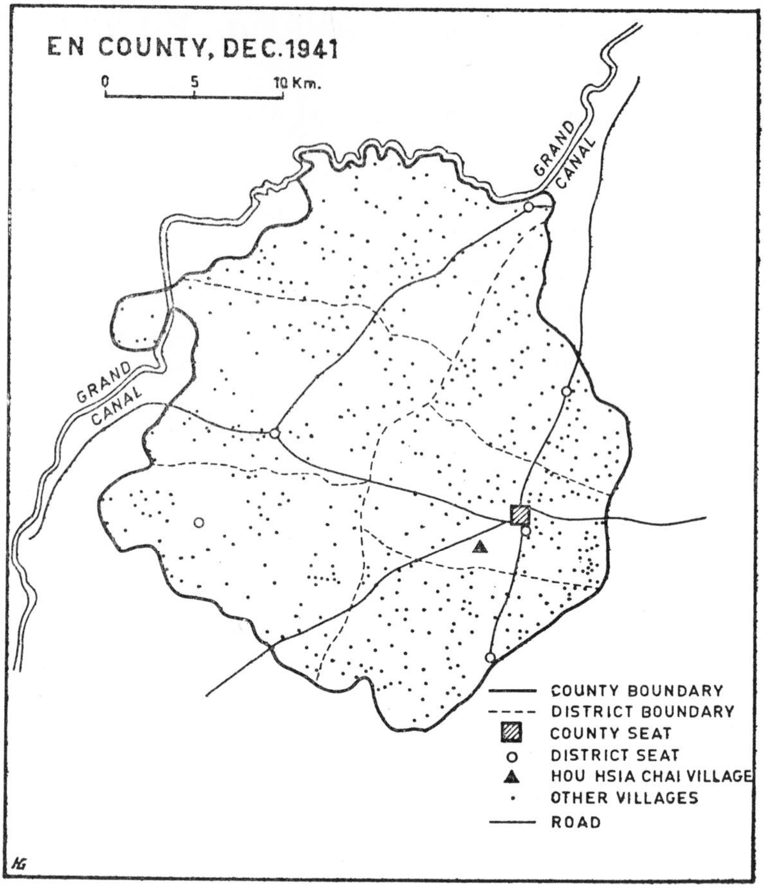

Map 7.

sand and making the soil highly saline.[8] However, crop yields for the village were slightly higher than the average yields reported for the county.[9] Sorghum, millet, wheat, peanuts, and cotton were the main village crops. Sorghum and cotton were planted in March and harvested in late August; wheat was planted in September and harvested in May. Sorghum, millet, and soybeans were then grown on the land formerly used for wheat.[10] Peanuts were planted in March, harvested in late August, and then sold to the peanut-processing mills in the county seat. A household owning 10 mow of land used 2 or 3 mow for raising peanuts or 1 mow for cotton. Thus, about 15 to 20 per cent of the land was used to cultivate these two cash crops, and the remainder was used for food and wheat. Before 1910 the peasants had cultivated the opium poppy in place of cotton and peanuts.

En County: Hou Hsia Chai Village

Land Tenure

The village did not have any households that lived solely by leasing land and collecting rents.[11] Only a dozen households rented land from other peasants who owned more land than they could efficiently farm.[12] Household farms were small. Seventeen per cent of the households had farms larger than 30 mow and accounted for 30 per cent of the village land. Sixty per cent of the households had farms between 10 and 30 mow making up 64 per cent of village land. Twenty per cent had farms less than 10 mow and accounted for only 6 per cent of village land. Three per cent of the village households did not own land.[13] Although land distribution was unequal, most households owned between 10 and 30 mow of land.

The number of households renting land changed very little each year. In 1942, 13 households rented land.[14] Ten owned less than 10 mow, and the remaining three owned 17 mow each. As a group, these tenant households only owned 7 head of livestock. Two had mortgaged some of their land for credit, and all except one rented land from other villagers. Most households had rented land for 2 to 4 years, but one household had rented for 15 years. There is not any evidence that the percentage of households renting land had changed greatly over the past half century.

The land tenure system of this village operated in the same way as in the other villages examined. Households with a few plots located in different sections of the village found that some plots were costly and unremunerative to farm. Greater monetary gain could be derived by leasing that land to nearby households owning very little land. A household with less than 20 mow might be able to farm additional land adjacent to its plots and realize some monetary gain. It thereby benefitted both households to agree on terms of rent, amount of land to be leased, and the period of tenancy.

Three rent systems existed. The most prevalent, paid by 7 out of 13 households, was the *tsu-ti* system, in which the tenant paid a fixed amount of rent per mow in kind, usually about three fifths of the crop for a normal harvest, to the landowner.[15] The *tsu-ti* tenant supplied his own capital and paid a rent deposit of two or three yuan per mow.[16] The tenant was free to use the land as he saw fit as long as he honored the terms stipulated in the original rent agreement. For example, if he had agreed to pay rent in millet or wheat and cultivated cotton or peanuts instead, he marketed these crops and purchased millet to pay his rent. Rent contracts were arranged by a third party and drawn up after the harvest; the contracts covered period of contract (usually a year subject to renewal), time of payment, and the amount and type of crop to be paid per mow. After signing this agreement, landlord and tenant did not meet until the rent was paid at the next harvest.

If the harvest was so poor that the crop per mow was worth less than the amount of rent to be paid, tenant and landowner divided the crop between them equally. If the harvest of millet amounted to only 100 catties per mow instead of the usual 140 catties, the landowner usually received 80 in rent and the tenant got the remainder. With a 30 per cent decline from the normal harvest, the landowner still had the right to collect his 80 catties, the remainder going to the tenant. But if the harvest fell below 80 catties per mow, landowner and tenant split the amount equally.[17] This rent system proved harsh at times of poor harvests, but with good harvests the tenant retained more than he would under the proportionate rent system. In this way the tenant had some incentive to improve the land. The landowner paid all taxes and levies on the land.

The second rent system was called *fen-chung;* rent was determined by dividing the harvest equally between landowner and tenant.[18] The tenant was not required to pay any rent deposit. If two or more crops were grown on the plot, the rent was determined by valuing the combined harvests at their current market price and converting this to equal shares in kind; tenant and landlord then jointly divided the crop between them. In former times this rent system had predominated; in case of several bad harvest years, tenant and landowner switched from the *tsu-ti* to the *fen-chung* system. The period of *fen-chung* lease usually ran about three years; land was rented only to peasants belonging to the same lineage group as the landowner. The landowner did not supply any capital to his tenant but gave him complete freedom to use the land as he wished.

The third rent payment system, which had not existed before 1910, was called *ta-fen-tzu* or *ehr-pa fen-tzu.* The tenant household received 20 per cent of the harvest and the remainder went to the landowner.[19] Several poor households owning less than 10 mow rented land on this basis. The landowner supplied all the capital, including fertilizer, to the tenant. A few wealthy peasants from other villages were reported to be interested in finding tenants to lease land under this arrangement. Apparently, these households had some capital to invest in a tenant, and they had found it profitable to have the tenant grow cash crops. They then acquired the lion's share of the harvest and marketed it at high prices. In this rent payment system middlemen were not used, and the landowner carefully picked the tenant he believed was trustworthy. The landowner told the tenant which crop he wanted grown on the land. In return, the tenant assisted the landlord at his home with repair work, preparation of fertilizer, and odd jobs.[20] If the tenant needed credit, he obtained it from the landowner.

Land tenure was not important in this village because so few households leased and rented land. Among the dozen-odd households renting land, there seems to have occurred the same shift from paying rent as a proportion of the harvest to paying a fixed amount per unit of land. We even note that two households were renting land and receiving assistance from landowners in much the same way that tenants and landlords in Japan cooperated with one another. It is impossible to say if such a new development was beginning to take place in this region, because so few households leased and rented land in this way. The *tsu-ti* and *fen-chung* rent payment systems still predominated as they had a century earlier, mainly because it was a convenient system for households holding different amounts of land. Households had adopted the *fen-chung* rent payment system because there were inherent advantages for both tenant and landowner when farm prices steadily increased.

Capital

Crop yields were high only if ample amounts of native fertilizer were used. This consisted of dirt and animal waste mixed into a compost and put on the fields in January. Good soil required about 500 catties of compost per mow, but twice that amount was needed on poor land. Each peasant prepared his fertilizer, and only a few households had extra cash to buy night soil from the county seat. Further, only a half dozen households had sufficient livestock and farming implements to care for their land.[21] There were 8 mules, 3 donkeys, 38 cows, 19 carts, 34 ploughs, and 13 harrows for 130 households. This meager capital stock had only increased slowly in recent years. There were five public wells of which only two provided drinking water. Although the county government in 1941 had ordered a dozen new wells to be built their construction had not yet begun.

Villagers shared their little capital between one another. Several households would pool their money to buy tools and livestock and share between them, or they would exchange labor services to use another household's tools during the busy farm season. The system of two or three households cooperating to purchase livestock was called *huo-mai*.[22] If only two households financed the purchase, the third cared for the animal. The animal was then rotated every ten days between the three households to complete the farm work during the spring sowing or fall harvest. When households simply assisted one another in the fields because labor was scarce, the practice was called *huo-chung*.[23] In another case three households might have only one harrow or plough between them, and in order to use this tool efficiently two households assisted the other using the harrow or plough. This was repeated for the other two households so that all had an opportunity to use the tool for the spring sowing. This custom was called *chia-huo*.[24] Finally, when a number of households pooled their money to buy a tool to be shared equally by each household, the system was called *ta-huo-mai*.[25] Many different cooperative arrangements were used by households to compensate for the scarcity of capital and money to buy capital. Households cooperating on the above basis did not draw up contracts between them nor was money exchanged between them. These capital share arrangements merely indicate that households found it to their advantage to cooperate, and indeed, a fairly high degree of mutual assistance existed.

Households cooperated in other ways. When building a home or assisting at a funeral or wedding, peasants of the same lineage group gathered and assisted one another in the manner described as "helping" or *pang-mang*.[26] However, when a natural disaster struck the village, households did not have any arrangement in which some would come to the assistance of others. They apparently regarded it unnecessary to establish any formal organization to protect the village — say, from locust attacks — possibly because natural disasters of this kind, when severe, were extremely rare.

Labor

Labor markets did not exist in En county market towns, but within villages peasants worked on one another's farms during the busy seasons of spring and fall. During the wheat harvest when the spring crop was also being planted, women and children in poor households of only 10 to 30 mow even worked in the fields because so much labor was needed. Households owning 30 to 50 mow had to employ several workers for a few days or even a week to accomplish what had to be done in the fields.

Villagers reported that after 1937, there had been an increase in the number of workers seeking short-term employment.[27] There are two possible explanations of this trend. First, in 37 cases households had divided their land between 1920 and 1941. This division produced new household farms and fragmented the farm land. Households with less than 30 mow had to supplement their farm income with non-farm income, and if more households of this size were formed after 1920, a higher percentage of households began to find it impossible to live by only their farm income.

A second possibility is rising living costs. In 1941 peasants reported that the price of grain was 4 to 6 times that of 1937 prices, peanut prices were 9 times higher, and cotton prices 12 times higher. A family of six needed only 600 yuan to live in 1937 but 1,000 yuan in 1942.[28] Although cash crop prices rose more rapidly than food prices, the price of yarn, cloth, matches, and oil rose more rapidly than cash crop prices. Peasants found it more difficult to buy the same consumer goods from the towns without giving up more in exchange. It was difficult to increase farm income without purchasing more inputs such as seeds, fertilizer, and tools, and the prices of these commodities also rose rapidly. Households turned to earning more non-farm income because of rising money wages in the market towns and cities.

Some households had always dispatched workers outside the village to work for long periods of up to a year or more. Before 1937 a dozen peasants had gone to Manchuria as coolie workers. Some had even worked there for as long as ten years.[29] They usually sent 50 to 60 yuan to their relatives in the village each year.[30] There were only four long-term workers in the village, three of whom had come from other villages. They received around a 100 yuan a year plus food and a week's holiday at New Year's. A poor peasant might ask another of the same lineage group to employ him, and out of sympathy that household provided food and lodging in return for acquiring a servant for an undetermined length of time. The total number of peasants working outside the village in 1942 at both short- and long-term employment was between 20 and 30 men. Some were employed in other counties as peddlers,[31] some worked as casual workers or clerked in stores, and some were still in Manchuria.

Village handicraft was another source of household income. About a dozen households wove baskets and sold them in the market in the county seat. These baskets were made of willows obtained from a village east of the county seat, located on a small river.[32] A weaver wove enough baskets during the three winter months to earn only 10 yuan. This handicraft activity demanded considerable skill, and for that reason alone only a few households were able to participate. Another activity was the making of bean cakes. Several families produced these cakes and sold them within the village.

Until the late 1930s the major village income came from farming, supplemented by wage and handicraft income earned during the idle months of the year. After 1937, more households dispatched workers to the market towns to take advantage of rising money wages. Whether rising commodity prices or a decline in size of farm, or some combination of the two, had brought about this new development is not certain.

Credit

In 1942, 8 out of every 10 peasants had incurred debt.[33] We know nothing about the size or period of debt or if the total debt had increased or declined in recent years. Although households were always borrowing various sums from one another or from moneylenders in the towns, debt only became serious in the village if large amounts of land were mortgaged to moneylenders outside the village or if land was sold to outsiders. When debt was held within the village and repaid, credit demand was not great. Villagers stated that most households borrowed when the harvest was poor, and cash had been exhausted by spring.[34] With good harvests, peasant incomes were higher, and spring borrowing declined. The annual demand for credit, then, depended greatly upon the year's harvest.

However, demand for credit also depended upon the frequency of ceremonies and contingencies. Every household expected at one time or another to spend as much as 150 to 300 yuan, or one fifth to one fourth its average income, for a funeral or wedding.[35] The necessity to purchase livestock and farm tools for farming, or medicine in the event of family sickness also compelled households to borrow.

The procedure for obtaining credit in Hou hsia chai was similar to that of the three previous villages. A small sum of 10 or 20 yuan was borrowed from a friend or relative and repaid without interest in a few weeks. A larger sum of 50 to 100 yuan could be obtained from a wealthy villager, a native bank in the county, or a moneylender. Land was pledged as collateral for these loans, and the loan had to be repaid within a year at an interest charge of 2 or 3 per cent per month.[36] This system was simply called *chieh-ch'ien,* or borrowing money.[37] A middleman or personal guarantor was required to provide the introduction and arrange the terms of loan.

Before 1937 the peasants were able to borrow from native banks in the market towns, but after 1937 these banks went bankrupt because of the war. The peasant then had to depend more than ever before on merchants and moneylenders for credit. Prior to 1937, the monthly interest rate had varied from 2 to 3 per cent, but by 1942 inflation had driven the rate to 5 per cent and sometimes 8 per cent.[38] If the peasant did not repay his loan after the harvest, the lender called upon the middleman to remind the borrower to hasten payment. If the peasant defaulted on his loan, the lender took the land previously offered as security. When small loans as little as 70 or 80 yuan were not repaid, the moneylender had the right to take the land.

Once a peasant pledged land as collateral, he was not supposed to secure another loan with the same plot. This breach of contract was difficult to prevent if the moneylender did not know the villager personally. Therefore, moneylenders insisted that middlemen arrange loans in order to reduce the risk of a borrower selling his land, pocketing the loan, and running off, or denying having borrowed money. The moneylender had little protection under the law in the county seat. It was exceedingly difficult for him to force a debtor to pay without recourse to the indirect pressure a third party could apply on the debtor. The peasant who had solicited a friend or relative to act on his behalf was particularly vulnerable to this kind of pressure and felt obligated to repay the loan. Moneylenders regarded the go-between as a deterrent against defaulting on loan repayment and providing the necessary security for their lending.

If the *chieh-ch'ien* loan could not be repaid on time or more cash was needed, the peasant mortgaged some land; in En county this was called *tang-ti.*[39] In 1942, of the village's 3,100 mow, about 500 mow had been mortgaged to five other villages.[40] Hou hsia chai's villagers held only 10 mow of land mortgaged by peasants in other villages. A large outflow of land had taken place in recent years. Perhaps frequent poor harvests caused by bad weather and locusts had forced many households to borrow more than they normally would have if harvests had been normal. Villagers claimed there had not been any large increase in households mortgaging land after 1937,[41] so that peasants would have had to incur debt sometime between 1911 and 1937. On the other hand, because mortgage contracts were usually for periods of three to five years, it is quite possible the bulk of this mortgaged land did not represent households borrowing cash in the 1920s. Instead, households might periodically have borrowed from outside villagers every so often, and in the process of different households mortgaging and redeeming land, the amount of mortgaged land remained constant over a long period.

When a peasant decided to mortage land, he requested a middleman to provide an introduction, give financial guarantee, and assist in drawing up the mortgage contract, some which covered a period as long as ten years.[42] If the borrower did not want to use the land and pay rent, the lender took over the land. It was first necessary to determine the land value in order to calculate the amount of land to mortgage for the cash needed. The value of mortgaged land ran about 50 to 60 per cent of the land's selling price. For good land it was as high as 70 per cent, and for poor land about 20 to 30 per cent.[43] Once the value and amount of mortgaged land were determined, a contract was drawn up stating the amount of the loan and when it would be repaid. The three parties affixed their signatures to the document, and the land passed into the lender's hands. The land tax was paid by the peasant cultivating the land.

The peasants of En county mortgaged land rather than pledged it as collateral for loans.[44] The reason for this practice is not clear. Perhaps, because banks loaned considerable amounts of money, they insisted that peasants mortgage their land as a better guarantee that loans would be repaid. On the other hand, households owned larger farms than in the three villages already discussed — the majority owned between 10 and 30 mow — and it may have been easier for them to obtain loans through mortgaging land. For loans exceeding 100 yuan, a household sought out a wealthy household or moneylender in another village or the market town. Even if a third party served as intermediary, a prospective lender might regard the risk too high and refuse to accept pledged land as collateral, insisting instead, that the borrower mortgage some land. In 1940 Hou hsia chai village experienced a poor harvest because of insects, but other villages had not fared badly. In 1941 many households needed cash in the spring to tide them over until after the fall harvest. The only way they obtained credit was to borrow from moneylenders in other villages or market towns, who insisted that land be mortgaged.

When borrowing was unsuccessful, land was sold. Selling land was a tedious operation and subject to great risk. The county did not have a land market where this transfer could be managed easily, adequate protection given to buyer and seller, and land properly assessed. When a peasant decided to sell, he sought out a reliable friend to find a buyer and arrange a profitable sale. The middleman first checked with friends and relatives, and if he was unsuccessful in finding a buyer, he then looked outside the village. Once he had found a buyer, the middleman obtained a small deposit from the interested buyer. After the land was surveyed and both parties agreed upon a price, a deed was drawn up indicating the amount of land, its location, and sale price. The middleman was paid a fee, usually 2 per cent of the value of the land sale, but often he merely accepted small gifts from the buyer and seller. The buyer then made a second copy of the deed to show ownership in the event a dispute arose later. He then went to the county seat tax office, paid the deed tax, and received a new deed showing payment of the deed tax and registration of the land. Many peasants never registered their land, and it was estimated that three or four out of every five buyers refused to register their land in order to evade paying the deed tax.[45]

A final source of credit was the *ch'ing-hui* or small revolving deposit associations made up of a dozen peasants.[46] Each peasant deposited a small amount when the association met, and a small fund amounting to 50 or 100 yuan accumulated. If a member wished to borrow for taxes, marriage or funeral expenses, or buy goods to peddle, he could borrow the full deposit amount and repay at 2 or 3 per cent interest per month. Each member took his turn to borrow. Only peasants owning land and paying village taxes were permitted to join. This arrangement eliminated the middleman and saved considerable time for the peasant.

Marketing

Before 1937, villagers did their marketing in a large village several miles away, but after 1937, a new market was established outside the county seat and closer to Hou hsia chai. Cloth, oil, matches, and tea were the principal commodities purchased. When a peasant went to market, he took several catties of cotton or peanuts to sell, and with that cash he then bought the consumer goods he needed. Sometimes cotton seeds were exchanged for peanut oil, so that some goods were still bartered.

Five or six villagers cooperated to buy cotton from other households and sell it to a ginning firm in the county seat. There were 20 to 30 of these ginning firms processing cotton and selling it to six large brokers, who packed the cotton and arranged its shipment to Tientsin or Chinan. The remainder of the cotton sold by the peasants passed directly to cotton brokers representing wholesale firms in Tientsin and Chinan. The same was true for peanuts, for brokers from as far as Tsingtao purchased in this part of Shantung. Price was competitively determined by bidding and haggling, and brokers competed with one another to buy as large a quantity as possible at the lowest price.

Land Inheritance

The household head was concerned primarily with maintaining continuity of the family line. The Chinese peasant believed that acquiring land was the most dependable way a family's fortune could be improved and security provided for the sons. The more land a household head could transfer to his sons, the easier it was for them to farm and acquire land. The household head would be greatly respected and honored through ancestor worship. The family line was perpetuated in this way rather than by keeping the farm land intact, in the name of a single family member. Another reason for dividing land was to prevent being singled out for theft or having to pay more taxes. The following is an interview with the peasant Wang Ching-ch'ang; Wang had divided the land between his sons and parents in 1936.

Question: Why do you divide the land equally generation after generation?

Answer: This has been the custom from early times.

Question: Is it not true that living conditions would be better if the land was not divided in this way?

Answer: This is probably so, but if one does not divide the land after accumulating a great amount, thieves will rob you and more taxes are demanded from you. This is an equally bad situation.[47]

This revealing statement shows that large landowners, of which Wang was formerly one, feared the consequences of being overtly wealthy for too long a period. If one's wealth became conspicuous, the risk of theft and taxation was great. In other words, protection of private property under the law did not, in practice, exist.

When sons demanded that family divide the land or the household head decided the time was opportune to transfer the land to his sons, the arrangements made were similar to that already mentioned in the three previous villages. A deed, or *fen-tan,* was drawn up specifying the distribution of shares and indicating the family had agreed to property division. For a brief period the family might still live in the same household, but the sons soon moved away with their families to establish their own households and to farm independently.

Villagers also practiced the custom of allotting a portion of land to the aged parents to cover funeral expense. The amount of *yang-lao-ti* land set aside for this purpose was usually one third of the total land being transferred to the sons.[48] When the sons lived separately after *fen-chia,* the parents moved into their homes for short periods on a rotation basis. After the death of the parents the *yang-lao-ti* land was sold to pay for funeral expenses, and if any land remained, it was then sold or divided between the sons. The custom of *yang-lao-ti* naturally made for further fragmentation of land.

Approximately half of the village households had divided the family wealth between the male heirs at least once within the past sixty years. This may be seen in Table 15, which is based on data from a household survey made in May and June of 1942. Each household was queried as to when it had divided the land and on how many occasions. I calculated the percentage of known cases of household division from the total number of answers and arranged these according to time period. Newly formed households which had not yet had time to divide the land are included in category three.

Table 15. Frequency of division of household land in Hou hsia chai, late nineteenth century–1942.

Type of case	Number	Per cent
Household division reported		
Before 1890	4	3.4
1890–1909	14	11.9
1910–1919	7	5.9
1920–1929	17	14.4
1930–1941	20	16.9
Cases reported as unknown	13	11.1
No household division reported	43	36.4
Total	118	100.0

Source: CN, IV, 557–563.

Household divisions by different time intervals fluctuated considerably, but it is quite apparent that during the 1920s and 1930s their number had increased. This pattern resembles that of Sha-ching and Ssu pei ch'ai villages. We do not have any information from these interviews about why household division had increased after 1920 and 1930. The increase could have been because of greater insecurity arising from civil war and the Japanese invasion. Again, it could have been due to the general demographic profile of households in which a larger number, established sometime in the late nineteenth century, were approaching the time when sons insisted upon establishing their family farms.

Village Leadership and Organizations

During the Ch'ing period Hou hsia chai had been organized into three groups of households according to their proximity to each other in the village. An undetermined number of households made up a group called a *p'ai* with its leader, the *p'ai-ch'ang*. The *p'ai-ch'ang* discussed village affairs with the assistant village head and the village headman, the *chuang-ch'ang*.[49] The main task of the *p'ai-ch'ang* had been to assist the headman to collect the *t'an-k'uan* from the villagers when it was levied after 1900. In 1938, the *p'ai* system was discontinued, and several years later the *pao-chia* system was instituted. The village was then divided into 13 *chia*, each containing 10 households; the *chia* heads conferred each month with the headman and his assistant on village affairs and the allocation and collection of the *t'an-k'uan*. This large group comprised the village council.

The headman, in 1942, was a 37 year old peasant who had been elected in February of that year. Previous headmen had not served for more than a term of eight years. They were fairly wealthy peasants owning between 30 to 50 mow.[50] Table 16 shows the previous six headmen, their periods of service, and the amount of land they owned.

Table 16. Period of service and land holdings of former Hou hsia chai headmen.

Headman	When elected	Years served	Amount of land (mow)
Wu Yu-heng	February 1942	–	30
Wang Ching-lung	July 1940	$1\frac{1}{2}$	30
Wang Wen-ching	mid-1938	2	–
Wu Yu-lin	1937	1	30
Wang Pao-yuan	1929	8	50
Li P'u	1922	7	30

Source: CN, IV, 404.

These headmen had been selected for their qualities of fair play, ability to arbitrate disputes, and a talent for dealing with local officials. They came from the largest village clans, but this does not mean that a particular clan dominated in the village leadership. From Table 16 it is evident that headmen other than from the Wang clan were selected by ballots cast by household heads owning land. A headman did not serve for any definite period and resigned if ill or too busy to continue as headman. Wang Ching-lung resigned because he had little time to manage village affairs, and Wang Wen-ching resigned for the same reason. Wu Yu-lin and Wang Pao-yuan disqualified themselves because they became ill. Headmen did not receive any salary, but each year villagers gathered contributions for a small sum as a token of thanks for their work.

The headman was assisted by the *ti-fang* or *ti-pao*, who were part-time farmers living in the village. During the Ch'ing period they were paid a salary by the village's three *p'ai*, and their main job was collecting taxes.

During the Republican period their job became less important and they were responsible to the village headman, serving as a runner between him and the *chia* heads. The village *ti-fang,* in 1942, was a former schoolteacher who could read and write. He was paid a small salary in kind after each harvest from the 13 *chia,* and his main job was to serve as liaison between the headman and *chia* heads.

Before 1911 the village headman's job had been easy because the *t'an-k'uan* was a very infrequent tax levy, and he did not have any village organizations to supervise. The most expected of him was to arbitrate disputes and see that households paid their land tax. As the local government demanded more taxes and attempted to extend its control deeper into village affairs, the village headman's responsibilities increased. He now had to collect the land tax and *t'an-k'uan* on a regular basis; select peasants for corvee labor outside the village; supervise the village school; take a census of village households; organize the village defense corps; take charge of the *pao-chia* organization. In addition, he continued to arbitrate between quarreling households and conducted the traditional ceremony prayer for rain when drought threatened.[51]

When the local government required more tax revenue, each district was notified of the amount it must pay. District officials convened the village headman and apportioned the levy burden to each village according to its ability to pay. Each headman returned to his village and assembled the *chia* heads to discuss what assessments each household owning land must pay in order to meet the village *t'an-k'uan* levy quota. Tenants were exempt from paying the levy. Once the *chia* heads and headman agreed upon household fees, they notified the households of their respective *chia,* and at a designated time all households brought the amount of levy forward. This was turned over to the headman, who then reported to the county officials. If some households in a village refused to comply, word of this invariably reached the county police. They quickly came to the village, and the household head was severely beaten until he promised to pay.[52]

The same procedure was used to mobilize village labor for county projects. When county officials decided upon the amount of labor required to complete a certain task, they required villages of certain vicinities to provide the labor. The headman and *chia* heads of each village convened to decide which households would supply the village's quota of workers. Each household provided an able-bodied worker on a rotation basis depending upon the amount of land the household owned. Again, the burden fell on households with the ability to pay.

In the early 1920s troops of the warlord Chang Tso-ch'ang had moved into En county and foraged off the countryside. Many villagers fled the area, and the loss of livestock and farm capital was great. Rural conditions were again turbulent in 1926–27 when remnants of warlord armies attacked villages in the southern part of the county in desperate attempts to obtain food and carts.[53] Although villages had not suffered great damage from these periodic harassments, the peasants had been compelled to organize self-defense corps, called *hung-ch'iang-hui* or Red Spears Societies to protect their villages. By 1930 these organizations had disbanded because external threat had receded. But in 1939, the county government ordered that villages create the same kind of defense corps, consisting of young men between 18 and 45 years of age but to be grouped on the basis of the *chia*. Each group was actually the *chia* head, who took orders from the corps commander, or the village headman. In Hou hsia chai the defense corps had been created but had not yet seen action; however, villagers referred to this organization as the Red Spears Society rather than the village self-defense corps.

Before 1920 the village used a system of crop watching called *I-p'o,* in which peasants, on an informal basis, watched their crops at night. Individual peasants merely went out with friends or relatives to watch their crops from mid-May until late August.[54] When a peasant employed another to watch his crops the arrangement was referred to as *k'an-ch'ing.* Sometime during the 1920s the village organized a system of night patrol, called *ta-keng,* with the specific purpose of watching the village crops. Each night 30 men patrolled the village.[55] This group was divided into four sections made up of seven peasants and a leader. While two sections patrolled the western and eastern parts of the village, the other two sections slept for part of the night, and then the patrolling was rotated. Men between 20 and 40 years of age were eligible for night watch. Each man was selected on the basis of the amount of land a household owned. A household with 10 mow provided one person, one with 20 mow 2 persons, and a household with less than 10 mow was exempted.[56]

The village had established a school in 1910, which accommodated between 20 to 30 pupils, all boys. Each household sending children paid a small fee for books and materials. If extra money was needed to maintain the school, funds were supplied by the village council when the *t'an-k'uan* was collected. The village council simply assessed households an extra amount to cover extraordinary village expenditures as well as the *t'an-k'uan.* In the same way, the village council financed the village temple and maintained the public wells.[57] Students were instructed in portions of the Chinese classics which they memorized by constant repetition after the headmaster. They were not taught simple arithmetic, fine arts, or scientific subjects. Only a handful of villagers could read or write, and newspapers did not circulate within the village.

Clan influence was extremely weak, and clans did not own land except a few plots for burial of their members. This land was referred to by the villagers as *tsu-ying-ti* or clan grave land, and it was not to be sold or divided when clan members transferred land to their sons.[58] At the annual Ch'ing Ming festival clan members assembled at the graves to pay homage to their ancestors, and a member was selected to farm the few mow around the graves for the coming year. He had the responsibility of caring for the graves, and the harvest obtained from the few mow of clan land were to reimburse him for his efforts. He was obliged to record the amount of yield, tax paid, and what he retained for himself as self-payment. He was not allowed to mortgage this land to obtain credit.[59]

Village and County Finance

En county had always been divided into districts and, until 1937, district officials dealt directly with village headmen who, in turn, managed village affairs through the village group, the *p'ai.* Sometime after 1937, districts were subdivided into *lien-pao* — groups of 15–17 villages — and these became the intermediary body standing between the district and the village.

From county tax data, we know that police were established in each of the six districts between 1920 and 1930, their main role being that of preserving order and enforcing payment of taxes. As county expenditures rose, it became necessary to raise more revenue in order to balance the budget, and so the police force was increased until in 1942 it totalled 180 men.[60]

The county budget had changed greatly between 1908 and 1942. In 1908 roughly 25 per cent of the total revenue collected to balance expenditures was spent for official salaries, and another 25 per cent was spent on general administrative overhead.[61] The remaining 50 per cent was divided between county education and public welfare and forwarded to the provincial finance office. In 1941, 90 per cent of the total revenue collected was spent on three items only: administration, county defense, and the police. Another 8 per cent was spent for education and county economic construction; the remainder was forwarded to the provincial finance office.[62]

On the revenue side of the budget, in 1908, the major county revenue was the land tax, and in 1941, although 90 per cent of total revenue came from land tax and *t'an-k'uan,* the latter supplied the largest share.[63] The estimated budget expenditure for 1942 was to be 770,000 yuan, as compared to the 1941 budget expenditure of 344,000, and roughly 720,000 yuan of this amount was to be collected by village *t'an-k'uan.*[64]

In 1941 revenue and expenditure were twice as large as they were in 1932. Most of this increase was due to a three- to four-fold rise in the price level on the expenditure side. However, the county administration had been extremely successful in balancing the budget each year by increasing tax revenue and by having any surplus transferred to the next fiscal year without recourse to deficit financing through borrowing.

There is insufficient budget data to construct a table showing annual revenue and expenditures change between 1937 and 1941, but scattered information can be interpreted to suggest the major sources of revenue and how they were collected. There were two main groups of taxes: taxes levied on the rural community and taxes levied on the merchants in the market towns and county seats. The greatest burden, probably 80 to 90 per cent of tax revenue, fell on the rural community.

Rural taxes were of two kinds: the land tax and the *t'an-k'uan* levy. Villagers paid the land tax, a fixed rate per mow of land, three times a year, to the county land tax office, which was called the *t'ien-fu cheng-shu-ch'u*. This tax had not been increased, and with the rise in farm prices and money income, it represented a very small part of the peasant's annual income. When a peasant sold land to another, the land tax was transferred to the new owner, who also paid a deed tax of 5 per cent of the value of the land purchase. After paying this tax, the new owner received an official copy of the land deed called a *hung-ch'i,* or red document, bearing an official seal and stating the sale had been recorded and the deed tax paid.[65] This document was proof of ownership and served as a record for the tax office. Many peasants preferred not to register a land transfer in order to evade paying the deed tax. Because village land taxes were frequently paid through the village headman, it was possible for new landowners to pay the land tax without being detected by the tax office as the new owners. Consequently, the land tax records in the county seat did not tally with the actual amount of farmed land and the names of households owning and farming the land.

A great deal of detail has already been presented about how the *t'an-k'uan* levy was collected. Its incidence was left to the villagers, and the village council apportioned the burden according to each household's ability to pay. It was collected with greater frequency after 1930; to enforce *t'an-k'uan* collection, the police force was increased and used frequently.

Merchants paid two groups of taxes: a business tax levied on each merchant called the *ying-yeh-shui*[66] and commodity excise taxes. The first tax fell directly on the merchant and was only partially passed on to consumer or groups from which the merchant purchased and hired labor services, because of the high degree of competitiveness that existed in each market. However, the business tax, paid as a fixed percentage of gross revenue earned, was easily evaded by merchants if they reported a lower gross revenue than actually earned. It was extremely difficult for police and tax officials to check on each merchant's earning to determine whether they were paying the full tax.

Numerous turnover taxes had been introduced since the early 1930s and were evaded by being passed forward to consumers in higher prices and to suppliers of goods and services in lower prices. A tax on peanut oil was paid by pressing mills to a tax collector, who made periodic rounds to collect. Mills passed this tax on to the peasants by offering lower prices for their peanuts. Although peasants could switch to marketing another cash crop if peanut prices did not rise, they continued to market peanuts because the price was higher than those of other grain and cash crops.

Animals and fowl were also taxed when slaughtered in the market, and a tax of 10 per cent of the sale value was paid when livestock were sold. There were 50 brokers in En county who purchased livestock, slaughtered it, and sold the meat. They were visited periodically by two officials who collected this tax.[67] There was also a tax on wine and tobacco, commodities sold by 33 merchants; these merchants were given special permits to sell these goods as long as they paid the prescribed duty to the police who checked on their stores periodically.[68] These brokers and merchants were able to pass much of the taxes on to consumers by marking up prices.

En county was reported to have had fewer merchants than neighboring counties,[69] and they were organized into a merchant association, which met in the county seat. Merchants with property valued at more than 500 yuan were permitted to join,[70] and this ruling excluded the large number of peasant-peddlers roaming through the market towns. The *t'an-k'uan* had not been levied on this merchant association, but many expected to pay the levy in 1943.

8. The North China Village: Summary

At the risk of some repetition, it seems necessary at this point to sum up the findings from these four village studies and to draw attention to certain uniformities that will be useful for further analysis of this peasant economy. Differences existed between these four villages in living standards, average size of farm, percentage of households dependent upon nonfarm income, and villagers' indebtedness, but these were differences of degree. Sha-ching was the poorest of the four. Although living standards did not deteriorate markedly in this village, at least until after 1938, households possessed few consumer durables, a large percentage had to send labor to work outside the village, and nearly a quarter of the village's income came from nonfarm income. Peasant debt to outsiders was great, and part-tenant households were numerous.

Conditions were quite the reverse in Ling shui kou, probably the village with the highest living standard of the four. In this village there were shops and artisans; only a small percentage of the village's households dispatched workers outside to earn nonfarm income; most debt was held within the village; and many households possessed some consumer durables such as bicycles.

Though villages differed in living standards, the difference cannot be explained by the hypothesis that they were at various stages of economic change that formed a single pattern within a region. Villages were naturally subjected to the influences of similar economic factors, but these differed because of location, resource conditions of the locality, and the frequency and duration of random disturbance such as war and climatic disasters. Therefore, various economic factors, which were in turn influenced by these variables, produced different types of village economic development rather than a single pattern of sequential stages of growth, maturity, and decay.

The economic factors, common to all villages, appear to have operated in the following way between 1880 and 1940. Population increased steadily at an annual growth rate of about 1 per cent. All arable land in the villages was cultivated by the 1920s or 1930s, so that since the late nineteenth century the increase in cultivated land had been only marginal and the average size of farm had declined. There were only slight improvements in farm technology, such as the introduction of the American cotton seed and new corn seeds. Additional wells had been constructed, and the supply of traditional fertilizer was increased. The capital stock of the average farm household remained unchanged. Because the number of households had increased, the supply of village capital stock increased slightly. These economic factors interacted and influenced productivity according to the natural resource base of each village, the village's location to urban centers of development, and random disturbances, such as a natural disaster or war, which inflicted minimal damage on the village.

There is not any evidence that peasant living standards before 1937 declined, and therefore, total farm production increased in order to support the rise in population. Even though household farms gradually diminished in size, average productivity was maintained. Furthermore, the manufacture of village handicrafts, the introduction of industrial crops, and the new opportunities of nonfarm employment in nearby cities enabled peasants to augment their income from cereal and vegetable production. If villages were fortunate enough to enjoy these advantages, levels of income could be maintained, perhaps even increased, and peasant living standard need not fall.

If villages suffered a series of poor harvests caused by bad weather, floods, and crop pests or a significant decline in the number of carts, animals, and able-bodied men because of marauding armies, their loss of wealth made it extremely difficult for peasants to regain former living standards. The inevitable consequences were increasing indebtedness, an increase in tenant and landless households, and even emigration. Villages suffered more from some major disaster, natural or man-made, than from any other combination of economic factors.

Five types of village economic development can be derived from these four village studies. These classifications are used to show the complexity of village change in this peasant economy and the danger of generalizing about a single trend. First, villages having a cash crop, handicraft, and an opportunity of off-farm employment earned more than enough income to compensate for any temporary loss in village income. Such a case is Ling shui kou which had a higher living standard than most villages. Second, villages possessing two or more of the above three sources of income might have experienced a series of poor harvests, but they eventually recovered their former living standards. Furthermore, the number of tenant and landless households had not changed. Such a case was Hou hsia chai of En county. Third, villages with two or more of the above alternate income sources, but experiencing poor harvests, suffered a slight decline in living standards, and the number of tenant and landless households increased. Village debt to outsiders rose, and considerable transfer of village land to outsiders took place. This was the case of Ssu pei ch'ai. Fourth, villages having only one additional source of income, off-farm wages, might experience few random disturbances. Although their living standards were lower than in the above village types, they had not declined over the past half century. Such an example was Sha-ching. Fifth, villages having only off-farm wages to supplement farm income might suffer from many random disturbances. Living standards declined, tenant and landless households increased, and some households were forced to move away. In the village survey materials I used, there was no example of such a village. However, other rural surveys undertaken in the early 1930s indicate that such villages in north China existed. It was quite common during the 1920s for warlord armies to devastate villages and force peasants to emigrate to the treaty ports and Manchuria.

It is difficult to say which type approximated the general conditions of north China villages. All types co-existed, and villages of each type could be found even in the same county. The time element is also important. Rural conditions of 1940 differed greatly from those of 1900, and it is quite likely that changes observed in villages in 1940 were more like the village types three, four, and five. This classification of village economic change shows that economic conditions within a village could be either on the decline, improving, or remaining the same.

Important Village Similarities

There are many similarities between villages, as observed in these survey findings, which suggest that rural change was basically the same despite the fact that different patterns of village development prevailed.

All villages, except Sha-ching, experienced the same shift from paying land rent as a percentage of the harvest to a fixed amount of the harvest. In Sha-ching, money rents had existed as early as the nineteenth century and before, because village land was located in former banner land area. Land owned by banner personnel had been leased to Chinese peasants who paid money rent. The custom of money rent payment persisted until this century. In other areas the change in land rents from percentage to fixed amount of the harvest was gradual, and both systems could be found side by side in the same village.

The land inheritance system made it impossible for large farms to remain intact for more than one or two generations. Farm land became increasingly fragmented and difficult to farm efficiently. When villages underwent a large number of household divisions at the same time, many households with little land were formed. Thus, more peasants had to leave the farm for short periods to earn nonfarm income.

Village boundaries were undefined until the establishment of village crop-watching associations around the turn of the century and after. Villages had always acquired and lost land depending on harvest fluctuations and village debt, and peasants lacked a strong sense of village identity. After the crop-watching associations were formed, the peasants became accustomed to regarding the area of land guarded by these associations as the village proper.

Village taxes in the form of *t'an-k'uan* increased greatly after 1920, and by the late 1930s it was the major source of revenue for local administrations. Village leaders had the difficult and disagreeable task of allocating this tax burden and seeing to its payment. They allocated the tax burden by assessing households a fee per unit of land. This was then collected through the village household organization, the *pao-chia*. By allocating tax burden according to a household's ability to pay — the amount of land it farmed — village leaders were able to equalize tax burden, ensure that the village pay higher taxes, and minimize social resentment against having to pay a greater tax.

Village organizations for agricultural development to construct wells, irrigate fields, produce fertilizer, and increase livestock supply were nonexistent. These matters were left to individual households. However, households cooperated with one another privately to purchase farm capital, share livestock and labor, or rent lands. These arrangements were worked out by informal agreement between household heads of the same lineage group, friends, or neighbors and were specifically intended to overcome scarcities of capital, labor, and land.

The influence of clan management in village affairs and farming was very small. Village leadership consisted of prominent and able owner cultivator household heads capable of dealing with local officials and handling village problems. This elite group's composition constantly changed from one generation to another and was not based upon hereditary succession. Change in village leadership very much approximated the rise and fall of households in the village.

Some General Findings

The household must be considered the basic economic and social unit. Clans were weak organizations in village life, and village leaders devoted their efforts primarily to tax collection, village defense, and settlement of household quarrels. Households were very responsive to farm price changes and attempted to put their land to the best economic use. They weighed the advantages and costs of leasing or renting land. They rationally considered various income alternatives to farming and how much labor to allocate between different tasks to maximize household income. Households were powerfully motivated to earn more income and buy land.

The land tenure system in all four villages functioned to enable households with different land holdings to farm more efficiently and obtain more farm income. Pure tenants made up a very small proportion of villagers, although many households owning land frequently rented plots for short periods. In this land tenure system landholders neither gave guidance nor material assistance to their tenants, and new techniques were not transferred from landholder to tenant. Few large landholders farmed their land, and the absentee landlords living in market towns usually acquired their land through the rural credit system.

The credit system was based upon households using land as security and near money. Households borrowed small sums by pledging some of their land as collateral or, if larger sums were needed, by mortgaging or even selling land. Considerable village credit was provided by households lending to one another. Some credit flowed from market towns to villages, and households used their land as security to obtain it. If loans were not repaid, households mortgaged their land. Creditors, rather than farming the mortgaged land themselves, preferred to have the debtor households rent and farm it until the original loans were repaid and the land redeemed. Risk was the great difficulty in this credit system, but this was reduced by recourse to a third party to provide personal introduction, character reference, and financial guarantee that the loan would be repaid. This made for greater trust and obligation between debtor and lender. Interest rates remained fairly constant at 2 and 3 per cent per month over this period except when inflation became serious after 1938.

Technological change and the improvement of the rural infra-structure such as schools, water control systems, and roads were very slow or nonexistent. Local officials were far more interested in collecting taxes and preserving order so as to maintain administrative power than in developing agriculture. Officials successfully taxed villages more heavily by using greater police power to impose frequent levies on villages. Tax revenue was divided between the provincial and local governments, with the latter spending mainly for official salaries and to enlarge the police force. Peasant distress was not apparent during this period in spite of increased taxes and the absence of any government investment to promote rural development.

There is every indication that, over the long run, land distribution did not change, and the inequality of land holding, already very great, did not become more unequal. The reason for stable land distribution was the inheritance system of dividing land equally between the male heirs.

There is little evidence that merchants, absentee landlords, and moneylenders blocked rural improvement and caused peasant misery. Their influence in villages appears to have been very weak. On the other hand, as local officials succeeded in collecting more taxes, their control over villages became greater because police power was used to collect village taxes. The allocation of tax burden was left to the village headman and council.

These various findings naturally need to be confirmed by empirical evidence gleaned from other rural surveys before the assertion can be made that they apply to all of north China. In the remaining chapters of this book evidence will be introduced to show that the general conditions in these four villages were quite typical of the north China countryside. The uniformities and regularities so far observed can then serve as the basis for theorizing about how this peasant economy evolved after the late nineteenth century.

III. The Peasant Economy of North China

9. Peasant Farm Organization: Labor

In beginning my analysis of the rural economy with the microcosm, the household and village, I have already described some important changes and institutions in four villages for a fifty year period. This approach is in keeping with Fei Hsiao-tung's theory that an intensive investigation of a small field will exemplify the importance of regional factors for analyzing various problems and will provide empirical illustrations.[1] But the facts, so far, have been drawn from one collection of materials, and any conclusion derived from them runs close to theorizing from scanty evidence representing only a small fragment of this rural economy. More evidence must be drawn upon to answer four basic questions. How was peasant household labor utilized as farms became smaller in size? Why did peasants refrain from investment in more farm capital beyond a certain size of farm? Why did peasants manage large and small size farms so differently? How did peasants use their land when commerce and industry began to develop rapidly in the towns after the 1890s?

New field survey data are organized around a broad framework showing the use and allocation of labor, capital, and land by peasant households. The starting point for discussion is the household unit. The activities of the peasant family farm can best be understood by postulating several assumptions about peasant behavior. These assumptions relate to the wants and satisfactions the household considered important and to the constraints that limited household efforts to achieve its goals. They will serve as the basis for analyzing the organization of labor on the household farm and the use of labor in the village.

The Size of the Peasant Household

The typical household farm consisted of husband and wife, one or two children, and an aged relative. Many households became large, with three generations living under the same roof. There is a close correlation between the number of persons per family and the size of farm,[2] because a family possessing more sons had more labor power to earn income to buy land. If a household had not had any serious family sickness and had few aged members to care for, hard work and frugality could increase its size of farm. When the sons married and their offspring increased, the family farm might have reached a certain size to provide income for all to live together. Buck's survey of several localities in Hopei and Shantung produced data which I have arranged to show the number of persons per size of farm. Table 17 shows that as the size of farm enlarged, the number of persons per household also increased.

A household is regarded as consisting of workers and consumers. A

Table 17. Relationship of size of farm to number of persons per household, according to locality.

Hopei							
Ch'ang-li		Cheng-ting		Ts'ang		T'ung	
Size of farm	Persons per household	Size of farm	Persons per household	Size of farm	Persons per household	Size of farm	Persons per household
1.02– 1.22	6.0	0.27–0.92	4.1	0.29– 1.07	5.3	0.25– 0.91	4.4
1.23– 2.45	6.5	0.93–1.84	5.6	1.08– 2.14	6.0	0.92– 1.83	4.8
2.46– 3.68	8.1	1.85–2.77	6.8	2.15– 3.22	7.4	1.84– 2.75	5.6
3.69– 4.91	8.0	2.78–9.73	10.4	3.23– 4.30	8.9	2.76– 3.68	6.1
4.92– 6.13	9.9			4.31– 14.36	10.4	3.69– 7.77	7.8
6.14– 9.82	9.9			14.37–128.58	13.6	12.55–31.64	12.0
9.83–14.81	10.5						
Average	8.6	Average	6.4	Average	7.7	Average	5.9

Shantung							
Ning-yuang		Shou-kuang		T'ai-an		I	
Size of farm	Persons per household	Size of farm	Persons per household	Size of farm	Persons per household	Size of farm	Persons per household
0.14–0.42	4.4	0.02–0.15	2.8	0.16– 0.49	6.5	0.56– 1.20	4.7
0.43–0.86	5.0	0.16–0.32	4.3	0.50– 1.01	7.3	1.21– 2.40	5.8
0.87–1.30	7.8	0.33–0.48	5.3	1.02– 1.53	7.0	2.41– 3.61	6.9
1.31–1.74	9.5	0.49–0.64	8.3	1.54– 2.05	9.6	3.62– 4.81	8.5
1.75–2.18	7.3	0.65–0.80	8.7	2.06– 2.57	9.8	4.82–13.18	9.0
2.19–2.62	7.0	0.81–1.72	12.3	2.58–13.33	7.8	15.92–24.59	11.5
Average	7.0	Average	6.1	Average	7.6	Average	7.2

Source: Buck, *Statistics*, size class of farms, p. 293; number of persons per farm, p. 300.

worker is defined as a male within the age group of 15 to 60 years of age who earns income for the household, and females within the same age category are considered to supply half the labor power of a male. This is an arbitrary age distinction, for in rural China boys of 8 and 9 assisted their parents in the fields during busy seasons. In order to simplify our calculations, and the results would not differ greatly anyway, males and females outside this age category will be counted as consumers adding nothing to household income. Although the number of persons per household could range from as low as one to as high as 20 with an average of around 5.2 persons per household,[3] the number of workers per household varied greatly within the household. In a very small sample of households, say a dozen or two, differences in sex distribution, age distribution, longevity of the aged, and the reproduction rate of wives produce irregularities making it impossible to see any relationship between the worker–consumer distribution and the number of persons per household. Only when our sample is large, covering all households in a village, important relationships emerge.

Table 18. Number of household workers and consumers in Chai-shan village of An-ch'iu county, 1940.

Size of farms (mow)	Number of households	Number of persons	Persons per household	Number of workers per household	Number of consumers per household	Worker to consumer ratio	Amount of land per worker (mow)
6 and above	4	45	11.2	3.9	5.7	0.68	1.9
4–6	22	158	7.1	2.7	3.2	0.84	1.8
2–4	79	405	5.1	2.2	2.1	1.04	1.4
Less than 2	41	165	3.5	1.5	1.6	0.93	1.1
Total	146	773	5.2	2.2	2.2	1.00	1.3

Source: Kahoku kōtsu kabushiki kaisha, *Tetsuro Aigoson jittai chōsa hōkokusho* (A survey report of conditions in Ai-huo village along the Chinan-Kiachow Railroad Line), statistical appendix 1.

In Table 18, data collected in 1940 are presented for Chai-shan village of An-ch'iu county in Shantung, which contained 146 farming families. Land distribution in this village was very unequal, and families farmed small plots. We observe that the number of persons per household increased as households increased their land. The number of workers per household and the amount of land per worker also increased as the size of farm grew larger. Finally, the worker–consumer ratio fell as households became large and owned more land, because the number of consumers greatly exceeded those in the work-force age category. Was this pattern typical in most north China villages? It probably was, but it is difficult to obtain household data for many villages to show this was the case.

When a household was formed, the worker–consumer ratio slowly rose as the children grew older, and if the household accumulated some land the amount of land farmed per worker increased. When a household was established it usually consisted of an adult male, his wife and child, and an aged parent. Assuming the household numbers four people, for the first few years the household head, sometimes assisted by an aged male parent supplies labor for field work but he will be assisted by his wife during busy periods.[4] When the first son is seven or eight he begins to help his father in the field, and very likely, a second child has now been born. As both children grow older they contribute more labor power to the household, and the worker–consumer ratio slowly rises to a peak, when the sons do full-time field work. The daughter assists her mother in sewing, preparing the meals, cleaning, helping in the fields, and perhaps doing household handicraft work. When the daughter is married, she will leave the household, but her place is soon taken by the wife of the son. The aged parents must be cared for and count more and more as consumers.

The number of workers in a household rises to a maximum about 10 or 15 years after it is established. Meanwhile, household income is gradually increased and land purchased. The household can now count on a constant labor supply for at least another 10 years, possibly longer, before the land is divided between the sons. After the sons marry and the wives' labor is integrated with that of the household, the land comes to be passed to the male heirs and new household farms are formed. This is the typical household reproduction cycle, but it varies greatly depending upon the household. What occurs for clusters of households takes place in villages. When a household sample of village size is examined, the relationships between the number of workers per household and the size of household and the worker–consumer ratio to size of household are clear and consistent throughout.

Labor Utilization in the Household

The household, guided by the male head, must be regarded as the basic economic decision-making unit. Niida Noboru has argued that "the rural household is a collective consuming and producing body,"[5] and indeed, that is precisely how we must regard this entity. The household's primary objective was to earn as much income as possible through farm labor and other resources or by work in crafts, trades, and other employments. The income was intended to preserve a line of descendants giving homage to their ancestors, carrying out the prescribed ritual related to festivals, marriages, and funerals, and achieving status for the household. Ancestor worship provided a set of working principles on which the rural family patterned its way of life, adopted goals to pursue, and formed basic values and attitudes toward life. The customs and institutions concerning child rearing, marriage, household economy, wealth inheritance, and religious rites that evolved and modified slowly over time reflected an intense desire by the family to live as a collective, harmonious working unit seeking to augment its wealth to provide security for its progeny.

Labor

Children were instructed early in life that "the family may not have enough to eat if [they] do not work hard." [6] They were urged to emulate the behavior of the wealthy families of the village who had worked hard and saved their money to buy land and livestock. Martin C. Yang recalls as a child in his Shantung village being told that "if he wants his family to have a big ox, a strong mule, two donkeys, three or four good houses, and many large and good pieces of land such as the P'an family," he must work hard and save his money.[7] Children were taught that hard work and frugality were closely related with the accumulation of wealth.[8] They were reared not to accept their lot in life and always remain poor, but to strive and achieve the same status and wealth of rich families in the village.

The household head was responsible for deciding who would work in the fields, labor for another household, or leave the village to find employment. A household owning little land was naturally eager to acquire more land. In order to earn the money to buy more land the household could rent land and use household labor to farm it or send labor to the market towns to earn nonfarm income or decide on some combination of the two. In determining what principles guided the household head in deciding which alternative to undertake or how to combine the two, given the available supply of labor in the household, some considerations immediately come to mind. He might compare income from land rental with income from work outside the village. To estimate the potential income from either alternative, or some combination of the two, it was also necessary to consider the amount of hard work involved. Farming necessitated long hours of toil, and the high risk — particularly when renting land usually meant farming someone else's poorer quality land — had to be weighed closely against the amount of sheer drudgery needed to produce a harvest. Working outside the village was neither easy nor without danger. A peasant separated from the household for weeks or months at a time faced loneliness and countless difficulties in working in an alien environment without friends or relative to turn to for help. Any comparison of income from alternative sources of employment, then, had to take into account the disutility of the work itself.

If various village surveys can be pieced together it may be possible to infer with some caution how much village labor was being allocated to farm or nonfarm work in this region. The first condition to establish is that the size of farm and distribution of the land were two major factors determining which households retained labor for farm work or dispatched labor from the village. For example, Shih chai hai village in Chi-ning county of Shantung was surveyed in 1941.[9] Located near the Grand Canal and specializing in soybeans and winter wheat, this village of 186 households farmed roughly 1,000 mow of land. About four fifths of the village's household farmed less than 20 mow of land. If households are ranked, as in Table 19, according to four groups of different size farms ranging from 0 to 2.2 mow,

5.3 to 10 mow, 15 to 24 mow, and 45 to 85 mow, and if the amount of farm capital, rural workers employed, and type of nonfarm employment of household labor for samples of households in each of these categories are shown, several observations can be made.

Table 19. Amount of labor employed, capital stock, and type of nonfarm employment for households according to size of farm in Shih chia hai village of Chi-ning county in Shantung, 1941.

Number of households surveyed[a]	Amount of land farmed (mow)	Number of agricultural workers hired	Number of large and small carts	Number of ploughs and harrows	Number of oxen	Number of mules and donkeys	Type of outside employment
Group A							
1	85	1	1	2	–	2	–
2	70	1	1	2	–	1	–
3	64	1	1	2	–	1	–
4	59	1	2	2	1	1	–
5	55	1	1	2	1	–	–
6	49	1	1	2	1	1	–
7	45	–	1	2	1	–	Day laborer
8	40	1	1	2	–	1	Peddler
Group B							
15	24	–	–	2	1	–	–
16	20	–	–	3	1	1	Day laborer
17	16	–	–	2	1	–	–
18	16	–	–	4	1	–	Peddler
19	16	–	–	5	–	1	Oil press worker
20	15	–	1	3	–	1	Oil press worker
21	15	–	–	1	–	–	–
22	15	–	½	3	1	–	Day laborer
Group C							
31	10	–	–	–	–	–	Day laborer
32	10	–	–	–	–	–	–
33	7.5	–	–	–	–	–	Day laborer
34	7.5	–	1	–	–	–	Day laborer
35	7.4	–	–	–	–	–	Day laborer
36	7.0	–	–	–	–	–	Day laborer
37	6.5	–	–	–	–	–	Day laborer
38	5.3	–	–	–	–	–	Day laborer
Group D							
44	2	–	–	–	–	–	Day laborer
45	2	–	–	–	–	–	Peddler
46	2	–	–	–	–	–	Day laborer
47	2	–	–	–	–	–	Day laborer
48	1	–	–	–	–	–	Day laborer
49	–	–	–	–	–	–	Day laborer
50	–	–	–	–	–	–	Day laborer
51	–	–	–	–	–	–	Day laborer

Source: Kokoritsu, *Santōshō Zainei kenjō o chūshin to seru nōsanbutsu ryūtsū ni kansuru ichi kōsatsu* (A study of agricultural commodity circulation in the county seat of Chi-ning county of Shantung province; Peking, 1942), pp. 83–88.

[a] Farms have been grouped by farm size. Group A farms range between 40 and 85 mow. Group B farms range between 15 and 40 mow. Group C farms range between 5 and 10 mow, and Group D farms include 0 to 5 mow.

Labor

Farms in the 15 to 24 mow and 45 to 85 mow categories owned capital, employed rural laborers, and sent few or no workers to work outside the village. These household farms were relatively large compared to the majority of households, but their percentage share of the village was not great. Farms owning less land possessed little or no capital, and every household sent someone to work outside the village. In this village very few households rented land from wealthier households. The reason seems to have been that wage income had been rising rapidly for a number of years, and the farm income obtained from rented land was less than that to be earned from outside the village for the same amount of labor and risk involved.

Assuming that households were primarily concerned with maximizing income in order to buy more land, did the average household farm become larger, smaller, or remain the same between the late nineteenth century and the 1930s? Given the available information on land prices, land rents, and farm prices during this period, is it possible to show how rapidly rural and nonfarm wages rose and which rose faster over time? By answering these questions something can be said about the trend of village labor seeking off-farm employment and the amount of land being rented.

Decline in the Size of the Family Farm

According to the findings of the National Land Commission's rural survey of the mid 1930s, the average size farm in Hopei was 17.5 mow and for Shantung, 14.3 mow.[10] From scattered data we know that peasants worked larger farms in the eighteenth and nineteenth centuries than during the 1930s. A Chinese agricultural handbook commenting on rural conditions in the mid-eighteenth century mentions that peasants in south China cultivated not more than 10 mow of land on the average, and at most 20 mow, and in the north a peasant cultivated from 70 to 80 mow but usually not more than 100 mow.[11] The *North China Daily Herald* reported that in north China the "bulk of the peasantry [did] not cultivate more than thirty mow a family" during the 1880s.[12] While traveling in north China Alexander Williamson remarked that in Shansi the peasants usually "cultivate from 5 to 20 acres" or probably around 30 to 120 mow, but at this time this province was less densely populated than Hopei and Shantung.[13] J. L. Buck provides data for four counties in Hopei and eight counties in Shantung showing that the size of farm declined between 20 and 30 per cent between 1870 and 1930. The percentage decline in size of farms was very large irrespective of the size of farm in 1870. In I county a decline of 65 per cent occurred and the farm size in 1870 was very large, whereas in Ning-yang county a decline of 50 per cent took place although the size of farm in 1870 was very much smaller than that of I county.

A sample of twelve counties out of a total number of 237 counties

Table 20. Change in size of farm, 1870–1930.

County	Crop area per farm (hectares) 1870	1890	1910	1930	Percentage decline, 1870–1930
			Hopei		
Ch'ang-li	2.17	2.06	1.95	1.73	20
Nan-kung	–	–	1.12	1.00	–
Su-shui	–	–	1.12	1.04	–
T'ung	1.88	1.76	1.62	1.49	20
			Shantung		
Fu-shan	0.94	0.85	0.71	0.58	38
I-shui	1.28	1.05	0.88	0.90	29
Lin-che	–	–	0.30	0.29	–
Ning-yang	1.45	0.97	0.90	0.73	50
T'ai-an	1.94	1.69	1.32	1.06	45
T'ang-i	–	4.82	2.37	1.70	–
Ch'i-mo	0.30	0.27	0.23	0.22	26
I	5.48	4.94	2.50	1.91	65

Source: Buck, *Statistics*, p. 288.

certainly may not provide representative coverage. Another approach can be used to estimate the reasonable limits in which a diminution in size of farm took place. I have made three estimates of the possible change in size of farm between 1890 and 1940 on the basis of reasonable assumptions inferred from data of local gazetteers and rural surveys. These estimates show that farm size declined, but the magnitude of change varied within fairly narrow limits.

If, in a hypothetical rural county, a population increase of 70 per cent in fifty years or an annual rate of increase of 1.07 is assumed, the rate of rural population increase is one that is confirmed by census data and household information in local gazetteers.[14] Let us assume also that urban population increased more rapidly so that its percentage share of total county population rose slightly, about one tenth over this period. This assumption corresponds with available information of urban population increase and may in fact actually understate this increase and transfer. Let us further assume that villages multiplied within the range of 8 per cent or 10 villages and 16 per cent or 20 villages. These changes in magnitude also seem to be in accordance with the increase in villages during the Ch'ing period as revealed in local gazetteer maps.[15] Three possible changes in the area of cultivated land will be considered: first, village land remained constant; second, it increased 12 per cent; and third, it increased 25 per cent. We can now estimate the changes in household farm area from these assumptions.

Rural surveys of the 1930s showed that a household required 25 mow of farm land to maintain a household of five people on farm income alone. This size of farm naturally varied according to different soil conditions, but let us use it as a rough benchmark to compare with our estimates of farm size in 1940 and 1890. The results for this hypothetical county are presented in Table 21.

Table 21. Change in size of farm for a hypothetical north China county, 1890–1940.

Village and population	1890	1940
A. County population (assuming a 1.07 per cent per annum increase or 70 per cent in 50 years)	100,000 people	170,000 people
Rural population (assuming a shift from 9/10 to 8/10 of population lives in rural areas)	90,000 people	136,000 people
Urban population (assuming a shift from 1/10 to 2/10 of population lives in cities)	10,000 people	33,000 people
B. Number of villages (assuming a size of 150 households) and an increase in 10 villages	120 villages	130 villages
1. Average village population	750 people	1,040 people
2. Average number of households (assuming 5 persons per household)	150 households	208 households
3. Average land owned per household assuming villages owns 4,000 mow of land	28 mow per household	19 mow per household
4. Average land owned per household assuming villages increase area from 4,000 to 4,480 mow of land	28 mow per household	21 mow per household
5. Average land owned per household assuming villages increase area from 4,000 to 5,000 mow of land	28 mow per household	24 mow per household
6. Necessary land for household of five to live from only farming	25 mow per household	25 mow per household
C. Number of villages (assuming an increase in 20 villages)	120 villages	140 villages
1. Average village population	750 people	971 people
2. Average number of households	150 households	196 households
3. Average land owned per household assuming villages own 4,000 mow	28 mow per household	20.5 mow per household
4. Average land owned per household assuming village increased area from 4,000 to 4,480 mow of land	28 mow per household	22.9 mow per household
5. Average land owned per household assuming village increased area from 4,000 to 5,000 mow of land	28 mow per household	25.5 mow per household

In 1940 the amount of land necessary to support an average household farm family by farm income alone, except in the case of a large increase in villages and cultivated land, was inadequate. Some income now had to be earned by work other than agriculture. In order for households to have sufficient land to farm, the area of cultivated land would have to increase from 480,000 to 700,000 mow, an unlikely achievement for any county during this period because there was probably not enough arable land for the cultivated farm area to be doubled. It is more realistic to assume that an increase between 20 and 40 per cent in cultivated farm land took place. We can only conjecture as to the range within which the actual change in farm size occurred. The percentage decline in size of farm falls within the range of 10 to 32 per cent, which is a percentage similar to that given by Buck (Table 20). The change in number of households ranged between 30 and 40 per cent for *B* (2) where households increased from 150 to 208 and in *C* (2) from 150 to 196. This range of increase appears to approximate the actual increase in farm households in villages during this period.

Evidence collected from a Japanese field survey of Wu li pao market town in Shantung in 1941 showed that one of the villages making up this town, Ch'en-chieh, contained 80 households in 1900 and 195 households in 1941.[16] In Table 22 data obtained from surveys of five villages show

Table 22. Change in number of households in villages of Hopei, 1931–1936.

County and village	Number of households 1931	Number of households 1936	Change in number of households	Per cent increase
Tsao Ch'iang county, She ya k'oh village[a]	84	98	+14	16
Nan-p'i county, Ta-ning village[b]	138	156	+18	13
Ts'ang county, Tai chia yuan village[c]	108	125	+17	15
Ts'ang county, Pai t'u chuang village[d]	401	412	+11	2
Kuang-tsung county, Pei seng pai chang[e]	86	92	+6	7

Source: Tenshin jimusho chōsaka, *Kahokushō nōson jittai chōsa shiryō* (Survey materials regarding conditions of villages in Hopei Province; Tientsin, 1937). a. pp. 46–50; b. p. 117; c. p. 181; d. p. 168; e. pp. 149–150.

that the number of households increased between 2 and 16 per cent for a period of only five years (1931–1936). If this time period were extended to fifty years, a percentage increase in the vicinity of 30 per cent would be quite appropriate.

Without more information on village population age structure, sex distribution, and the ratio of workers to consumers it is difficult to comment on the seriousness of rural overcrowding. The formation of many new households was the relevant factor reducing the size of family farm.

Commodity Prices, Rural Wages, and Land Price, 1900–1930

If the rural population increased about 70 per cent between 1880 and 1930, the number of households increased between 20 and 30 per cent, and the size of farm declined, can significant conclusions be deduced from the trend in commodity prices, rural wages, and land price about overall agricultural development? Much depends upon the trend of urban and commercial growth that took place. Let us first examine the hypothetical case of little urban and commercial development in which little farm labor could find employment in the cities and let us deduce the likely trends for various rural prices. Then let us examine the case in which urban commercial growth provided rural labor with considerable employment opportunity and deduce the likely trend for various rural prices. After presenting these alternative conditions, various rural prices will be presented for confirmation of one or the other case.

With little urban commercial development, an increase in the rural population by as much as 70 per cent would greatly expand the rural work force and yearly farm laborer wages would probably show little increase, perhaps remain constant or even decline. The price of land would rise relative to other prices as more households competed to buy land. Land rents would also rise, and the difference in rent between high and poor quality land would widen. Farm commodity prices would rise rapidly depending upon the proportion of farm costs divided between rents and wages and on which of these components rose more rapidly. Without transport development, villages would be unable to carry crop specialization very far, and as population increased, more land would be used solely to supply food. If we further assume that farm capital stock and technology changed little over the period, a dwindling of average size of farm and a further increase in the rural work force would compel households to farm their land more intensively to offset a decline in living standards.

Assuming that urban commerce and industry slowly develop, foreign trade and urban expansion will now determine the course of agricultural commodity prices, except in the short run when the harvest fluctuates. Rising urban demand will encourage more peasants to seek employment in the towns, and rural households will be able to augment their farm income with wage income. Increased urban demand for food and industrial crops will raise prices and increase farm household income, and transportation improvement will encourage greater specialization between food and industrial crops in the countryside. Land hunger is greatly alleviated because the rural population through increased crop specialization and exchange and through more nonfarm income can more easily prevent living standards from declining in spite of the fact that farm capital and technology have not changed greatly. Land prices need not rise as rapidly as

Table 23. Price, wage, farm costs and land price indices in the winter wheat–sorghum-producing region, 1901–1933.[a]

Year	(1) Prices received by farmers	(2) Prices paid by farmers	(3) Terms of trade[b]	(4) Wages of farm-year labor	(5) Price of labor animals	(6) Land prices
1901	–	–	–	34	–	32
1902	–	–	–	34	–	29
1903	–	–	–	33	–	29
1904	–	–	–	34	–	31
1905	–	–	–	33	–	32
1906	37	71	52	37	37	33
1907	40	67	60	52	41	37
1908	41	57	72	53	42	38
1909	48	50	96	56	45	41
1910	52	50	104	56	47	44
1911	54	56	96	58	49	46
1912	53	63	84	73	60	49
1913	62	60	103	76	67	54
1914	60	60	100	79	68	56
1915	64	64	100	81	73	61
1916	73	65	112	84	78	64
1917	81	72	113	88	81	65
1918	79	78	101	89	79	68
1919	74	79	94	92	75	72
1920	89	81	110	87	71	74
1921	98	85	115	89	81	78
1922	104	88	118	90	85	80
1923	111	98	113	95	88	84
1924	107	110	97	92	90	88
1925	107	109	98	96	95	94
1926	100	100	100	100	100	100
1927	95	99	96	109	108	100
1928	118	114	104	118	112	105
1929	154	132	117	124	121	115
1930	150	141	106	131	124	114
1931	126	147	86	133	123	113
1932	114	120	95	132	–	–
1933	76	–	–	–	–	–

Source: Buck, *Statistics*. (1) p. 149; (2) p. 150; (3) –; (4) p. 151; (5) p. 153; (6) p. 168.

[a] The year 1926 is the base year by which these indices were compiled. Therefore the index for 1926 has been set equal to 100.

[b] Prices received by farmers divided by prices paid by farmers equals terms of trade.

other farm prices. In contrast to the above case, labor wages will rise, perhaps as rapidly as commodity prices.

These two cases can be tested with the historical price data collected by Buck and his colleagues for 1900 and 1930. Long-term data on land rents are not available, but there is no mention made in the field survey literature that money rents rose more rapidly relative to other farm prices. In Table 23 price data are presented for this region in index form with 1926 as the base year. In Table 24 indices of land price, rural wage, and farm capital price are presented for four counties in Hopei and six counties in Shantung in order to relate to the magnitude of decline in size of farm for these same counties.

Price trends for the winter wheat-sorghum region, which includes Hopei and Shantung, show a very gentle rise until the late 1920s and then a great surge between 1928 and 1930, when the civil war raged. Prices decline thereafter. Prices farmers receive for their goods rise nearly two and a half times between 1906 and 1926 compared to only one and a half times increase in prices paid for goods purchased from the towns. Over a twenty-five year period, the wage for annual rural laborers rose at about the same magnitude as commodity prices. However, a sharp upswing can be detected for the very late 1920s and must be attributed to the scarcity of labor created by the civil war. The price trend for farm labor animals shows the same trend as for wages. Finally, we note that the price of land rises in much the same way and at the same speed as do general farm prices. This moderate increase in the price of land must be interpreted to mean that demand for land had not become intense, and the shortage of land, if a decreasing size of farm can be considered to reflect a condition of increasing land scarcity, was not so severe as to have bid land prices up greatly.

Similar conditions can be observed from many of the county examples, but there are several exceptions which require some explanation. In Ch'ang-li county, the fivefold increase in rural wages as compared to the moderate rise of other rural prices can be explained by the facts that this area borders south Manchuria and rural workers continually migrated to Manchuria. Although the size of farm declined and the labor supply increased, more peasants migrated to the cities and Manchuria and a supply condition which did not satisfy demand at wage levels existing in the recent past was created.

In Nan-kung, Su-shui, and T'ung counties, rural prices and wages rise moderately as the average size farm diminishes gradually. In Shantung for I-shui county, where the decline in average size farm was quite large, we note that rural wages only rose 100 per cent; possibly the magnitude of population increase and the numbers entering the work force age enlarged the rural labor supply and increased its size fairly rapidly. However, land

Table 24. Indices of land price, price of labor animals, and wages of farm-year labor for ten counties.

County	Year	(1) Price of land	(2) Price of labor animals	(3) Wages of farm year labor
	Hopei			
Ch'ang-li (20 per cent decline in size of farm 1870–1930)				
	1905	–	–	17
	1906	38	50	17
	1907	41	51	17
	1908	41	55	20
	1909	44	55	20
	1910	44	59	20
	1011	47	56	25
	1912	51	63	25
	1913	54	68	25
	1914	54	69	26
	1915	58	67	32
	1916	59	68	33
	1917	60	69	35
	1918	64	71	37
	1919	65	71	38
	1920	67	72	45
	1921	69	75	49
	1922	76	80	49
	1923	82	76	64
	1924	90	108	69
	1925	92	83	79
	1926	100	100	100
	1927	102	88	108
	1928	105	88	126
	1929	111	90	131
	1930	114	–	–
Nan-kung (5 per cent decline in size of farm, 1910–1930)				
	1901	30	–	28
	1902	30	–	28
	1903	30	–	28
	1904	30	–	29
	1905	30	–	29
	1906	30	38	31
	1907	30	41	33
	1908	34	41	34
	1909	34	45	34

Table 24 (Continued)

County	Year	(1) Price of land	(2) Price of labor animals	(3) Wages of farm year labor
	1910	35	45	36
	1911	36	51	36
	1912	41	51	40
	1913	41	57	42
	1914	42	61	47
	1915	43	66	48
	1916	45	68	51
	1917	17	37	55
	1918	30	50	60
	1919	32	50	64
	1920	20	35	43
	1921	40	74	71
	1922	78	81	75
	1923	78	86	87
	1924	78	87	87
	1925	95	95	98
	1926	100	100	100
	1927	116	109	109
	1928	121	116	117
	1929	136	130	122
	1930	136	145	131
Su-shui (7 per cent decline in size of farm, 1910–1930)				
	1901	28	–	31
	1902	28	–	31
	1903	28	–	31
	1904	29	–	32
	1905	31	–	33
	1906	32	40	35
	1907	32	40	36
	1908	33	40	37
	1909	35	43	40
	1910	35	46	40
	1911	37	52	43
	1912	39	53	45
	1913	41	54	45
	1914	41	58	53
	1915	46	59	53
	1916	47	61	54
	1917	47	66	59
	1918	47	67	63

Table 24 (Continued)

County	Year	(1) Price of land	(2) Price of labor animals	(3) Wages of farm year labor
	1919	47	70	68
	1920	53	31	86
	1921	74	69	78
	1922	74	77	80
	1923	82	81	85
	1924	95	86	90
	1925	95	93	97
	1926	100	100	100
	1927	111	103	100
	1928	121	112	108
	1929	126	107	110
	1930	133	114	117
T'ung (20 per cent decline in size of farm, 1870–1930)				
	1901	28	–	33
	1902	30	–	33
	1903	31	–	33
	1904	32	–	33
	1905	36	–	36
	1906	36	33	36
	1907	36	33	38
	1908	41	35	39
	1909	43	38	39
	1910	45	42	41
	1911	48	43	44
	1912	53	48	44
	1913	58	51	44
	1914	45	30	47
	1915	64	52	48
	1916	68	57	48
	1917	68	67	50
	1918	76	69	56
	1919	64	44	56
	1920	85	49	56
	1921	86	73	66
	1922	93	75	66
	1923	93	81	66
	1924	100	88	84
	1925	100	95	84
	1926	100	100	100
	1927	113	105	100

Table 24 (Continued)

County	Year	(1) Price of land	(2) Price of labor animals	(3) Wages of farm year labor
	1928	115	112	109
	1929	110	107	125
	1930	–	114	–
	Shantung			
I-shui (29 per cent decline in size of farm, 1870–1930)				
	1906	31	29	59
	1907	31	31	67
	1908	22	23	62
	1909	52	32	73
	1910	53	32	77
	1911	60	33	81
	1912	72	34	82
	1913	74	35	84
	1914	79	36	85
	1915	77	36	87
	1916	74	40	103
	1917	75	39	92
	1918	106	40	110
	1919	110	43	120
	1920	108	44	120
	1921	98	42	120
	1922	85	81	111
	1923	88	84	108
	1924	92	91	96
	1925	97	95	95
	1926	100	100	100
	1927	97	106	105
	1928	92	87	128
	1929	110	108	115
	1930	112	111	123
Ning-yang (50 per cent decline in size of farm, 1870–1930)				
	1912	75	112	153
	1913	92	135	170
	1914	97	138	174
	1915	103	145	180
	1916	112	149	188
	1917	120	151	194
	1918	114	138	190

Table 24 (Continued)

County	Year	(1) Price of land	(2) Price of labor animals	(3) Wages of farm year labor
	1919	126	150	198
	1920	116	134	177
	1921	109	123	161
	1922	106	117	154
	1923	106	117	150
	1924	94	86	130
	1925	97	93	112
	1926	100	100	100
	1927	105	108	93
	1928	107	108	91
	1929	122	133	93
	1930	122	133	93
T'ai-an (45 per cent decline in size of farm, 1870–1930)				
	1912	72	75	133
	1913	81	81	148
	1914	84	84	156
	1915	93	90	167
	1916	97	95	179
	1917	98	98	183
	1918	102	101	187
	1919	101	100	181
	1920	93	92	165
	1921	110	108	195
	1922	88	88	154
	1923	84	86	153
	1924	85	89	119
	1925	92	95	121
	1926	100	100	100
	1927	108	101	92
	1928	108	112	96
	1929	127	128	100
	1930	133	132	104
T'ang-i (65 per cent decline in size of farm, 1890–1930)				
	1901	57	–	38
	1902	57	–	38
	1903	57	–	39
	1904	57	–	40
	1905	57	–	44

Table 24 (Continued)

County	Year	(1) Price of land	(2) Price of labor animals	(3) Wages of farm year labor
	1906	59	34	45
	1907	61	34	47
	1908	61	35	51
	1909	61	39	51
	1910	63	40	52
	1911	65	44	55
	1912	65	45	59
	1913	65	48	59
	1914	74	50	63
	1915	74	53	65
	1916	74	55	66
	1917	77	61	73
	1918	77	62	76
	1919	77	66	77
	1920	87	69	79
	1921	87	76	80
	1922	89	83	86
	1923	89	88	88
	1924	97	90	94
	1925	100	91	97
	1926	100	100	100
	1927	108	101	106
	1928	108	100	109
	1929	115	102	109
	1930	116	103	114
Ch'i-mo (26 per cent decline in size of farm, 1870–1930)				
	1906	–	55	–
	1907	42	57	127
	1908	47	59	125
	1909	46	66	132
	1910	58	62	137
	1911	57	58	134
	1912	66	58	141
	1913	71	61	147
	1914	70	62	146
	1915	69	66	142
	1916	67	70	145
	1917	44	70	144
	1918	53	70	146
	1919	54	70	144

Table 24 (Continued)

County	Year	(1) Price of land	(2) Price of labor animals	(3) Wages of farm year labor
	1920	60	75	71
	1921	67	73	76
	1922	79	80	81
	1923	79	83	86
	1924	87	89	89
	1925	100	94	97
	1926	100	100	100
	1927	115	108	104
	1928	142	110	115
	1929	142	115	118
	1930	142	128	123
	1931	162	–	133
I (65 per cent decline in size of farm, 1870–1930)				
	1912	38	128	134
	1913	38	155	149
	1914	49	161	152
	1915	54	166	158
	1916	59	169	162
	1917	61	168	163
	1918	49	152	149
	1919	61	160	150
	1920	57	139	131
	1921	61	128	118
	1922	71	118	110
	1923	76	115	107
	1924	76	100	95
	1925	88	106	97
	1926	100	100	100
	1927	100	95	107
	1928	100	96	107
	1929	145	133	109
	1930	161	–	112

Source: Buck, *Statistics.* (1) p. 168; (2) p. 153; (3) p. 151.

prices do not show an upward increase; pressure to buy and rent land was perhaps minimal.

In Ning-yang and T'ai-an counties, the wage level is very high in the early period, rises for a number of years, and then gradually declines.

Labor

In the late nineteenth century, war reduced the population causing a scarcity in laborers so that wage levels were higher than in other counties. As population recovered and gradually increased, more young people entered the work force and the trend of wages moved downward slightly. Perhaps rural demand was strong enough to retain laborers in the village and prevent them from seeking urban employment. In T'ang-i county there occurred a 65 per cent decline in average size of farm, yet rural wages only rose 150 per cent and land prices only 100 per cent. Similar trends are discernible for Ch'i-mo and I counties.

We may conclude our empirical inquiry by stating that there seems to have been enough development of industry and commerce in county seats, larger cities, and the treaty ports to provide off-farm employment to peasants. Many were attracted to these centers to work for brief periods or to join the urban work force as factory workers or unskilled laborers. The great drift of peasants to Manchuria, particularly during the war-torn 1920s, created labor scarcity in many counties. An upward drift in farm wages occurred, and a similar rise in price of labor animals also took place. The reason for the rise in price of labor animals is that the supply did not increase rapidly, and during the late 1920s many were killed.

Our most important finding is that, without any evidence that land rents rose more rapidly than other prices but given that the price of land rose only moderately, we may conclude that there must have been only a modest increase in demand to rent land. In spite of a substantial growth of rural population, there did not occur any great increase in the percentage of tenant households or landless peasant households wanting to rent land. The large increase in the number of peasants seeking to work outside their villages is due to the expansion of new urban work opportunities and a larger number of households seeking to increase their size of farm. Households regarded it to their advantage to obtain income from nonfarm sources rather than rent land, and for this reason too we observe little increase in rented land. These conclusions, based upon the analysis of rural price trends just mentioned, confirm the validity of the second hypothetical case mentioned at the outset of this section.

The Increase in Farm Production

It appears likely that a slight structural change in this regional economy took place between 1890 and 1937. The rural population increased at an annual growth rate of around 1 per cent, and the urban population increased at an annual rate of roughly 3 per cent or more (see Table 41). By what amount the nonfarm population increased is not known, but its share of total population must have risen over this period, perhaps by as much as an additional 5 or 10 per cent. For this to have occurred, farm production would have had to rise, food imports increase, or some combination of the two occur. In Chapter 11 it will be demonstrated that food imports merely fluctuated during the twenties and thirties without any significant trend. It was the gradual expansion of farm production that enabled this modest structural change to take place.

Although farm capital stock per household more than likely remained the same, traditional farming technology may have continued to improve gradually as it had in the past. Households farming less land were able to utilize their labor more efficiently and farm more intensively. Though the cultivated area only increased slightly, an increase in labor effort combined with improved traditional technology conceivably raised yields so that average product per rural worker did not decline.

In Table 25 I attempt to measure the yield of sorghum and wheat for the years 1910–11 and 1930–31 to determine to what extent food production might have risen. There will naturally be considerable difference in yield variation for different crops because households gave more attention to some crops than others. Furthermore, in calculating food production we run the risk of using inaccurate cultivated area data because of the great under-reporting of farm land to local officials by peasants trying to evade land tax payment. This need not constitute a serious bias in the data if we are comparing yields for a reasonably short period when cultivated area did not change greatly. The degree of bias stemming from under-reporting would be the same for both years.

We confront a major difficulty in trying to compare the 1910 and 1930 data because weight and area unit measurements differed. A conversion ratio had to be obtained by which the measurement units of one year could be standardized with that of the other year. This was done by converting the Chinese measurement units of 1910 to Japanese measurement units of

Table 25. Comparisons of crop productivity and the rate of increase of yield, 1910–1930.

		1910–11		1930–31		
Province	Crop	Number of districts compared	Average productivity (catty/mow)	Number of districts compared	Average productivity (catty/mow)	Yield increase (per cent)
Shantung	Wheat	40	77.8	107	117.9	51
Shantung	Sorghum	103	109.7	105	156.7	43
Hopei	Wheat	108	64.8	128	103.3	60

Source: Data for 1910–11, from *SSJT*, vol. I, in sections devoted to Shantung and Chihli provinces; data for 1930–31, Tŏa kenkyūjo, *Shina nōgyō kiso tōkei shiryō* (Basic statistical tables for Chinese agriculture; Tokyo, 1940), I, 41, 43.

that time, which remained standard throughout this period. These conversions were then made equivalent to Chinese weight and area units for 1930. The conversion ratio obtained was then used to make the unit measurements of 1910 and 1930 comparable. This procedure was used for wheat and sorghum in 107 counties in Shantung and 108 counties in Hopei. The average yield was derived by first dividing the output by the cultivated area for each county and then obtaining an average for the province. The number of counties for which data were obtained for these two crops and the statistical results are presented in Table 25.

The results show that the yield of wheat increased between 50 and 60 per cent over this 20 year period and sorghum yield rose 43 per cent. If we also assume that their cultivated area remained constant because households used additional land for cultivating industrial crops, the rate of output growth would be 2.1 per cent per annum for Shantung wheat, 1.8 per cent for Shantung sorghum, and 2.4 per cent for Hopei wheat. These growth rates exceed that of population expansion. Yet, it is conceivable that considerable error produces an upward bias in these growth rates. Such a margin of error can be attributed to the conversion factor used to standardize measurement units, yield estimates, and the alleged constancy of cultivated land. Even by trimming the growth rates by 0.5 per cent to compensate for these sources of error, we are still left with a growth rate of food production large enough to have supported the small percentage increase of nonfarm population which occurred.

Labor Utilization in Villages

Farming is a seasonal occupation with household labor being used more intensively during some months of the year than others. The demand for labor within villages was determined mainly by crops cultivated and the crop rotation system used. Although crop rotation systems varied and were quite complex,[17] three standard patterns can be observed. The first is the fruit- and vegetable-growing system; the second is the multi-grain crop system; the third is the food and industrial crop rotation system.

Villages near cities specialized in growing fruits and vegetables, and if weather permitted, three vegetable harvests were often possible.[18] Vegetables could be grown as early as February and as late as October in many areas, and the produce easily marketed. The demand for labor to plant, weed, harvest, and market crops was fairly continuous throughout the year, and peasants had few idle days on their hands. Buck observed that in Ping-hsiang county of Hopei "an intensive crop, such as vegetables, provides a greater amount of labor per farm and at a time when this labor supplements rather than interferes with other crops." [19]

In districts where winter wheat, millet, and sorghum were the chief crops, peasants rotated their land between different cereals to prevent excessive exploitation of the soil. After the fall harvest, winter wheat was sown on a portion of the land, and the remaining land was left fallow. When wheat was harvested in the spring, the remaining village land had already been sown for sorghum, millet, soybeans, and vegetables. After the wheat harvest, that land might be permitted to lie fallow or soybeans were planted, because the peasants realized that this legume, which had nitrogen-fixing properties, restored the soil to its former fertility. The demand for labor was more intense in the early spring and late fall because of the winter wheat planting and harvest.

In districts specializing in cotton or peanuts but growing wheat, more labor was required for field work than where grain alone was cultivated. The crop rotation system used enabled the peasants to obtain three harvests every two years. In the first year, grain and cotton were planted in different plots. After the fall harvest, wheat might be sown on land formerly used for grain, and land used for cash crops was left fallow for a season. In the spring, grain and cash crops were planted on the fallow land, and soybeans and vegetables were grown in the place of winter wheat. After the harvest in year two, wheat was planted where grain and cash crops have been cultivated, and the remaining land was left fallow. Plots were rotated to grow different crops on a seasonal basis. Growing cotton required much more labor than was necessary to grow grain. The land had to be better prepared, weeding had to be more intensive, irrigation had to be maintained, and the harvest required many more hands. In villages which adopted cotton, more labor was required during planting and harvesting time than if only grain was grown. The same was true when potatoes were substituted for millet and wheat as a food crop in the 1920s and 1930s, although growing potatoes required considerably less land.

Villages supplied a quantity of labor for non-agricultural employment depending on the distribution of land, size of farm and amount of capital, and the type of crops and crop rotation system used. The case of Shih-chai village in Lin-ch'ing county in Shantung was studied in November of 1941.[20] The distribution of land was very unequal, with 11 per cent of the households owning 41 per cent of the land while only 38 per cent of the land was owned and farmed by 70 per cent of the households. The average size farm of the village's 115 households was around 20 mow, and the majority were able to live by farming. Since 1925 more land had been used to grow cotton, and by 1937 two thirds of the village land was devoted to this crop.[21] Although demand for labor was strong and fairly continuous throughout the farming year, the inequality of land distribution made it necessary for households with little capital and land to send workers outside the village to earn wages.

After war broke out in 1937 the amount of labor leaving the village for temporary employment increased greatly because the village switched from cotton to growing millet and sorghum for food. The marketing system had been disrupted, and households could not sell their cotton to buy the amount of grain they needed. Cultivating grain required less labor, and more manpower was released to work outside the village. The war had also reduced the supply of livestock, and a household which had lost a mule or donkey could not prepare the same amount of land for spring sowing as before. Many households, now unable to farm their land, leased some of it and sent workers to the market towns to earn wage income.[22] The loss of farm capital and the switch to a new crop rotation system meant that less labor was needed in the village, and the supply of labor for urban employment was increased. Figure 3 has been constructed from village data to show how labor was allocated during the busy and slack farming season. Three groups of households ranked according to size of farm owned, number of persons in the household, and amount of farm capital are arranged with *A* group of households owning more land and capital followed by *B* and *C* groups with less land and capital.

We observe that during the slack farming season, *C* household group sent labor to the market towns to find employment or used farm labor to produce fertilizer to sell to other households. During the busy season they exchanged their labor for the capital of more wealthy households. Households in *B* category also sent some labor to the market towns, but *A* category households with more land did not find it necessary to send much labor outside the village. During the busy farm season the exchange and use of labor became more complex. The market town labor market received and allocated peasant labor to work in different villages or at jobs in town, and households exchanged labor services and farm capital in order to plant and harvest the crops. All households had to pay the *t'an-k'uan* levy and send labor, when officials demanded, for corvee work somewhere in the county. This use of labor, however, did not exist before 1937 except during the civil war period of the late 1920s.

Households which had lost land or were newly formed and owned little land depended upon nonfarm income to remain in the village. If these households were successful over time in acquiring some land, they sent less labor to work outside the village. If land distribution became more unequal in a village or the size of household farm decreased, the village provided more labor for temporary employment in the towns and cities. These conditions differed greatly according to time and place, so that the percentage of households having full time and part-time employment varied greatly. The peak farming periods when labor demand was most intense came in April to May and August through October, but during the months of January, February, November, and December households found it difficult to find work for the able-bodied workers. According to Buck, in villages investigated the percentage of able-bodied workers having full-time work ranged from as low as zero to 75 per cent.[23] The unusually high percentage of workers with only part-time employment means that the majority of

Fig. 3 Use and allocation of labor in Shih-chai village, 1941.

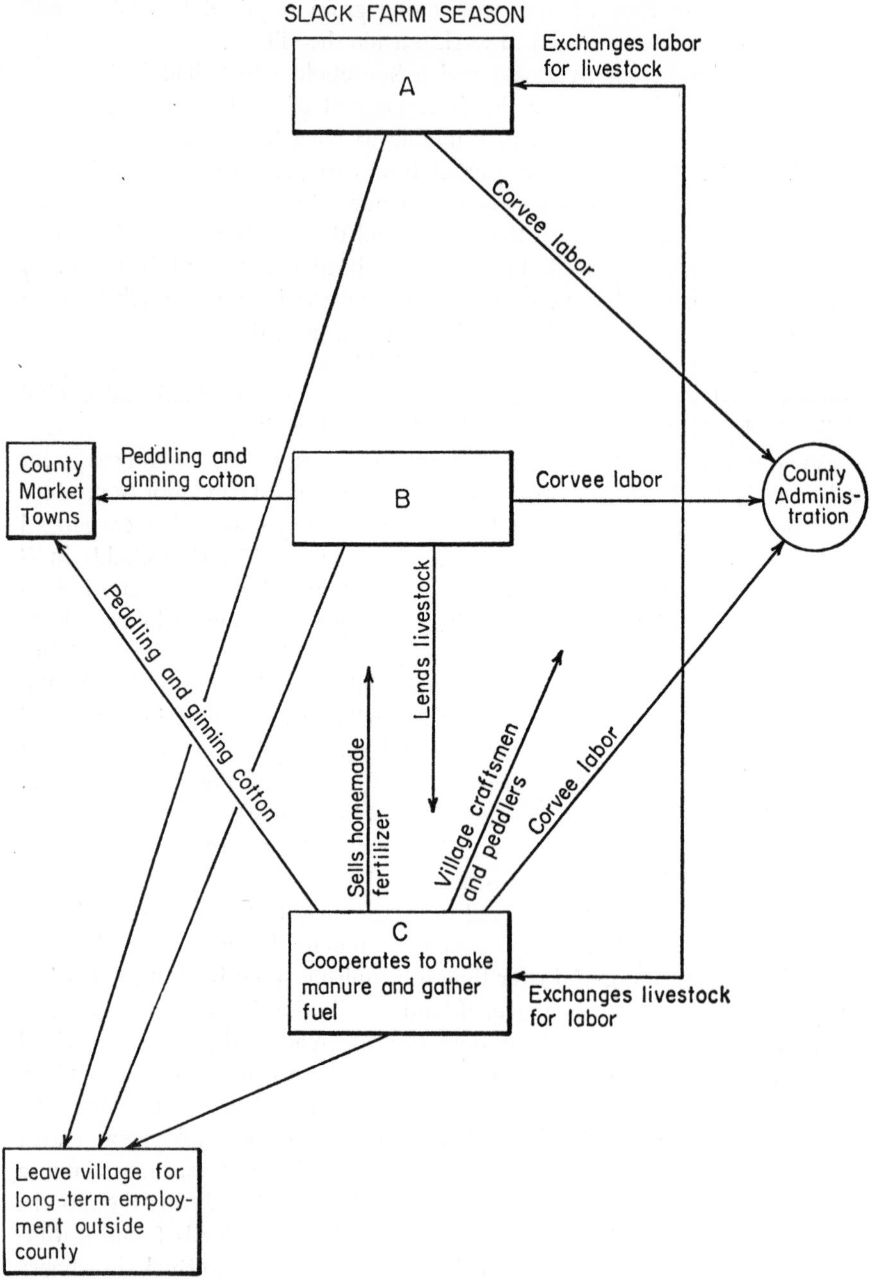

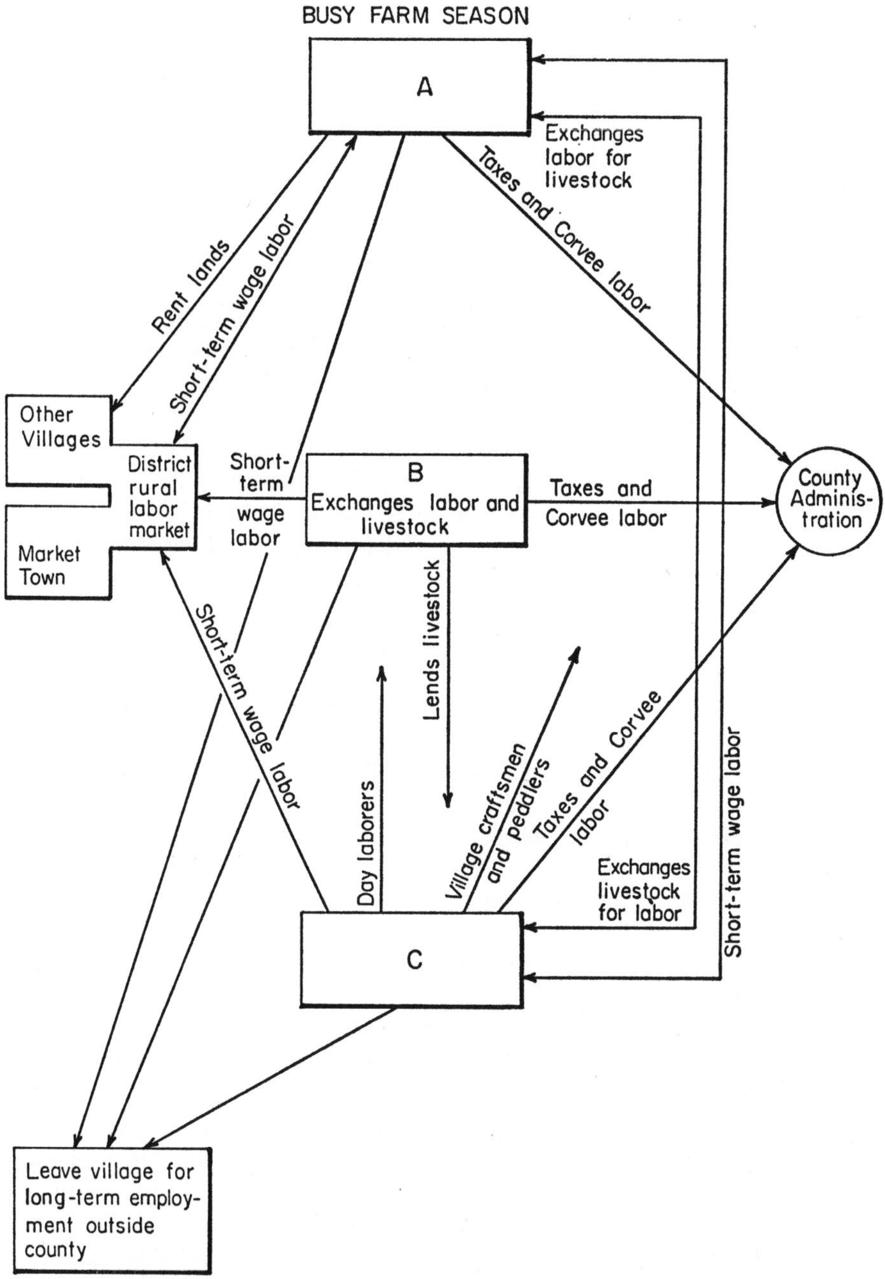

A. FOUR HOUSEHOLDS OWNING 2 HEAD OF LIVESTOCK AND 69 KUAN-MOW OF LAND PER HOUSEHOLD.
B. THIRTY-FOUR HOUSEHOLDS WITH ONE HEAD OF LIVESTOCK AND OWNING BETWEEN 19 AND 65 KUAN-MOW PER HOUSEHOLD.
C. SEVENTY-TWO HOUSEHOLDS WITH NO LIVESTOCK AND OWNING LESS THAN 19 KUAN-MOW PER HOUSEHOLD AND 5 HOUSEHOLDS WITH NO LAND AND NO LIVESTOCK.

households were compelled to find work outside the village, particularly during the slack farming season.

Field surveys of the 1930s showed that a household of five persons had to have at least 25 mow of fairly good land to live by farming alone.[24] In the mid 1930s it seems that the majority of households did not own or rent enough land to support themselves without additional income being earned from nonfarm employment.[25] As households multiplied in the villages, cities expanded, and the urban demand for skilled and unskilled labor rose rapidly. Customs officials commented that in Tientsin "the cost of the ordinary essentials of life has doubled between the years 1911–21, and has been followed by a rise of about 50 per cent in wages." [26] However, wage increases differed according to skills. Wages of masons and carpenters nearly doubled between 1911 and 1921, while "the daily wages of ordinary skilled workmen [were] about the same irrespective of trade." [27] The *Tsingtao Gazetteer* reports that agricultural workers were paid a daily wage of 0.20 yuan compared to masons and carpenters who received 0.45 and 0.50 yuan respectively.[28] In 1921 rural laborers earned 0.27 yuan per day compared to .80 yuan per day for carpenters. In 1924, after a currency change, coolie transport workers, who earned slightly more than rural workers, received 36 cents a day as compared to a dollar a day for carpenters. The wage differential between skilled and unskilled workers probably widened gradually during this period.

Such a wage differential, in fact, also reflects the large wage difference between the average wages paid in the cities and the villages. Buck's rural wage data for this region show that between 1901–1926 rural day laborers received a 150 per cent wage increase over this period or an increase of 3.7 per cent per annum. This increase corresponded roughly to the rise in the price level and indicates that large numbers of able-bodied workers were leaving the villages for the cities to find work. Their influx into the city labor markets kept wages of unskilled laborers lagging continuously behind those of skilled workers. The large increase in migration to Manchuria after 1911 also meant a departure of young laborers for long periods of time. As rural population increased, the percentage of able-bodied workers between the ages of 15 and 60 in the rural population probably remained the same or declined slightly during this period because of the large migration to towns and to Manchuria. The income they earned and remitted to the villages was spent primarily on consumption and taxes.

We have no way of knowing to what extent more households came to send labor to work outside the village after the 1880s and 1890s, but even in the absence of reliable statistics, there is little evidence in gazetteers, eye-witness reports, and farm surveys that a great increase in rented land within villages occurred, whereas there is every indication that more households recognized the advantages of earning nonfarm income and made every attempt to use their labor for this purpose.

10. Peasant Farm Organization: Capital and Technology

The north China family farm was not a single spatial unit enabling the household to manage its land easily and efficiently. A farm consisted of scattered strips and pieces, located in diverse sections of a village or nearby villages. When a household increased its land, it did so by adding bits and pieces to those it already possessed, rather than by consolidating plots to form an integrated farm. When a household needed money, it mortgaged or sold one of its scattered plots.

The time spent moving from plot to plot to tend the fields was great, particularly if a dozen or more plots were located far from the households. Buck estimates that the average distance between plots in north China was roughly a half mile, and households had to use carts to haul fertilizer to the fields and harvested crops to the farmstead. Plots varied in number and size, and wealthy households could own as many as a score or more of different sizes. Table 26 shows a wealthy farm in Luan county of Hopei owning 23 plots of different size located between a quarter mile to a mile and a half from the household.

As farms increased, so did the average size of plot. There were some exceptions, but in the majority of counties surveyed by Buck, this situation seems to have been common (see Table 27). Some efficiency in farming was gained by the household when the size of farm expanded, but this gain must have been very small considering the time spent and energy exhausted in transferring labor and capital from one plot to the other.

Fen-chia or the System of Dividing the Land Equally among Male Heirs

Not only did the prospect of acquiring higher village status and more wealth motivate the household head to accumulate land, but the veneration received by his sons if he left them more land than he had received from his father was a strong incitement for the household head to work, save, and favor the birth of sons. The fact that the land would eventually have to be divided between the sons did not disturb the parents. "When a son is born even to a poor family, he is not looked upon as someone who will further divide the family's land, but as one who will add to it. When a second son is born, the parents do not worry that their small piece of land will be divided into two parts. Instead, they begin to hope that when their sons are grown up, one will be a hired laborer, another a mason, and that they will earn not only their own living but add fifty dollars or so to the family every year. In two or three years, they can buy one more mow of

Table 26. Number of plots and their distance from the household of a wealthy peasant in Luan county of Hopei, 1941.

Plot number	Size of plot (mow)	Distance from household (li)
1	9.00	0.5
2	7.80	1.5
3	7.50	1.0
4	8.77	1.0
5	3.00	0.5
6	13.50	0.5
7	8.40	1.5
8	19.50	0.5
9	17.00	1.0
10	6.50	0.5
11	36.58	1.0
12	16.00	0.5
13	8.40	3.0
14	2.00	1.0
15	7.50	4.5
16	4.00	4.5
17	10.47	4.5
18	16.00	3.0
19	7.40	1.5
20	16.00	4.5
21	24.00	1.5
22	6.80	0
23	5.27	0
Total	261.39	

Source: Nishimura Koichi, "Kahoku ni okeru daikeiei nōka no genkin shūshi" (Cash income and expenditures of a large-scale farm in north China), *Nogyō keizai kenkyū*, 20.1:29. (December 1948). One li is approximately equivalent to 1,890 feet English measure.

land with their savings. Thus when the parents are old, they will be better off than they now are. This expectation increases with each son born."[1] More sons meant more family income, which in turn enabled the household to buy more land. Because aged parents were cared for by their sons, it made no difference if the land was divided and each given a portion of household wealth to start a career as farmer, as long as the process was repeated successfully each generation.

Whereas household division may have served as a powerful stimulus for the accumulation of land by individual households, it also served as a brake slowing down land accumulation by wealthy households. Although a wealthy household might accumulate a considerable amount of land,

Table 27. Size of parcel and field by size of farm for eight countries, 1930–1933 (hectares).

Hopei							
Ch'ang-li		Ts'ang		Ch'ing		T'ung	
Size of farm	Average crop area per parcel	Size of farm	Average crop area per parcel	Size of farm	Average crop area per parcel	Size of farm	Average crop area per parcel
1.01– 1.22	0.13	0.29– 1.07	0.27	0.35– 1.15	0.18	0.25– 0.91	0.34
1.23– 2.45	0.23	1.08– 2.14	0.32	1.16– 2.30	0.24	0.92– 1.83	0.41
2.46– 3.68	0.21	2.15– 3.22	0.34	2.31– 3.46	0.30	1.84– 2.75	0.52
3.69– 4.91	0.26	3.23– 4.30	0.39	3.47– 4.61	0.35	2.76– 3.68	0.48
4.92– 6.13	0.28	4.31– 14.36	0.55	4.62– 9.63	0.37	3.69– 7.77	0.98
6.14– 9.82	0.34	14.37–128.58	1.19	16.42–20.96	0.78	12.55–31.64	1.34
9.83–14.81							

Shantung							
En		Ning-yang		Shou-kuang		I	
Size of farm	Average crop area per parcel	Size of farm	Average crop area per parcel	Size of farm	Average crop area per parcel	Size of farm	Average crop area per parcel
0.27– 0.90	0.21	0.14–0.42	0.13	0.02–0.15	0.04	0.56– 1.20	0.31
0.91– 1.81	0.25	0.43–0.86	0.20	0.16–0.32	0.06	1.21– 2.40	0.38
1.82– 2.72	0.36	0.87–1.30	0.26	0.33–0.48	0.07	2.41– 3.61	0.45
2.73– 4.54	0.49	1.31–1.74	0.24	0.49–0.64	0.07	3.62– 4.81	0.51
4.55–13.58	0.51	1.75–2.18	0.29	0.65–0.80	0.08	4.82–13.18	0.62
		2.19–2.62	0.44	0.81–1.72	0.10	15.92–24.59	1.02

Source: Buck, *Statistics*, pp. 104, 293.

which was divided and passed into the hands of two or three sons, the probability was that these recipients of the land eventually sold it. The progeny of a successful and large landowner became small holders. Several examples show how this occurred in large landowning families.

In 1906 in the village of Tung fan liu of Chang-chiu county in Shantung, there were 7 large landowners of which the largest, T'ai Ho-t'ang, owned 472 mow.[2] Four households owned between 30 to 60 mow, 63 owned between 15 and 30 mow, and 46 owned less than 15 mow of land. T'ai's grandfather had slowly accumulated 351 mow in the late eighteenth century, and in 1793 he divided the land between his two sons, giving each 175.5 mow. In 1870 T'ai received 164 mow from his father, and by 1905 he had increased his holdings to 515 mow, most of which was owned in Tung fan liu village. T'ai employed 13 year-round laborers and from 20 to 40 short-term workers during the busy season to manage the land. He owned 4 donkeys and 4 mules, 2 ploughs, 3 large carts, 8 small carts, and a large number of ducks and pigs. In addition to his farm wealth he owned a number of small businesses in the market towns. In 1907 he divided his land and commercial wealth between his sons. This property was gradually sold by his sons, and in 1928 T'ai's descendants had been reduced to small owner-cultivators with about 20 mow.

There is another case of what household division can produce on land distribution in Ping-ku county of Hopei over six generations of peasants belonging to the same lineage group. The data is presented in Figure 4. Chang Fu's son, Wan Ts'ang, successfully increased his small inheritance of 16 mow to 800 mow, which he in turn divided equally between his four sons. Two sons increased their holdings, but in the case of Lin and Yung their holdings declined. When these four sons in turn divided their households, their land was divided into nine households managing many scattered plots. After these nine households conducted household division, 19 farming households were created with an average holding of 48 mow. As more households divided, we see the gradual creation of many family farms with less than 10 mow, the typical feature of this rural landscape. By the end of the sixth generation, land cultivated by the Chang lineage group had increased greatly but only a few households had large farms, and the majority had only very small farms. We do not know the change in land distribution of other lineage groups in Pei ta kuan village, but similar loss and acquisition of land must also have occurred.

Some household heads, possessing luck, foresight, and the ability to work hard and save, increased their land, but their sons or grandsons invariably lost the land. For example, the Te Ch'ien family (Fig. 4) increased their farm 100 per cent before it was divided between their four sons. One of these sons, Feng Lou, then trebled his size of farm, but after he divided it between his three sons, none was able to acquire more land. In fact, one son lost land.

Fig. 4 Equal division of land in the Chang clan over six generations in Pei ta kuan village of Ping-ku county of Hopei, 1936.

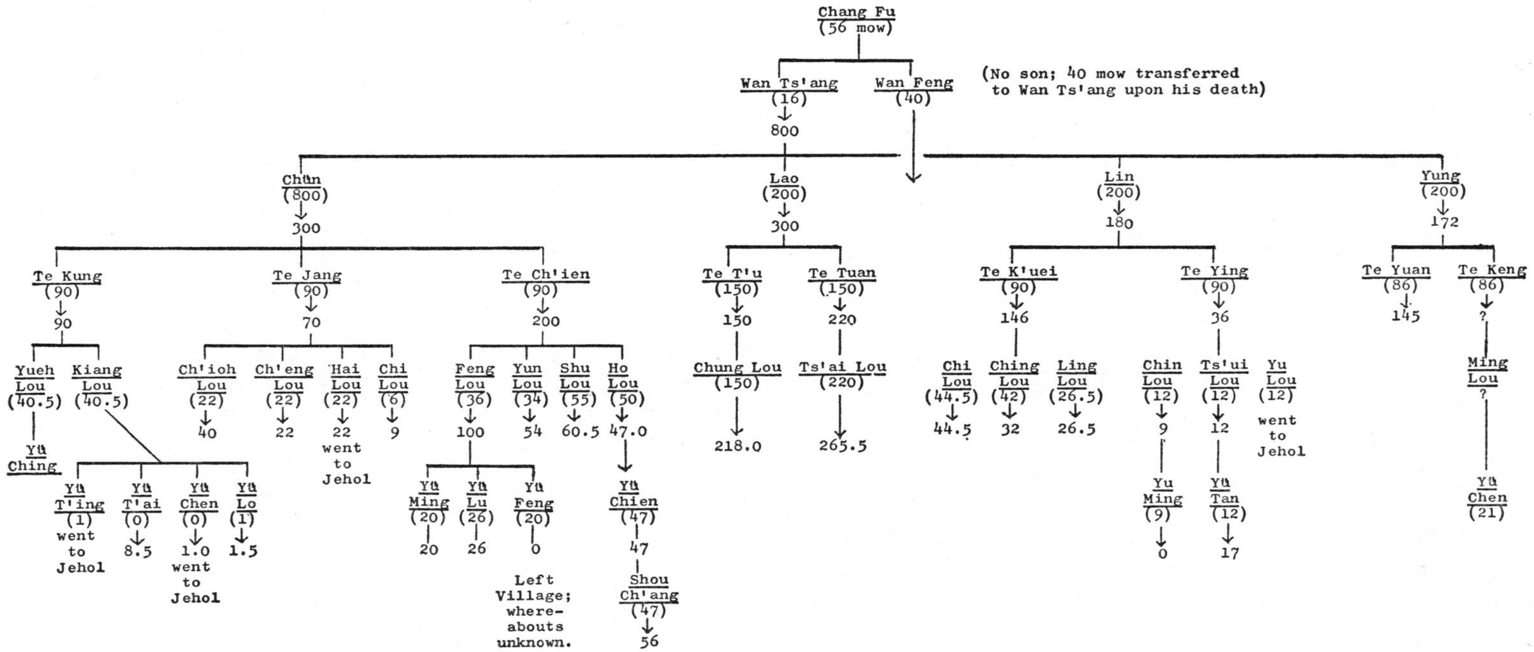

Source: Muramatsu Yūji, *Chūgoku keizai no shakai taisei* (The social structure of the Chinese economy; Tokyo, 1949), pp. 305–306.

More important, perhaps, is the disappearance of large landholders through *fen-chia*. Isoda Susumu relates how the grandfather of Li Juh-yuan of Sha-ching owned over 200 mow in the late Ch'ing period, but when the land was divided equally between his two sons, Li's father managed to keep his share intact to divide it between his five sons.[3] Li Juh-yuan received 20 mow in the process which enabled him to become a farmer. Martin C. Yang observed that family fortunes rose and declined in his native village, T'ai-t'ou, near Tsingtao. "A farm family's rise is largely accomplished by the buying of land, its fall occasioned by the emergencies that force the sale of land. It is interesting to note that no family in our village has been able to hold the same amount of land for as long as three or four generations." [4] South Manchurian Railway Company researchers examined Lo hsin village of Cheng-ting county in 1941 and found that of 259 households, only 6 farmed plots exceeding 50 mow, and the majority farmed only a few mow of land and rented no land.[5] Around 1900 ten households of the Wang clan in this village farmed plots between 50 and 60 mow in size. "Through household division, the land was divided and sub-divided until in 1941 only 6 households in the village had over 50 mow of land, of which only three households were members of the Wang clan." [6]

Equally important was the fact that household division created new household farms with less land to farm. In Hsi han k'o village near Tsingtao, there were 170 households in the village around 1900, several of which farmed 50 mow, but the average size farm was only 6 or 7 mow.[7] In 1938 the village had 262 households with no household farming more than 30 mow, and the average size farm was now only 4 mow. Population had increased about 1.5 per cent per year, many more households had been formed, little increase in the stock of farm capital per farm had taken place, and farm technology remained unchanged. Households were able to remain in the village at relatively the same living standard as 40 or 50 years ago because more household labor worked outside the village.

In Table 28 it is possible to see how household division created more households between 1931 and 1936. In two villages in Wang-tu and Ts'ang counties in Hopei the largest increase occurred in the size of farm category 10 to 30 mow, and large farms between 100 and 150 mow were divided into several small farms.

The reason for dividing land equally between the sons is a problem separate from that being examined here. The best study of land inheritance in north China concludes that disputes between brothers was the main reason why households finally divided their land.[8] Quarrels between other family members also created unbearable tensions and violent disputes which raged incessantly, ultimately forcing a division of land in order to restore calm. A household free of dissension and argument might keep its wealth intact for a long period, perhaps two generations, but eventually an ambitious and clever son contrived to press for a division of the family's wealth.[9]

Table 28. Distribution of land in two villages of Hopei, 1926–1936.

		1926		1931		1936	
County and village	Size of farm (mow)	House-holds	Per cent	House-holds	Per cent	House-holds	Per cent
Tung yang ch'iu, Wang-tu county[a]	0– 5	–	–	15	10	13	8
	5– 10	–	–	29	20	30	19
	10– 20	–	–	54	38	58	38
	20– 30	–	–	20	14	24	16
	30– 50	–	–	18	13	21	14
	50–100	–	–	4	3	6	4
	100–150	–	–	3	2	2	1
	Total			143	100	154	100
Hsiao chu chuang, Ts'ang county[b]	1– 4.9	0	–	0	–	5	9
	5– 9.9	1	3	2	5	10	18
	10– 19.9	3	8	4	10	15	27
	20– 49.9	15	38	18	45	13	23
	50– 99.9	15	38	14	35	13	23
	100–200.0	4	10	2	5	0	–
	over 200–300	1	3	0	–	0	–
	Total	39	100	40	100	56	100

Source: Tenshin jimusho chōsaka, *Kahokushō nōson jittai chōsa shiryō*. a. p. 2; b. p. 197.

Contrary to the general opinion that the Chinese household was a stable and enduring institution, it seems that the typical family was beset with tensions that threatened to divide the household at any time. The Chinese household, on both economic and social grounds, rested on very insecure foundations where it might disintegrate or fragment at any moment.[10] As it became more difficult to earn a living from farming and the sons left for uncertain periods to earn income to supplement what was earned from the land, it became increasingly harder to maintain family harmony. The paradox was that if a household worked collectively to amass wealth only to have it dispersed between the sons, each act of accumulation planted the seeds for future domestic rivalry in which each son demanded his share of the collective wealth.

Household division did not take place regularly but fluctuated. In the village studies section, it was pointed out that during the late 1920s and 1930s there had occurred a sudden increase in households dividing the land. Niida Noboru has pointed out that in the Communist controlled areas of the northwest, rural households during the 1930s and 1940s divided their wealth more rapidly and at an earlier date than had been usual in former times.[11] Some Western observers believed household division was more frequent among poorer peasants than among the wealthy.[12] If a household head recognized that the family fortunes were fast disappearing, he might hasten to divide everything between the sons before nothing was left. Peasants of Ch'en-chieh village remarked that "the necessity of evading the rapacious squeezing of local officials and the hope of being missed by marauding bandits were additional factors obviously responsible for the increase in household division" in that village in recent years.[13]

The demographic profile for villages also made households divide their land more quickly in some areas than in others. A village with a large percentage of its population below fifteen years of age could expect to experience within a decade or two a massive outbreak of household division unlike a village with a large percentage of aged and a small percentage of young. In areas subjected to terrible natural calamities bringing harvest failures and the predatory attacks of warlord armies, the village birth rate declined greatly in a matter of a few years. This was the case for many villages around Peking during the 1920s.[14] Many contained fewer young people, and a long period had to elapse before the percentage of young again bulked large in the village population. Household division and the formation of new households did not occur for a long time even though population increased slowly. After a long period of population and village household expansion resulting from household division, war and famine might reduce the birth rate so drastically that the number of households actually declined over a short period.[15] In these areas, household division would not influence the distribution and size of land for a long period of time.

Capital Accumulation and Investment

Income not spent for consumption and maintaining the farm was used to buy land. If a household accumulated more land, it usually increased its farm income and more land could be purchased. The problem for the household was to decide how much land it could efficiently farm and how much it should lease to other households. Closely related to this matter was the additional problem of what proportion of income should be used to buy more land, invest in farm capital, and satisfy family consumption needs. As household income increased, decisions had to be made periodically as to how much income to allocate between these alternatives.

Our task is to examine field survey data to determine if any relationships are observable between the amount of farm capital and the size of farm and amount of farm output produced. If relationships are observed, it would be possible to advance some propositions about how present households decided to use their income and what factors determined the amount of land they farmed.

In this study land carries two meanings depending on how the household used it. First, land represented a form of savings or near-money for the household because of the type of credit system that existed (see Chapter 15). Second, land which had been reclaimed, irrigated, and tilled represented capital for the household. I define this modified land as capital because it is an intermediary commodity producing an assortment of goods that provide for the welfare of the household and the care and upkeep of the land. I will classify land as a form of fixed capital because its value and size does not change during the period of annual productive use. The period of productive use can vary greatly, but for our purpose we will regard it as one year. Other forms of fixed capital are buildings and orchards which remain fixed in supply throughout the production period. Other forms of capital such as seeds, livestock, fertilizer, irrigation facilities, and tools, I will define as variable capital. These are forms of capital which can be varied during the production period according to household decisions about how much income to invest in their purchase and maintenance.

These definitions are arbitrary, and I make them only for purposes of classification and comparison to show that different categories of capital varied in amount according to the size of farm. By defining farm land as capital and distinguishing between farm land as capital and the means of production used in different amounts at various stages of farming, two important relationships can be observed: total capital per farm increased in value as the size of farm expanded; the proportion of total capital allocated as variable capital begins to decline when the proportion of fixed capital rises and the size of farm expands.

The first relationship can be observed from the following field study results. In Ma village of Huo-lu county near the large railway junction of Shihmen, peasants owning over 20 mow possessed more capital in the form of buildings, land, trees, and variable capital than peasants with farms of less than 20 mow.[16] In Hui-min county of Shantung two village surveys of Ho p'ing hsiang and Sun chia miao showed that peasants with farms larger than 20 now owned more variable capital than peasants farming less than 20 mow.[17] A survey of Lao wa chuan village of T'ai-an county of south-central Shantung showed similar findings.[18] In Suan chuan chen and Mi ch'ang villages of Feng-jun county in eastern Hopei, peasants with farms of 40 mow and more had more capital than peasants with farms of 15 or 30 mow of land.[19] In Ta san li village in Lin-ch'ing county of southeast Shantung households with more than 30 mow were able to employ more farm workers because they could provide them with more variable capital than households with farms smaller than 20 mow.[20]

An example of the second relationship between variable capital and the

Table 29. Value of farm capital according to size of farm for Nan-ying village of Shen-che county, 1933.

		Per cent of total capital							
		Fixed capital				Variable capital			
Size of farm (mow)	Total capital (yuan)	Land	Buildings	Fruit trees	Total fixed capital	Live-stock	Tools	Seeds and fertilizers	Total variable capital
Under 9.9	619.94	73.0	22.6	1.0	96.6	1.0	2.7	0.7	3.4
10 to 19.9	919.40	73.8	18.4	1.0	93.2	1.5	3.6	1.4	6.8
20 to 29.9	1,541.00	74.9	14.3	1.0	90.2	2.4	4.7	1.9	9.8
30 to 59.9	2,701.85	73.6	16.9	1.1	91.6	2.4	3.8	2.2	8.4
Over 60.0	5,964.90	73.4	16.7	1.5	91.6	2.7	3.9	1.8	8.4

Source: Mantetsu chōsabu, *Kita Shina no nōgyō to keizai* (Agriculture and economy of north China), II, 603. Data from this source has been arranged differently in this table to show the difference between fixed and working capital values according to size of farm.

size of farm may be seen in Table 29. The results were obtained from a survey of Nan-ying village in Shen-che county of Hopei in the early 1930s. Fixed capital as a percentage of total farm capital is at first large, falls, and then rises to remain constant. Variable capital as a percentage of total capital first rises, falls, and then remains constant. As more land is acquired, it is apparent that households are not investing in more variable capital to farm the additional land. A point is reached when beyond a certain size of farm, land is simply leased to other peasants and that land cannot be considered household capital any longer. Another illustration of the relationship between variable capital and size of farm can be seen in Table 30, which was compiled from data collected from two villages in

Table 30. Amount of investment in variable capital per mow of farm land according to size of farm for two villages in Feng-jun county, 1938 (yen).

Size of farm (mow)	Ferti-lizer	Fodder	Seeds	Live-stock	Tools	Other mate-rials	Total
Under 10	1.04	1.28	0.19	0.08	0.15	–	2.74
11–20	1.72	0.06	0.30	–	0.26	–	2.34
21–30	–	–	–	–	–	–	–
31–50	4.15	0.75	0.07	–	0.19	0.14	5.30
Over 51	2.27	0.30	0.23	0.54	0.16	0.01	3.51

Source: Mantetsu chōsabu, *Kita Shina no nōgyō to keizai*, II, 606. A 50-mow farm was not the ceiling at which investment in variable capital per mow began to decline in all counties. Much depended upon skilful farm management, quality of soil, and the availability of variable capital. The size of farm for which variable capital investment per mow declined varied from area to area.

Feng-jun county in Hopei. The results show that the amount spent by farms for variable capital first rises as the size of farm increases, but after a certain point — in this case 50 mow size farm — the amount of variable capital per mow of farm land declines rapidly.

There seems little doubt that the pattern of household investment was one of spending a smaller percentage of total income for variable capital the larger the farm became as may be seen in Table 31, which was compiled

Table 31. Household income and investment in variable capital by size of farm, according to household sample for Mi-ch'ang village of Fen-jung county of Hopei, 1938 (yen).

Size of farm (mow)	Total annual household income of households sampled	Investment	Percentage of total income
Under 13	124.77	83.96	67
14–40	360.07	239.52	66
Over 41	1,172.74	644.41	55

Source: Mantetsu Hoku-Shi keizai chōsajo, *Shōwa jūsan nendo nōka keizai chōsa hōkoku* (A survey report of the farm household economy in 1937), Tientsin, 1940, pp. 26–34.

from household budget data from a village survey of Feng-jun county in 1938. Household investment and capital accumulation behavior seem to have followed a common pattern. A household spent a certain amount each year to maintain the physical and spiritual well-being of its members and another portion went to manage the farm. Some income had to be set aside to pay taxes, repay debt, and provide for family sickness or emergency. Suppose that the household realized a windfall gain from either a good harvest and rising farm prices, or additional wage income earned by the sons working outside the village. It was used most likely to buy land, and the same outlays for consumption were maintained. To farm additional land, the household would also have to spend an extra amount for variable capital, and so some increase in farm management expenditures takes place in the next year. This could be financed by credit, from savings, or from the windfall gain. As the new land provided extra farm income, a portion could be saved to invest in variable capital, but after a certain size of farm was reached, the household decided to spend a smaller percentage of household income for variable capital. From Buck's field data it is possible to explain why households were able to farm efficiently a certain size of farm, and beyond that size they leased land and invested in nonfarming activities.

Farm Output, Income, and Investment according to Size of Farm

When Buck surveyed localities in north and east-central China between 1921 and 1925, he attempted to determine which size farm operated most efficiently and earned most income. A major conclusion of his study was that large farms whose range varied from over 21 mow to over 201 mow were more profitable and earned more income than farms which were smaller.[21] In the light of Buck's 1930–1933 study and other rural surveys, this conclusion must be modified greatly. The major failing in the 1921–1925 survey was that farm size was restricted to five categories, which in themselves were too small.[22] This defect was corrected in Buck's later study where classification was made to include eight sizes. Buck was thus misled by his early survey data to conclude that large farms were more profitable, for had he included more classes he would have found that

Table 32. Income per mow of farm land according to farm size for three villages in north China, 1930s.

	Hopei	
	Shen-che county	
Size of farm	Li-yuen village	Nan-ying village
(mow)	(Chinese dollars per mow)	
Below 9.0	13.30	15.41
10–19.9	12.44	11.38
20–29.9	11.47	10.49
30–59.9	11.60	9.53
Over 60.0	11.27	9.56

	Shantung
	An-ch'iu county
Size of farm	Chai-shan village
(mow)	(yuan per mow)
Below 2	95
2.1–4	106
4.1–6	109
Over 6.1	105

Source: Data for Shen-che county, A. K. Chiu, "Recent Statistical Surveys of Chinese Rural Economy, 1912–1932, unpub. diss. (Harvard University, 1933), p. 403; data for An-ch'iu county, Kohoku Kōtsu, *Tetsuro Aigoson jittai chōsa hōkokusho*, p. 130 and section 2 of statistical appendix.

beyond a certain size, depending upon the locality, farm output and income per unit of land declined. Although Buck did find several examples of this in his early survey, he felt compelled to explain these by unusual conditions existing in the locality, and he did not cite this as a major trend for farms in general.[23]

I have found data for three villages which show that beyond a certain size farm income per unit of land begins to decline. Income per mow of land either rises as the size of farm rises and then declines, or is high for the category of smallest farm size and then declines as the size of farm increases. This may be seen in Table 32. Over a small range of sizes, and the size varied depending upon the particular rural conditions of an area, farm income first increased and then declined. Though more labor could be applied to sowing, irrigating, weeding, and harvesting, there was a definite limit to the amount of man-hours that could be applied per unit of land. At this point some change in the complementary factor, capital, must occur if the land is to be made to yield more. Water, seeds, and fertilizer were the important resources necessary to increase output. The supply of water was determined by the number of village wells and availability of rain fall. The number and quality of seeds depended upon the previous year's harvest or the appearance of new seed varieties in the market towns. The supply of fertilizer depended upon the number of labor animals, other livestock such as pigs, and human excrement. It is difficult to say which was the more important factor preventing output per unit of land from falling beyond a certain point. There is some indication, however, from survey data of the 1930s that had more fertilizer per mow been applied on larger size farms, yields would have been maintained equivalent to that of smaller size farms. This observation is based on the data collected from Buck's 1930–1933 survey. I have grouped data on amount of fertilizer produced per crop hectare, labor animal units per crop hectare, and the crop yield by index according to size of farm for four counties in Hopei and four counties in Shantung. The data appear in Table 33.

Several interesting relationships stand forth. First, the amount of fertilizer per crop hectare quickly declined as the size of farm expanded. The same holds true for the number of labor animal units per crop hectare.[24] The amount of fertilizer produced is closely correlated with the number of labor animals. Farming conditions of this region suggest that as farms became larger, there were fewer labor animals per crop hectare to supply fertilizer and so the supply per crop hectare also declined. Although fertilizer was obtained, in part, from human excrement mixed with dirt, this constituted a very small percentage of the fertilizer applied to fields. This is borne out in the study of Sha-ching village.

The trend in crop yield related to size of farm varied according to county. In some counties yield rose as the size of farm increased, leveled off, and then declined abruptly, as the size of farm was further enlarged. In other

Table 33. Amount of fertilizer produced on farm, labor animal units per crop hectare, and crop yield by size of farm for eight counties

County	(1) Size of farm (hectares)	(2) Amount of fertilizer per crop-hectare (kg.)	(3) Labor animal units per crop-hectare	(4) Crop yield by index for farm size[a]
		Hopei		
Ch'ang-li	1.01–1.22	14,811	1.09	58.7
	1.23–2.45	6,510	0.60	91.6
	2.46–3.68	4,036	0.35	83.0
	3.69–4.91	4,850	0.48	131.2
	4.92–6.13	2,832	0.26	103.4
	6.14–9.82	2,376	0.25	97.2
	9.83–14.81	1,888	0.19	95.5
Ts'ang	0.29–1.07	4,065	0.56	110.4
	1.08–2.14	4,037	0.38	81.5
	2.15–3.22	3,105	0.28	98.5
	3.23–4.30	3,146	0.29	94.7
	4.31–14.36	2,297	0.11	92.7
	14.37–128.56	1,002	0.26	88.4
Ch'ing	0.35–1.15	8,213	0.76	88.5
	1.16–2.30	5,878	0.56	97.8
	2.31–3.46	4,814	0.50	96.0
	3.47–4.61	4,165	0.46	102.4
	4.62–9.63	3,607	0.41	99.1
	16.42–20.96	2,595	0.30	104.6
T'ung	0.25–0.91	2,132	0.44	93.9
	0.92–1.83	2,539	0.28	98.0
	1.84–2.75	2,116	0.19	99.8
	2.76–3.68	1,676	0.17	99.3
	3.69–7.77	1,530	0.16	97.4
	12.55–31.64	1,286	0.12	99.2
		Shantung		
Hui-min	0.61–1.38	3,763	0.47	99.7
	1.39–2.76	3,244	0.35	99.3
	2.77–4.15	3,258	0.33	99.6
	4.16–5.54	2,710	0.29	102.3
	5.55–8.76	3,648	0.36	98.9
Ning-yang	0.14–0.42	3,834	1.19	99.9
	0.43–0.86	3,262	0.56	101.7
	0.87–1.30	3,521	0.35	95.2
	1.31–1.74	3,153	0.24	92.5
	1.75–2.18	2,300	0.22	108.2
	2.19–2.62	2,777	0.29	80.8
	2.63–8.57	2,641	0.24	107.5

Table 33. (Continued)

County	(1) Size of farm (hectares)	(2) Amount of fertilizer per crop-hectare (kg.)	(3) Labor animal units per crop-hectare	(4) Crop yield by index for farm size[a]
Chi-ning	0.17–0.77	4,925	0.62	114.9
	0.78–1.55	4,424	0.41	91.1
	1.56–2.32	5,170	0.46	108.6
	2.33–4.66	3,318	0.34	101.7
	4.67–10.34	1,968	0.20	87.8
I	0.56–1.20	2,366	0.39	110.4
	1.21–2.40	3,344	0.32	110.8
	2.41–3.61	2,775	0.28	113.9
	3.62–4.81	3,022	0.29	110.9
	4.82–13.18	1,932	0.22	95.2
	15.92–24.59	1,870	0.23	88.1

Source: (1) Buck, *Statistics*, p. 293; (2) Buck, *Statistics*, p. 137; (3) Buck, *Statistics*, p. 299; (4) Buck, *Statistics*, p. 295.

[a] In (4) the crop yield index was derived by Buck in the following way. He averaged all crop yields for the region and set this equal to 100. He then compared in index fashion the yield for each locality survey. These indices only show whether output in a given locality is above or below the average yield for the region. The magnitude of index change is unimportant for our purposes. However, the trend upward or downward according to farm size is extremely useful for measuring the land productivity of different size farms.

instances the crop yield, already high for the smallest size farm, slowly declined as the size of farm increased. In a few counties crop yield slowly rose as the size of farm increased, and then leveled off, fluctuating mildly (T'ung and Ning-yang counties). In no case, however, do we observe yield to rise continuously as the size of farm expands.[25]

There is little question that crop yield was affected by the availability of fertilizer, but other considerations undoubtedly entered the picture, such as the greater efficiency obtained from managing larger size farms. This factor appears to have been sufficiently strong to have raised yields beyond the size farm where labor animal units and the quantity of fertilizer per hectare declined. But in the final analysis, the scarcity of fertilizer must be a critical factor explaining why yield declined. Although there is little data to suggest it, the importance of fertilizer for farming in this region has been mentioned frequently by competent observers.[26] Greater investment in livestock and fertilizer production, the variable capital essential for raising yield and income per unit of land, was necessary for the household to make farming a more profitable venture.

Table 34. Population density and average farm size in which crop output declined, according to farm size in twenty-four counties of Hopei and Shantung.

Locality	Size of farm (mow)	(1) Average farm size (mow)	(2) Number of persons per household for average farm size in which output declines[a]	(3) Number of persons per square mile of crop area
		Hopei		
Su-shui	36.90–94.50	65.70	8.3	1,329
Cheng-ting	41.70–145.95	93.82	10.4	873
Ch'i	22.80–165.60	94.20	8.4	976
Fou-p'ing	70.04–130.05	100.05	8.5	1,300
Ch'ang-li (1)	92.10–147.30	119.70	9.9	539
Chiao-ho	91.20–172.35	131.78	9.8	578
Nan-kung	58.50–256.05	157.28	11.5	764
Ch'ang-li (2)	92.10–390.75	241.43	12.8	733
Ch'ing	246.30–314.40	280.35	17.5	622
T'ung	188.25–474.60	231.43	12.0	505
Ts'ang	215.55–1,928.69	1,072.12	13.6	352
		Shantung		
An-chiu	9.75–26.40	18.08	7.1	3,235
Shou-kuang	12.15–25.80	18.96	12.3	3,867
Ch'i-mo	12.45–24.90	18.68	11.9	4,610
Fu-shang	29.40–59.25	44.33	9.5	1,813
Lai-yang	41.40–79.80	60.60	9.7	1,339
Wei	39.15–83.55	61.35	9.4	979
I-shui	37.35–102.30	69.83	8.0	212
En (2)	27.30–127.80	77.55	7.8	1,233
T'ang-i	62.85–95.85	79.35	8.7	645
Ning-yang	39.45–128.55	84.00	12.0	1,090
Hui-min	83.25–131.40	107.33	11.9	552
Chi-ning	70.05–155.10	112.58	11.8	1,212
T'ai-an	38.70–196.95	117.83	7.8	2,132
En (1)	68.25–203.70	135.98	11.7	715
I	238.80–368.85	303.83	11.5	443

Source: (1) Buck, *Statistics*, p. 293; (2) Buck, *Statistics*, p. 295; (3) Buck, *Statistics*, p. 423.

[a] The crop index for which number of persons per household for average farm size was compared was based on the average of most frequent yield in Buck, *Statistics*, p. 211.

It is also interesting that the size of farm in which a decline in crop yield occurs varied greatly depending upon county conditions. In Table 34 I have ranked the average farm size in which yield first declines from low to high and then compared this to the number of persons per household for that size of farm and the population density, measured as the number of persons per square mile of crop area. The first important point to be observed is that the range for average farm size in which yield begins to decline varies enormously depending upon the county and bears some correlation with population density. In other words, where the size of farm is small, population density appears to be greater and vice versa. There are some exceptions, notably in Shantung, but the general relationship appears to hold true in Hopei. This point is worth stressing because it is unlikely that soil fertility variations were extreme in this region, because similar climatic and topographical conditions existed. The second important point is that the number of persons per household rises as the size farm in which yield begins to decline becomes larger. These two conclusions, when taken together, suggest that population density and persons per crop area were very important in determining the size of farm which could be attained and efficient operation.

The cross-sectional data in Table 34 of ranked average farm size for output decline can be compared to density of animal population, the amount of fertilizer produced, and the average productivity of important crops to show that households with larger farms invested less for variable capital (labor animals and fertilizer) than households with smaller farms. In Table 35 we observe that the average productivity of main crops in each county is closely associated with the number of labor animals and amount of fertilizer: average productivity tends to be higher in counties where animal units per hectare of crop area and amount of fertilizer produced per hectare are higher and vice versa. This close correlation between productivity, fertilizer, and animal population for cross-sectional data of different average farm size on a county basis shows again the importance of size of farm and household investment in farm variable capital. It also suggests that a much improved animal husbandry would have enabled farmers to obtain larger yields from their land.

Greater income could be earned as the household work-force increased in number, and with proper planning and saving, more land was purchased. Yield could also be increased depending upon the investment in livestock, supply of fertilizer, and availability of water, but eventually a size of farm was reached in which yield and income per mow began to decline. We observe that out of Buck's 26 cases of different size farms in which output declined, 50 per cent covered size of farms below 100 mow, and 77 per cent covered size of farms below 150 mow. Because population density varied greatly and farm management could be conducted with more or less efficiency given the availability of resources, the range in farm size for which

Table 35. Animal population density, amount of fertilizer produced, and crop index according to counties ranked on the basis of size of farm where crop yield begins to decline.

Counties ranked by order of size of farm in which yield declines	(1) Size of farm (hectare)	(2) Animal units per hectare of crop area	(3) Amount of fertilizer produced (kg. per hectare)	(4) Crop index based on average of most frequent yields by important crops
		Hopei		
Su-shui	2.46–6.30	0.62	2,686	123.2
Cheng-ting	2.78–9.73	0.57	4,100	154.7
Ch'i	1.52–11.04	–	–	75.4
Fou-p'ing	4.68–8.67	1.41	13,953	111.7
Chang-li (1)	6.14–9.82	0.34	1,888	118.3
Chia-ho	6.08–11.49	0.64	3,235	100.9
Nan-kung	3.90–17.07	0.55	3,665	119.7
Ch'ang-li (2)	6.14–26.05	1.15	7,878	90.6
Ch'ing	16.42–20.96	0.53	2,595	116.7
T'ung	12.55–31.64	0.31	1,286	85.6
Ts'ang	14.37–128.58	0.24	1,002	74.0
		Shantung		
An-chiu	0.65–1.76	1.28	9,038	343.0
Shou-kuang	0.81–1.72	1.64	11,938	289.1
Ch'i-mo	0.83–1.66	1.75	10,340	146.2
Fu-shan	1.96–3.95	0.55	3,704	92.3
Lai-yang	2.76–5.32	0.70	3,733	76.5
Wei	2.61–5.57	0.53	3,238	135.1
I-shui	2.49–6.82	–	–	111.4
En (2)	1.82–8.52	0.60	3,150	117.3
T'ang-i	4.19–6.39	0.31	2,377	82.1
Ning-yang	2.63–8.57	0.41	2,641	68.2
Hui-min	5.55–8.76	0.55	3,648	117.7
Chi-ning	4.67–10.34	0.61	1,968	84.8
T'ai-an	2.58–13.13	1.27	10,196	42.6
En (1)	4.55–13.58	0.33	3,150	79.1
I	15.92–24.59	0.35	1,870	78.0

Source: (1) Buck, *Statistics*, p. 293; (2) p. 136; (3) p. 137; (4) p. 211.

output declined was rather large. Farms rarely increased in size beyond 150 mow, or around 23 acres, because this was the optimum size which could be managed profitably. As this optimum size was approached, households invested a smaller percentage of farm income in variable capital.

Capital and Technology

Why did households not make this investment? One reason is that peasants had limited knowledge of managing large farms efficiently. The larger the farm became the more difficult it was for the household to put land and capital to their most profitable use. When a household found that it was unable to cope with the technical and managerial problems of farming a larger size farm, it simply leased poorer land, with inconvenient access, to other households. Rather than invest in additional capital the household used its income to invest in urban commerce and handicraft or lend money to other peasants.

An excellent example of this may be found in Ching and Lo's study of 131 large farms in Shantung for the 1890s. Their results show that the majority of these households were large farming households owning between 100 and 500 mow of land; a few households even managed farms larger than 500 mow or 75 acres in size.[27] These 131 farms owned a total of 231,878 mow, but they only farmed 46,772 mow or 21 per cent and leased the remainder, about four fifths of their land, to other households.[28] At the same time, they invested in handicraft and mercantile enterprises in the market towns.

Households undoubtedly weighed the various investment alternatives and expected rates of return open to them. Farming more land became unattractive when the technological limits of this agrarian system were reached. This was the obstacle which had to be removed before yields could be increased and larger farms be managed.

Farm Capital and Technology

Farm tools used in the early 1940s were similar to those sketched in the agricultural guidebook, *Nung-cheng ch'üan-shu,* circulated among county magistrates in the fourteenth and fifteenth centuries. Tools were "simple and crude, and their construction was extremely poor," [29] yet they were appropriate for the dry farming conditions of this region and suitable for labor intensive methods of farming. There were 15 different types for preparing the ground, 30 types for weeding and caring for crops between sowing and harvesting, 7 types of implement for cutting and gathering the crop, 20 types for processing grain, and 30 miscellaneous tools.[30]

These tools had existed for many centuries, yet why had the supply of labor animals never increased so that hand tools could be modified and partially replaced by implements drawn by animal power? At some time in China's early agricultural history, population had increased to a certain size where the existing cultivated land could not support more people without reducing the supply of livestock. Competition between humans and livestock for what the land produced became intense, yet a balance was maintained. The farming techniques known and practiced at that time and thereafter limited the number of livestock that could coexist with people.

War often altered this balance, perhaps favoring one or the other, depending upon the extent to which the supply of labor animals and the number of people were greatly reduced, but soon afterwards a balance was restored. Households multiplied, new villages emerged, and the countryside again became densely populated. However, farms continued to be operated mainly with labor power. What were the farming techniques and system of land utilization which restricted the increase of livestock on the family farm?

The methods of soil preparation to preserve moisture were better suited to the use of small hand tools than to large implements drawn by labor animals. The farming methods for this region were first systematized in a remarkable agricultural treatise called the *Ch'i-min yao-shu,* written by Chia Ssu-hsien of the northern Wei dynasty sometime in the first half of the sixth century.[31] Chia not only formalized in clear and simple terms the many techniques known in his day but made novel suggestions of how to improve upon existing methods. The key problem at that time, as now, was how to ensure that the soil retained its moisture throughout the year. Limited rainfall and cold temperatures during the winter combined to dessicate the soil quickly and make it powdery, and dry winds removed the rich top soil. Chia's advice was that autumn ploughing be deep to prepare the soil for wheat, but shallow in the spring to prepare for millet, soybeans, and sorghum. This rule, still observed by peasants even in this century, was to prevent "the evaporation of moisture from the surface of the earth" and "to plough the fertilizer into the soil." [32] The peasants would then take their harrowing implements to break the large clods of soil to prevent further evaporation and "to overcome the unfavorable conditions of the early north Chinese spring and bring the crops to fruition." [33] The soil was hoed and raked to preserve its moisture and nutritive qualities, weeds were removed, and the crops were thereby permitted to grow more rapidly. Light ploughing required a single labor animal. Intensive harrowing and hoeing did not require animal power, only that considerable labor be applied continuously.

Another factor influencing the livestock supply was the periodic introduction and spread of certain cash crops, which limited the amount of food which could be produced for livestock. When wheat and cotton were introduced into the land rotation system, they used land which otherwise would have been devoted to supporting livestock. Because these crops could be cultivated with the available hand tools of the period, it was only necessary that an ample labor supply be on hand. Again the demand for livestock was severely limited.

Scholars disagree on when wheat became a prime crop in north China. Yonada Kenjirō argues that evidence can be found in the *Ch'i-min yao-shu* and interpreted to show that wheat was already used widely in the crop rotational system of the Wei and Sui dynasties.[34] According to Yonada, wheat was planted in the fall, harvested in the late spring, and legumes such as soybeans were then planted, followed by millet and sorghum the subsequent year. This cycle was repeated so that the three crop in two year rotation system was already well known before the T'ang period.

Nishijima Sadao contends that though wheat may have been known and even cultivated, it did not displace millet as the basic crop in this region until the middle of the T'ang period.[35] The controversy centers not on the existence of wheat at an earlier time, but on when wheat became widely cultivated. Nishijima believes that no suitable method of grinding wheat to make flour was available before the T'ang period. The high cost of grinding wheat by hand was an obstacle which first had to be removed before the supply of flour for urban consumption could be greatly increased and wheat widely cultivated.[36] Only after government restrictions regulating the use of water-operated milling wheels were removed and large estates were permitted to mill wheat with these grinding stones, did the supply of flour for urban markets increase rapidly. Estates were encouraged to increase the supply of flour because large metropolitan centers like Chang-an had emerged, and the demand for wheat flour to make noodles and other dishes had risen enormously. Supply and demand freely interacted with an important technical bottleneck now removed, and by the middle of the mid-T'ang period, wheat began to displace rice and compete vigorously with other grains for growing space.

Cotton was introduced into north China sometime around the twelfth century and after, but it was not until the fifteenth and sixteenth centuries that it had spread rapidly to many districts and become an important cash crop.[37] Amano Motonosuke has traced the diffusion of this crop through various counties for the major provinces in both the Ming and Ch'ing periods with evidence found in local gazetteers. In the early sixteenth century counties in southern Hopei were growing cotton, and in Shantung it was cultivated widely in six administrative departments.[38] Officials estimated, by the mid-eighteenth century, that cotton occupied 20 to 30 per cent of the cultivated land in Hopei.[39] In some counties like Luan-ch'eng it took up 60 per cent of the farm land and peasants imported grain from other areas. The crop also spread to Nan-kung, Chao, and Hsing counties, which later became prime cotton-producing areas. In Shantung cotton became an important cash crop in En, Chi-tung, Li-chin, P'u-t'ai counties and in districts along the Grand Canal to the southwest.[40] The spread of cotton cultivation was slowly accompanied by the development of new fertilizers, improved seeds, and better irrigation methods, which enabled the peasants to maintain soil fertility; where cotton was rotated with grain, these new methods kept harvest yields fairly stable.[41]

Peasants were eager to adopt new cash crops because they gave households additional income. However, farming methods and work schedules had to be modified to ensure that these new crops would not rob the soil of its fertility. For cotton, peasants had to plough the land carefully in the fall, fertilize the land more heavily than for grain crops in early winter, irrigate more intensively when sowing seeds, and take special care to weed during the spring and summer months.[42] As a result, peasants expended more labor and time than they customarily used for growing grain. Households specializing in such cash crops were unable to give consideration to increasing their livestock number.

But more important, the land used for cash crops could not be used to grow the grain that normally went to supply livestock with food, as was observed by Japanese researchers' surveying Sun chia miao village of Hui-min county of Shantung in 1940. They reported that after peasants switched to growing more cotton and potatoes, the supply of sorghum and millet, important livestock food, declined.[43] In 1930 this village had 36 cows, but in 1940 it had only 19. Many animals had been sold or slaughtered because it had become impossible to feed them. For the time being, however, villagers did not need to increase their livestock supply because cotton and potatoes provided the village with enough income and food.

Another factor which governed the supply of livestock was the practice of dividing the land and farm capital equally between the sons to form new family farms. When several smaller farms were created, the balance between livestock and land was altered slightly. Different schedules of work and methods to farm the land had to be fashioned, and these could seriously affect the maintenance of farm animals. In the event the new farm was extremely small, grain might still be purchased from wage income, but the household could find it very difficult to encourage the number of livestock to multiply. Consequently, it often was very difficult for households to care for and increase the supply of livestock when farms were continually being fragmented into smaller farmsteads. Some evidence of this may be seen in Table 36 for three villages in Hopei where change in the supply of livestock can be compared with the division of households taking place within a ten year period.

In Ta-ning village households increased from 132 to 156 between 1926 and 1936, but the number of livestock declined from 143 to 135. Households owning more than one head of livestock in 1926 declined in number by 1936 because of household division. The same decline occurred in Hsiao-chu village where households increased from 44 to 51 between 1926 and 1936. Further, households without livestock became more numerous, and those having more than one animal also declined. In Pei se p'a chang village the number of livestock remained constant between 1931 and 1936 when households increased from 86 to 92. The number of households with 4 and 5 animals declined and those without livestock increased. Some households in all three villages must have sold livestock. It is also significant that in each of these three villages the cultivation of a cash crop, cotton or peanuts, increased between 1926 and 1936, whereas land devoted to sorghum and millet declined. More potatoes were grown as a supplementary

Table 36. Change in number and distribution of labor animals by household in three villages of Hopei as household division occurs, 1937.

County and village	Labor animals per household: Number of animals	Labor animals per household: Households	Number of households: 1926	Number of households: 1931	Number of households: 1936	Number of livestock: 1926	Number of livestock: 1931	Number of livestock: 1936
Nan-p'i county, Ta-ning village[a]	0	0	23	29	35	0	0	0
	1	2	24	24	32	12	12	16
	1	3	0	3	6	0	1	2
	1	1	50	45	54	50	45	54
	2	1	27	30	25	54	60	50
	3	1	5	4	3	15	12	9
	4	1	3	3	1	12	12	4
	Total		132	138	156	143	142	135
Kuang-tsung county, Pei se p'a chang village[b]	0	0		30	34		0	0
	1	2		4	2		2	1
	1	3		3	0		1	0
	1	1		30	36		30	36
	2	1		10	14		20	28
	3	1		3	2		9	6
	4	1		5	4		20	16
	5	1		1	0		5	0
	Total			86	92		87	87
Ts'ang county, Hsiao-chu village[c]	0	0	2	2	8	0	0	0
	1	2	2	4	2	1	2	1
	1	1	10	19	36	10	19	36
	2	1	13	10	5	26	20	10
	3	1	12	15	0	36	45	0
	4	1	5	0	0	20	0	0
	Total		44	50	51	93	86	47

Source: See Tenshin jimusho chōsaka, *Kahokushō nōson jittai chōsa shiryō:* a. pp. 119–120; b. pp. 149–150; c. p. 198.

crop. We can conclude that where cash crop cultivation reduced the amount of grain harvested and household division created more family farms of smaller size, the growth of the livestock force was arrested, and in many instances it even declined.

In Western agricultural development a major innovation commonly associated with the rise of livestock supply, the increase of soil fertility, and the rise in yield of grain crops, was the introduction of legumes like clover, sanfoin, alfalfa, and lentils into the crop rotation system.[44] These legumes first made their appearance in the lowlands of Europe during the fifteenth and sixteenth centuries and then spread to England and later France where they in turn revolutionized farming. They restored nutrients to the soil quickly and increased the supply of fodder for feeding livestock during winter. More labor animals could be maintained, and their numbers increased more rapidly. Farms had more animal power to use in soil preparation, harvesting, and transportation. Farm tools were slowly modified and improved. One improvement led to another, and the cumulative result was an agricultural revolution taking place within a century and a half.

We do not observe the introduction and widespread adoption of similar legumes in China. It is not yet certain whether these legumes were known or if they had been introduced and found unsatisfactory for Chinese soils. The problem awaits more research. The botanical sections of local gazetteers contain evidence of the various plants grown and how long they grew in certain districts. These passages could be analyzed to determine which legumes were grown when and for which crop rotation systems. The findings could then be used to construct maps, and perhaps even charts, to show the diffusion of certain plants throughout the country and what factors promoted or retarded their diffusion.

The introduction of new seeds and farming methods to rural communities seems to have been the responsibility of local officials. In the early Ming and Ch'ing periods when local administration had to contend with a small rural population and functioned more efficiently, officials instructed peasants to use new seeds and reclaim land.[45] These same officials studied agricultural guidebooks and, after learning the proper methods, encouraged the peasantry to adopt and practice them. What seems to have taken place after a half century or more was a relaxing of these efforts. Meanwhile, rural population doubled, and the costs of administration rose so that taxation occupied the minds of local administrators. As corruption spread through the ranks of lower officials, the bureaucracy in turn devoted fewer resources to promoting agricultural development.

The expansion of towns and markets undoubtedly increased the demand for rural products and provided the necessary stimulus for rural households to look for better methods of production. Very little research so far has been devoted to the means by which new agricultural techniques spread through rural markets and became adopted by villages. At this stage of our knowledge it is impossible to generalize whether the rural marketing system impeded or accelerated the diffusion of new farming methods throughout the country. From our previous village studies, however, it is obvious that few new farming methods and seeds were made known to the peasantry through local markets. Although peasants frequented market towns several times a month and learned about the outside world, rural markets were probably a very slow means of transmitting new farming knowledge from one part of the country to another. Certainly, it was not as rapid as the introduction of new farming methods to villages by local officials.

Large farms may have needed new farming methods to raise yield, but from what we have seen of the land tenure system in our previous village studies, it is obvious that landowners made no serious efforts to instruct tenants in the proper methods of farming their land. Aside from borrowing new seed varieties from abroad, the principal way in which new farming technology evolved was by the method of trial and error. Peasants selected the best seeds, which seemed drought resistant, gave a higher yield, and ripened more quickly. They experimented with different kinds and amounts of fertilizers and learned when it was best to plant seeds and how to take care of the young shoots when they first appeared.

In a culture where farming knowledge passed from father to son the production of new agricultural technology was bound to be painfully slow. This was not a system or environment that could produce new seed varieties rapidly and the supply of complementary capital to grow these seeds efficiently. What was required to bring about this kind of technological change was a system of farm research and extension service.

Several experimental stations, like that of Litsun in Shantung, were eventually established, and they made remarkable progress in selecting and improving native seed varieties and distributing these to peasants in the surrounding districts. But these stations received little support from the provincial authorities, their research was frequently disrupted by war, and they were not linked to villages so that new findings could be transmitted to the peasants.[46]

The trend toward smaller and more fragmented farms need not have impaired the peasants' ability to manage their land efficiently and raise output had there existed some means of promoting farm research and instruction. For example, in Taiwan, by superimposing a farm research and farm extension system upon a village economy with institutions and farming methods similar to those of China, the Japanese were able to increase farm output greatly.[47] What was sadly lacking in north China was some way of expanding farming knowledge and evolving new techniques. Still, the system that did exist for this purpose performed remarkably well considering that it was the peasantry which bore the responsibility of promoting agricultural development.

11. Peasant Farm Organization: Land Utilization and Commercial Development

The task now is to relate peasant household economic behavior to the expansion of the market between the 1870s and 1930s. The basic questions around which the materials in this section are organized are: How did households respond to the market changes induced by foreign trade in the late nineteenth century? What prompted peasants to extend the cultivation of cash crops, and was a tendency toward commercialization of agriculture taking place in this region? With the demise of the Ch'ing dynasty, what trends in agricultural development and urban expansion were taking place?

The Household Farm and Land Use

In attempting to increase farm income, households had to decide which combination of crops was to be grown, what amount of land was to be devoted to each, and how to finance the cultivation of new crops. There is very little information to determine how households decided these matters, but it would seem that households behaved rationally with respect to use of land, particularly within the physical and economic constraints in which they had to operate.

Households first made certain enough food was produced and a certain quantity of the harvest could be marketed to buy the things they were unable to produce for themselves. Enough surplus also had to be produced to maintain livestock and provide enough seeds for the next farming cycle. Households had to decide how much land to allocate between food and cash crops, and such a decision in turn depended on the quality and amount of land available, existing irrigation facilities, the extent of market development, and the relative prices prevailing between different crops.

Land was used differently in various counties depending on these conditions. Buck's data, for example, show that the percentage of land devoted to major crops such as wheat, cotton, sorghum, millet, and peanuts varied greatly depending upon the area. It is impossible to say why one district elected to devote more land to one principal food or cash crop than another. The evidence presented in Table 37 merely shows that differences were very great.

Households allocated certain amounts of land for different crops depending upon the quantities they hoped to market. They sold and retained different percentages depending upon the state of the market and the farming conditions appropriate for certain combinations of crops. Data in Table 38 for four counties in Hopei and four in Shantung show the per-

Table 37. Percentage of land devoted to main crops for specific counties in Hopei and Shantung, 1929–1933.

	Percentage of land for winter crops	Percentage of land for spring crops		Percentage of land for summer crops planted after winter crops	
County	Wheat	Cotton	Sorghum	Millet	Peanuts
		Hopei			
Ch'ang-li (1)[a]	5.4	2.4	46.1	0	0
Chiao-ho	40.5	0.0	4.6	0	0
Cheng-ting	23.9	34.7	12.5	12.1	0.4
Nan-kung	19.2	43.8	11.1	0.2	0
		Shantung			
An-ch'iu	47.7	0.2	17.2	0	0
Chi-ning	83.9	0.1	9.4	0	0
En (1)[a]	34.1	11.4	14.8	0.6	0.1
T'ang-i	34.5	36.2	15.7	0	0

Source: Buck, *Statistics*, pp. 192, 196.
[a] The number in parentheses denotes the first locality survey.

centages of crop sold, retained, and stored by farms for three main crops. Many more crops could have been listed, but three should be sufficient to show that great variation existed between districts as to the shares marketed and used on the farm.

Three main patterns of market dependency existed, although there could have been others, and perhaps variations of these three also existed. The most typical pattern appears to have been that of household use of most of the land to produce for its own consumption, with only a plot or two used for a cash crop, which, once sold, paid for necessary consumer goods. For example, wheat was a prime cash crop, but it was integrated into the crop rotation system so as not to interfere with spring and summer planting. A small percentage of winter crop land was used to cultivate wheat, and it was sold for cash to purchase necessary consumer goods. A household might begin to use a little land for cotton or peanuts and after the harvest market small amounts from time to time as cash needs arose. With this arrangement peasants purchased their seeds in the market town or from other villagers.

Second, there were districts where for a century or more peasants had specialized in a cash crop and a high percentage of land was used for this crop. Because markets were well established and middlemen supplied grain from surplus producing counties at a low cost, these districts had gradually become dependent upon selling their cash crops to buy food. Examples are

Table 38. Percentage of three main crops used for different purposes according to county, 1929–1933.

County	Barley			Sorghum			Peanuts		
	Per cent sold	Per cent used on the farm	Per cent held over	Per cent sold	Per cent used on the farm	Per cent held over	Per cent sold	Per cent used on the farm	Per cent held over
Hopei									
Ch'ang-li (1)[a]	11	89	0	2	98	0	65	35	0
Cheng-ting	0	100	0	5	95	0	93	7	0
Su-shui	57	42	1	11	86	3	–	–	–
T'ung	82	15	3	22	74	4	86	13	1
Shantung									
Hui-min	0	100	0	23	58	19	–	–	–
Ning-yang	5	95	0	11	89	0	89	11	0
Chi-ning	0	100	0	7	90	3	–	–	–
I	4	96	0	17	74	9	92	8	0

Source: Buck, *Statistics*, pp. 229, 235, and 236.
[a] The number in parentheses denotes the first locality survey.

counties like Luan-ch'eng, Chao, and Kao-ch'eng in the cotton-producing zone of central Hopei. Households retained enough of the harvest to obtain seeds for the next year's harvest, so that each farming cycle was financed by the household. This form of cash crop specialization had taken considerable time to develop and had been achieved principally by households financing greater crop specialization.

Finally, some districts after 1900 began to specialize rapidly in a single cash crop. This trend was encouraged by railroad development and export expansion. Foreign and native merchants advanced new seeds and credit to peasants to promote cash crop cultivation. Examples are to be found in Wei and I-tu counties in Shantung where tobacco was quickly adopted by many villages as the principal crop so that nearly all farm income came from this crop. The adoption of peanuts in counties of northeast Shantung is another instance of this extreme form of specialization. This pattern is of interest because of the speed with which households suddenly shifted to the new crop and the important role played by merchants to provide the necessary capital for households to make the switch.

Households had to consider the amount of water, fertilizer, and labor time and effort required to grow cash crops. For example, cotton and tobacco demanded much more capital and labor than wheat or millet and sorghum. Because households of larger farm size possessed more labor and capital and could hire labor when needed, they were often able to devote a higher percentage of land to cash crops and less to grain and vegetables than smaller farms. An example of this pattern, in Table 39, shows land use according to size of farm in 1941 for Tai san li village in Lin-ch'ing county of Shantung. In this case as late as 1941 three fourths of the spring planted crop consisted of cotton. The larger farms devoted a higher percentage of land to growing cotton and less for food and vegetables. It cannot be asserted from their example alone that as farms grew in size they tried to specialize in cash crops. Other village surveys suggest that beyond a certain size farms did not attempt to specialize entirely in one crop.[1]

An expanding market economy and the acquisition of new knowledge of how to grow and market crops determined the sequence of crops which peasants cultivated. In the nineteenth century peasants quickly adopted the opium poppy when it was found to be very profitable in inferior soils. After railroad development and export expansion during the 1890s opium cultivation declined, to be replaced by greater cultivation of cotton, peanuts, and soybeans. This change in land use was the result of households responding to price change and new marketing opportunities.

Changes in Land Utilization between the 1870s and 1930s

By the 1870s new products like Western manufactured yarn had begun to penetrate local markets. The impact of this new market development on

Table 39. Percentage of land devoted to different crops according to farm size in Tai san li village, 1941.

Size of farm (mow)	Number of house-holds	Percentage of land										Total amount of land (mow)
		Cotton	Millet	Sorghum	Corn	Soybeans	Sesame	Potatoes	Onions	Melons	Total	
Under 10	42	76.1	11.0	9.4	2.1	1.1	0.1	0.1	0.0	0.0	100	224.3
11–30	37	79.2	9.8	5.6	0.7	2.0	0.3	0.6	0.3	1.5	100	814.7
31–50	8	91.3	4.1	3.0	1.0	0.6	0	0	0	0	100	296.5
51–100	3	94.7	5.3	0	0	0	0	0	0	0	100	226.2
Above 100	1	100.0	0	0	0	0	0	0	0	0	100	117.0
Total	91											1,478.7

Source: Amano, *Chūgoku nōgyō no shomondai* (Problems of Chinese agriculture), II, 47.

handicraft spinning and weaving was considerable, but trade also brought another new product to north China: the opium poppy. Despite imperial injunctions issued in 1800, 1831, and 1839 to prohibit cultivation of the poppy, peasants quickly realized that demand for this product was increasing and considerable profit could be made by switching from grain to poppy cultivation. It was estimated that in Hopei the poppy yielded 40,000 to 50,000 copper cash per mow whereas wheat only produced 10,000 copper cash per mow; in Szechwan the profit from growing the poppy was nearly twice that of wheat.[2] By 1870 the poppy had spread throughout Fukien, Kwangtung, Chekiang, Yunnan, Kweichow, Szechwan, Shensi, Shansi, Hopei, Shantung, and Manchuria. In June of 1872 it was reported that the poppy was being grown extensively in Shantung, even though it had only made its appearance there two years before.[3] In 1886, an American consular official in Chefoo remarked that "the native production of opium appears to be rapidly driving the Indian drug from the market; the demand for which is infinitesimally small as compared with former years."[4] In July of 1880, the poppy was reported to be grown throughout Paoting-fu in Hopei.[5]

The speed with which peasants switched to the poppy as a cash crop shocked the court and worried European merchants whose profits depended upon the import of opium from India. Officials feared that specializing in the poppy to the exclusion of growing grain would damage the country's grain storage system. The *Peking Gazette* in 1878 declared that "Ever since the poppy began to be cultivated on a large scale, the supplies laid by as a provision against times of scarcity have been gradually drawn upon until at last there was scarcely grain enough in store for half a year's consumption."[6] The severity of the great famine of 1877 in north China was, in fact, attributed to the extensive cultivation of the poppy.[7] Some Western observers like T. R. Banister of the China Maritime Customs agreed by pointing out that, with the spread of the poppy, "Granaries were everywhere left unfilled, and neither in town nor village was there the necessary reserve for a natural catastrophe of this sort."[8]

Other Western observers like Von Richtohofen rejected this view, claiming that "the Chinese prefer to supply first their rice and other grain before they seek to plant those crops which are not for their direct use, but by the sale of which they may acquire the funds for purchasing their food."[9] This assertion confirms the point made above that typically households first supplied their basic needs before using land to grow a marketable crop. Yet, it is possible that in many districts households did plant too much poppy, which in times of normal grain harvest would not have been serious, because the market transferred grain from surplus producing areas to counties deficient in grain. But if a prolonged drought also ruined the harvest in these surplus producing districts, households specializing in the poppy suffered, and grain normally imported became unavailable.

Soil conditions probably determined the area and extent of specialization in poppy cultivation. In Szechwan, "The more favourable conditions for agriculture and the more fertile the ground, the smaller is the ratio in which the poppy is planted." [10] Because the poppy grew exceptionally well in sandy soil and did not require much water, it was widely cultivated in southwest Shantung and in districts which flooded every five or six years.

In the early 1900s, the court finally achieved some success in reducing the area under poppy cultivation. Perhaps its task was made easier by the fact that foreign trade had also increased, and exporters now offered attractive prices for cotton, peanuts, soybeans, and tobacco. Their prices rose relative to food crops, and households which formerly used land to grow the poppy now switched to growing one or more of these cash crops.

In order to obtain some idea of the rapid change in land use between 1910 and 1930 I have constructed Table 40 and maps 8 and 9. I have

Table 40. Change in land use for counties in Shantung and Hopei, 1910–1930.

Type of change in land use	Number of counties in Shantung	Number of counties in Hopei
Introduction of cash crop into rank of top four crops	40	50
Decline of a cash crop in rank or disappearance from rank of four main crops	7	10
Change in rank of two or more grain crops in four main crops	12	28
Change in rank of one grain crop in four main crops	19	6
No change observed	1	0
Unknown	18	36
Possible change in land use	11	9

Source: Data for 1910, Shinkoku nōkō shōbu, *Shina seisan jigyō tōkeihyō* (Statistical Tables of Chinese Enterprises); for 1930, Tōa kenkyūjo, *Shina nōgyō tōkei.* Data on peanuts for Hopei were obtained from an independent survey conducted in 1924. I attempted to plot agricultural commodity prices on provincial maps and relate this to cultivated area, but there was insufficient price data.

designated cotton, peanuts, tobacco, and various beans of the soy genus as cash crops. The most important four crops in terms of their cultivated area were ranked on the basis of 1910 survey data and compared with the top four crops ranked in order of cultivated area from 1930 survey data. This was done for every county in Hopei and Shantung for which data existed. The purpose was to show the change that occurred in the ranking of the top four crops and the crops displaced by cash crops. I adopted several other categories to show crop change and these are listed in Table 40.

Of Shantung's 108 counties 40 showed a preference for cash crops, and in 31 counties there was minor change in ranking of grain crops. In 7 counties, cash crops declined in importance and more land was given over to food crops. For 18 counties, the quality of data does not permit comparison, and there remain 11 counties for which some change in land use might have occurred. Of Hopei's 129 counties there were 50 counties indicating a preference for cash crops, and 34 having change in grain crop ranking. In 10 counties, cash crops declined in importance, and in 36 counties the results are unknown. There remain 9 counties for which some change in land use might have taken place. We may conclude that considerable crop change took place. The quality of our data does not permit an econometric measure of the supply response of peasants to price change, but ranking crops and comparing these for two time periods suggests that peasant supply response was great.

In Map 8 there are no specific areas in Shantung where a decisive shift to cash crop cultivation occurred to indicate that a strong tide of commercialization swept through rural districts. In the counties along the Grand Canal in western Shantung, in the northwest and northeast, and south of the Chinan-Tsingtao railroad, peasants had begun to switch to cash crops, but this pattern is irregular and erratic. In districts where traditional transport was replaced by railroads, peasants shifted to more profitable crops even though they had to be shipped longer distances. Some districts near railway lines adopted tobacco because of the vigorous efforts made by outsiders to introduce this crop. The British Tobacco Co. introduced Virginia tobacco to several districts in central Shantung in 1913, and it was quickly accepted by the peasants. By 1922, the value of tobacco produced around Tsingtao had increased fourfold.[11] Peanuts were introduced by an American missionary in 1892, and by 1930 they were grown extensively in that province and in southern Hopei.[12]

Similar happenings took place in Hopei. From Map 9 it can be seen that in the northeast, peanuts found ready acceptance among the peasants because of the favorable soil and transport conditions. In the counties along the Peking-Hankow railway peasants also began to cultivate more cash crops. But in the cotton belt of eastern Hopei substantive changes had not occurred beyond those of the Ch'ing period. No fixed pattern can be found in this province whereby counties around major cities or along transport routes specialized in cash crops.

Buck cites evidence that a gradual switch to cash crops had taken place after 1900.[13] Tang Chih-yu also points out that after 1900 "acres and acres of land formerly devoted to poppy culture were gradually transformed into cotton and tobacco culture." [14] Was this trend something new in this region's agricultural history and did it mean that peasants had become more

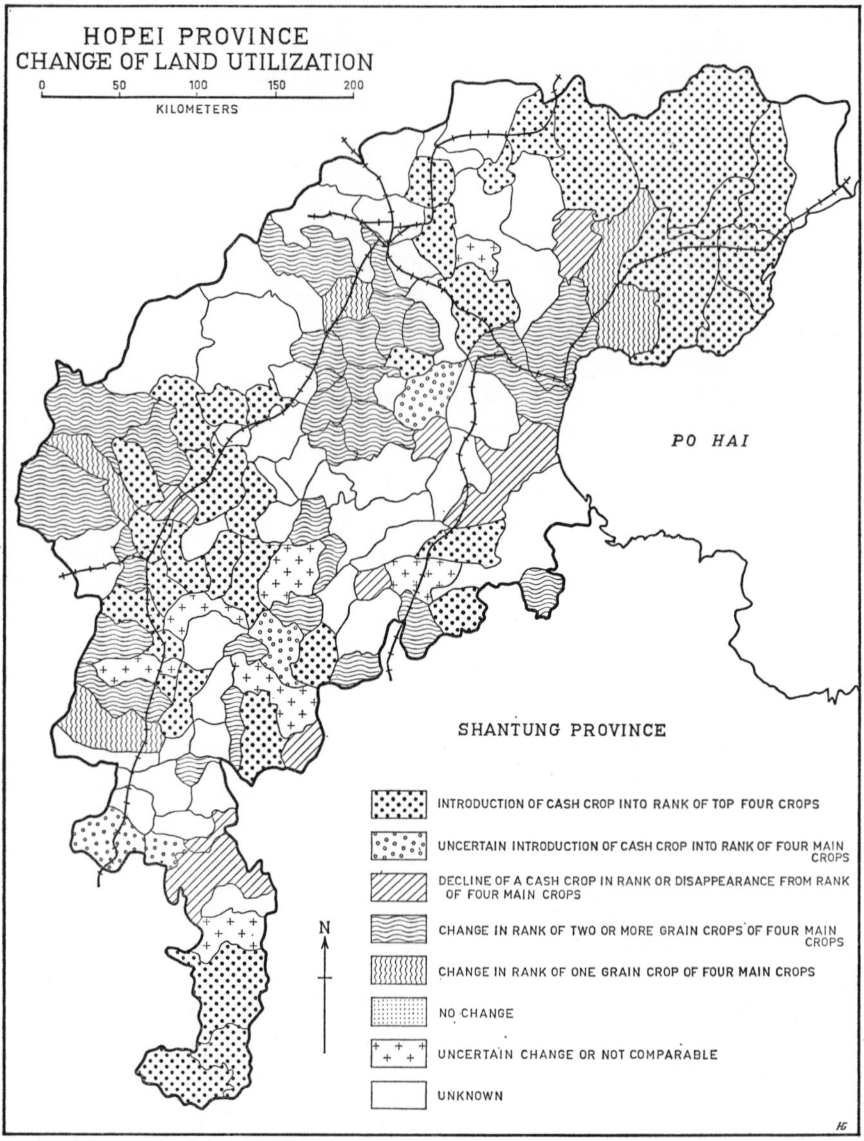

Map 8. Comparison of top four crops according to order of cultivated area for counties of Hopei province, 1910–1930.

oriented toward the market? Had this shift in land use engendered changes in farming organization? This hardly seems to have been the case. We have already pointed out the spread of wheat during the T'ang period and the adoption of cotton during the Ming and Ch'ing periods. We also know that peasants quickly seized upon the opium poppy and began to cultivate that plant in the latter half of the nineteenth century. Peasant households usually reacted quickly to changes in market price and crop income and

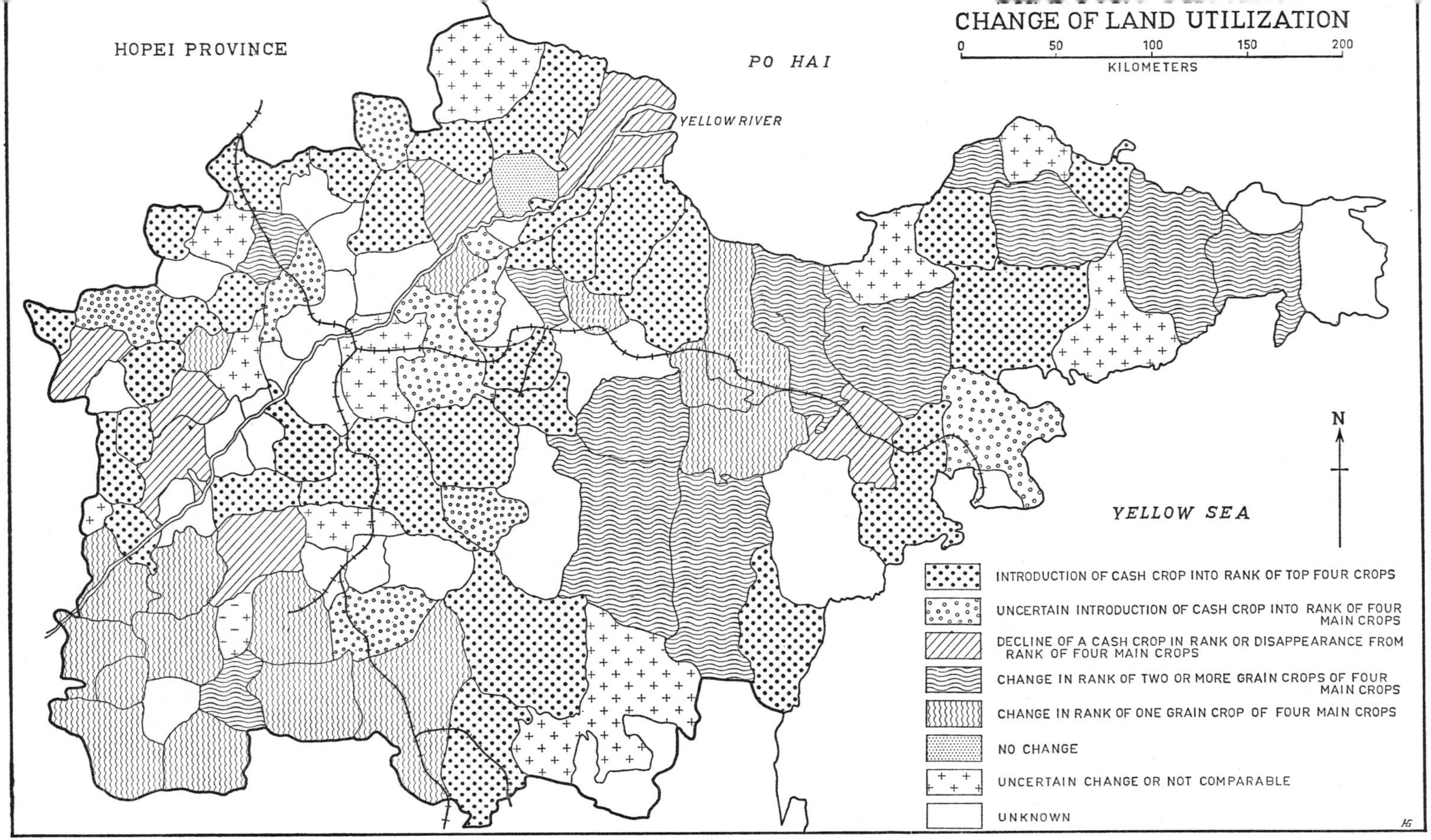

Map 9. Comparison of top four crops according to order of cultivated area for counties of Shantung province, 1910–1930.

rationally chose that crop which provided more income even though occasionally more labor effort was required. What was new for the peasantry, perhaps, was the improvement in transport, the expansion of trade, and the growth of cities. These new developments provided households with greater opportunity to supplement farm income at a time when it was becoming evident to all that overcrowding had become serious in villages.

Transport Improvement, Trade Expansion, and Urban Growth

Transportation during the Ch'ing period had been a key bottleneck obstructing the expansion of internal trade. By the late nineteenth century it was obvious to the Westerner that road building and repair lagged far behind the organization of inland trade. Three writers comment that "In view of the small extent and uncertain character of the waterways of the northern provinces, and the fact that from the earliest times the inhabitants have been accustomed to the use of wheeled vehicles, it might have been supposed that some care would have been bestowed on the roads which here form the only possible means of inter-communication. Neglect here, however, culminates." [15] And indeed the roads, such as they were called, were shockingly poor. In 1908 the third secretary of the British Legation in Peking traveling to Jehol complained, "Villages are numerous, but all are mud-built and poor looking in spite of the wealth of crops everywhere. The roads are vile." [16]

Poor transport raised the prices of goods between districts separated only by short distances. An American consular official remarked how "Coal in reasonable quantities can be bought at any time at the mines at Tzu-chou (Hopei) for less than $1 per ton but so limited and imperfect is the means of transportation across the country that in consequence thereof, it doubles in price every twenty miles it is transported. So that by the time it reaches Tientsin, the nearest market, it cannot be sold profitably for less than $13 per ton." [17]

In districts in which profitable cash crops were traditionally grown, local officials did not make any attempt to encourage their production and export, so that in the silk production areas of Ching-chou fu in Shantung, transport "as elsewhere in the province [was] rapidly falling into decay from mere neglect." [18] Even after the treaty ports were opened in Shantung and prosperity from trade was evident to all, local officials did not take advantage of these new opportunities to connect inland markets with ports by better roads or canals so that trade could be increased. In 1901 James V. Carroll, Commissioner of Customs in Chefoo predicted that "the future prospects of Chefoo depend entirely upon the encouragement to progress set to the people by their officials." [19] Thus, when the Tsingtao-Chinan railway was constructed, it was the port of Tsingtao which prospered and Chefoo which stagnated. Perhaps the backwardness of transport never appeared so glaringly defective as during the great 1875–76 famine that swept across five provinces taking about 12 million lives. To relieve the misery of the population the court purchased many grain vessels with their cargoes intact and routed them to Tientsin, but "so slow and imperfect [were] the means of transportation" that grain merely accumulated and rotted on the Tientsin docks.[20]

Between 1898 and 1912 European engineers built 5,733 kilometers of railway line connecting Peking with south Manchuria and Hankow, Tsingtao with Chinan, and Tientsin to Pukow.[21] These trunk lines cut through both provinces and linked the hinterland more closely to Peking and the treaty ports of Chinwangtao, Tientsin, and Tsingtao than had ever been possible with traditional transport. However, the treaty ports were still not linked with the interior through roads, and railway junctions within the interior were not connected to districts with feeder lines. In 1921 "modern roads outside the city areas of Tientsin and Peking [were] still in their infancy." [22] Custom officials in Chefoo complained the port was "still without either railway or road." [23] The same officials in Tsingtao remarked that "roads in the Shantung province are in the same deplorable conditions as elsewhere in north China." [24] In Chinwangtao of northeast Hopei, "Nothing had been done to improve the bad conditions of roads for cart traffic, which greatly impeded transportation of goods to market at inland places dependent upon this port for their supplies of imported goods." [25] Without roads and a feeder rail system, the impact of railroads upon inland trade was greatly minimized.

There is no question but that railroads were profitable, particularly before 1920, but during the 1920s civil war and periodic military takeover of the lines reduced revenue earnings and made their repair and upkeep costly and difficult, if not nearly impossible. Between 1903 and 1906 the Imperial Railway running from Peking to Shanhaikuan showed a gain in passenger and freight revenue from 3.5 to 6.9 million Tls. The ratio of new earnings to investment, after interest payment to creditors was made, rose from 4.75 to 18.25 per cent.[26] The Tsingtao-Chinan line earned 2,881 Chinese dollars per kilometer of line in 1906, and by 1911 the sum had risen to 5,549 dollars per kilometer. The most profitable line was the Peking–south Manchuria line, mentioned above, which carried staples and minerals from the northeast to north China. Expenditure per kilometer increased more rapidly than revenue per kilometer after 1920. In 1930 the line again made profits, and in 1933 it transported 7 million tons of goods of which three fifths consisted of minerals, 12 per cent finished goods, and the remainder agricultural products.[27] The earnings of north China railways for selected years may be seen in Table 58 of the statistical appendix.

Merchants in Wei county of Shantung soon realized after the completion of the Tsingtao-Chinan line in 1905 that more goods would move directly to Tsingtao than would pass through their hands onward to Chefoo. A Western traveler commented that "The big traders have gradually realized, too, that cheap, speedy, and regular transit is a factor against which they have never reckoned, and against which 'old custom' cannot hold its own. Since the opening of Chefoo to foreign trade, the province has found its natural outlet in this port, and it has held a practical monopoly leaving only a minor share to the Grand Canal and the small waterways of southern Shantung. No sooner was the Tsingtao railway completed, however, than it was realized that a large portion of the Chefoo trade had been diverted into the new channel." [28] In Hopei, railroads quickly increased their share of goods by diverting traffic from the river trade. In 1912 railroads hauled 53 per cent of all goods whereas the Grand Canal and the rivers Hsi Ho, Pei Ho, and Tung Ho carried 44 per cent. In 1921 railroads hauled 70.5 per cent, and these same rivers transported only 25.5 per cent.[29]

Customs officials in the treaty ports were quick to point out that railroads had begun to stimulate rural areas to sell more to the urban markets than before. Officials in Tsingtao in 1911 remarked that "Produce which formerly could not bear the expense of the laborious cart journey to the coast now finds a ready market, and is produced in yearly increasing quantities. Prosperity is visible everywhere in the districts along the line and beyond, and the railway, at first bitterly opposed, is now pronounced a blessing, and extension in other directions is eagerly looked for." [30]

One important impact of railroads on the rural economy was to divert trade from local market centers and ports to the treaty ports serviced by railroads thus giving the appearance of stimulating an increased flow of grain and cash crops from the interior to large market towns and the treaty ports. It is very difficult to say precisely how much of the increased flow of commodities arriving in treaty ports represented additional marketed product produced by rural households and how much was diversion from inland market centers. On the other hand, it is obvious that railroads diverted traffic from river transport to railroads so that river traffic contracted considerably.

Because of the change in land use that took place after 1900, we can probably assume that some increase in farm product sold on the market took place, although we must be very cautious in claiming that a substantial shift occurred. However, data for regional trade suggest that improved internal transport had greatly assisted in transferring some of the surplus produced by peasants to the treaty ports for export. The record shows that after 1890, the rate of trade expansion accelerated greatly. Before 1890 few goods trickled through Tientsin and Chefoo into the interior. Their volume was so small that internal disturbance to trade such as poor harvests and famines hardly affected imports. T. A. Bannister, writing about the relationship of the 1875–76 famine to foreign trade, claimed that before 1890 China could have survived easily without foreign trade. "Yet the direct effect of this terrible famine upon the mount of foreign imports was less than might have been expected. The net import of piece goods only declined about 6 per cent in both quantity and value. This was generally supposed to indicate that foreign piece goods were not in demand among the common country people, those stricken by famine, but only among the town-dwellers and the well-to-do who were not directly affected. In view of the vast population of China, even this statement was perhaps short of the truth. In the enormous cloth requirements of the country, foreign importations contributed as it were but one drop to the bucket. Foreign cloth was wanted only for special, not ordinary purposes; had the entire foreign trade of China suddenly ceased in the year 1877, the economic life of the country would have been affected but little." [31]

When we measure the expansion of trade, we observe that indices for yearly exports, net imports, and total net value of trade rise abruptly during the 1870s, and by 1900 their index value is twice that of levels in the 1880s.[32] I have plotted these changes on semi-log graph in Figure 5 to show trade expansion in north China between 1890 and 1936. The corresponding increases in the wholesale price level are also noted.

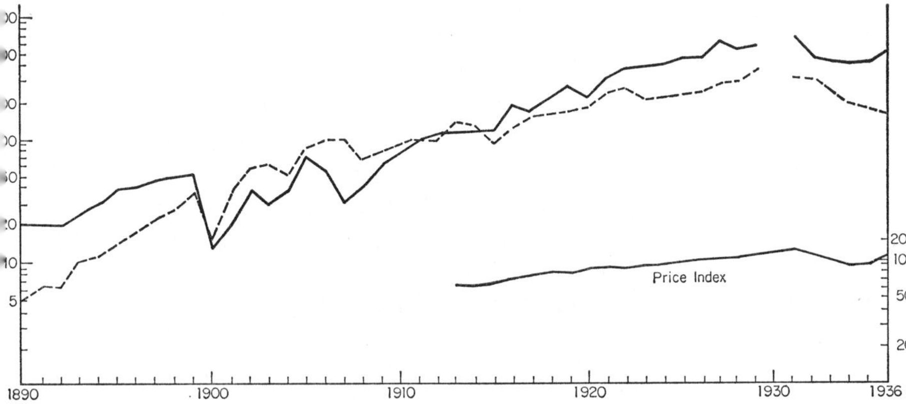

Fig. 5 Trend for exports, imports, and retail prices for north China, 1890–1936.

Exports ————————
Imports – – – – – – –

Exports greatly exceeded imports during the 1890s, but imports increased more rapidly than exports. Trade fell off during the Russo-Japanese War period, but by 1911 had resumed its original level and rate of increase although imports now exceeded exports. Between 1910 and 1920 trade expansion continued with exports beginning to exceed imports and give the region a favorable trade balance. Price increase contributed partially to the rapid rise in value of exports. World depression reduced exports and imports, but by 1936 their trend was again upward.

Part of this expansion in trade must be attributed to strong foreign demand for semi and fully processed raw materials. Many products such as cotton, soybeans, hides, straw braid, and peanuts were greatly demanded by industrial countries. These same products also sold at cheap, attractive prices because of the falling rate of exchange. Exports and imports were valued in the monetary unit called the Haikwan tael. In 1890 one Haikwan tael exchanged for 5s 8 ½d in English currency and $1.38 in U.S. currency compared to 2s 5 5/15d and $0.66 in 1910.[33] China remained on the silver standard while other countries adopted the gold standard, and because of the continued increase in supply of silver, China automatically experienced continued devaluation of her currency relative to the currencies of the Western nations. Although foreign buyers found it cheaper to buy north China's exports, devaluation should have curbed imports because these became more expensive for importers to buy. This does not seem to have taken place in this region or anywhere else in China.[34] A possible explanation for this is that considerable investment and new construction was taking place in the treaty ports during this period, in anticipation of large profits. Demand for materials and commodities was so vigorous that the steady rise in import prices in no way dampened this boom.

After the 1890s soybeans and their derivatives, peanuts and their oil, hides and meat, cotton, and tobacco became important export staples leaving north China ports. The supply of these goods did not really increase until after 1900 when a number of processing enterprises had been established and a commercial network had come into existence to purchase and move these goods from the interior to the treaty ports. Handicraft articles such as straw braid, vermicelli, and native cotton cloth were produced in increased quantities and exported at the same time. Between 1892 and 1901 total trade at Chefoo increased from 13.3 to 37.6 million taels with imports consisting chiefly of cotton yarn and piece goods and the major exports being silk, beans, bean cake, and vermicelli.[35] After Tsingtao was occupied by Germany in 1898, the trade of that port rose from 3.9 million in 1900 to 8.7 million taels in 1901. This provided convincing "proof that a systematic and honest administration can, without the imposition of heavy taxes, raise the native customs revenue to a height which would have been impossible under the old regime." [36] Between 1902 and 1911 exports rose from 8.5 to 25.5 million taels.[37] In Tientsin for the same period exports rose from 14.7 to 39.3 million taels, an increase based mainly on the export of raw cotton to Japan.[38]

From 1912 to 1921 trade increased in fits and starts. High freight rates, lack of tonnage during the war, and political unrest in the interior made it difficult for goods to move from the hinterland to the treaty ports to be shipped abroad. After 1920 trade advanced more rapidly. In Chinwangtao the net value of trade between 1922 and 1931 rose from 16.2 million to 36.7 million taels.[39] Large shipments of coal, peanuts, and beans pushed export values to high levels. Trade in Tientsin also rose steadily from 244.5 million in 1922 to 350.2 million taels in 1931 despite the disruption of commerce in north China because of the Shensi famine (1928–1930), the acquisition of outer Mongolia by the USSR (1927), and civil war (1927–28). "Almost every important item of the staple" such as raw cotton, hemp, eggs, peanuts, pigs, and sheep intestines, straw braid, walnuts, and horsehair increased.[40] In Shantung "products tended to gravitate towards the railway connecting the provincial capital with the port of Tsingtao in preference to being forwarded by the longer road journeys to the northern Shantung ports" of Chefoo, Lungkow, and Weiyuanhui.[41] Between 1922 and 1931 trade through Tsingtao rose 120 per cent.

This increased volume of trade and the recent improvements in inland transport made it attractive for many peasants to move to the larger cities and treaty ports. For the inland cities of over 50,000 we have few reliable data on how rapid their populations increased, but some statistical information, presented in Table 41, is available for the north China treaty ports and Peking showing that the rate of population increase between the 1890s and 1931 was indeed very rapid. Peking had the largest population, but it was expanding more slowly than the population of the treaty ports. Growth rates in these centers ranged between 4.8 to 9.3 per cent per annum. Friedrich Otto has calculated that between 1913 and 1928 the population of the 31 treaty ports covered by the Maritime Customs rose from 7.5 to 12.8 million, an increase of 70 per cent or 3.6 per cent per annum.[42] Much of this increase must be attributed to the influx of peasants seeking part-time work. Jean Chesneaux has shown with maps that the largest portion of the urban work force during the 1920s came from the peasantry.[43] In 1917 "About 10 per cent of the Chinwangtao population [were] natives, the remainder immigrants from other districts and provinces." [44] In Peking males in the age category of 16–40 years of age made up 48 per cent of the city's population, and the male to female ratio was exceedingly high, with 1.7 male to every female.[45]

The Adoption of Cash Crops by Villages

We have assumed that peasant households tried to increase their income by using their labor, land, and capital for various work tasks to maximize total income with the least expenditure of labor time and effort. Household income was divided between consumption, investment, paying taxes, repaying debt, and a portion might even be hoarded. The bulk of income was derived from farming. A portion of farm output was consumed on the farm and the remainder was sold for cash. Did households market a larger or smaller share of farm output in the nineteenth century as compared to the 1930s? Buck found that between 30 and 55 per cent of grain and cash crops were marketed depending on the type of crop.[46] Because cash crops

Table 41. Population increase in eight large cities of north China.

	Treaty port cities of Shantung				
Year	Chefoo	Tsingtao and municipalities	Tsingtao city	Lungkow and municipalities	Lungkow city
1891	32,500	–	–	–	–
1901	57,120	–	14,000	–	–
1911	–	–	54,459	–	–
1921	–	240,200	83,272	65,000	5,603
1931	–	400,025	–	130,000	11,524
Percentage of population increase	5.8	5.2	9.3	7.3	7.5

	Peking and two treaty port cities of Hopei		
	Tientsin	Chinwangtao	Peking
1900	320,000	–	–
1912	–	5,849	725,235
1921	837,000	12,829	863,209
1931	1,388,747	20,000	1,419,099
Percentage of population increase	4.8	6.6	3.6

Source: Data for Peking, H. O. Kung, "The Growth of Population of Six Chinese Cities," *Chinese Economic Journal and Bulletin* 20.3:304 (March 1937). Data for other cities, Decennial Reports for each treaty port for years when data was available.

had been adopted rapidly after 1900, Buck's data could be interpreted to mean that peasants were becoming more oriented toward the market. But we know from the studies of Katō Shigeshi and Skinner that historically a fixed number of villages were always serviced by a rural market, and that peasants visited markets three or four times a month. Peasants were already dependent on markets long before commercial developments after the 1890s. The question is not whether peasants had become more or less oriented and dependent on markets, but why villages should adopt the cultivation of cash crops so rapidly after 1900?

My explanation is really a hypothesis requiring more study before it can be accepted, and my only justification for introducing it at all is that some village data suggest it might have some validity. Land used for cash crops had to be fertilized heavily and worked intensively to prevent a decline in soil fertility and crop yield. The decision households had to make was whether the additional income to be earned from these crops justified the additional expense, the extra labor associated with their cultivation, and the risk of soil deterioration. The matter was made more complicated by the fact that though industrial crops sold at higher prices than a food crop like wheat, they required more inputs of labor and capital than did the food cash crops. Households had to decide which cash crops were best to grow as well as how much resources to devote to cash crops and crops for household consumption.

The decision to cultivate cash crops depended upon more than just the size of farm and household income. Motivation was important. Households were strongly motivated to earn more income to buy the yarn, cloth, matches, and kerosene which began to circulate in local markets after the 1890s. But greater demand for these goods may only partially explain why some households switched to growing cash crops. Another reason may have been the periodic formation of new household farms through *fen-chia* and the decline in average size farm.

After partitioning of land, many new small farms might be too small to earn enough farm income to support the household, and this forced some household labor to be dispatched to work outside the village for an indefinite period of time. Although households considered this a great hardship, this alternative would be weighed and compared to the prospect of cultivating a cash crop, which involved hard work for the family, possible decline in soil fertility, and financial risk in the event of a decline in crop price. Given the fact that household labor could be employed for both purposes, households with small farms often combined both alternatives and used some land for growing cash crops and dispatched labor to the cities during the idle farm season.

In some village data, there seems to be a close correspondence between the switch to cash crops and the formation of new household farms through *fen-chia*. In two villages surveyed by Japanese researchers in 1936 this relationship can be clearly observed. In Tung yang ch'iu village there were 13 new households formed between 1932 and 1936 and a definite increase in cotton and potato cultivation at the same time. In Pei tung tun village 17 households were created between 1931 and 1936, and there was also a steady increase in the cultivation of cotton. However, peanut production declined because the price fell during the early 1930s. These two changes suggest that when population pressure on limited land had become acute, newly formed households and existing ones began to cultivate higher income yielding crops in spite of the fact that this entailed more expense of labor by households. The results of these two village surveys can be seen in Table 42.

Our data is hardly sufficient to show convincingly that population pressure, as reflected by the increase of new households, compelled peasants to adopt cash crops. Signs of overcrowding had long existed in some villages

Table 42. Land use change in two Hopei villages, 1913–1936.

County and village	Type of crop	Year introduced	Cultivated area in 1927 (mow)	Cultivated area in 1932 (mow)	Cultivated area in 1936 (mow)
Wang-tu county, Tung yang ch'iu village[a]	Potatoes	1913	90	210	300
	Native cotton	1930	0	12	46
	American cotton	1934	0	0	316
			1926	1931	1936
Ts'ang county, Pei tung tun village[b]	Millet	–	300	350	550
	American cotton	–	0	10	50
	Corn	–	150	100	50
	Peanuts	–	80	40	15

Source: Tenshin jimmusho chōsaka, *Kahokushō nōson jittai chōsa shiryō*; a. p. 8. Number of households increased from 143 to 154 between 1932 and 1936; b. p. 197. Number of households increased from 108 to 125 between 1931 and 1936.

and few cash crops were cultivated, possibly because of unfavorable soil conditions or because handicraft and nonfarm income was easy to earn or peasants lacked the knowledge of how to grow new cash crops.

North China's Food Supply

Since Yuan and Ming times the imperial government had imported large quantities of grain from other provinces to feed the population of its principal metropolitan centers. During the Ch'ing period the court designated eight provinces to supply grain to the capital, and the amount set by law was not to be less than 3.5 million piculs or about 280,000 tons.[47] Shantung and Honan were included among the tributary provinces, and the heaviest burden fell upon Kiangsu and Chekiang. The provinces of central China were the surplus food-producing centers at the time.[48] When north China had a poor harvest and grain prices rose, private merchants were permitted to ship grain from south Manchuria to Hopei and Shantung.[49] In the late Ch'ing period the court abandoned using the Grand Canal to transport grain tribute in favor of importing grain on a commercial basis via the sea. We have no way of measuring whether grain requirements changed during the Ch'ing period and to what extent imports of food from other provinces varied with harvest fluctuations in north China.

Except for the capital and certain large cities, the countryside was able to supply the grain it needed. After 1900 the demand for food increased because urban population rose, and a larger percentage of the region's population had to be provided with food from the countryside. But during periods when poor harvests had caused famine in wide sections of the region and civil war had disrupted the transportation system, the supply of food was inadequate for the towns at prices which had prevailed in the recent past. Food prices rose, and importers and merchants purchased grain from abroad and sold it for a profit. Table 43 shows rice, wheat, and flour imports into north China between 1913 and 1931. When these imports are correlated with regional food prices, nearly four fifths of the variation in

Table 43. Quantity of food imports into north China ports, and index of food prices, 1913–1931.

	Imports (in piculs)				
Year	Rice	Wheat	Flour	Total	Food price index (1926 = 100)
1913	372,044	20	203,186	575,250	64.27
1914	404,536	7	76,446	480,989	63.86
1915	325,366	21	4,536	329,923	64.20
1916	281,871	74	8,193	290,138	66.36
1917	535,327	7,789	140,855	683,971	71.30
1918	156,223	–	8,040	164,263	68.30
1919	19,139	1	11,292	30,432	66.72
1920	98,187	4,697	39,841	142,725	82.47
1921	882,245	12,973	20,389	915,607	82.24
1922	1,413,374	929	368,236	1,782,539	79.92
1923	1,351,766	354,676	1,451,696	3,158,138	84.96
1924	529,315	110,077	1,167,143	1,806,535	89.24
1925	1,322,155	31,695	599,237	1,953,087	95.89
1926	1,224,362	46,486	1,620,606	2,891,454	100.00
1927	2,087,903	43,564	1,802,747	3,934,214	106.95
1928	1,721,398	113,248	3,011,327	4,845,973	113.07
1929	1,315,286	120,616	6,229,163	7,665,065	116.07
1930	1,390,357	34,655	1,980,027	3,405,039	119.72
1931	1,507,164	441,370	2,038,500	3,986,974	114.39

Sources: Food price index, *Shang-hai chieh-fang ch'ien-hou wu-chia tzu-liao hui-pien, 1921–1957* (A collection of Shanghai price data before and after the Liberation, 1921–1957; Shanghai, 1958), p. 175. This index may be influenced by imports of previous years, but it was compiled on the basis of domestic prices. Data for quantities of rice, wheat, and flour imports into north China ports, Wu Pao-san, *Chung-kuo liang-shih tui wai-mao-i ch'i ti-wei ch'ü-shih chi pien-ch'ien chih yüan-yin 1913–1931* (The causes of fluctuations and trends of food grain in China's foreign trade; Shanghai, 1934), statistical appendix.

food imports are observed to have been caused by changes in regional food prices.[50] In 1922 and 1923 imports rose greatly because of the north China famine, and between 1927 and 1929 imports again rose because civil war had caused a partial breakdown in the production and distribution of grain.

What was true for north China applied equally to other regions. After 1911 total food imports increased, and during the late 1920s and throughout the 1930s their rise was considerable. Civil war, floods, and the invasion by Japan were the principal factors affecting the production and distribution of grain within China. In 1932, food imports were valued at $329 million Chinese dollars, but the figure declined to only $49.2 million in 1936 when internal conflict was reduced and the government spent heavily to improve transport and promote flood control.[51] When war broke out in 1937, imports again rose; in 1938 they climbed to $130 million, $223.6 million in 1939, and $358.6 million in 1940.[52]

For the country as a whole, there is little correlation between the trend for harvests and food imports between 1912 and 1930. In other words there seems to have been no tendency for agricultural production to be displaced by imports. A large flood naturally increased imports, but only temporarily. If values are assigned for the state of the harvest, for example, 1 for a highly satisfactory harvest, 2 for a good harvest, 3 for a fair harvest, and 4 for a poor or no harvest and if harvest change is correlated with food imports on a yearly basis between 1918 and 1933, little correlation between these two variables is observed (see Table 59 in statistical appendix). However, when domestic food prices are correlated with food imports a high degree of correlation is obtained. Similar findings are obtained when wheat imports are correlated with world wheat prices, although the rice price series used for world rice prices does not provide a very high correlation with rice imports. Wickizer and Bennett in their study of rice price and output trends in Asia have shown that between 1920 and 1940 net imports of rice into China and India are inversely related.[53] When India had a rice surplus she exported rice and reduced her imports. In most instances this was timed with an increased purchase of rice by China. Availability of supply and a lower price seems to have determined the volume of rice flows between these two countries.

Food was imported into China for the following reasons. When war or great floods disrupted supply and distribution, food prices in cities tended to rise. Importers competing in a free foreign exchange and trade market purchased food from foreign sellers and distributed these supplies to wholesalers in the large cities. Internal and external grain prices dictated the flow of grain, but the availability of supply in foreign countries determined the amount which China could actually import. Civil war in the 1920s was a major factor in a decline in cultivated areas and dislocated internal trade. It "not only dislocated the means of transportation, but drove many farmers away from their land." [54] The decline in cotton area was accompanied by a reduction in grain cultivated area. Throughout the 1920s there were complaints in Hopei that the "production of foodstuffs were totally inadequate to meet home consumption, and there was no surplus for export." [55]

For this reason the results of national food surveys undertaken in 1927 must be evaluated with extra caution. In that year C. C. Chang of the Bureau of Statistics in the Legislative Yuan conducted a survey of annual production and consumption of food in China. By using questionnaires he obtained sufficient information to construct a food balance sheet for fourteen provinces.[56] His results showed that only Manchuria produced more food than it consumed and that the other provinces consumed more food than they produced. The north China provinces of Shansi, Hopei, Shantung, and Honan accounted for 80 per cent of the total food deficit for the fourteen provinces. The year 1927 was one of civil war, and agricultural production and distribution were greatly disrupted. These conditions undoubtedly account for Chang's gloomy results.

When harvests were normal and distribution channels functioned properly, the cities received sufficient food and food imports declined to a very low volume. Under these conditions agriculture produced enough for the countryside and the towns, as may be seen in results obtained in 1942, a normal harvest year, from a Japanese survey of grain markets in countries along the Peking-Hankow and Tientsin-Pukow railroads to determine the rural population's capability of supplying enough grain for its needs.[57] Estimates were made of the total grain supply and of the amount of grain each person required for a year in 115 counties along the Peking-Hankow line and in 69 counties along the Tientsin-Pukow line. The results set forth in Table 44 show that all counties were self-sufficient in grain, and they had extra grain to export to the cities.

Villages were able to increase the food supply and ship a larger quantity of industrial crops to the cities. This was achieved not only by the gradual increase in total farm output but by substituting inferior foods like potatoes and millet for wheat. The spread of potato cultivation is a sure sign that land was being used more intensively than in the past to support the expanding rural population. Observers who knew the north China countryside well reported that after 1930 there was a definite shift to potatoes as household food to supplement grain. "It should be emphasized that very recently, potato production has increased, and the potato has become an important food item for the north China peasant. Potatoes do not require a lot of labor, nor do they need much fertilizer, and for these reasons its production has increased greatly and it now supplements the present food supply." [58]

North China's food supply problem was never critical. The occasional importation of food only showed the ability of the regional economy to turn to outside sources of supply when war and natural disasters had disrupted home production. Under normal conditions the peasants produced enough

Table 44. Grain production and consumption in counties along the Peking-Hankow and Tientsin-Pukow railroad lines, 1942.[a]

Railway line	District (*tao*)	Number of counties	Grain area per person (mow)	Output of grain per person (catties)	Yield (catties per mow)
Peking–Hankow railway	Pao-Ting	22	3.3	518	157
	Chen-Ting	21	3.2	514	162
	Shun-te	15	3.5	610	174
	Ch'in-nan	14	4.1	744	181
	Yu-pei	25	3.4	606	177
	Yu-tung	18	3.9	664	169
	Total	115 (average)	3.6	605	170
Tientsin–Pukow railway	Wu-ting	13	3.3	622	187
	Chi-man	7	2.3	476	209
	T'ai-an	8	2.4	540	222
	Yen-chi	12	4.3	996	234
	Ts'ao-chou	12	3.9	824	211
	Ssu-pei	17	4.1	1142	276
	Total	69 (average)	3.6	867	240

Source: Kokuritsu, *Kyō-Kan ensen*, pp. 4, 16.
The necessary amount of grain per person per year is 450 catties.

for their needs and those of the cities. This was achieved by changing land utilization and the ability of the peasants to farm more intensively. Farm output would naturally have risen more rapidly had technological change taken place and peace prevailed.

12. Changes in Peasant Living Standards

To what extent had towns and villages in north China changed between 1880 and 1937 to have influenced living standards for better or worse? Tsingtao, Tientsin, Chinan, and Shihmen cities had grown to great size in terms of population, commerce, and new industries. Living standards in these centers were considerably higher than in the countryside in terms of food, shelter, and clothing. What had formerly been quiet sleepy market towns in the late nineteenth century now had become sprawling cities with shops, factories, storage houses, railway terminals, and markets.

Villages such as Sha-ching or Hou hsia chai were larger in size but, on the surface, conditions had scarcely changed. Peasants tilled their land, carted their goods, and lived in their straw-thatched and earth-made homes as their ancestors had done. The customs pertaining to lending money, mortgaging, exchanging, inheriting, and renting land, and managing village affairs remained roughly the same as in the past. However, certain subtle underlying changes began to occur. The present size of villages indicated that many more households farmed the land than fifty years ago, but they farmed fewer and smaller plots. Although farming techniques had scarcely improved, peasants earned more farm income because they cultivated new cash crops. More crop specialization had taken place. Finally, more peasants left their villages to earn income to supplement their farm earnings.

Did these various developments reduce or raise peasant living standards? The scraps of evidence available can only be pieced together to give an incomplete picture of changing rural living standards. This must suffice until more evidence becomes available. The best data on living standard changes were collected by Buck and his associates between 1929 and 1931. These data, tucked away in his voluminous statistical volume, have been ignored by scholars, who have asserted that rural living standards steadily declined after the late nineteenth century. The main thrust of my argument so far is that where normal conditions prevailed rural living standards did not decline. I use Buck's data to confirm this assertion.

Buck's data show consumption, nutrition standards, dietary changes, and living standard trends. They were collected from interviews of sample households in the village selected in each of the localities designated for field work. One particular set of questions was related to change in living standards of households in "recent years." The term "recent years" seems to indicate a time period of several decades which would be suitable for identifying living standard changes between 1910 and 1930. Table 45 evidence is presented for localities in Hopei and Shantung to show whether or not living standards increased, fell, or remained the same between 1910 and 1930. Data are also supplied to indicate the reasons for changes in living standards.

Table 45. Changes in peasant living standards, 1910–1930.

County[a]	Change in living standards			Indicator of rise in living standard				Indicator of fall in living standard
	In-crease	De-crease	Con-stant	Kero-sene	Tile roof	Better clothes	Better food	Banditry and taxes
				Hopei				
Chengting (1)	+			+				
Chengting (2)	+						+	
Chiaoho	+			+			+	
Nankung	+						+	
Hsun-i	+			+		+	+	
Ting	+					+		
Ch'ing	+					+	+	
Foup'ing (1)	+							
Foup'ing (2)			+					
Foup'ing (3)			+					
				Shantung				
Chanhua	+			+			+	
En (1)	+					+	+	
En (2)	+					+	+	
Fushan	+				+	+	+	
Huimin (1)	+						+	
Huimin (2)	+					+	+	
Lich'eng (1)	+			+		+		
Lich'eng (2)	+			+		+		
Lich'eng (3)	+				+	+	+	
Linch'ing (1)	+					+	+	
Linch'ing (2)	+				+	+	+	
Tang-i (1)		+						+
Tang-i (2)	+					+	+	
Te (1)	+					+	+	
Te (2)	+					+	+	

Source: Buck, *Statistics*, pp. 400–401.
[a] Numbers in parentheses indicate first, second, or third survey.

Peasants in 22 out of the 25 localities examined stated that their living standards had risen. In two localities of Foup'ing living standards had not changed, and in Tang-i a decline had occurred because of bandit activity and increased taxes. Indications of improvement in living standards are the facts that peasants discarded oil lamps in favor of kerosene, tile roofs were constructed instead of thatched roofs, city-made clothing was purchased, and better food was eaten. Because so many counties were affected by civil war and warlord taxation during the 1920s, it is surprising that peasants could report any improvement in their living standards. However, the number of localities in the sample is small, and the sample covers slightly less than 10 per cent of the counties of these two large provinces.

Buck's surveys also yield considerable information about food consumption, which relates to the changes in land utilization discussed above. Peasants in some districts ate better than peasants in other areas. We find that food intake measured as the amount consumed per person per day consisted of a different assortment of principal crops like yams, sweet potatoes, sorghum, wheat, corn, and millet. In Shantung, for example, peasants in Ch'i-mo and Lai-yang counties consumed mainly sweet potatoes, in Chining wheat, in T'ai-an sorghum and sweet potatoes, and in Shoukuang sorghum, wheat, and millet.[1] In Hopei the main foods consumed in Ting county were corn and millet, in Tung corn, in Ts'ang sorghum and corn, in Chengting yams and millet, in Ch'ang-li sweet potatoes and sorghum, and in Yencheng wheat, millet, and sweet potatoes.[2]

In counties where peasants mainly consumed sweet potatoes and yams population density was high and land was used chiefly for growing industrial crops. In counties where peasants consumed sorghum, corn, or millet, land was used to produce wheat as a cash crop. In several areas where soil and climate were appropriate for wheat, the peasants consumed much of the wheat produced. Counties could be ranked to show different peasant living standard levels by the main foods they consumed, but this ranking is open to conceptual difficulties. In counties where peasants consumed sweet potatoes, millet, or corn, living standards as measured by the quality of housing, clothing, and other consumer goods may have been fairly high because the cash crops gave these peasants more farm income than was earned in areas where better quality grain foods were grown.

Table 46 shows the changes in food consumption after 1904 for important crops of a sample of 32 counties in the winter wheat-sorghum region

Table 46. Trends in consumption of important food crops, 1904–1930 (in percentage of 32 county sample).

Food crop	Increase	Decrease	No change	No data
Barley	0	2	98	–
Corn	43	5	43	9
Sorghum	2	43	45	10
Millet	21	7	62	10
Sweet potato	17	0	74	9
Wheat	21	7	62	10

Source: Buck, *Statistics*, p. 82.

of north China, which includes Hopei and Shantung. It is observed that many counties reported an increase in land used for wheat, corn, millet, and sweet potatoes. Wheat became an important cash crop for some districts because of its rising price. Corn, millet, and sweet potatoes were inferior food crops adopted so that more land could be devoted to industrial crops and wheat. However, a large number of counties reported no change in food consumption. The two main reasons given for the decline in food consumption were that peasants had been offered high prices for other crops, and they had quickly responded by planting less of the low-priced crop, or that bad harvests had forced peasants to reduce the planted area.

Peasant households usually contained three to six rooms although large farmsteads sometimes had as many as eight or more rooms.[3] Households were furnished with an assortment of simple chairs, tables, beds, cupboards, and benches. A few even had mirrors and windows. The amount and quality of furniture depended upon the size of farm.[4] We are poorly informed about matters of health, although from the standpoint of sanitation, conditions were far from desirable in comparison to health standards in Japan and Western countries at the time. Compost piles were constructed near the household, and it was relatively easy for parasites to be transferred into the household. There were few drinking wells, and water for the most part had to be boiled. Peasants had acquired from experience their own customary preventative measures to ward off disease and care for the ill. These seemed to have worked satisfactorily except during famines when physical resistance was greatly weakened and communicable diseases quickly reached epidemic proportions.

Peasants blamed banditry and warlord soldiers for affecting rural living standards in the localities surveyed by Buck.[5] Further evidence will be presented in a later chapter dealing with random factors which influenced agricultural production. There seems little doubt that civil war and social disorder were the two main causes for deterioration in peasant living standards. Of course, prolonged poor harvests which produced famine conditions like those of 1920 and 1921 in Hopei also had a serious effect on living conditions. But peasants seemed to recover quickly from these disasters and commence farming again.

It may be concluded that peasant living standards over the period did not decline except during times of prolonged poor harvests and war. If we accept Buck's data we can even admit the possibility of a slight improvement in living standards for this region. This was made possible by the expanding commerce and industry of the treaty port–market town economy.

13. The Peasant Economy: Summary

The north China peasant was rational and calculating in using his meager resources to derive a living from the land. He was very responsive to changes outside his immediate surroundings and attempted to adjust his use of resources accordingly if he was sufficiently informed about these changes. This rural economy was essentially a household economy, and the household must be regarded as the basic economic decision-making unit. The peasant household tried to maximize its income by using to the best of its abilities the resources at hand and the accumulated knowledge of farming of previous generations. Without a thorough understanding of the conditions under which peasants lived, their behavior often appears irrational and devoid of purpose in the eyes of outsiders. The following should correct that impression and show the operating principles which guided peasants in the use of their resources.

The supply of household labor was directly related to the size of the farm. The household allocated its available labor to field work and nonfarm employment according to the amount of effort and risk involved to earn the largest income. If farm land and capital were scarce, the household dispatched more labor to work in other villages and market towns. If the farm was large and had capital, more labor was retained for farming. In reality households worked out the combination of these two alternatives which provided the largest income.

Households used their savings from farm and nonfarm income to buy land and increase the size of farm. Beyond a certain size of farm, households leased land to other peasants and used their wealth for moneylending or investing in handicraft and commerce. The decision to invest less income in farming was determined by the existing technology and the managerial skill of the household. When the rate of return from greater farm capital became unattractive in comparison to the rate of return from alternative investments, more household wealth flowed to nonfarm activities. The rate of return from farming was chiefly determined by the level of technology, the managerial skill of the household, and the amount of investment. The amount of land a household decided to manage depended upon its quality and location, the supply of farm capital and household labor, and the technical skill and farming knowledge of the peasants. If a household acquired more land than it could efficiently farm, it put the land to the next best economic use, that is, leasing it to other households.

The land which the household managed was allocated among different uses. Some land would be allotted for growing high income crops for the market, and the remaining land was used to grow crops vital for the household's consumption. The decision of how much land to allocate between these two categories of crops depended upon the peasants' knowledge of which crops grew best, the existing soil conditions which permitted certain crops to grow better than others, and the opportunities to exchange crops for goods that could not be cheaply produced on the farm. As a result, some districts specialized in industrial crops, and others in food crops. Households also decided which cash crop or combination of cash crops should be grown. Such a choice depended upon the labor supply and household's ability to provide additional capital in order to prevent a decline in soil fertility.

The above decisions were ultimately determined by the foresight, experience, and knowledge of the peasants. Some households made better decisions than others and were able to earn more income and accumulate land. In every village a few wealthy households could be found. Households which made bad decisions inevitably became poorer.

The Process of Agricultural Development

Between 1880 and 1940 the average size of household farm declined. Farms were increasingly fragmented depending upon the rate of population expansion and the periodic transfer of land from the household head to the male sons. The inheritance system made it extremely difficult for farms to remain intact over the course of more than one or two generations. The credit system and the slow expansion of nonfarm employment opportunity in traditional China made it impossible for the eldest son to inherit the farm.

Population increased between 60 and 80 per cent during this period, and the proportion of population living in cities by 1940 was probably 5 or 10 per cent more than in 1880. Farm output rose slightly more rapidly than the rate of population expansion, and it was possible for cities to grow. Although imports rose for short periods in the 1920s and 1930s, their amount fluctuated because food production and distribution were disrupted by war and poor harvests.

Urban commercial and industrial growth accelerated because of foreign trade expansion and the increased investment in new cottage industry and manufacturing by foreign and native capitalists. These developments increased the demand for industrial raw materials and labor. As more peasants migrated to the cities, the demand for food rose. Urban economic growth provided expanding employment opportunity for peasants and enabled households to substitute crops of higher prices for those of lower prices. Because household income rose, small farms survived and living standards did not decline.

In a comparison of the trends of rural wages, land price, and the price of farm capital, the results show that land did not become critically scarce and the rural workforce was not excessively enlarged with underemployed and landless peasants. Rising values should not be interpreted to mean that peasants were prospering. The steady increase in population and the gradual rise in farm production probably just enabled households to maintain their living standards. At no time did production increase rapidly enough to permit large stocks to accumulate. The region barely supplied its needs. At certain times, particularly during the war-torn years of the 1920s, great numbers of people were forced to flee the region. There is no evidence to suggest that large sections of the countryside became so impoverished that their living standards in the mid-1930s were lower than in the 1890s.

It was a major triumph for this peasant economy to provide additional labor to the cities, increase the supply of industrial staples and food, and yet maintain living standards comparable to those of the recent past. It was only the rural households that invested in farming, and their managerial decisions alone made this process possible. This is remarkable considering that so little new technology from outside was introduced into agriculture during this period.

Technology and Agricultural Development

Farm technology increased very slowly because of the low level of farming education and the disinterest of officials and scholars in farming problems and ways to promote new farm technology. When a scholar or official took the trouble to collect information on how to farm efficiently and publish his results, the impact on farm technology was considerable because more backward areas learned the best techniques of advanced areas and farming knowledge was better systematized for future generations. Unfortunately, there are too few examples of this in Chinese agricultural history. The more usual method of generating technical advance was for peasants to use trial and error methods of selecting better seeds and farming methods suited to the immediate environment. This was a very slow and tortuous way of advancing knowledge and educating successive generations of peasants. As was shown in Chapter 10 there was no channel or institution for introducing new farming techniques to villages from the outside.

The only way that a decisive break with traditional technology could take place was for the educated classes and those with authority to establish research stations, a farm extension system, and schools and agricultural colleges. Given peace and time, these organizations could quickly raise the levels of farming skills of the peasantry. The difficulty for our period of interest is that north China lacked a stable political order. Equally important, the urban oriented leadership did not regard agriculture as sufficiently important to be developed. Nor did this leadership properly understand what was involved to raise productivity. Agriculture was merely an industry to exploit.

An important finding in this section was that certain inferences could be deduced from the relationship between household investment and the size of farm. It was observed that beyond a certain size of farm, output and income per unit of land declined. Associated with this trend was a decline in the percentage of household income invested in variable capital. More household wealth was invested for nonfarming activities or used for consumption, and the household leased more land to other households. Increasing the size of household farm would not have changed household economic behavior or made farming more profitable in terms of raising output and income per unit of land. Improving and raising agricultural production could take place without altering the size of household farm.

The improvement could be achieved simply through technological change, such as new, high-yield seed varieties, chemical fertilizers, pesticides, improved tools, and a stable water supply. Without improving these inputs and increasing their supply, households were compelled to use age-old techniques and a limited supply of farming inputs. Inadequate knowledge and limited managerial skill restricted investment to a small, fixed percentage of income and limited the size of farm that could be managed efficiently. Without knowledge of more efficient farming, wealthy households found it more profitable to invest outside agriculture and to lease their land to other farmers.

Low income and savings were not crucial factors deciding peasant households to invest less in farming and more in nonfarming activities. Nor did the size of farm and periodic fragmentation of land through *fen-chia* account for this investment behavior and low productivity of larger farms. Rapid technological improvement of the inputs used by households would undoubtedly have directed more household income to farm investment because the rate of return from farming would have risen.

We can only speculate at this time whether or not at some previous time in China's agricultural history the introduction of new legumes and better soil preservation methods would have increased the supply of labor animals and improved land fertility so that new seed varieties could have been selected. Had this occurred, perhaps China would have experienced a genuine revolution of agriculture. Why such a revolution did not take place still remains an important problem for future research. Although only modest technical advances were generated within agriculture and farm production increased just enough to support an expanding population, these developments alone still attest to the remarkable vitality and energy of this agrarian system.

IV. Village and Market Town in North China

14. Landlord and Peasant

In the 1930s many scholars were convinced that the inequality of land ownership and the land-renting system greatly affected peasant farm production and income. From their writings emerges the paradigm that income distribution in Chinese society was determined by socioeconomic class relationships and that not only landlords but moneylenders, merchants, and officials operated as a powerful pressure group to exploit the peasantry. The economy developed slowly because the income retained by the peasantry was insufficient for investment and improvement of agricultural techniques. Furthermore, low farm income made it impossible for the peasants to increase their purchases of commodities produced in the cities, and therefore, rural demand was inadequate to encourage urban capitalistic development.

The Disintegration of Large Estates

In the late seventeenth century the amount of land controlled by the Manchu military and government in north China was enormous. Roughly 14 million mow of land had been given to Manchu military men or bannermen in Hopei. The government had also decreed that in Hopei and Shantung, respectively, another 7.5 and 2.9 million mow be allotted as military encampments for the stationing and support of Manchu troops at various garrison command posts.[1] In Hopei another 27,800 mow were set aside for the military to guard the Grand Canal, and in Shantung 608,691 mow were set aside for the same purpose.[2] After Manchu military units settled in these encampments, they intermarried with the Chinese and villages sprang up. By the nineteenth century most of this land had already passed into Chinese hands. Large estates were held by three groups during the early Ch'ing period: displaced Chinese landowners from around Peking who had been given land north of the capital; banner army personnel; public and private school land.

When the Manchu armies swept into north China, they introduced the same organizations for feeding and maintaining their armies that they had developed in the areas they conquered and settled in Manchuria. After establishing their capital in Peking, the Manchu leaders ordered that all land within a radius of approximately 175 miles of the capital be confiscated and redistributed among Manchu banner personnel in order to support their armies.[3] This land was referred to as *po-pu ch'i-ti* land. Chinese landowners, merchants, and officials owning land in this radial zone were granted other land farther from the capital in what is today known as southern Chahar, Jehol, and northeast Hopei.

Once settled, these displaced landowners leased their land to the many landless peasants, and from their rents they paid the land tax. The new tenant class that emerged gradually reclaimed waste land and devoted more of its time and effort to tilling this land than farming their rented land. As a result, output did not increase rapidly on rented land, and the new landowners found it more and more difficult to increase their rents at a time when they needed more cash because of rising commodity prices. Many landlords returned their land to local magistrates rather than continue to pay land tax on it. The government preferred to collect tax revenue rather than accumulate tracts of land it could not use. To discourage landowners from returning their land, the government permitted them to pay taxes only on land where they resided, which meant a considerable reduction in their tax burden. Rather than lower rents to tenants, many landowners continued to insist that their tenants pay even higher rents. If some tenants incurred debt, they had to sell the little land they had privately developed in order to pay their rents. Bitterness increased between absentee landlords and their tenants, and violent disputes were frequent.

By the early eighteenth century the government intervened between landowners and their tenants and ordered officials to collect tenant rents on behalf of the landholders, deduct taxes owing from these rents, and refund the remainder to the landowners. Local officials continued this practice throughout the century, but by the early nineteenth century there were few tenants farming these lands. Former tenants had either acquired private land and ceased renting land, or landlords had mortgaged and sold their land. Many landholdings were also divided between members of landlord families and later sold. Inevitably, nearly all land passed into the hands of a freehold peasant class living in villages and farming scattered plots.

In the area around the capital, the *po-pu ch'i-ti* land was supposed to be used exclusively for the support of a Manchu military man and his family. This was tax-exempt, free land given to officers and soldiers as partial payment for military services rendered. These land grants were also intended to support a large peacetime army without spending large sums from the government's treasury. When the Manchus expanded their area of control in Manchuria, they had acquired slaves to supervise and farm their land. After the banner army personnel obtained *po-pu ch'i-ti* land around Peking, they turned it over to be farmed by stewards and slaves brought from Manchuria.

The Manchus were trained for military service, they knew little about farming, and they were uninterested in developing the land themselves; thus, they preferred to leave the management of the land to their stewards. Labor was scarce in north China in the late seventeenth century because war and the confiscation of land for bannermen had driven many people to other parts of the country. Captured prisoners and slaves from Manchuria were used at first to farm this land, but the income earned from the land was insufficient for bannermen needs. The method adopted to remedy this problem was to rent land to tenants. A situation was soon created where, "in the banner lands around Peking, rents were collected from tenants to support the bannermen. Consequently it became difficult to differentiate between land farmed by these tenants and that tilled by the slaves of the bannermen households." [4]

A recent study of eighteenth century banner land rent books shows that an unusually large amount of rent was paid in money.[5] Only about one third of the money rents were collected in silver, the remainder in copper cash, the preferred media of exchange among the common people.[6] In the early eighteenth century the shortage of copper cash caused a decline in the market rate of exchange of silver for copper so that copper was greatly overvalued.[7] Considerable amounts of copper had been withdrawn from circulation and made into copper implements, which sold for a profit. The government frequently found it could not pay banner troops in copper at the designated times, and they became even more eager to rent their land and receive rent in copper cash. These rent books also show that tracts of land ranging between 100 and 1,000 mow were rented to tenants;[8] clearly the bannermen were leasing large portions of their estates.

The process by which rural China was gradually monetized during the Ch'ing period and the causes for the upward movement in commodity prices deserve more discussion and analysis than has been possible with the available research. The upward movement of commodity prices and the bannermen's constant need for cash compelled them to rent their land, yet the earnings from rents and farming estate land with slave labor did not leave enough profit at the end of the year to satisfy them. Commodities became more expensive, and family expenditure invariably exceeded revenue. At first this was not serious, but as land rents lagged behind commodity prices, many bannermen sons had to borrow by using their land as security. By the 1680s, and afterwards, large amounts of land had already been mortgaged to Chinese moneylenders, who gradually began to acquire this land as their own when bannermen failed to redeem it.[9]

By the 1720s, the government had decided it must take action to prevent the entire loss of banner land. It ordered a survey of all existing banner land and that records be made showing the amount and location of this land. The survey revealed a great decline in original banner landholdings and considerable land under mortgage. By the 1740s, the government redeemed much of this mortgaged land and reclassified it to a category making its transfer to private hands illegal. These steps proved successful, and by the 1780s banner land increased by one million mow over the existing amount in the first decade of the century.[10] For a brief period the bannermen had been saved, but these stop-gap measures failed to arrest the process by which this problem became serious in the first place. By the early nineteenth century banner land was again declining and passing into private hands through mortgage, and by the end of the Ch'ing period nearly all banner land was in private hands.

Large tracts of land were also owned by private and public schools: 41,700 mow in Shantung and 142,000 mow in Hopei. Private school land expanded rapidly, and by the late eighteenth century it was one and a half times as much as public school land in some areas such as western Shantung.[11] When private and public schools found they could not meet their expenses by raising school fees, they also leased land to the peasants. Rents were usually collected in money because schools needed cash to operate. The amount of rent collected was determined by fixing a certain amount per mow according to how the land was classified.[12] A large amount of school land was also mortgaged and eventually sold. Although the amount of land owned by private and public schools was fairly small, they are examples of large estates that ultimately declined as land passed into private hands through mortgage and sale.

Changes in Land Distribution

In writing up his field notes of Ting county in Hopei in 1930, Li Ching-han stated that "the crux of the problem of the Chinese village economy is the shortage of land."[13] Li and many other scholars who had examined the village economy at first hand were disturbed by the great inequality of land ownership and the fact that the overwhelming majority of peasants farmed plots too few and too small to provide a reasonable living standard. The inequality of land distribution was alleged to be the product of the land tenure system. Before examining the different systems of renting land, it is necessary to know whether land distribution in villages became more or less unequal or remained the same between the late nineteenth century and the 1930s. The reason for dealing with this question is that it was frequently claimed by those who argued that the peasantry was exploited by landlords and the urban power groups that land distribution had become more unequal over time. The powerful landowning class by virtue of its wealth had sufficient leverage to acquire more land, which was then used as a means to enhance their social status and increase their economic power. This argument can only be verified by examining the change in land distribution during the period of most rapid urban economic growth: 1880–1937.

On the basis of existing evidence I intend to argue that land distribution either remained relatively constant or became more equal, but most certainly did not become more unequal. First, I will present data to show that land distribution in the late nineteenth century was already very unequal before railroad development and trade made any strong impact on this rural economy. Second, I will show that in the case of some villages, evidence exists to show that land distribution changed very little. Third, I will compare land tenure conditions for villages in Shantung for the late nineteenth century and 1930s to show that the percentage of tenant and farm laboring households may have even declined.

In the 1880s the *North China Daily Herald* commented that in north China villages "Of three hundred families, about eight families may perhaps have 400 mow each, about thirty families may have over 100 mow, many have less than 20 mow, and not a few own no land of their own at all, but rent two or three acres from others or work as farm hands." [14] In the 1890s, a U.S. consular official in Tientsin remarked that "the average size of farm in this province does not exceed two acres [roughly 13 mow of land] and the wealthiest farmers seldom own above a score of acres [150 mow]." [15] In 1905 eleven villages in Sheng-tu county of Hopei showed land distribution conditions similar to those of the 1930s: a few peasants owned over 100 mow, a smaller number owned 30 to 80 mow, and the majority farmed around 10 mow or less. These results are shown in Table 47.

Table 47. Land distribution in ten villages of Sheng-tu county in Hopei, 1905.

Village	Amount of village land (mow)	Number of households	Number of households owning land measuring between: 0–10 mow	30–80 mow	100–150 mow	150–500 mow
Pei kao ling	800	100+	40	60	1–2	–
Yeh-yang	1,000	100+	100	–	1–2	1
Hou-t'o	900	100+	100	–	1–2	–
Nan t'ao ch'iu	1,400–1,500	70–80+	50	8–9	3	–
Shih li p'u	1,000	78+	71	4–5	2	–
Yung-mo	1,000	90+	?	?	?	–
Tung-kuan	1,000	100+	?	?	3	–
T'ang-hui	1,000	70+	?	?	1–2	–
Hsiao-hsiang	1,000–1,200	90+	?	?	1–2	–
Chang-chuang	4,000	300+	65	–	1	–
T'ien-hsing	3,000	100+	majority	?	1–2	–

Source: *CC*, I, 196; for Yung-mo village, *CC*, I, 662. The plus sign (+) indicates that the number of households is only a rough estimate.

Sidney D. Gamble gathered data for a village in Hopei to show that in 1910 there were 134 households farming 3,678 mow, and twenty-one years later there were 173 households farming 4,323 mow.[16] Village population increased at a rate of 1.2 per cent per year, whereas village land had increased by 17 per cent. When a Lorenz curve is fitted to the data, we observe that land distribution between 1910 and 1931 became more equal

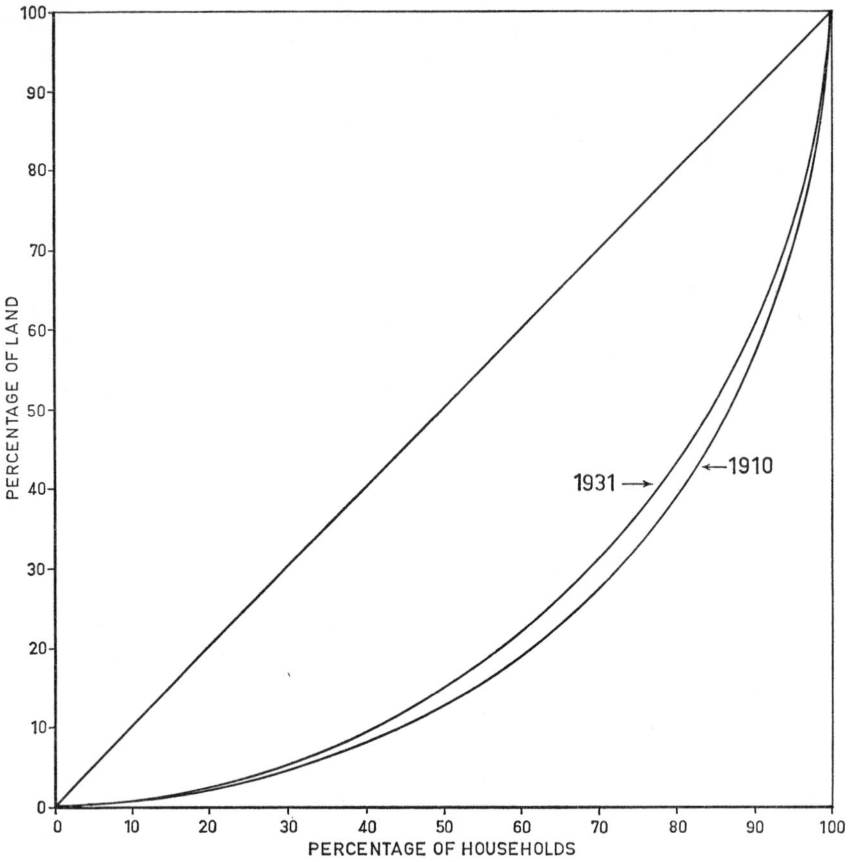

Fig. 6 Lorenz curve showing land ownership and land distribution of a village in Shu-lu county of Hopei in 1910 and 1931.

(see Fig. 6). This corresponds to our information about Sha-ching village where land distribution also scarcely changed.

In 1957, two Chinese scholars published the results of their historical research of 131 large landholding households in 197 villages in 42 counties of Shantung during the 1890s.[17] I have arranged their 1890 data into three classes according to the number of households surveyed in different villages. The results are then compared to those of a provincial survey of the early 1930s to show land tenure conditions at these two dates. The data of the 1930s are arranged according to the corresponding county for which 1890 data exist.

Three categories of farm, shown in terms of percentages, were compared: agricultural-laborer, tenant, and part-owner and owner. These percentages are derived according to the number of households obtaining income from farming and nonfarming activities. A household obtaining most of its income from wages is considered an agricultural-laborer household. A household renting land and obtaining most of its income from farming is

Table 48. A comparison of land tenure conditions in selected counties of Shantung, 1890s–early 1930s.

		1890s[b]				1930s[c]			
County[a]	Villages (number)	Farming households (number)	Agricultural laborer households (per cent)	Tenant households (per cent)	Part-owner and owner households (per cent)	Farming households (number)	Agricultural laborer households (per cent)	Tenant households (per cent)	Part-owner and owner households (per cent)
A. Ch'ang-ch'iu	32	4,164	12	6	82	37,560	10	20	70
T'ai-an	15	2,904	16	12	72	149,355	9	10	81
P'ing-tu	3	2,122	13	17	70	182,678	3	–	97
Hsia-chin	5	1,918	14	8	78	49,317	2	1	97
Po-hsing	8	1,886	33	30	37	37,116	4	1	95
Pin	16	1,613	35	3	62	45,256	2	4	94
Chu-ch'eng	3	1,186	5	48	47	148,870	1	14	85
I-tu	9	1,178	16	12	72	149,355	9	10	81
B. P'ing-yin	7	790	7	16	77	33,814	1	4	95
Fei-ch'eng	5	768	21	23	56	63,378	12	16	71
Tung-p'ing	9	585	19	28	53	142,954	32	37	41
Chiao	7	505	24	21	55	100,000	10	30	60
C. Ch'ang-i	4	498	4	42	54	99,800	7	4	89
Li-ch'eng	3	474	27	7	66	79,800	3	17	80
Tzu-ch'uan	4	387	22	–	78	61,695	18	10	73
P'eng-lai	5	383	5	45	50	58,365	–	–	100
Ho-che	2	378	9	10	81	85,664	15	20	65
Fu-shan	2	370	23	35	42	29,500	14	7	79
Tsou	3	370	8	–	92	74,394	10	10	80
Hui-min	1	350	43	–	57	63,166	18	1	81
Lin-i	5	325	39	13	48	17,600	5	2	94
Liao-ch'eng	6	300	6	15	79	24,500	12	14	74

[a] *A* group includes 1890 data, for sample households numbering between 1,000 and 1,500; *B* group consists of households numbering between 500 to 999; *C* group consists of households numbering between 300 and 499. There were many households less than 300 which could have been listed, but their number were so few that it is questionable they could be considered representative of the county.

[b] *Ibid.*, Ching Su and Lo Lun, appendix I, pp. 1–4.

[c] *Chung-kuo shih-yeh chih*, vol. 3, chap. 1, pp. 53–59 (Shanghai 1933).

regarded as a tenant household. A household owning land but renting a small portion or renting no land and obtaining most of its income from farming is a part-owner and owner household. The problem is that agricultural-laborer households might be understated in the 1930s if their numbers were estimated on the basis of a fixed amount of land, say less than 5 or 10 mow. In the 1890 data households with 10 to 15 mow obtaining income from nonfarm employment were counted as agricultural-laborer households, and quite possibly a major discrepancy exists between the estimates for these two dates.

In Table 48, of 22 counties only 6 showed a decline in the percentage of part-owner and owner-cultivator households. In three quarters of the sample of 22 counties, which in turn is about one fifth of the provincial counties, more households came to own and rent land. This could merely mean that more households formerly owning land now had to rent some land to earn farm income. We cannot say whether more households acquired or lost land. If the size of farm declined, it seems reasonable to argue that fewer households had large farms, and even those that were large experienced a slight decline in their size of holdings.

Thirteen of the 22 counties showed a decline in the percentage of tenant households, and 17 showed a decline in the percentage of agricultural-laborer households. The large decline of the latter may be an error, due to the discrepancy pointed out above. It is generally believed that the percentage of tenant and agricultural-laboring households rose in rural areas where the impact of treaty port commercial development was strongest. The counties listed in Table 48 were located in Shantung near the Chinan-Tsingtao railroad. Perhaps the percentage of tenant and agricultural-laboring households did not increase because many households shifted to cultivating new cash crops to increase farm income or because handicraft income increased. Whatever the reason, the evidence suggests that the percentage of tenant and agricultural-laboring households did not rise and that a higher percentage of owner-cultivator households probably began to rent some land. Under these circumstances it is quite possible land distribution became more equal and farms simply became smaller in size.

Another reason why it is possible that land distribution did not become more unequal is that households with large farms over 100 mow gradually diminished as a percentage of large landowners. When Ching and Lo's data of 121 wealthy households owning over 100 mow of land are compared with similar data obtained by the 1937 National Land Survey Commission the following facts emerge. Although our sample for the 1890s is only one eleventh of the number of households for the mid-1930s, let us assume both samples are randomly selected and the distributions within each sample are similar. We note that in 1936 the percentage share of households owning more than 500 mow was smaller and the percentage of households with farms between 100 and 200 mow more than doubled. In 1890 about

Table 49. Distribution of land according to size of farm over 100 mow and number of households in Shantung, 1890–1936.

Size of farm (mow)	(1) Households in 1890 Number	Per cent	(2) Households in 1936 Number	Per cent
100–199	37	31.6	1,234	85.9
200–299	20	17.5	116	8.2
300–499	38	31.4	46	3.2
500–2,000	26	19.5	35	2.7
Total	121	100.0	1,431	100.0

Sources: (1) Fujita, p. 19.
(2) T'u-ti wei-yuan hui, p. 28.

half of the sample households farmed more than 200 mow, and nearly one fifth farmed over 500 mow. In 1936 only slightly more than four fifths of the largest landholders farmed land between 100 and 200 mow, and only a little over 2 per cent farmed more than 500 mow.

One more example can serve to support the argument. So far, considerable evidence has been presented to show that land distribution in many parts of north China was already very unequal before 1900. Several examples of village land distribution show that little change took place. Finally, a comparison of samples of large landowners for both dates showed that the percentage of very large landowners declined by the mid 1930s. It must now be shown that if these conditions prevailed between 1880 and 1930, they would produce the conditions observed during the 1920s and 1930s: namely, the majority of households owning from 5 to 20 mow. Two examples of land distribution for 1880 and 1930, which though arbitrarily made, approximate the conditions of both periods. If the average size of farm declined and large farms declined, a large increase in small household farms took place; further, it is quite likely that land distribution did not become more unequal, but in fact became more equal.

Let us assume that in a hypothetical village between 1880 and 1930 the amount of cultivated land increased by 10 per cent, land distribution in 1880 was already very unequal with roughly 20 per cent of village households owning 80 per cent of the land, the percentage of large landowners declined, and the average size of farm became smaller. We will first consider that the percentage of households owning no land did not change, and then we will assume this percentage doubled by 1930. The data are set forth in Table 50.

In 1880, 20 per cent of households owned 80 per cent of the land, whereas in 1930, 15 per cent owned 52 per cent of the land. Land ownership distribution in both cases is still very unequal. More households are

Table 50. Land distribution in a hypothetical north China village, 1890 and 1930.

Size of farm	1880[a]				Percentage of landless households unchanged 1930[b]				Percentage of landless households doubled 1930[c]			
	Households		Total land		Households		Total land		Households		Total land	
	Number	Per cent	Mow	Per cent	Number	Per cent	Mow	Per cent	Number	Per cent	Mow	Per cent
0	7	5	0	0	10	5	0	0	20	10	0	0
More than												
0– 10 mow	68	45	100	3	100	50	675	20	100	50	675	20
11– 30 mow	45	30	500	17	60	30	925	28	56	28	925	28
31– 70 mow	15	10	950	32	20	10	825	25	16	8	825	25
71–100 mow	9	6	700	23	10	5	875	27	8	4	875	27
100–150 mow	6	4	750	25	0	0	0	0	0	0	0	0
Total	150	100	3,000	100	200	100	3,300	100	200	100	3,300	100

[a] Average size farm = 21.0 mow.
[b] Average size farm = 17.4 mow.
[c] Average size farm = 18.3 mow.

without land although the percentage in the case of 1880 households remained constant. What is interesting is the great increase in households in the categories of farm size 11–30 mow and below 10 mow. In the 1920s and 1930s, surveys showed that the majority of households owned land within these two categories of farm size. In this example very few farms were larger than 100 mow, and it was assumed these farms disappeared. In 1930 many more households dispatched labor to work outside the village as compared to 1890 because the majority of households were in the category of farm size, 1 to 30 mow.

In the case of 1930 households, the number without land has increased greatly. If these households are excluded, we note that land distribution in 1880 was one of 21 per cent of households owning 80 per cent of the land and in 1930, 13 per cent of households owning 52 per cent of the land. This is analogous to land distribution in 1880. Note the clustering of households in the more than 0–10 mow, 11–30 mow and 31–70 mow categories, which characterized rural conditions of the 1930s. It is impossible to say precisely what percentage change of landless households took place, but from the four village studies already mentioned and the evidence in survey literature of the 1920s and 1930s, there is no evidence that a great increase in landless households took place in villages. What did happen was a great increase in households in the farm size category of less than 30 mow of land and the decline in large farms of over 100 and 200 mow.

If the percentage of households and land owned for both examples of 1930 are plotted on the Lorenz box diagram, it would be observed that both curves showing land distribution for 1930 show greater equality of land distribution than for 1880. In effect, what has taken place is a trend toward more equal land distribution. The removal of large landowning households with small change in the percentage of landless households has produced a clustering of households in the middle categories.

Types of Renting System

A land tenure survey conducted in 1936 shows that three rent systems co-existed in this region: money rents; rent in kind as a fixed amount of the harvest; rent in kind as a share of the harvest.[18] In Hopei, about three fifths of the peasants renting land paid money whereas in Shantung this proportion was only one fifth; in Hopei about one fifth paid rent as a fixed amount of the harvest, and in Shantung it was slightly over one third; and in Hopei only 16 per cent paid rent as a share of the harvest, but in Shantung two fifths of the peasantry paid this rent. Money rents were more widespread in Hopei during the mid 1930s, but in Shantung rent as a share of the harvest predominated.

The existence of money rents in Hopei does not mean that commercialized agriculture developed more rapidly than in Shantung. By commercialized agriculture, I mean peasant households selling 40 per cent or more of their output, developing large-scale farms, employing a large agricultural workforce to assist in the farming of land, and leasing land on strictly a commercial basis. In Hopei, more land had been confiscated by the government early in the Ch'ing period, and as this land was gradually leased by estate owners and institutions, the custom of collecting money rents became widespread. Eventually this land was mortgaged and sold, but the new owners continued the practice of collecting money rents when they leased land. Taxes were also higher in Hopei, and this may have spurred landowners to insist that their tenants pay money rents.[19]

Paying rent in kind as a percentage of the harvest was called *fen-i.*[20] Tenant and landlord agreed upon the share of the harvest to be divided between them. The tenant usually paid between 30 and 65 per cent of the harvest to the landlord. Rarely did the landlord supply capital and credit to his tenant. Once tenancy terms were decided, the landlord did not interfere with the tenant's management of the land. Japanese investigators found that *fen-i* was usually practiced where land was poor and villages had suffered poor harvests, because landlords and tenants were guaranteed some crop share even though land productivity was exceptionally low.[21]

If the harvest yield was stable and the soil good, the peasants preferred to pay rent in kind as a fixed amount of the harvest. This was commonly called *wu-na ting-e,* but there were many terms for this system depending upon the district.[22] Landlord and tenant agreed upon a fixed amount of crop per mow of land depending upon the type of crop grown. The normal procedure was to pay rents after the spring wheat harvest, the summer vegetable harvest, and the fall harvest.

Landlords only canceled rents if the harvest was a complete failure. If the harvest was poor, a landlord might allow a postponement of rent until the next year, but this invariably made for disagreement between tenant and landlord. The landlord insisted the tenant pay two years' rent in one year, and the tenant retorted it was impossible for him to do so. A compromise arrangement was frequently used where, if the harvest was 50 per cent below normal, tenant and landlord split the produce equally, but if the harvest was less, the tenant paid his rent and bore the loss.

This fixed rent system benefited tenant and landlord when harvests were stable and farm prices were rising steadily. As landowners became accustomed to prices rising each year, they could estimate the selling price of their crops and farm income with greater certainty. The collection of a fixed rent removed the uncertainty of rent fluctuations unless, of course, the harvest fluctuated greatly. The tenant also benefited, because anything produced over the stipulated rent accrued to him, and rising farm prices netted him additional income.

Between 1913 and 1938, farm prices rose about 40 per cent or a rate of 2.4 per cent per year.[23] A major price fluctuation occurred between

1931 and 1935 when prices fell because of economic depression, but after 1937 prices began to rise rapidly, and by 1941, prices in major cities were four times higher than their 1937 level.[24] Sometime between 1913 and 1920, many peasants began to switch to the fixed rent system, and this trend continued even into the 1930s. This was very likely accompanied by some improvement in agricultural techniques because of the incentive received by peasants to increase output. "In the land tenure system where rent is a fixed amount payable in kind, tenants are inclined to use more fertilizer. As a result, income rises and any extra goes entirely to the tenant. Under the share rent system, even though the tenant introduced more fertilizer, only a part of the increased gain in productivity went to him while the remainder went to the landlord. The tenant had little incentive to add more fertilizer, and good management of the land developed more slowly." [25]

A uniform rent system did not exist in any village.[26] For example, in Sha-ching, the system of paying money rent before the tenant farmed the land predominated, but some tenants also paid rent in kind as a percentage of the harvest. In Ssu pei ch'ai more peasants paid fixed rents in kind depending upon the type of crop grown, yet the *fen-i* system also existed. The same was true in Ling shui kou and Hou hsia chai. Data on land tenure conditions in each county of Shantung also indicate that different rent systems coexisted in the same village.[27]

Kawano Shigetō has suggested that progressive improvement of the harvest accounted for the shift from share to fixed rent.[28] Because harvests in north China were generally poor between 1880 and 1910, most peasants favored the *fen-i* rent system, but after 1911 harvests improved, and peasants gradually shifted to the fixed rent system. Kawano argues that in some years when harvests were again poor, peasants reverted to the former *fen-i* system. It is hard to accept Kawano's explanation because he has not shown evidence that a cluster of bad harvests occurred during the late Ch'ing period, followed by a series of good harvests. It is more likely that when farm prices rose more rapidly because of increased urban demand, landlords and tenants became convinced it was to their best interests to fix rents. Although many peasants switched gradually to the fixed rent system, peasants frequently reverted to the share rent system in years of poor harvest.[29] The changes that occurred in this land tenure system after 1880 hardly enable one to say that a development toward capitalist farming was taking place and landlords and tenants were entering an era of closer cooperation.

Landlord Economic Behavior

It has already been pointed out that tenant and landlord agreements lacked personal warmth and were short-lived; besides that, landowners did not encourage long-term cooperation with their tenants and frequently changed tenants. Isoda Susumu has referred to these kinds of relationships as being essentially pre-modern.[30] This may be true, but this categorization is not helpful in explaining landlord behavior, because it is not clear what is meant by a traditional or modern landlord. For our purposes, it will be useful to specify the two types of landlord that existed and what they were trying to achieve.

The wealthy farm household leasing land to other households was primarily interested in how much income it could earn each year by expending a minimum amount of labor and using as few resources as possible. When the household had decided how much land to farm for the coming year, it also had to plan the amount of labor required to manage each plot, the expected income from each plot's harvest, and the household's expected outlays. Any remaining land which the household regarded as too costly and difficult to farm—because the soil was poor or plots were located far from the farmstead—would be leased and an expected rent from each plot calculated. The household head probably made a subjective calculation and comparison of the income to be earned by renting these plots or farming them, and it was only a matter of seeking a prospective tenant.

It was unwise for the household to lease too much land, because it never knew when extra cash would be needed. If expenditures suddenly exceeded income, the household could mortgage or sell a plot for ready cash. This could not be done if all land was tied up in long-term lease. Households regarded their land as near-money, and for that reason they took the precaution of not committing too much land to long-term lease.

The point seems worth stressing again that households having little land but extra labor had the option of renting land to increase farm income or sending more labor outside the village to earn nonfarm income. Households probably tried to calculate if more or less income could be obtained by renting land after deducting costs and rent than from earning wages from nonfarm employment after considering the disutility of work. Many considerations naturally entered into making this sort of decision, but the choice ultimately depended upon relating the anticipated income reward with the amount of labor effort expended.

Villages also were characterized by an imbalance between the distribution of land ownership and household labor. A few households had more land than they could manage with their available labor, and many had more labor than was required to farm their land. Households which had accumulated land were bound to possess inferior plots which were best leased to other peasants. Yet, their stock of capital might be too small to share with their tenants to help them develop the land. Furthermore, the landlord household might not be able to spare extra labor to supervise its tenants closely. Limited household capital and labor made it difficult for landowning households to cooperate closely with their tenants.

Landlord and Peasant

Wealthy farm households accumulated land in three ways. First, a household through hard work and practicing rigid economy each year might be able to save enough to buy extra plots. If this same household were free of family sickness and there were several working hands in the family, it could increase the size of farm. Second, a household head might save money by working in Manchuria or a distant city. With hard work and careful saving, this same individual might be able to start a small business in a city or market town. If this business prospered, the proceeds could be used to buy land in the householder's former village. Finally, a peasant household might be fortunate enough to obtain a windfall gain of cash from a relative or through some strange quirk of fate.[31]

The first two methods of acquiring land were most common. However, with the rapid development of cities and their industries, it is most likely that after 1910 households began to acquire more income from outside the village with which to buy land. A good example of this may be seen in Hou chia ying village of Ch'ang-li county.[32] In 1900 the village contained several large landowners possessing 200 to 300 mow of land, but by 1942 these households had become poor, and a new group of landowners owning be-

Table 51. Principal landlords of Hou chia ying village of Ch'ang-li county, their origins, size of landholdings, and management of land, 1942.

Landlord	Origins of wealth	Period of holding wealth and amount of land owned	Management of land
Liu Hsi-hsing	Opened a porcelain shop and gradually purchased land	Had been wealthy for many years	Leased to 6 or 7 tenants
Hou Ching-ch'ang	Worked in Manchuria and returned to buy land	Formerly a poor peasant owning only 10 mow; in 1942 owned 180 mow and leased 100 mow	Leased to 15 or 16 tenants
Hou Tsan-lien	Worked in Manchuria and returned to buy land	When his father was living, Hou was a poor peasant; in 1942 he owned 117 mow and leased 6 mow	Farmed most of the land by himself
Hou Yuan-wen	Worked in Manchuria and returned to buy land	Formerly poor but in 1942 Hou owned 30 mow and leased 10 mow	Farmed his own land
Hou Ch'uan-wu	Formerly an official who saved his money and gradually bought land	Formerly poor but in 1942 Hou owned 30 mow and leased 10 mow	Leased to 2 or 3 tenants
Hou Yuan-hung	Worked in Manchuria many years, saved his money, and bought land	Formerly poor but in 1942 Hou owned 30 mow and leased 10 mow	–
Hou Yuan-lai	Worked in Manchuria and returned to buy land	Father was a poor peasant and peddler; but in 1942 Hou was wealthy	Leased to 5 or 6 tenants
Hou Yun-chung	Father worked in Manchuria, saved money, bought land, and increased landholdings through farm earnings	Formerly a peasant of modest means	Farmed land himself
Liu Pin-k'uei	Owned a porcelain shop and gradually bought land	Formerly a wealthy household, but in 1942 Liu owned 170 mow and leased 30 mow	Farmed most of his land by himself

Source: CN, V, 151, 179.

tween 100 and 180 mow had emerged. The majority of these large landowners had acquired income by working as day laborers in Manchuria or managing shops outside the village. After saving a certain amount, they returned to their native villages and purchased land. Table 51, based on village survey evidence, lists the main households which leased land, the origins of their wealth, the length of time which they had held their wealth, and how they managed their landholdings.

The other important group of landholders consisted of absentee landlords living in the market towns and treaty ports and engaged in commerce, industry, and moneylending. A rural study of Chi-ning county of southwest Shantung in 1941 shows that of the 420 absentee landlords in the county seat, the ten largest owned over 3,000 mow and lived in Tientsin, Chinan, or Tsingtao.[33] They hired superintendents to manage their lands and collect rents. Of the remaining landlords with land scattered about the county in various villages, 10 owned between 2,000 and 3,000 mow, 100 owned between 1,000 and 2,000 mow, and another 300 owned between 500 and 1,000 mow. Similar conditions prevailed in every county.

These landlords reinvested their earnings to expand and diversify their business holdings and, on occasion, loaned money. The way in which most of these landlords acquired land was through the rural credit system. Peasants often borrowed large sums from the wealthy in the market towns in preference to borrowing from wealthy villagers because they could obtain larger sums at slightly lower interest terms. They used their land as collateral, and in the event of defaulting on their loan, some land was mortgaged. Sometimes this same land had to be sold. Gradually a moneylender accumulated land which he then leased to other peasants. The following examples show this clearly.

Wu-tien village, consisting of only 50 households, was located near the county seat of Liang-hsiang county south of Peking.[34] Half of the villagers worked outside the village, many going to Peking in the winter to seek work. Bad harvests between 1921 and 1942 forced many peasants to borrow, and when they could not repay their loans, their land reverted to urban moneylenders. Peasants continued to farm their former land as tenants as long as they paid rent in kind to the absentee landlords. These landlords were primarily concerned with their city businesses, and they did not have time to manage their land and assist their tenants. One of the wealthiest absentee landlords was a former county magistrate of Anhwei named Wu, who had amassed 3,000 mow by the time he retired from office.[35] Wu owned 30 mow in Wu-tien, which he had purchased from a farmer in the 1920s. He paid the land tax for his land from his rents, but other taxes such as the *t'an-k'uan* were paid by his tenants.[36] Wu employed a superintendent to manage his lands and collect rents. This superintendent stated that if a tenant failed to pay his rent within the short grace period allowed, he threatened the tenant with a legal suit and this invariably hastened rent payment.[37]

In a survey of absentee landlords in P'eng-te county in northern Honan very near the Hopei border and on the Peking-Hankow railway line, Japanese researchers found 43 absentee landlords living in the county seat and owning 1,735 mow of land in the county.[38] Each landlord owned an average amount of land of 29 mow. Seventy three per cent of this land had been acquired from peasants who had mortgaged their land because of their inability to repay loans and had not yet redeemed their land. In two villages located several miles from the county seat the majority of tenant households had formerly become indebted to some wealthy person in the county seat. When these households failed to repay their loans they continued to farm their land and paid rent in kind as a percentage of the harvest to the new owner. The absentee landlords had little interest in managing their landholdings because they were mainly engaged in managing shops and lending money.

The abstentee landlord Li Ho-tang of Luan county in Hopei, between 1880 and 1922, purchased banner and private land totaling 5,000 mow.[39] Li acquired this land from peasants who had formerly borrowed money from him, mortgaged their land, and failed to redeem it at the proper time. Most of these debtors had then sold their land to Li. In this way Li had purchased 422 plots of which the smallest was 5 mow and the largest 50 mow.

A merchant in Chang-ch'u county of Shantung in the early nineteenth century operated a money shop and loaned money in the county seat. He accumulated 960 mow by acquiring land when peasants defaulted on their loan repayments.[40]

There were also wealthy individuals who used various stratagems to acquire land and, in so doing, built a financial empire of considerable size. A wealthy absentee landlord of Ch'i-hsia county of northeast Shantung is a good example.[41] The landlord Mou Jen-heh used his landholdings to move into commerce, moneylending, and handicraft. In the early Ch'ing period Mou's grandfather owned only 300 mow, but Mou's father managed to increase his holdings to 1,000 mow, which he was able to pass to Mou Jen-heh intact. With this estate Mou built a fortune consisting of 60,000 mow of farm land, numerous pawn shops, stores, banks, and enterprises selling silk, grinding flour, and pressing oil. Mou's household consisted of 49 people, many of them servants, consuming this wealth.

Mou's early windfall gains were acquired from a speculative venture. During a great famine in 1917 the peasants of Ch'i-hsia county were reduced to eating bark off the trees. At the height of the famine Mou loaned grain to peasants in exchange for plots of land. In this exchange he gave only 230 *shih* of grain for 3,500 mow. In later years the annual rent collected from these lands yielded 650 *shih* of grain. Each year Mou practiced arbitrage in the grain market to increase his earnings from the grain trade. During the harvest months when prices were at rock bottom, Mou purchased large amounts of grain and stored it in his granaries to sell during the spring months when prices rose. Mou had the reputation of cheating his tenants by having his rent collectors use grain measuring rods longer than those used in market towns. However, Mou devoted most of his efforts to managing his urban commercial and industrial holdings. The land he acquired by speculation was later converted to cash to finance urban business holdings.

The above does not exhaust the examples that show a large absentee landlord class using its wealth and managerial activities in the market towns and cities. In spite of the wealth and urban based business operations of these landlords, their domination of the rural community was exceedingly limited. Land passed into the hands of landlords but eventually was resold to peasants in the villages. Much land simply passed back and forth between villages and market towns.

Under these conditions, it is understandable that landlords and tenants had little relationship with one another. Wealthy villagers had neither the time nor resources to assist their tenants, and absentee landlords were too busy with their urban businesses to care about their tenants except that they pay their rents. Both groups regarded land as a form of near-money to be mortgaged or sold depending upon the need for cash. The transfer of land from one household to another was mainly associated with the need for cash and the inability of debtors to repay their loans. The acquisition of land by households did not mean that wealth concentration continued each generation, for land was always being divided and transferred to new owners through mortgage and sale. Wealthy peasant households acquired their land by working outside the village as much as by farming.

The land tenure system did not retard agricultural development by adversely affecting income distribution and farm management. As will be seen shortly the percentage of tenant households was small. Those households which rented and leased land were merely attempting to use available land more efficiently to maximize household income. Where land was transferred to another party as a by-product of the credit system, it did not lead to undesirable consequences for the rural economy, because land as a form of near money played an important role in the transfer of credit from lender to debtor. Without such a rural credit system, farm households would not have been able to farm throughout the year and reclaiming land would have been impossible.

Farm Tenancy in North China

According to the 1936 land tenure survey about three fourths of the peasantry in Hopei and Shantung owned their land, and if we include landowning peasants who also rented land, this constitutes a little over four fifths of the peasantry.[42] The remainder consisted of pure tenants and agricultural workers. About three fifths of the peasants owning land farmed holdings of less than 20 mow, and another one fifth farmed between 20 and 50 mow or 3 to 8 acres.[43]

These peasants used their extra income to buy land, but when situations arose where households needed cash, they mortgaged and even sold land. Although their landholdings then declined and farm income failed to cover outlays, they were still able to get by with wage income from alternative employment or renting land from other owners. Sometimes they did both. As long as opportunities existed by which farm income could be supplemented, the percentage of tenant households in villages changed little in spite of population increase and the formation of new farm households in villages. There is little solid evidence that the percentage share of tenant households increased between 1880 and 1937 in north China. The reasons for this were increased farm income from cash crop and greater nonfarm income from the growth of handicraft and nonfarm employment. Treaty ports development and urban expansion along the main railway lines provided the new off-farm employment opportunities to peasants. The final factor influencing the growth and decline of tenant households was the frequency of natural and man-made catastrophes.

After the 1850s peasants began growing the opium poppy; from the 1890s on more households began to grow soybeans, cotton, peanuts, and tobacco. Villages with suitable soils located close to market towns benefited more than those villages situated in remote areas where transport costs made commodity exchange expensive and difficult. A good example of this is shown in a survey of two villages conducted in 1941 of I-tu county in central Shantung.[44] One village lay close to a market town and had adopted tobacco cultivation sometime in the 1920s. The number of tenant households gradually declined and part-owner households increased because tobacco provided more farm income from which households could buy extra land. The other village, located in a hilly section of the county far from any market town, depended mainly on cereal production. It marketed a small share of the wheat and millet harvest in exchange for consumer necessities, but there had not been any change in the proportion of tenant households whose percentage was higher than in the tobacco growing village. Another village survey conducted near the Chinan-Tsingtao railroad found that after tobacco had been introduced, more peasants had been able to earn income from which they could buy as much land as they formerly rented, and the number of tenants declined.[45]

After the 1880s, new handicraft enterprises developed in the villages and market towns. The import of foreign yarn and the introduction of cheap weaving looms by merchants in districts such as Kao-yang and Paoti of Hopei and Wei in Shantung provided new employment and income for peasants.[46] Market towns supported a large variety of handicraft establishments which received an impetus to expand when railroads linked them closer to the treaty ports. In Ting county for example, one out of every four villages had an organized handicraft industry producing dyes, flour, noodles, or medicines,[47] and many of these owed their growth to expansion since the turn of the century. Some handicrafts, such as spinning, suffered a severe setback because of keen competition with yarn imports. However, expanding market demand and gradual urban development stimulated considerable village handicraft which previously did not exist.

There is no need to comment on the new opportunities for off-farm employment for peasants. These had existed even in the nineteenth century, but railroad construction, the building of new urban dwellings, mining, and transport absorbed ever increasing numbers of peasants for temporary work. I will comment on the impact of natural disasters and war on rural life in Chapter 17, and all that needs to be stressed at this point is that villages suffering prolonged natural calamities and war were deprived of some of their labor, livestock, labor animals, tools, and carts. These disasters plunged many households into debt, and invariably peasants sold their land, joined the ranks of tenants, and even fled the villages.

The opportunity to switch to cash crops, the expansion of new handicraft production, the growth of nonfarm employment, good harvests, and peace and security were the necessary conditions enabling villagers to increase their income, buy land, repay debt, and rent less land. A decline in cash crop prices, the collapse of rural handicraft, a fall in nonfarm employment, several poor harvests, and war forced peasants to mortgage and sell their land.

One or more of these factors combined with varying intensity to cause either a reduction or an increase in the number of tenant households. Table A-7 is a table with field survey data to confirm this proposition. Data from many village studies were assembled to relate the percentage of tenant households with the existence or nonexistence of opportunities for peasants to earn income from handicraft production, grow cash crops, and obtain nonfarm employment. The results indicate that in villages where tenant households comprised more than 5 per cent, villagers had very little opportunity to supplement their farm income. Yet, there are also cases where random disturbances occasionally destroyed the peasants' basis for earning income. In Ssu pei ch'ai village poor harvests forced many peasants to mortgage land, become tenants on their own land, and even sell some of their land.

The percentage of tenant households in villages could increase, first, because households were unable to earn enough nonfarm income to farm only their small farms. They were compelled to increase their farm income by renting land from households which had more land, or they rented land previously mortgaged to moneylenders. Second, households experienced a reduction in farm income due to poor harvests or war and had not found means to restore income to its former level. This had forced many into debt, and if land had been mortgaged or sold, the household might have decided to rent additional land from another household.

Severe calamities which led to several years of poor harvests or the loss of labor and capital due to war and pillaging were the principal reasons why some areas had higher percentages of tenant households than others. I was first led to believe that the percentage of tenant households was strongly determined by the existence of opportunities for earning nonfarm income and that this relationship could be observed spatially by mapping counties and their percentage of tenant households. I also considered rural population density to be important, believing that extreme pressure on the land would lead to considerable leasing and renting of land between households. None of these expectations or hunches were confirmed by the results found from mapping the data.

I discovered, instead, that some counties had a high percentage of tenant households even though considerable land was devoted to cash crops and peasants had access to nonfarm income. Several of these same counties could be regarded as having low population density. Nevertheless, the maps are of interest because they show the great complexity of patterns of high and low percentage of tenant households by county.

The data were arranged in four categories. The first represented counties having less than 5 per cent of rural households as full-time tenants; the second category was rural households with tenants between 5 and 15 per cent of rural households renting the land they farmed; the third category was rural households having more than 15 per cent of rural households renting land; the final category represented counties for which inadequate information existed. Shantung data were obtained from a 1934 provincial survey of economic conditions.[48] Hopei data were most incomplete, and I had to obtain scraps of information from four separate county surveys: J. L. Buck's 1929–1933 farm survey;[49] eight counties surveyed by Chu Chih-sheng in 1932;[50] a survey of 23 counties in north and northeast Hopei in 1934;[51] and an individual survey of Ch'ing-yuan county in 1930.[52] The results may be seen in maps 10 and 11.

The hilly areas of north and northeast Hopei contained the highest percentage of tenant households. This might be explained by conditions of poor transport, little handicraft, and the few cash crops grown in the area. On closer inspection I also found that in some counties, particularly Tien-chin, An-tzu, and Wu-ch'ing, the percentage of tenant households exceeded 5 per cent even though households extensively cultivated cotton, peasants had easy access to employment in the cities of Tientsin and Peking, and commodities could be cheaply marketed. One would have normally expected the percentage of tenant households here to be less than 5 per cent. Ho-chien county of central Hopei contained less than 5

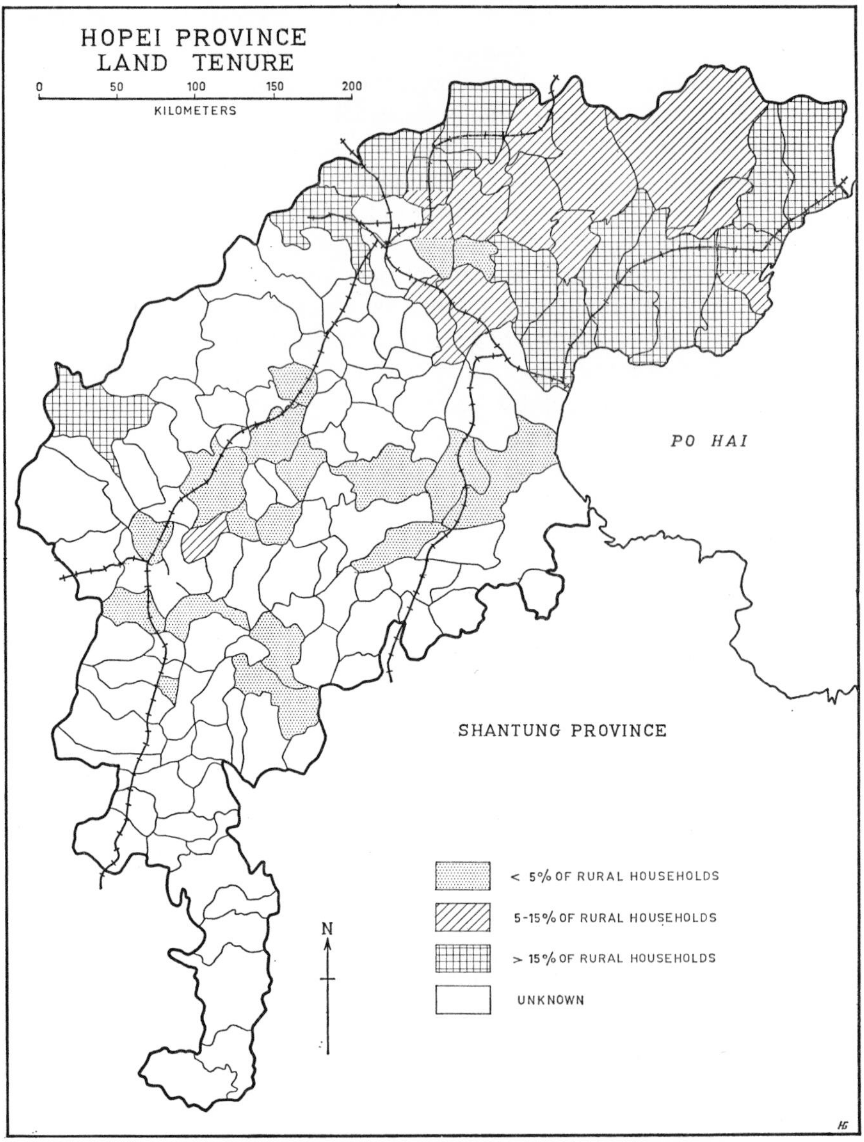

Map 10. Percentage of tenant households according to county in Hopei province, 1930s.

per cent tenancy and much of its land was devoted to soybeans and cotton. On the other hand, less land was devoted to growing cotton in Ho-chien than in Wu-ch'ing, and it was located further away from the major markets than Wu-ch'ing.

It appears that northwest and northeast Shantung, specializing in cotton and groundnuts respectively, had fewer tenant households than the south-

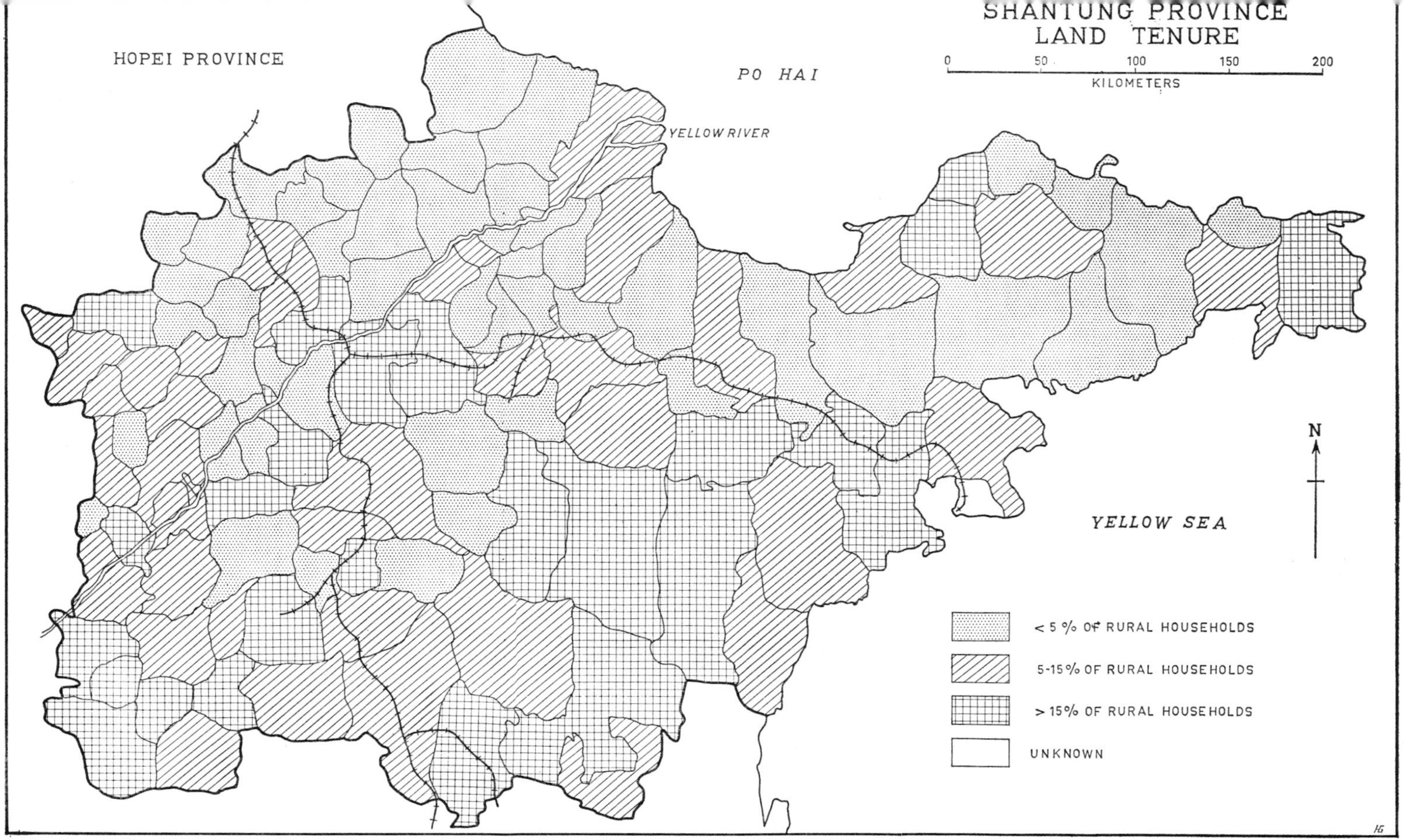

Map 11. Percentage of tenant households according to county in Shantung province, 1930s.

ern and central highland areas. However, Ch'u-fu county located near the Tientsin-Pukow railroad line with a low population density contained over 15 per cent tenant households. Lin-ch'ing county, with most land devoted to cotton, was a high tenancy district. Chiao county, near Tsingtao and the second biggest peanut-producing district, had over 15 per cent tenancy.

Many counties having high tenancy also specialized considerably in cash crops, peasants had access to nonfarm income, and often population density was not as high as in counties with fewer tenant households. We find little correlation between tenancy, population density, and the amount of land devoted to growing cash crops. In one respect the high correlation between counties growing cash crops and having high population density supports the proposition introduced in Chapter 11 that households adopted cash crops if a large increase in household division had taken place in villages. Yet, inconsistencies remain and cannot be explained by simple reference to rural households being unable to increase their income in various ways. Random disturbances in the past must have also affected the level of tenancy from district to district. The results of this mapping test do not entirely refute the notion that the availability of nonfarm income was important in allowing peasants to manage small plots without renting land from other households. Random disturbances also determined the spatial pattern of tenancy. We must accept the fact that extreme variation in tenancy existed throughout this region and makes single factor explanations very questionable indeed.

We may conclude that buying or leasing land depended on the level of household income, and where very small plots were either owned or leased, the acquisition of extra land depended to a large extent on the opportunities to earn income through cash crop cultivation, handicraft, off-farm employment, favorable harvests, and long periods of peace and stability. In the process by which small family farms gained land and large family farms lost land, it was still possible for a high percentage of rural households to survive on very small family farms and for the percentage of tenant households to remain fairly constant over a long period of time.

15. Moneylender, Merchant, and Peasant

Scholars have written unsympathetically of the merchant and moneylender of rural China. They have been described as parasitic and more responsible for the backwardness of the rural economy than contributing toward its improvement. In fact, so many emotionally charged statements have been made about their role and behavior that the credit and marketing systems are little understood. The subject deserves re-examination.

The Supply and Demand for Rural Credit

I have already stressed the importance of peasants using land to acquire credit. Peasants did not have any place to store their money safely except in a hiding place somewhere on the farmstead. Market towns did not provide them with any savings deposit banks, and merchants were unwilling to hold the personal savings of their countless customers because of the risks involved. Peasants might hoard copper cash or silver for short periods, but as the rate of exchange between these two currencies always fluctuated, peasants could not predict with certainty which currency they should hold. There was no such problem where land was concerned.

Land appreciated in value as the price level rose.[1] Buying land meant exchanging money for an asset easily converted into money if the need for cash arose later. Finally, land represented a safe store of value. Land had some of the attributes of money: it was a store of value and commanded purchasing power in terms of the credit or cash it could obtain. For the merchant or moneylender, land constituted a stepping-stone to greater wealth, served as a safeguard against commercial loss, and made one's wealth appear small to the eyes of venal officials. For the official, acquiring land meant preserving intact the gains from years of speculation. For the peasant, purchasing land meant security for his family, ensured continuation of the family line as land was transferred to sons, and brought social status.

According to the National Land Survey Commission Report of 1937 land was the principal form of security used by peasants in Hopei and Shantung in 1936 to obtain credit.[2] Over half the peasants borrowed on the basis of their land as collateral, and in some counties nearly three quarters of the peasants borrowed in this fashion.[3] Small loans of less than 50 yuan could be obtained from friends and relatives without security, but larger sums of 100 to 150 yuan could only be borrowed by offering the moneylender land as security.[4]

It was rare that land reverted to the moneylender if these small loans were not repaid. The peasant mortgaged additional land to pay his debt. The period to repay and redeem depended upon the district: in Manchuria there were areas where land could be redeemed any time;[5] in Ting county a grandson could redeem land which his grandfather had mortgaged; during the nineteenth century land could still be redeemed after 30 to 40 years in many districts; but by the twentieth century more peasants insisted the redemption period be shorter. After mortgaging their land to moneylenders, debtors were usually allowed to work as tenants and pay a fixed or proportionate amount of the harvest as rent.[6]

Selling land was a difficult and tedious business, because a formal land market did not exist. The law required that peasants make a deed of land transfer, which the buyer took to the county tax office to be notarized and pay the transfer deed tax. In some districts a fee was paid to officials recording land transfers.[7]

The waiting period to receive income after planting their crops was long for the peasants, and unless additional income could be earned, cash had to be borrowed during the spring months to buy grain until the fall harvest. The habit of borrowing during spring was as prevalent during the eighteenth century as during the 1930s.[8] Harvest fluctuations greatly influenced the volume of borrowing each spring. A poor harvest forced many peasants to mortgage and sell their land in order to survive until the next harvest. A good harvest enabled peasants to repay old debts and accumulate a small surplus making it unnecessary to borrow the next year. Unexpected expenditures for a funeral, wedding, or family sickness usually plunged peasants deep into debt because their meager savings were not enough to cover these outlays.

We can gain a rough idea of how many peasants borrowed money from the land tenure survey of 1936, which was a fairly normal harvest year in north China. In Hopei about three quarters of the peasant households earned less than 150 yuan a year, and only 4 per cent earned over 400 yuan; in Shantung a little over four fifths earned less than 150 yuan per year and only 2 per cent earned over 400 yuan.[9] The majority of peasants earned an annual income equivalent to the sum usually borrowed for a wedding, a funeral, or purchase of grain and livestock.[10] Nearly two fifths of the rural households in Hopei and one quarter of them in Shantung spent more than they earned during a year.[11] Even in a normal harvest year an average of one third of these households had to borrow because their expenditures exceeded income. The reader needs little imagination to conceive of the extent of borrowing under conditions of poor harvests. About 43 per cent of Hopei's rural households and 28 per cent of Shantung's households were in debt.[12] This is a larger figure than the percentage of households whose expenditures exceeded income, so that households which had incurred past debt must also be included in the number of debtor households. We do not have similar data for an earlier period to show whether the percentage of rural households in debt increased, declined, or remained the same over time, but the problem can be approached from another angle.

Moneylender, Merchant, and Peasant

If a greater percentage of peasants were forced to borrow, this would increase the demand for loanable funds supplied by moneylenders and shops in market towns. Without growth of trade and towns, we would expect interest rates to rise. There is historical evidence that monthly interest rates for the late eighteenth century were 3 per cent for Hopei and Shantung;[13] for the late nineteenth century these monthly rates were roughly the same;[14] and during the 1930s they ranged between 2 and 4 per cent.[15] Interest rates naturally fluctuated on a seasonal basis according to the harvest and supply of cash, but monthly rates calculated as an average for a year appear to have been quite constant over a period of two hundred years.

Although commerce and handicraft grew slowly during the eighteenth and nineteenth centuries, the supply of credit in market towns must also have expanded. The growth of agriculture was merely the division of households and the formation of new family farms and the extension of the area of farm land. As long as household income consisting of cash from farm sales, handicraft income, and wages also rose slowly, household demand for credit could be supplied by other households or from moneylenders in the market towns without bidding up the price of loanable funds. Over the long run the proportion of rural households borrowing and repaying debt probably did not change very much except when the harvest was poor. Such fluctuations were offset by periods of prosperity when loans were repaid, stocks accumulated, and the supply of loanable funds again increased.

Household income, however, was still so low that in many districts credit was used to buy grain during the spring to enable the household to survive until the next harvest. Li Ching-han reports in his Ting county survey that half of village debt went to repay former debt incurred mainly for consumption purposes.[16] Amano Motonosuke reports that villagers in Kung county of Shantung borrowed mainly to buy grain until the next harvest.[17] Although examples of this sort abound, there were rural districts with higher income where credit was obtained primarily for purchasing commodities for weddings, funerals, and even to buy labor animals and farm implements.

Although peasants borrowed mainly from friends and relatives,[18] credit was also obtained from market towns. The reason for this was that larger loans could be more readily obtained at better terms than wealthy villagers could provide.[19] Market town merchants charged slightly lower interest rates than private moneylenders. In Table 52 I have grouped Shantung's counties into five areas and compared the interest rates charged by both lenders.

Interest rates charged by private individuals scarcely differed between regions, except for the northwest. Interest rates charged by merchants and shops were generally lower than those charged by private moneylenders. Interest rates in the regions of the treaty ports of Tsingtao, Chefoo, Yentai,

Table 52. Monthly interest rates by region for Shantung, 1934 (in per cent).

Region	Rates charged by private individuals	Rates charged by merchants and shops
1	2.6	1.8
2	2.6	2.5
3	2.6	2.7
4	2.6	2.1
5	1.8	1.7

Source: Chung-kuo shih-yeh chih (Shantung) chap. 1, pp. 90–97.

Region 1. includes Tsingtao and nearby counties;
2. counties along railways and in northwest portion of province, which is a cotton and peanut growing region (this region would also include the tobacco growing areas of central Shantung);
3. counties in southwest of province that border old grand canal;
4. counties in central and south central portion of province on Kiangsu frontier;
5. counties in northwest Shantung, a hilly and backward region except in vicinities around Chefoo, Weiyuanhui, and Yentai.

and Weiyuanhui were lower than for other regions. However, we do not see any great difference in interest rates between areas of the hinterland.

Other suppliers of credit were pawn shops, money changers, and native banks. Pawn shops existed long before the Ch'ing period, but by 1900 they had declined numerically as native banks increased and expanded their operations. In 1931 a survey reports there to have been 65 pawn shops in 25 counties of Hopei with a total capital of 613,000 yuan, but in Shantung province there were only 28 shops.[20] It is not clear whether this survey included very small pawn shops in market towns or only in the major cities.

Native banks, located principally in Tientsin, Chinan, Peking, Shihmen and Tsingtao, had branch banks in the county seats of districts specializing in wheat, cotton, and peanuts. Their loans to merchants played an important role in financing the growth of these staple trades. With native bank credit merchants were able to send their brokers to various market towns to purchase industrial crops and grain. This bank credit made for a large share of their working capital to make purchases, hold stocks, and then sell to factories, exporters, and other merchants. Merchants did not extend loans to peasants. Native bank credit was restricted to financing trade rather than production.

A study of Tientsin native banks reveals that between 1910 and 1940 a weeding-out process had been taking place in which a large number of banks periodically went bankrupt. Those that survived could attribute their success to tailoring their loans to enterprises they knew very well and trusted. These banks loaned credit for unlimited periods, but they also attracted a large flow of deposits from their customers and other merchants. They also managed to keep their operations small, efficient, and cheap. In a sample of 60 Tientsin native banks studied, it was found that 64 per cent of their capital came from deposits of Tientsin merchants, 28 per cent from officials, and 8 per cent from absentee landlords.[21] The main revenue earned by these banks was interest on their loans, and their biggest outlay was the interest paid to their depositors.[22] These banks maintained a high ratio of loans to deposits and used their customers' deposits for making loans. Banks occasionally assisted one another when depositors requested withdrawals, but the lack of a central bank did not give them any protection when panic hit the business community. In 1937–38 an unusually large number went bankrupt because grain merchants could not repay their loans and depositors demanded that their deposits be refunded.[23]

In 1923 a new credit institution, the rural credit cooperative, appeared in north China,[24] and by 1933 there were 952 cooperatives in Hopei with 23,753 members loaning around 90,000 yuan to their members to buy capital and repair homes.[25] The majority of cooperative members only deposited about 5 to 10 yuan, which represented a very small fraction of their household income. Peasants were reluctant to deposit most of their savings with the cooperatives despite the fact that they received an interest of 5 per cent on their deposits and higher rates for deposits left over longer periods. However, it is still significant that within a decade fairly firm foundations were established, and cooperative expectations at the time were that membership could be increased and more cooperatives created. It is not known if these cooperatives mobilized savings and loaned more efficiently than other institutions and private individuals, but the fact remains that villagers now had another source of credit.

The Study of Rural Markets by Skinner and Solomon

A most neglected area of study in Chinese economic history has been the structure and operation of rural markets. The appearance of G. W. Skinner's study of marketing and social structure in rural China marks the first attempt to describe comprehensively the function and spatial characteristics of rural market towns.[26] Skinner's study, which applies the principles of Lösch's location theory, seeks to explain the operations and genetic process by which standard market towns multiplied and declined. The standard market town was the periodic rural market town with fixed days allotted for marketing. Market towns and their areas "fit together in the manner of hexagonal ceramic tiles" [27] forming two patterns of development. The first is where each standard market town depended on two higher-level market towns, and the second covers cases of dependency on three higher-level market towns. Skinner refers to several regions of Szechwan province as proof these two patterns existed. An important conclusion reached by him was the derivation of a model area per standard marketing community of 52.5 square kilometers with an average population of 7,800 people.[28]

What interested Skinner was why markets in the past had multiplied in number while in recent years their number had declined in certain areas. Skinner's hypothesis was that long before the twentieth century markets on alluvial and coastal plains had increased in number, market areas had narrowed, and market day scheduling had intensified because of population increase.[29] He used this market structure type to predict a certain rural population density and village to market ratio for the Ningpo area in Chekiang and various counties in Shantung. His results showed higher population densities in larger marketing areas than he had expected. Skinner explained this by citing further evidence that traditional rural markets had declined in number because their functions had been taken over by several large markets. He interpreted this change as a step toward creating a modern economy; he then used these examples to estimate how many rural markets throughout China had been affected in a similar way.

Skinner's study clearly describes how market towns functioned and the different market–village relationships that emerged on the rural landscape under different geographical conditions during the Ch'ing and Republican periods. His account explains the trend detected some years ago by the great Japanese economic historian Katō Shigeshi. The relationship between market towns and larger urban markets and changes in commodity exchange between them after the introduction of railroads and treaty port development have not yet received the attention they deserve. A useful analytic approach to this problem was worked out by M. R. Solomon in an essay setting forth a useful typology to analyze the operation of various kinds of markets.[30]

Solomon classified markets according to types of commodities: a personal service market, perishable produce market, agricultural staple market, manufactured consumer goods market, and capital goods market. He analyzed each market in terms of the number of sellers, their control of price and output, and new sellers' abilities to enter each market. Solomon used data of the 1940s for China, India, and southeast Europe to test his model. He believed that about 70 to 100 per cent of rice and cereal in the rural staple market passed through the hands of the landlord class before entering the staple market.[31] A handful of landlord sellers with numerous peasant sellers controlled supply in the rural staple markets. Landlords were able to influence prices greatly by hoarding, and this produced "relatively wide swings in the price quotations of the very thin local market." [32] The meagerness of the market naturally facilitated this price manipulation but made the sudden disposal of large inventories difficult. Because peasants had limited resources to expand their output, the output of staples was inelastic with respect to price when prices moved upward. The staple then passed into the hands of merchant wholesalers with oligopolistic and oligopsonistic market power. They had considerable financial resources by which to influence price. By being able to hold large inventories, these wholesalers speculated in futures and made huge profits. As a result, prices fluctuated widely and large price differentials existed between areas. Under these circumstances it had been impossible for a large-scale, specialized distribution system to develop. Market conditions were characterized by a large degree of market power concentrated in the hands of a few buyers and sellers.

Solomon's description of the operations of the rural staple market will be tested against the available information about markets in north China between 1880 and 1937. I will refer to the markets for three principal staples and an important consumer good, cloth. First, it will be necessary to sketch the general market structure of the region on the eve of railroad building.

Rural Market Structure before Railroads and Treaty Port Development

During the late Ch'ing period cotton goods, coal, iron products, and vegetable tallow were exported from north China and rice, sugar, tea, and silk were imported from the southern provinces.[33] But some northern provinces like Hopei only produced a small quantity of commercial goods for export and depended for its food supply primarily on tribute exacted from other provinces. "Chihle is the most sterile province of the empire, but the establishment of the court within its jurisdiction is some compensation for its natural defects. It has, however, scarcely any exports, excepting a very inferior kind of date, and some kind of agate stone, and salt." [34]

The Grand Canal passed through northern Kiangsu and western Shantung, and in the eighteenth and nineteenth centuries this important transport route stimulated considerable commercial growth of towns and the development of handicraft production and cash crop specialization in adjacent rural areas.[35] In central Shantung there were also large market towns in Chang-shan,[36] I-tu, and Wei counties.[37] The main markets near the Grand Canal handling grain shipments lay in Chi-ning, Kung, and I-shui counties in the southern sections of the province. Cotton was assembled in Chi-tung, Lin-i, Lien-ch'eng, and Yun-ch'eng county seats in the northwest area above the Yellow River. Tobacco was grown and marketed in Chi-ning and Yen-chou in the southwest. Peanuts were produced and processed in I county.

However, these commodities were mainly consumed within this large regional market, and Shantung only exported special products such as fruits, vegetables, and felt. "The principal manufactures are felt, the caps worn by the Chinese in winter coming invariably from this province; and this is a very important branch of trade, employing several millions of capital. The inhabitants weave also tolerable carpets, and moreover, manufacture a kind of silky hemp-cloth, much worn by the lower orders, as a general article of dress." [38] The merchants of Hopei and Shantung were unimportant in the commerce of other provinces. Peng Chang places Chihli and Shantung thirteenth and fourteenth when he ranks China's eighteen provinces according to commercial importance and the power of each province's merchant clubs.[39]

Guilds and merchant clubs exercised considerable control over trade in the large coastal markets.[40] These organizations fixed price, controlled the volume of trade, collected taxes for local officials, and maintained and enforced standard commercial practices of its membership. We know less about the relationship of these groups to the many inland traders who gathered in the market towns of the interior to assemble and package goods for shipment to the coast or to large provincial cities. Many middlemen or brokers represented the guild merchants of the coastal cities, but others operated independently, preferring to deal with guild merchants on a private basis. These middlemen were referred to as *ya-hang*. They performed many functions to ensure the movement of goods from the interior to coastal markets:[41] they advanced credit to their sellers, provided lodging and storage facilities for their customers, and introduced buyers and sellers. Whether or not the *ya-hang* had sufficient economic power to fix prices and control supply in the rural market towns and large inland cities, or secondary markets, is a matter awaiting further study.

It is quite likely that the brokers buying goods in inland markets and selling in coastal markets had some economic power to maintain sufficiently wide price differentials between their buyers and sellers to net a good profit. Yet their risk was great, and shortage of working capital frequently plunged them into debt and even bankruptcy. It seems that guilds and merchant clubs were only able to preserve price control in a restricted market, namely in their selling markets or the commercial centers of southern provinces. For several reasons their power was insufficient to influence price in the interior. First, they depended on middlemen with experience to move goods by water or over land for long distances. Second, they needed buyers with an intimate knowledge of the market conditions such as weights, measures, commercial customs, product quality, and suppliers' bargaining power in the interior. By leaving the hinterland market in the hands of brokers and independents, the coastal merchant groups could then concern themselves with the problem of exporting to the southern markets.

After 1890 railroads diverted traffic from the Grand Canal and markets near the canal to new secondary markets and the terminal centers of Tientsin and Tsingtao. It was observed in Hopei that "The internal trade of the countryside with Tientsin before railroads was conducted by water and roads. In spite of the excessive costs of shipping by rail, it was safer to ship goods by rail than by conventional means. Gradually, about 20 per cent of the goods arriving in Tientsin from the interior came by rail while the remainder was shipped by water and overland. Merchants soon realized that greater profits could be made by shipping by rail once tracks were built to connect Peking with Hankow and Chahar. By 1905, 44 per cent of the inland traffic with Tientsin was carried by rail, 51 per cent by canal, and 5 per cent by road." [42]

The railway enabled more raw materials to be collected in hinterland markets and shipped to terminal markets on the coast. Commercial activity that had been formerly centered in markets along the Grand Canal now shifted to the secondary markets of Shihmen, Paoting, and Chinan.[43] The railway made commercial ties between these new secondary markets and the treaty ports stronger and reduced the price differentials between the two. In 1907 commodity prices in the ports of Chefoo, Weihaiwei, and Tsingtao ranged between 25 to 50 per cent higher than in Chinan and Ch'ing-chou.[44] In 1930 cotton, wheat, and peanut prices in Tsingtao were only 10 to 15 per cent higher than in the markets of central Shantung.[45]

The impact of this new mode of transportation on the function and behavior of inland merchant groups is far from clear and is difficult to measure. Without a clearer understanding of the inland market structure for rural staples and handicraft products than we presently possess, we must be cautious about assigning too great a role to railroads in altering the traditional market structure. What is certain is that guilds and provincial merchant clubs in the treaty ports declined in power and importance after 1900 because of commercial expansion and industrial development. Widening of the market made export trade of the rural staple even more competitive, and market price became more dependent on business conditions in foreign markets.

Commodity Markets in North China after Railroad and Treaty Port Development

Cotton. In Hopei the major cotton-producing areas were the basin of the Tung-pei river in northeast Hopei, a half dozen counties located in south-central Hopei, and Wu-chiao, Nan-kung, Ning-chin, and Wei counties of eastern Hopei.[46] These areas produced 18, 64, and 18 per cent respectively of the province's total supply of cotton. In Shantung, cotton was produced in two regions of the northwest: Wu-ch'eng, En, Te, P'ing-yuan, and Lin counties straddling the Grand Canal, and Chi-tung, Ch'ing-ch'eng, Hui-min, and Chi-yang on the lower reaches of the Yellow river. In the extreme southwest lay a third region consisting of Ch'eng-wu, Ho-che, Ting-t'ao, and Ts'ao counties.[47] These three regions produced 61, 28, and 10 per cent respectively of the province's cotton supply.

The staple market of cotton consisted of three markets which I will refer to as primary, secondary, and terminal. Primary markets consisted of marketing towns and county seats in cotton-producing districts where peasants marketed their cotton in exchange for cash to buy consumer goods. The buyers in this market consisted of brokers acting independently, small wholesalers, ginning firms, peddlers, and representatives of buyers in secondary and terminal markets.[48] After the harvest suppliers and buyers convened in the market towns of the cotton-producing districts to bargain on price and quantity of cotton to be exchanged. Absentee landlords collected rents in cotton and grain which they sold for cash, but the amount they supplied was small relative to the volume marketed, because their claims to the land were only a small part of what was harvested. Many different buyers competed with one another to buy cotton. Some buyers intended to sell to merchants in other towns, others to buy and sell directly to consumers. They had to bid competitively for the cotton according to the price and profit margin they expected to obtain. They did not collude to fix price. Working capital and knowledge of the market were necessary prerequisites for merchants or brokers to enter the market and compete. The price set and the quantity exchanged were determined by the daily bids of buyers and producers.

Secondary markets were located at large railway centers or on rivers where cotton was easily collected from the primary market and shipped to terminal markets. Shihmen and Paoting of Hopei served as important secondary markets, while Chinan and Changtien were the main secondary markets in Shantung. Here brokers and merchants delivered their cotton to new buyers who also competed with one another to buy and then sell to their customers located either in secondary or in terminal markets. Some buyers represented local spinning factories and merchant shops; others represented wholesalers, exporters, and garment producers in the terminal markets. Buyers bid according to the price they believed could be sold to make a profit. There is also little evidence that a few buyers in these markets colluded to fix price.

After 1900 the number of wholesalers in the emerging secondary cotton staple markets increased rapidly, suggesting a trend toward a competitive rather than oligopolistic market. In 1909 only three large cotton wholesalers operated in Chinan, but in 1921 their number exceeded 20 firms shipping 300,000 piculs of cotton a year to Tsingtao. By 1933 their number had increased to over 50 and more than a million piculs were shipped each year.[49]

By the 1920s banks are first observed to enter the cotton trade. The large number of middlemen buying in the primary market needed advance credit. Banks like the Chung-kuo yin-hang in Chinan owned storehouses for accepting cotton as security against loans. Between 1932 and 1936 this bank increased its loans to cotton merchants and brokers from 3,744 to 2.1 million yuan.[50]

Despite large fluctuations in annual prices, the pattern of supply and price variation on a monthly basis was the same each year. Between 1935 and 1940, for example, the annual quantity of cotton supplied to the Chinan market fluctuated greatly depending upon the harvest in the primary market districts. When monthly cotton supplies in Chinan are plotted on a graph for each year, we observe that the quantity of cotton supplied increased between August and December, fell off sharply until early March, rose slowly although to a smaller peak than previously in April, and then gradually fell off through the summer months until the fall harvest. This cycle repeated itself each year, although the twin peaks attained in December and April differed each year because of the harvest.

Seasonal variations for cotton prices were similar although the amplitude of fluctuation differed greatly.[51] Prices gradually rose from a low level in late winter, leveled off slightly in March and April, and then rose to a year's high in late summer, to fall off rapidly in the early autumn months when the harvest was marketed. Prices declined to a year's low in December and January. The inverse relationship between price and quantity on a monthly basis reflect a highly competitive market where holding and unloading inventories determined the price plateau and secondary surge of marketed cotton in the early spring months. If merchants had not kept large inventories to unload in the spring, seasonal price fluctuations between the fall and spring months would have been more severe. Inventory speculation kept prices lower during the spring when supply was normally scarce.

Tientsin and Tsingtao were the terminal markets for Hopei and Shantung. Nearly three quarters of the cotton flowing into Tientsin was exported, but only 32 per cent was consumed by the local textile industry.[52] Cotton exports from Tientsin rose rapidly during the late nineteenth century, and by 1931 nearly 900,000 piculs were exported annually with Japan taking 80 per cent of the trade. The short cotton staple, averaging one half inch in length, white, stiff, and thick, was exported because it was not suitable for fine spinning. The Tientsin textile industry imported a longer staple cotton, principally from America, which was combined with finer grade cotton from Hopei for spinning. In Tsingtao one third of the cotton supplied was imported before 1927, and the province did not become self-sufficient in cotton until after 1930.[53] During the 1930s Shantung exported about 20 per cent of its harvested cotton. Demand conditions in both terminal markets were highly competitive with local mills, native exporters, and foreign buyers bidding against one another. In Tientsin there were 55 export firms of which the seven largest handled only three fifths of the amount exported.[54] Cotton prices in Hopei were strongly influenced by export demand, whereas in Shantung prices were mainly determined by the demand of

Table 53. Comparisons of cotton prices at supply and final distribution and estimates of market costs for Hopei and Shantung.

Supply and distribution centers	Yuan/picul	Per cent
Hopei		
Shih chia chuang to Tientsin, 1927[a]		
Supply price at source	35.000	80.5
Marketing costs	9.617	22.1
Profit	−1.139	−2.6
Tientsin selling price	43.478	100.0
Hantan to Tientsin, 1927		
Supply price at source	34.000	78.2
Marketing costs	7.960	18.3
Profit	1.518	3.5
Tientsin selling price	43.478	100.0
Shu-lu to Tientsin, 1927		
Supply price at source	36.000	82.8
Marketing costs	7.397	17.0
Profit	0.081	0.2
Tientsin selling price	43.478	100.0
Ankuo to Tientsin, 1927		
Supply price at source	34.000	78.1
Marketing costs	7.370	17.1
Profit	2.108	4.8
Tientsin selling price	43.478	100.0
Nankung to Tientsin, 1926		
Supply price at source	34.000	78.2
Marketing costs	8.311	19.1
Profit	1.167	2.7
Tientsin selling price	43.478	100.0
Shantung		
Pin to Tsingtao, 1930s		
Supply price at source	40.00	88.8
Marketing costs	4.55	10.1
Profit	0.48	1.1
Tsingtao selling price	45.03	100.0
Lin-ch'ing to Chinan, 1930s		
Supply price at source	42.00	89.74
Marketing costs	4.30	9.20
Profit	0.50	1.06
Tsingtao selling price	46.80	100.00

Sources: For Hopei, T. S. Chu and T. Chin, *Marketing of Cotton in Hopei Province*, pp. 34, 37, 38, 39. For Shantung, Wu Chih-i, "Shan-tung sheng mien-hua chih sheng-ch'an yü yün-hsiao" (Production and circulation of cotton in Shantung province), *Cheng-chih ching-chi hsüeh-pao*, 5.1:65, 66 (October 1936).

[a] The year 1927 produced high cotton shipping costs because of civil war; therefore cotton was shipped by boat instead of rail and profit was negative.

Tsingtao's weaving mills. There is little evidence that prices in terminal markets were determined by price agreements set between a small number of exporting and weaving firms.

Table 53 shows that merchants in terminal markets did not absorb the lion's share of the trade's profits and had little market power to influence price and output. In Hopei the difference between primary and terminal market price, or market costs, accounted for roughly one fifth of the final sale price.[55] In Shantung market costs were only one tenth of the final sale price. In Hopei transport costs, brokers' fees, and taxes made up three fifths to four fifths of total marketing costs; in Shantung marketing costs were lower but taxes, middlemen's fees, and shipping costs remained the outstanding cost items. Profits were lower for merchants in Shantung than in Hopei. High marketing costs meant that brokers and middlemen absorbed a large share of the trade's profits. Yet these middlemen were vital to the trade because the absence of standardized market procedures and weights and measures made it necessary for merchant groups with specialized knowledge to operate in these primary markets and provide the connections with the secondary and terminal markets.

The demand for cotton in Tientsin was inelastic,[56] and similar demand conditions probably held for Tsingtao. As demand for cotton increased and prices rose over the long run, unusually large profits accrued in the trade, but easy entry and highly competitive market conditions often reduced profit margins for enterprises. This prevented a few firms from becoming powerful and dominating the market. A decline in export demand and a slump in textile manufacturing in the early 1930s sent prices tumbling and merchants suffered huge losses. The large number of bankruptcies in the trade stemmed not only from a high competitive market but also from large price swings caused by inelastic demand and supply conditions. Had quasi-monopoly conditions prevailed, more merchant firms would have been able to cover their loss. After accumulating profits again, some might have been induced to improve marketing methods, but this was not the case.

The introduction of the American cottonseed and the promotion of higher quality cotton did not come from merchants but was introduced by a few experimental stations. Foreign buyers perennially complained of the high moisture content of Chinese cotton caused by adulteration in various markets.[57] A merchant or broker could not be dissuaded from adulterating his cotton because he knew others would continue the same practice even if he desisted. During the 1920s the cotton-spinning associations tried to eliminate this practice but without success. Merchants did not have associations to promote such improvements.

Wheat. Wheat occupied about one third of the cultivated area of Hopei in the 1930s, but the province was occasionally short of wheat and had to import it from Shansi and Honan. A good harvest enabled Hopei to export between 10,000 and 200,000 piculs.[58] In Shantung wheat was only grown in the north central counties near the railroad and in the west.[59] Wheat was an important food staple for the urban population, and millet and sorghum were consumed by the peasants.

Wheat was first collected in market towns and then shipped to the secondary markets of Shihmen, Paoting, and Chinan. For example Chining county seat, south of Chinan, collected grain from surrounding counties and its 51 markets. The county seat market serviced villages within a radius of about 15 miles, and the remaining market towns serviced villages within a defined radius. Chining annually exported 48,000 tons of wheat as well as large quantities of sorghum and millet to Chinan.[60] Before railroads were built, grain was shipped to northern Kiangsu by the Grand Canal, but after the Tientsin-Pukow line was constructed about 95 per cent of all marketed grain flowed northward to Chinan.[61] After 1938, war disrupted railway traffic, and the Grand Canal was again used to transport wheat.

In the secondary markets banks financed grain merchants, who employed brokers to purchase wheat in grain-growing districts or from other provinces. Like the cotton staple market, the grain market was a highly competitive market consisting of many sellers and buyers. In the late 1930s, Paoting, with a population of 280,000, had to obtain much of its grain from Honan and Shansi. There were eighteen merchant houses in the city, which sent brokers to these provinces to buy grain and arrange shipment to Paoting.[62] These houses sold their grain to flour mills, shops, breweries, buyers from Tientsin and Peking, and brokers representing grain dealers in areas where cotton was produced.[63] In Shihmen, another large grain exchange and consumption center, population had risen from 63,000 to 167,000 between 1936 and 1940. In 1940, about 40 per cent of the city's grain came from Honan and 60 per cent from Shansi.[64] Merchant wholesalers called *huo-chan* sold a third of their grain to city dealers, and the remaining two thirds was shipped to Paoting, Peking, and Ch'angte. The city had 76 merchant firms importing and selling grain in that year.[65]

In 1941, there were 246 grain storehouses in Chinan serving middlemen and arranging grain shipments between county and city merchants. Most of these firms operated with a working capital of between 2,000 to 30,000 yuan and the five largest firms had capital of over 50,000 yuan.[66] The average firm's staff consisted of only six to ten persons. When they purchased grain, they bid according to their expected costs and sales to other buyers. One third of the required working capital was supplied by the firm and the remainder by deposits by merchants and banks.[67] A wealthy merchant or native bank deposited a certain sum of money with the grain wholesale firm for safekeeping and collected interest. The firm used this deposit as working capital to finance grain transactions. A high turnover of grain had to be maintained in order that cash be available to pay interest on creditors' deposits and meet depositor withdrawals. Risk was great, but if prices were accurately predicted and sufficiently large amounts of grain were bought cheaply and sold at higher prices, profits were large. The grain trade became very profitable after 1938 when food prices continued to rise, and many new firms were encouraged to enter the market. From earned profits firms paid interest on deposits. Depositors usually invested their funds with two or three grain wholesalers rather than with any single firm in order to minimize risk and ensure quick withdrawal.[68]

In the terminal market of Tientsin, large wholesale firms, originally established in the foreign concession areas, traded in grain. Prior to 1931, these firms were too small and weak to influence market price, and they possessed little working capital of their own.[69] When grain prices fell in 1931 many merged to prevent bankruptcy and after 1937, they began to make large profits as grain prices rose. Some achieved sufficient size to diversify their businesses and handle other agricultural goods when grain imports declined, but necessity rather than their economic power forced them into this new line. A large group of Tientsin wholesalers called *mi-chuang* handled rice and flour imports and arranged distribution of these goods throughout the city and its environs.[70] Another middleman group, the *tou-tien* or brokerage firm, brought buyer and seller together to arrange transactions.[71] These firms originated in the early nineteenth century, and possibly earlier, but after 1911 many merged to form associations in which each firm paid fees, and the association paid taxes on behalf of their membership. The *tou-tien* measured grain, advanced credit, arranged sales, provided storage services, reserved quarters for traders, and handled shipments for wholesalers, exporters, merchants, and various manufacturing firms producing oil and liquor. After 1938, the *tou-tien* made huge profits when prices rocketed. Many outsiders were attracted into this trade, and the number of firms in this segment of the grain market greatly increased.

Peking in the 1930s, with over 1.5 million people, required a tremendous quantity of grain and flour each day. More than 2 million quintals of grain were imported annually and distributed through the city's seven large markets where brokers and merchants arranged and managed grain transactions.[72] Rice and flour arrived from Tientsin, and wheat was imported from surrounding counties and Shihmen. Many merchants complained of the extreme price fluctuation in the city's grain markets, which seems to have been due to the inability of grain dealers to hold large inventories to cushion price. Storage facilities had simply not kept pace with the great increase in population after 1900. Another complaint was the low quality of north China wheat, which compelled many dealers to import their wheat from Shanghai and abroad.[73]

Because entry into the grain trade was easy, the influx of middlemen at different stages of marketing kept profit margins low. Yet inefficient handling and a large number of unnecessary transactions moving grain from primary to terminal markets also kept market costs high. For example, grain shipped from Ta-ming county in southern Hopei to Tientsin was priced at 8.48 yuan at the primary market, which amounted to 77 per cent of the Tientsin selling price (11.00 yuan).[74] Marketing costs came to 2.02 yuan or 18.33 per cent of the sale price. The Tientsin merchant purchasing grain from Ta-ming made only 0.40 yuan or 4.58 per cent of the final price. Taxes and brokers' fees accounted for another 3 and 2 per cent respectively of the sale price and constituted the largest items of market cost. Merchants in the terminal markets had to rely on different middlemen in the primary market, because they understood the different weights and measures used and were more familiar with local conditions. Merchants found it difficult to accumulate large profits in this highly competitive market structure.

Peanuts. Peanuts grew well in the moist climate and sandy soils of Shantung, and this province supplied about one third of China's peanut exports. About three million mow was devoted to this crop's cultivation in the northern counties of Yung-ch'eng, P'ing-tu, Wen-teng, Chu-ch'eng, and Chi-mei.[75] In Yung-ch'eng alone nearly one quarter of the land was used for peanut cultivation.[76] Peasants brought their crop to markets and sold it to brokers and representatives of exporters in the ports of Weihaiwei, Shihtaoerh, and Tsingtao. Export demand determined the peanut price at the secondary market, because middlemen were only able to buy within a fixed range as set by export price, their costs, and expected profits. Within local markets peanut prices were competitively determined by the haggling of many buyers and sellers. Peasants were hard hit if the peanut price fell, because the hilly land and poor soil limited the crops that could be substituted for the peanuts. Brokers were in similar straits too, because their livelihood depended entirely on the trade.

Once collected in secondary markets, peanuts were shipped to terminal markets, processed into oil and other derivatives and eventually exported. About 45 per cent of the final product was shipped to other provinces, 44 per cent was exported, and the remainder consumed within Shantung. Not only did foreign demand greatly determine prices, but the trade depended to a large extent upon numerous brokers with their knowledge of local market conditions in the primary markets.[77] Their services were indispensable, but their large number increased marketing costs and reduced profit margins for all concerned.

After 1911, the cultivation and export of peanuts advanced rapidly until 1931 when foreign demand slackened and exports declined. Production and export revived after 1933, and by 1936 the trade again flourished. About three fourths of the market cost of shipping peanuts from primary to terminal market accounted for export duty, customs surtax, and general excise tax. The trade was excessively taxed, and some in Shantung feared that "owing to this heavy burden of taxation on peanut oil exports in Tsingtao" [78] the trade would pass to Indian and African suppliers just as the tea and silk trade had been lost to Japan in the late nineteenth century.

Cotton Yarn and Cloth. In the 1880s and after, native spinning declined and hand weaving developed on a large scale because of the import and distribution of Western manufactured yarn throughout north China. Some areas began to specialize entirely in weaving and export of native cloth. Weavers mixed Western yarn with native yarn and produced a durable, cheap cloth which found a ready market in both city and village. Western piece goods circulated but were purchased mainly by the wealthy. When native textile mills gained a firm footing in Tientsin and Tsingtao after 1920, they produced and sold yarn to various handicraft weaving centers located in Hopei and Shantung.

Different merchants specialized in the import of manfactured yarn, the purchase of Western cloth, and the export of native cloth. Vertical and horizontal integration did not characterize merchant groups involved in these separate activities. In Lin-ch'ing county of Shantung one merchant group, called *pu-tien,* imported yarn from Tientsin and Chinan and distributed it to weavers. Another group, called *pu-t'an,* imported Western piece goods and sold directly to the wealthy in the county seat. The last group, the *pu-fan* merchants, purchased native cloth from village weavers and exported it to other markets in Shantung and outside the province.[79]

In Pao-chih county of northern Hopei similar functions were separately performed by different merchant groups. One merchant group purchased yarn from Tientsin spinning mills and sold to cloth merchants, who distributed it to weavers. These same cloth merchants later purchased the finished cloth and exported it to other counties.[80] The same compartmentalization can be observed in marketing functions in Kao-yang county of Hopei and Wei county of Shantung. The market structure for yarn and cloth consisted of separate markets with numerous suppliers and sellers, and on the supply side, different merchants providing different services in what appears to have been the same distribution system.

Traditional guilds lingered on, and in some areas they exerted considerable control over commodity price. In Ting county Gamble reports that cotton cloth was gathered in six markets and passed through 45 merchants belonging to a guild. The guild rigidly fixed the export price of cotton cloth and refused to adjust it even when demand greatly declined. Between 1892 and 1915 cloth exports rose steadily, but between 1915 and 1921 cloth exports declined from 4 million to 950,000 pieces, a fall of 75 per cent.[81] In these same six years the guild increased price several times hoping to recoup the earnings lost through declining demand. Whether guilds operated in a similar way in other rural markets is not exactly clear. There were some market conditions where merchants collaborated to fix prices, but in the principal staple trades such monopoly power did not exist.

16. Bureaucrat and Peasant

Three important studies of local government political control have been recently published, and they clarify and explain better than any previous works on this subject the complex relationships between the peasantry and officialdom in nineteenth-century China.[1] The authors, Hsiao Kung-ch'uan, Chang Chung-li, and Ch'u T'ung-tsu, have drawn on a wide range of official and privately written sources to present a convincing case that long-run stability of the social order can be attributed to the existence and operation of a complex bureaucratic local administration made up of trained officials and a scholar class.

These studies are a point of time description, however, rather than a genetic treatment showing how this structure changed during the Ch'ing period. Hsiao Kung-ch'uan comes closest of the three to a historical analysis of the key control devices which the Ch'ing rulers took over from their Ming predecessors and modified to suit their own purposes. What is still missing is an examination of how these organizations were transformed. To what extent did they flourish, atrophy or disappear from the rural landscape? The answer may never be known because of the scarcity of information about village economic and social life.

To answer this question for the twentieth century is less difficult because some information is available, and the purpose of this chapter is to apply it for our region. Before doing so, several points should be made.

The first concerns the residence and activities of the scholar or gentry class. Rarely, if at all, could they be found in the villages of the early twentieth century. Scholars and their families "tended to move to the administrative centers" [2] and assisted officials by providing services to the administrative unit with which they were affiliated. Hsiao claims that "socially, the inhabitants of a village often fell into two major groups, *shen* and *min* (or gentry and common people)," [3] but from the surveys of Sidney Gamble and the Mentetsu researchers, there is no evidence that the gentry resided in villages or played any role in village affairs.[4] This is not to say that early in the Ch'ing period conditions were the same.

The second point concerns the argument of this chapter. Our main intent is to show that after 1900 local government exerted new pressures on villages to pay taxes and ordered that new village organizations be created. Local government definitely attempted to establish closer ties with villages. These efforts were only partially successful. Local government officials continued to rely on the traditional system of collecting taxes and maintaining order. This system was fragile, subject to gross tax evasion, and failed to provide protection and security for the large rural population. However, new village organizations were formed and greater tax revenue was collected by officials. Because of the steady rise in farm prices, this did not necessarily mean a greater tax burden for the peasantry. Civil war and the Japanese invasion prevented officials from using these funds for local development purposes.

Village Leadership and Organizations

Each village was governed by a council of half a dozen or more peasants, who selected a headman and his assistant from among their numbers. Although after 1920 peasants were instructed to elect their headman by yearly ballot, in practice the same narrow selection method persisted. Members of the village council were chosen on the basis of the socioeconomic ranking of their family or clan in the village, and changes in village council membership over a period reflected changing clan or family fortunes within the village. Hatada Takashi has emphasized this point by tracing membership of the Li family in the Sha-ching village council.[5] The former council member Li Chen-tsung owned 200 mow of land in the nineteenth century; he divided it among his three sons, who, in turn, divided it among their sons. By the 1930s the grandsons of Li owned little land and none sat on the village council. Gamble shows a similar situation of revolving elites characterizing village councils. In a village near Peking between 1837 and 1932, "Thirty-seven men, from 21 families, had been association heads during this period. No single family had been represented during the entire time." [6]

Headmen were selected on a rotation basis in Shansi but served indefinitely in Hopei and Shantung until illness or dissatisfaction with their responsibilities forced retirement. Whether village leadership lay with the headman or council is not clear, as the headman was required to consult council members on all important decisions. The headman was typically selected for his wealth, education, and abilities. Education was essential in those districts where the county magistrate insisted that headmen record village land transactions. After 1920, administrative ability also became an important criteria because the headman's duties multiplied when the *t'an-k'uan* levy increased.[7]

In villages which had developed elaborate means of water control, household organizations for the rationing and use of water were quite separate from the authority vested in the village council and local government,[8] contrary to the belief that water control organizations greatly determined the character of village administration. North China villages were irrigated by wells, river water, and meagre rainfall. Some wells were communally owned, but where village wells were privately owned, nearby households were permitted to use them. It was only in villages located near rivers that peasants built sluices and flood gates and appointed peasants, called *ho-lao* or *ho-t'ou,* to guard and control the irrigation system. Households using the same sluice formed a group called a *cha,* and the *cha* selected the *ho-lao* to patrol and maintain the sluice, although additional labor was recruited from each household to dredge the sluice or repair flood damage.[9]

In theory the *ho-lao* was selected by the *cha* households each year, but in actual practice he retained the post for many years, and in some villages the job was hereditary.[10] Within the *cha,* schedules were fixed by which each household received certain quantities of water at prescribed times. Sometimes a village council member served as *ho-lao,* but this appointment had no bearing on village administration.[11] A peasant with the ability to organize others for cooperative work and devise schedules to share water without disputes was a natural selection for the *ho-lao* position. If he could arbitrate between feuding households, other households regarded him as a born leader and organizer. It was this kind of peasant, experienced and respected by the *cha* group, who managed the storage and distribution of water for the village.

Many of the large irrigation works providing water to the clusters of villages in Hsing-t'ai county and others like it had been built during the middle of the Ming period. By the mid-eighteenth century, local officials had already successfully mobilized villages to repair, improve, and even enlarge this system,[12] but officials usually only interfered in the management of the irrigation system when disputes broke out between villages, and the headmen were unable to achieve a peaceful settlement.[13] The successful operation of water control depended on the cooperation of households within each *cha,* not on any guidance offered by village leadership. Households recognized the necessity to share water equitably and, as in any cooperative venture, those with judgment and experience became leaders.

The first significant organizational change in villages after 1880 was the establishment of the crop-watching associations. What spurred the peasants to organize a formal association to guard a fixed area of land were increased taxes levied by the county administration and increased village expenditures for schools, night patrol, village militia, and the *pao-chia* system. Village councils decided to fix the area of village land that could be assessed to raise the necessary funds villages needed for taxes and other expenditures. The example of Sha-ching is described by Hatada: "We may regard the establishment of fixed boundaries for collecting taxes in Sha-ching as a necessary step for the villagers to ensure the village had a source of revenue. When finding a source of revenue became a real problem for the villagers because village expenditures had increased and revenue had to be found, villagers became more deeply concerned about the precise area for collecting taxes. The rise in village expenditures was the fundamental reason for fixing the village boundaries so that taxes could be collected. This rapid increase in village expenditures took place in villages throughout Shun-i county in the late Ch'ing and early Republican period. This increase was not only due to the new tasks which villages began to undertake but was directly related to the great demand for tax revenue by the government. Crop-watching associations were organized in villages because the government tried to collect more taxes." [14]

Villages recognized that having a formal association to guard a village perimeter made it possible for the council to assess all households owning land within this zone. Land was assessed by the association, but this method of raising funds quickly became the prime means for paying the village *t'an-k'uan* and maintaining the village temple, supporting the village school, and any other activity requiring financing.[15] By keeping a careful watch over the standing crops before the harvest, pilfering was prevented, and villagers retained more from the harvest to pay their assessments.[16]

The council assessed land according to village needs and the level of village economic welfare. In Wu-tien and Sha-ching villages a large percentage of households sent adults to work outside the village during the winter months, and peasants owned little land because population increase and land fragmentation had advanced to a serious stage. As time passed, more peasants found they could not support their families by farming alone. The village crop-watching associations assessed any peasant farming land irrespective of whether he rented or owned land, because landowners were already very poor and constituted a declining percentage of the village.[17] The tax burden had to be equitably distributed among all who used the land rather than penalizing only the landowners. In Ssu pei ch'ai and Ling shui kou villages where economic conditions were better and the peasants grew cash crops and received income from handicraft, the crop-watching associations only assessed landowners.[18]

That population and fiscal pressure on villages was less rather than more intense before 1900 may be seen from the existence of several customs which were widely practiced when village crop watching was still conducted privately. The very existence of these customs indicates that village leaders had not found it necessary to protect village resources. For example, villagers were permitted to gather sorghum leaves for brief intervals before the harvests, and peasants wandered from one village to another and took advantage of this opportunity. Arthur Smith reports that this custom was quite prevalent in the 1890s, and it gave the poorer peasants a chance to share the wealth of those who owned more land.[19] Hatada argues that this practice enabled wealthy peasants to hire fewer crop watchers than would otherwise have been necessary.[20] Villagers also allowed outsiders to collect grain stubble from surrounding land during the winter and graze their animals on the open fields.[21] Villagers only became jealous of outsiders encroaching on their land when they had to pay the village *t'an-k'uan*. After 1910 the peasants made a more concerted effort to identify and designate what land belonged to their village.

When warlord armies formed and conflicts broke out in north China after 1911, villages around the large metropolitan areas where troops were stationed formed night patrols and militia to ward off punitive attacks. By 1930 peace was restored, and many of these organizations were abandoned. Provincial authorities then decreed that schools be established in villages, sanitation measures be adopted, villages be merged to form new administrative units, and local development projects commence.[22] Few, if any of these measures, were successfully carried out. After 1937 counties under Japanese puppet government control reinstated the *pao-chia* system and revived the organizations of night patrols and militia. These organizational changes followed closely upon the vigorous efforts of officials to collect the *t'an-k'uan*.

At the risk of distorting the events of this period, I have constructed an index in Table 54 to indicate when new village organizations were created after 1880. The data was obtained from the field studies of Gamble and Mantetsu researchers. The tabulation is rough, and my periodization is only approximate. We must not forget that considerable unevenness of official control characterized the countryside. Around the large metropolitan areas local officials had more power over villages, but in remote districts their authority was weak, and because villages could avoid complying to administrative orders, village organizations emerged only after a considerable time lag. I have tried to show when these organizations were created by noting when the majority of sample villages established an organization.

Table 54. Village organizational changes in sixteen north China villages.

Type of organization	1880–1890	1890–1912	1912–1928	1928–1937	1937–1942
Village defense	0	0	+	0	++
Crop watching and night guard	–	0+	++	++	++
Granary	+	+	+	0	0
Village political organization (*pao-chia*, etc.)	0+	0+	0+	++	++
Village schools	0	+	++	++	++
Village labor corvee	0	0	0	+	++
Village military and extraordinary tax collecting organizational change (*t'an-k'uan*)	0	0+	++	++	++
Village temple management	0	0+	+	++	++

Source: Data for six villages in the CN, vols. 1–5; data for 10 villages from Sidney D. Gamble, *North China Villages* (Berkeley and Los Angeles, 1963), pp. 144–303.

Legend: ++ = organization firmly implanted in village; + = organization just emerging; 0 = organization is non-existent; 0+ = organization in partial existence.

Bureaucrat and Peasant

Beginning around 1890 and shortly thereafter, government pressure to pay more taxes appears to correspond with the formation of new village organizations. After 1911 when unified political control in north China collapsed and warlords ascended to power, demands on the peasantry to pay higher taxes become more intense. After 1928, provincial officials ordered county officials to merge villages and extended their control into the village. This control also produced an organizational response, seen after 1937 when village leaders found that the revival of the *pao-chia* system gave them greater control over village affairs than at any time in the recent past.

Local Government Fiscal Behavior

In the early Ch'ing period government fiscal policy operated on the premise that if agriculture developed, greater tax revenue would be collected for supporting the military and strengthening the state. Land was reclaimed and new settlements were encouraged by tax relief and public spending to restore order and rehabilitate the economy. Farm output slowly increased, cities grew, and population expanded. Land tax and poll tax were combined, and in 1712 the government announced it would not increase the tax quotas in proportion to any subsequent increase in the population but would take the figures reported in 1711 as the basis for permanent quotas.[23] For the next century government obtained the tax revenue it needed, and the economy prospered and grew.

By the early nineteenth century, government administration had become more expensive because prices had risen and personnel and duties had increased manyfold. Revenue still covered expenditures if famine and rebellion did not occur, but when the empire was rocked with internal revolt as in the mid-nineteenth century, the government was forced to spend heavily to smash the insurgents, but at the same time it was deprived of considerable tax revenue in the areas captured by rebels. By the late nineteenth century, the government was forced to spend more to repay foreign loans and to finance specific projects for modernization. Thereafter, it was continually short of tax revenue and seemed incapable of relying on the same methods to increase revenue, which had worked so well in the early Ch'ing period.

After 1900 government attempts to increase tax revenue are characterized by squeezing more taxes from any existing economic organization or activity irrespective of its importance in the economy. Between 1911 and 1928, most tax revenue was collected to finance warlord armies and the administrative machines collecting these taxes. After 1928 the Kuomintang made vigorous efforts to collect more tax revenue for promoting education, improving transport, and assisting industry, but considerable revenue still had to be used to support the large bureaucracy which had grown up over this period. After 1938, the local puppet governments controlled by the Japanese military collected taxes mainly for maintaining peace and security, keeping transport open, and constructing an intricate defense system of trenches and blockhouses around railway junctions and along railway tracks.

Tax revenue was increased by raising the land tax, introducing levies on commercial associations and villages, increasing taxes on land transfers and mortgage deeds, and elevating excise taxes as well as adding new taxes.

Between 1911 and 1930 violence erupted in province after province, and by the late 1920s conflict was raging in fourteen provinces of the country.[24] Counties in Hopei and Shantung receiving the direct brunt of this violence had to pay higher land taxes. Between 1912 and 1931 the land tax on dry field land in 116 counties of Hopei rose 40 per cent, and in 96 counties of Shantung it increased 60 per cent.[25] Amano Motonosuke has estimated that in Shantung the average land tax per mow of land rose from an index base of 100 in 1902 to 268 in 1925 and to 468 in 1927.[26] On irrigated land in Hopei the land tax made up 1.19 per cent of the land value in 1912 and rose to 1.37 of the land value in 1936. In Shantung the ratio of land tax to value of land per mow rose from 1.79 per cent to 2.26 per cent between 1912 and 1936.[27]

Increasing the land tax in some counties was done simply by raising the original land tax schedules. For example, in Ting county, the basic rate was doubled in 1914.[28] The usual practice was to levy a surcharge on the old land tax rate and collect this separately at another time. Surcharges were gradually increased, but during the 1920s very large increases took place. In Chi-tung county of Shantung the land tax in 1930 was only 2.20 yuan per mow, but the surcharge collected was 16.21 yuan or eight times higher.[29] In Ch'ing-hai county of Hopei the land tax surcharge was increased 140 per cent between 1921 and 1931, and in 1934 it was 180 per cent higher than the 1921 level.[30]

The periodic levy or *t'an-k'uan* has been used frequently in Chinese history, and the government relied upon it heavily during the Taiping rebellion and after the first Sino-Japanese war. In the latter case each province was ordered to pay an extra lump sum in addition to normal taxes to pay for the war. Each province collected this amount by apportioning it to counties, which in turn apportioned a share to each village.[31] This became a standard practice for raising additional revenue to cover unexpected expenditures which could not be met from current tax revenue. Warlord armies in the 1920s adopted this method and called it *ping-ch'ai*. They levied fixed amounts on villages but usually bypassed merchants.[32] Between 1929 and 1931, 130 counties in Hopei and 77 in Shantung supplied armies with this levy. In addition to sums of cash, villages were also ordered to give carts, animals, and peasant labor.[33] In some counties the amount of cash collected by this method accounted for 50 to 80 per cent of the land tax collected.

These levies continued to be collected in the early 1930s, and in some cases their share of county revenue amounted to nearly 50 per cent of total revenue.[34]

There was also a great increase in tax revenue collected from land transfers and mortgage deeds after 1912. In Ting county these taxes yielded 13,907 yuan in 1916, but in 1934 nearly 22,000 yuan was collected.[35] New excise taxes on commodities exchanged in marketplaces were introduced and gradually increased. In Ch'ing-hai county the tax on slaughtering animals was introduced in 1915 and surcharges on that rate were levied in subsequent years. These taxes and surcharges levied on the volume of goods handled by brokers yielded 3,725 yuan in 1925 but by 1933 nearly 16,000 yuan was being collected.[36] In 1915 Ting county collected surcharges of a similar type amounting to 6,222 yuan but in 1934 this amount was increased to 28,151 yuan.[37] Brokers dealing in hemp, cotton, livestock, cloth, fuel, fruit, and vegetables were ordered to pay increased fees as a percentage of the value of goods sold. Brokers easily passed this tax on to their buyers by simply raising their prices, and ultimately the consumer bore the brunt of this commodity turnover tax.[38] Because these excise taxes were levied on raw materials marketed by peasants, the bulk of this tax burden must have fallen upon the urban consumer who purchased these commodities in either raw or finished form.

At the provincial level the administration collected a great deal of revenue from government property, state-managed enterprises such as salt, tobacco, and the maritime customs house.[39] The provincial tax office was greatly dependent upon the sums forwarded to it by the county tax offices. Such fiscal decentralization had always characterized Chinese financial administration and had hindered counties from spending on projects to improve the infrastructure and local industries.

The Tax Burden on the Peasantry

Whether the increase in various taxes meant a real rise in tax burden on the peasantry is a very difficult question to answer. Even if income data were available, it would not be easy to estimate tax burden for different groups of peasant households without making certain assumptions about the amount of cultivated land taxed and the amount of income derived from farming. If excise taxes levied in market towns are excluded and if only the land tax, surtax, and *t'an-k'uan* are considered as the major tax burden on peasants, an attempt may be made to measure whether or not the tax burden increased. It should be clear from the previous description of village taxation that households were taxed on the basis of the amount of land they owned or farmed. It can safely be assumed that village taxes were proportionately allocated to households according to their land or farm income. This does not necessarily mean that the village tax burden was actually equalized between households. Households earning a larger percentage of nonfarm income paid less tax than households depending upon farm income, irrespective of the size of farm they owned and managed. It is impossible to measure tax burden in any meaningful way for different categories of households by farm size without making assumptions about the share of income each derived from farming and nonfarming.

For our purposes we will consider the tax burden on the village. Tax burden will be estimated by calculating village income and taxes over a thirty-five-year period, from 1910 to 1945. This method cannot take into account the variations of village income and tax depending upon village location and wealth that existed naturally. I have chosen two types of village development, which should represent a large portion of the countryside, and the deviations should be regarded as minimal. Even this approach does not make an estimation of village income and tax easy because certain assumptions must be made with respect to the amount of change in prices and taxes. The estimates I use are based upon field survey evidence and have some basis for truth.

The two hypothetical cases presented in Table 55 are not actual examples of villages but should be regarded as rough approximations of what took place at the upper and lower limits of the widely varying village conditions. I have assumed the land tax, surtax, and *t'an-k'uan* per mow to be the same for both villages. Tax data for 1910 to 1932 were obtained from Buck's surveys, and the tax data for the remaining period were estimated on assumption of a constant land tax and surtax and an increase in the village levy according to amounts recorded in the village studies of Part Two.

In village *A* I assume there is no change in cultivated land and that the peasants successfully evaded paying tax on 20 per cent of their land. I have also assumed that village population increased about 0.9 per cent per annum. I calculated income per mow on the basis of household income, the average size of farm, and various assumed rates of price rise. I assumed a modest rise in price of 2 per cent per annum between 1910 and 1931, price decline between 1931 and 1934 of about 20 per cent, recovery to 1930 price level by 1937, and rapid inflation thereafter. Village income measured in terms of income per mow rose 32 per cent between 1912 and 1930 because of rising farm prices and modest productivity increase, declined between 1930 and 1932 because of price deflation, and rose to the 1930 level in 1937 because of general economic recovery. Income per mow rose rapidly thereafter because of inflation.

Nonfarm income rose more rapidly because as the average size of farm declined more peasants worked outside the village. Village tax burden did not really rise until the 1925–1930 period, which was one of civil war and general breakdown in supply and distribution. The village tax burden fell in the early 1930s because village levies were reduced greatly but by 1937 they had risen again because local authorities were demanding more tax

Table 55. Estimate of tax burden for two hypothetical villages, 1910–1941 (in Chinese silver dollars).

	Tax per mow				Village tax	
Year	(1) Land tax	(2) Surtax	(3) Levy	Total tax	(4) Village A	(5) Village B
1910	0.80	0	0	0.80	640.00	640.00
1920	0.68	0.08	0.10	0.86	688.00	688.00
1925	0.65	0.14	0.30	1.09	872.00	872.00
1930	0.91	0.55	0.10	1.56	1,284.00	1,284.00
1932	0.93	0.75	0.10	1.78	1,424.00	1,424.00
1937	0.93	0.75	0.12	1.80	1,440.00	1,440.00
1941	0.93	0.75	0.60	2.28	1,824.00	1,824.00
1945	0.93	0.75	0.90	2.58	2,064.00	2,064.00

Income and Tax Burden in Village A

	Number of house-holds	Income per mow	Culti-vable area (mow)	Tax-able land (mow)	Farm income	Non-farm income	Total income	Village tax burden (per cent)
1910	100	8.8	1,000	800	8,800	2,200	11,000	5.8
1920	110	9.8	1,000	800	9,800	3,345	13,245	5.9
1925	115	10.5	1,000	800	10,500	4,975	15,475	6.0
1930	120	11.6	1,000	800	11,600	5,290	16,890	8.0
1932	122	9.7	1,000	800	9,700	7,186	16,886	7.3
1937	128	11.9	1,000	800	11,900	7,420	19,320	7.0
1941	130	13.5	1,000	800	13,500	9,320	22,820	9.9
1945	130	17.0	1,000	800	17,000	10,300	27,300	9.0

Income and Tax Burden in Village B

1910	100	8.8	1,000	800	8,800	2,200	11,000	5.8
1920	110	10.1	1,050	800	10,605	2,640	13,245	5.9
1925	115	11.6	1,075	800	12,470	3,005	15,475	6.0
1930	120	12.3	1,100	800	13,530	3,360	16,890	6.0
1932	122	10.8	1,150	800	13,470	3,416	16,886	7.3
1937	128	12.9	1,200	800	15,480	3,840	19,320	7.0
1941	130	14.5	1,200	800	17,400	4,420	22,820	9.9
1945	130	18.2	1,200	800	21,840	5,460	27,300	9.0

Sources:

(1) Buck, *Land Utilization in China*, p. 324.
(2) *Ibid.*, p. 324.
(3) Estimated on basis of levy increase in villages discussed in Part Two.
(4) Derived from survey data on average farm annual income in T'u-ti wei-yuan hui, p. 43.
(5) This tax burden corresponds roughly with that on households from village surveys conducted by Japanese in Feng-fun county. See Mantetsu chōsa bu, *Kita Shina no nōgyō to keizai*, I, 710.

funds for development projects. During the first few years of the war the tax burden rose slightly. The reasons for this were an increased *t'an-k'uan* and a decline in output caused by the disruption of local markets, loss of livestock, tools, and labor, and transport stoppages. As inflation continued and villages adjusted to production under wartime conditions, the village tax burden probably remained unchanged.

The increase in tax burden was greater or less for villages depending upon how rapidly household and village income had risen. I assumed a 50 per cent rise in household money income between 1910 and 1937, which seems to be a reasonable assumption based upon the changes that occurred in villages over this time. In 1937 the average household paid roughly 7 per cent of its money income for tax. Table 55 shows that the increase in tax burden was small, but for households having difficulty in saving from one year to the next, an increase of even 1 per cent meant foregoing some commodities.

In village *B* I have assumed the same increase in rural population as in village *A*. But in village *B* I have permitted the amount of cultivated land to increase 20 per cent so that income per mow increased more rapidly than in village *A*. However, nonfarm income did not increase as rapidly as in village *A*. The tax burden is the same in both villages. I have simply assumed two cases where village income increased the same amount but in different ways.

The approach is artificial and abstract. Its main defects are having to estimate magnitudes of price, income and tax change and a tax burden increase which may have been greater than I have shown. I see no way around these difficulties. On the basis of field research evidence I have tried to construct several probable cases of tax burden measurement and to show that the burden only increased when the production and distribution systems were disrupted.

The County Fiscal Structure

The local finance office of each county had a tax collection bureau staffed with personnel who were not paid a fixed salary to record land transfers and the amount of land tax and surcharges collected. Their job was made more complicated if the land was classified according to many grades with different tax rates. A county was divided into zones for tax-collecting purposes. Each zone had an agency called the *liang-fang*, where peasants paid their land tax. In Luan-ch'eng county there were seventeen such districts, two in Li-ch'eng and four in Shun-i.[40] Peasants paid their land tax three times a year. The land tax varied greatly from county to county and bore little relationship to the value and productivity of the land.[41]

Each county used semi-officials called *she-shu* or *li-shu* to record changes in land ownership and the amount of taxable land. Their records became the source materials which the county used to collect taxes and introduce surcharges on the land tax. In some counties the *she-shu* calculated the expected tax receipts and prepared records showing the area of taxable land and the amount of tax.[42] They received no salary. Villages usually assessed their households a certain amount to pay the *she-shu* each year, which we may regard euphemistically as "thank-you money." The *she-shu* calculated the district's taxes on the basis of the area of taxable land in their records. A *she-shu* visited villages to learn from the headmen what changes had occurred in land ownership, but this was not the standard practice for every county. The *she-shu* had to be able to read and write. He typically obtained the position from a parent, but it could also be purchased. In 1935 only a few counties began to discharge their *she-shu* and transfer their functions to paid clerks in the county tax office. This slow change indicates how extensively counties still relied on the traditional tax collection system. The system was wide open to manipulation, bribes, and irregular practices, which produced inequities of tax burden and discouraged the peasants from having honest dealings with officials.

We have a good example of how the *she-shu* system worked in Ch'ang-li county of northeast Hopei.[43] The *she-shu* recorded the tax collected, entered names of new landowners into the tax records, accepted payment of their registration fees, and reported to the county finance office the households that had not paid their land tax. They did not receive an official salary but obtained payments from villages. Nearly three quarters of the county land tax passed through their hands before arriving at the county finance office. Ch'ang-li county required about 80 *she-shu* to supervise the collection and recording of taxes on county land and land owned outside Ch'ang-li by residents of the county. The land tax only amounted to about 4 to 6 per cent of the value of the land's output,[44] but the introduction of surcharges on the basic land tax schedules and the collection of *t'an-k'uan* increased taxes greatly.[45] Police checkpoints in Ch'ang-li were established in 1914, precisely the year levies began to be collected.[46] By the late 1930s the surcharges on the original land tax had been greatly increased. In 1941 this amounted to 22 *fen* per mow and increased to 45 *fen* in 1942 compared to 6.4 *fen* per mow in the early Republican period.[47]

In 1939 the Ch'ang-li administration, pressed by the Japanese, carried out a land survey. The survey was repeated in 1940 with 50 officials selected to visit each village and ascertain the true amount of land, the number of residents and their names, the amount of land tax they paid, and the amount of land not registered for tax purposes. In the village of Hou chia ying the Japanese found that the amount of taxable land could be increased from 2,000 to 3,000 mow of land. For the entire county the taxable land was 1,900,000 mow compared to the 310,000 which was taxed. The *she-shu* system was abolished: only a few were transferred to the new tax office, and in 1942 the remainder were discharged. Villages containing between 80 and 300 households were combined to form units called *hsiang* or *lien-pao,*[48] and peasants paid their taxes to the *hsiang* administrative unit.

In the traditional fiscal system, non-paid clerks called *pao-cheng* were below the *she-shu* and supervised the collection of the land tax. Their position was also hereditary.[49] Every tax-collecting district had a *pao-cheng,* who met with village headmen at tax collecting time to make certain taxes were paid on time. Before taxes were collected the *pao-cheng* was notified of the expected amount by the finance office. He in turn notified villages in his district. He kept a careful record of households that did not pay. *Pao-cheng* received from each village an amount of grain valued between 20 and 100 yuan per year in lieu of salary. If the county collected the planned amount of tax, the *pao-cheng* received a small bonus from the administration.

Below the *pao-cheng* was a group called the *ti-fang* or *ti-pao,* whose task was to encourage households to pay their taxes.[50] The *ti-pao* beat drums in the villages during the tax-paying period. They also kept a strict watch over delinquent tax-paying households. The *ti-pao* lived in the villages and obtained their position by applying to the local government office. Once appointed they received no salary but were paid a small amount of grain by households at the end of the year.

The final tax-collecting group was the police. The first police training school in China was established in 1905 by a Japanese named Kawashima Naniwa to train a cadre of police officers.[51] In that year county police organizations were formed in many parts of the country. After 1911 the Ministry of Internal Affairs supervised the provincial and municipal police forces, but their number increased in a very uneven and irregular manner. In 1915 a law was passed fixing the number of county police at 300 for large counties and a minimum force of 100 for small counties. Because the government never defined their role nor carefully supervised their activities, their number depended largely upon a county's ability to support them. After 1935 many counties tried to cut their police budget but found this difficult to do. When war broke out several years later, their number were significantly increased.

The county police force became the right arm of the county officials. They were paid a fixed salary but given no increments when prices rose. They were sent to recalcitrant villages to force tax payment. Their arrival meant considerable village expense because they had to be feasted and entertained. Village councils made every effort to placate them and send them scurrying elsewhere. Amano Motonosuke reports that in Mou county of Hopei, the county budget only permitted a salary for 100 police, but actually the force totalled 1,000, who obtained their wages by squeezing extra cash from households of each village they visited.[52] This is undoubtedly an exceptional case of police corruption. The size of the force was usually smaller. In 1940 we find that Li-ch'eng had only 34, Shun-i had 10, and Luan-ch'eng had 8.

Local Government Expenditures

The tax revenue obtained from villages was used mainly for the military, the police, and for administrative purposes. Between 1912 and 1919 it was estimated that 30 to 40 per cent of central government revenue of China went for military affairs.[53] In 1923 half of Hopei's expenditures went for military activities whereas in Shantung the amount was 59 per cent. In 1931 police and county defense spending in Hopei still absorbed 39 per cent of total expenditures, and another 38 per cent went for education.[54] If the expenses necessary to maintain local administration are included, "the three principal items, police, education and self-government, took up almost nine-tenths of the total local government expenditure with the remaining one-tenth devoted to reconstruction, party administration, financial administration, weights and measures administration, relief, etc." [55]

When the civil war ended in 1929–30 local government began to give more attention to standardizing markets, promoting education, and providing peace and security. There were three major problems that local government did not have time to solve adequately before war engulfed the region once again. First, local officials overextended their activities by trying to accomplish too much with limited resources. This can be observed in the area of local police control. Frequently expenditures went for salaries rather than equipping a smaller police force to perform more efficiently. In Ch'ing-hai county in 1932 the police force of 150 men only possessed 64 rifles and barely 4,000 cartridges, but police outlays amounted to 33 per cent of the total local government expenditures.[56] In other instances local government spent too much for expanding the police force and not enough for building roads and fostering local industry. In 1935 Feng Hua-te reported his findings of a detailed study of local government spending in north China. His conclusion was that most of the extra tax revenue was being spent on the county police or for hiring additional officials; that is, it was merely "maintaining the existence of the local bureaucratic organizations." [57] In attempting to do so much, the bureaucracy became enlarged, inefficient, and extravagant in its use of public monies.

The second problem was that as local government attempted to regulate and promote education, establish new industry, and encourage transportation and communication development, it became increasingly involved in debt management. At the provincial level the biggest expenditure in the budget during the early 1930s was debt repayment. Bonds were continually being issued, and in order to make them attractive to banks the provincial governments offered high interest rates. In 1934 the debt charge paid for bonds was the foremost expenditure item in provincial budgets.[58]

Finally, local government officials still relied on the traditional tax collection system which was inefficient and corrupt. The tax collection system depended upon individuals inheriting the semi-official positions without official salary. This opened the system to corruption and bribery. Peasants naturally reacted with their personal interests foremost in mind. They used every means at their disposal to cheat and evade paying their taxes; for example, they refused to report the true amount of land they farmed. Feng Hua-te tells of villages owning two and three times the amount of land they reported to the county tax office.[59] When peasants purchased land, they only registered half or a third of the true amount purchased.[60] They also evaded paying the deed tax levied on land mortgaged or sold. Buyer and seller understated the value of the land so that the tax payable as a per cent of the land's value would be correspondingly low.[61] Another trick was for buyer and seller to draw up a mortgage deed instead of a land transfer deed when land was sold, because the tax on a mortgage deed was lower and payable within two years whereas the tax on a land transfer deed was higher and payable within six months.

Local officials between 1930 and 1937 had to rely upon the old tax collection system. The defects and abuses inherent in this system were well known. Competent officials had few trained personnel to assist them in managing a rural county, whose population might range from 50,000 to 100,000 people. Consequently, their control barely reached the village. Until the supply of local officials could be increased and the tax-collecting system reformed, it was impossible for the public sector to acquire sufficient funds to finance economic development and sponsor reform. These steps naturally required more time before the local government could become an engine for economic development.

17. Random Disturbances to the Rural Economy, 1890–1949

While traveling from Chefoo to Peking selling Bibles and preaching sermons, the Reverend Alexander Williamson commented that the north China plain looked like "an extended 'carse' with not a hill to relieve the monotony; the trees were few, and far from imposing. When I took a walk along the banks of the canal, my eyes met the same boundless expanse of winter wheat, patches of tobacco here and there, with rows of caster oil plants to mark off the field. As we approached villages, there were always vegetable gardens on the banks, in which were the fine white Shantung cabbage, carrots, red-topped and white turnips, thick-necked onions, and a variety of other culinary plants. The people, too, have everywhere the same appearance and follow the same employments." [1] Western travelers touring the north China countryside in the late nineteenth and early twentieth century reported a farming region of great crop diversity and dense population. Their observations do not contain any hint of impending poverty and a collapse of the rural economy. On the contrary, they sketched a picture of an area having a fair degree of rural prosperity.

Europeans were at first impressed by the countryside's fertility. In 1859, Rear-admiral Hope, commanding a squadron sent to evaluate Chinese military strength along the north China coastline, reported that "This part of the county [around Ninghai] is apparently the most fertile which I have seen in China — wheat, millet and maize are mainly grown — dotted over with villages and trees. It appears to enjoy considerable prosperity and a high state of cultivation." [2] In the late 1860s, John Markham, traveling from Chefoo to southwest Shantung to visit the birthplace of Mencius, pointed out that "Cereals of every description are largely grown in all the plains and valleys. Hemp, tobacco, pulse and fruit of all sorts are most plentiful. A great deal of pulse oil is also made in many districts and forms a very important article of export." [3]

In 1908, the British Consular official Garnett traveled through Fou-p'ing in northwest Hopei and later wrote that the countryside had "many signs of cultivation everywhere, newly sprung up wheat, groves of caster oil plants, recently harvested 'kaoliang' an Indian corn drying on the roofs of houses. But the cultivation is entirely confined to the valleys. There seemed to be an ever-increasing number of temples and shrines in the valley or on the peaks above us." [4]

What perhaps impressed foreign observers most was the great population the countryside supported. The consular official Campbell setting out for Jehol in June of 1894 described the rural districts around Peking in this fashion: "A more populous plain than this it would be difficult to pitch upon. It is sown broadcast with villages, large and small, and so thickly that you are rarely a mile away from one. Each is marked by what looks like a copse from the distance, but is in reality a sparse picture of willow, elm, pine, poplar, and locust trees (*Sohora Japinoca*), many of which shelter the tombs and cemeteries." [5] Because of overcrowding, remote areas had the appearance of being backward but not suffering from chronic poverty. One observer traveling in eastern Shantung commented that "The villages all look very poor, though they are frequently well built, and the houses constructed of stone and mud bricks, and the whole village surrounded by a wall. Nearly every one owns a little land, which he cultivates, and the produce of which he lives on, taking the surplus to the local market for sale. Though the people are so poor, yet beggars are rarely seen." [6]

Areas which had formerly experienced economic prosperity but had declined because of change in transportation had the characteristics of rural poverty which many observers cited in the 1920s and 1930s. In a letter written in the spring of 1897 a missionary in P'an-chia village near the Grand Canal in En county describes the region as follows: "The people are almost wholly agricultural, a quiet peaceable folk, who never stir up troubles unless 'assisted' by literati or officials. There is almost nothing to export in so densely crowded a region — the average population is at least 500 to the square mile — except cotton, and a few coarse vegetable oils, besides the products of cotton. The country is too poor to take many foreign articles of any sort. Most of the cities in this part of China which lie along the 'Grand Canal' have been decaying since the transfer of the rice tribute from the south to ocean going vessels." [7]

These reports describe an area producing a large variety of crops and in certain areas already specializing in several crops. The rural landscape was dotted with clusters of households making up numerous villages connected only by a dirt road wide enough for a cart to pass. Already the rural population seems to have been enormously large. Some districts were poor because they were either too far from major centers of commerce or trade had shifted to other areas. Where the harvest was normal and peace prevailed, villages appeared to be well off and not suffering from lack of food. The only serious problem at this time was the damage to agriculture caused by periodic floods along large rivers like the Yellow River.

Although there seems to have been a definite increase in flooding in the late nineteenth century, there was no fundamental change in climate to affect the harvest. North China had always been extremely vulnerable to floods and droughts.[8] During the nineteenth century Shantung had 30 droughts and Hopei had 47, and once every ten years a drought of unusual severity had occurred, causing famine for some districts.[9] Between 1822 and 1910 Hopei experienced only 58 good years without a major climatic fluctuation afflicting some areas; Shantung had only 51 years.[10] Historically, Chekiang and Kiangsu led all provinces in reported numbers of floods and droughts, but there was under-reporting in other areas. After the eleventh century these two provinces became the primary grain-producing areas for the northern provinces, and excessive attention to reporting weather changes and their effect on harvests may account for the alleged regional disparity in number of poor harvests.

The major reasons for drought and flooding in north China are the monsoon[11] and silting of rivers flowing from mountains inland toward the sea. In the early Ch'ing period the provincial governments managed to dredge the large rivers and build dikes where needed so that for sixty years there were no disastrous floods. Where the Grand Canal crossed the Yellow river flood control was managed by an independent water conservancy agency called the Yellow River Administration (YRA). The success of the YRA to minimize flooding during the eighteenth century was due primarily to "the active participation of the local officials, the economic and efficient employment of the corvee, and the general well-being of the empire in its earlier and less bureaucratic days." [12]

During the eighteenth century the YRA expanded and divided into two separate groups with 400 regular officials and numerous supernumeraries. Decision making within this organization became clumsy and inefficient, and it failed to acquire technical personnel who knew their business of controlling unruly rivers. The emperor frequently interfered and made bad decisions which so paralyzed the lower ranks with fear that they were unable to act decisively or forward new ideas to their superiors. The YRA became more incompetent and slow to anticipate floods, and it failed to take correct preventive steps to minimize damage once they occurred. As time passed the YRA demanded greater tax funds and spent more without improving water control. As an enormous parasitic sponge sapping the fiscal vitality of the empire, the YRA eventually produced conditions "in which its original objectives became incompatible with the vested interests of the people who served in it. Hence the most important phase of river control, the preservation of dikes, was deliberately neglected so that they would 'rot faster, decay faster, and be carried away faster,' thereby justifying the request for more appropriations." [13]

By the end of the late nineteenth century the government lost effective control over the Yellow river and did not regain it until the middle of the twentieth century. The efficiency and ability that characterized the YRA's activities of the early Ch'ing period was gone. Flooding became more frequent after 1858 when the Yellow river broke through its northern dikes and flowed into Shantung to empty into the Gulf of Po Hai.[14] During the 1880s the court's inability to bring the river under proper control by dredging its lower reaches and constructing better dikes along the river's shores elicited critical comments by Westerners on the government's ability to bring the river under man's control again. With some exasperation the *North China Daily Herald* wrote on June 18, 1886, "We have seen so many memorials on the state of the Yellow river, and the necessity of repairing its banks so as to restrain it when in flood and for the approaches to the sea, that we are not inclined to be very sanguine about the recent deliberations on the subject." [15] In every decade thereafter, there were at least two or three major floods along this river and other large rivers causing tremendous damage to agriculture and an unknown loss of human life and property in dozens of rural counties.

This peasant economy was particularly subject to four main types of external shock of which the peasants were not forewarned and had little power to control. I refer to these as random disturbances because they were not connected with the general pattern of internal development and cyclical change, and they occurred suddenly, without warning, to produce severe consequences for the rural economy. These disturbances were natural disasters, wars, increased taxation, and price fluctuations. Floods, droughts, hail, and insects, common in north China, frequently reduced the size of harvest, thereby depleting the peasants' reserves. Once the supply of seeds and food had been greatly reduced, the area of sown land also declined, and famine threatened.

When war broke out, armies moved through the countryside, living off the land. When they bivouacked in a county seat, they took pigs and poultry from nearby farms to feed their troops, seized labor animals to carry weapons and munitions, and even took young men to carry equipment and serve as military laborers. When households lost livestock, they were deprived of an important source of fertilizer and animal power. Pigs were essential to the farmstead because they contributed to the supply of fertilizer. In order to fertilize the land as heavily as before to prevent a decline in soil fertility, less land was sown and in turn, reduced the subsequent year's harvest. Where labor animals and able-bodied men had been taken for military service, households were unable to prepare the soil, sow seeds, irrigate the land, weed, and harvest as efficiently as before. As a result, output fell, the cultivated area devoted to crops for marketing declined, and peasants shifted to producing food crops for their own consumption. An even more serious consequence of this process was the desertion of villages and the influx to towns of families which had lost their wealth and had had to sell their land and seek work. There arose the peculiar paradox, so often observed in China after 1938, of labor shortage in the villages and a superfluity of labor in the market towns and large cities.

When local officials began to increase local taxes, households lost income which otherwise would have been spent for farm capital and consumer goods. The effect of a tax increase was varied and complex. At first, households might be induced to work harder to offset the loss of income through taxes. If levies were continued and further increased, peasants might be discouraged from investing and replacing their farm capital, which in the long run forced them to substitute labor for capital and lowered productivity and output. Continued taxation might reduce the amount peasants were willing to market.

Finally, a fall in farm prices due to commercial depression reduced farm income. If the price decline continued for long, households reduced their purchase of new capital and replacement of existing capital. The effects could be serious but were usually temporary, because severe price decline was infrequent and did not last long when it occurred. A great rise in prices created by a breakdown in transport and commodity shortages in the cities reduced peasant purchases in the market towns and what they offered on the market. This occurred because the prices of consumer necessities rose more rapidly than that of the food and fibers peasants were marketing. When peasants were squeezed in this way, they relied less on the market, preferring to produce more for their own consumption.

Warlordism and Its Impact on the Rural Economy

Several studies of political disintegration and the emergence of warlord cliques with their satraps and military units to control them have already been written, but a thorough study of the phenomena of warlordism has yet to be written. No other phenomena between 1911 and 1937 caused such upheaval and misery in the countryside as that of dissident military units wandering about pillaging and warring with one another. To be sure, the 1920–21 famine which concentrated its fury mostly in Hopei[16] and ravaged 317 counties across north China was a disaster of major proportions caused mainly by poor harvests in 1920 and 1921. But the emigration of millions of peasants from north China to Manchuria during the 1920s was principally due to the breakdown of peace and order in the countryside and the great loss of property at the hands of warlord armies. The Japanese army reported that between 1925 and 1927 areas around Chining in Shantung were devastated by fighting, and peasants lost an estimated 213,000 head of cattle and labor animals totalling 120,000 mules and 440,000 donkeys.[17] Nearly five million people in thirteen countries were affected by this conflict, and emigration from this region was great.

In the same period traffic along the Tientsin-Pukow and Chinan-Tsingtao railway lines was reduced by as much as 25 per cent because of fighting.[18] The rural staples such as cotton, wheat, and peanuts, which normally flowed from villages into the main markets of T'ai-an, Ta wen k'ou, ch'u-chou, and Yen-chow declined, and as a result stocks of these raw materials in Chinan and Tsingtao dried up. This forced manufacturing enterprises to operate at only one third or half capacity.[19] Employment declined, and many villages which depended upon this wage income suffered. Urban prices rose two and three fold in a matter of a year or two. Villages immediately reverted to producing food for household consumption, and cities became partially isolated from the countryside, a prelude to the disaster which would overtake this region after 1938.

A more serious problem was the hordes of uncontrolled and undisciplined troops roaming about demanding food and shelter. A study conducted by the South Manchurian Railway Company in 1930 estimated that in Shantung there were 192,000 troops in 21 locals, 290,000 unorganized troops without formal leadership and attachment to any military organization stationed in 54 locals, and nearly 20,000 bandits in 46 counties.[20] These groups supported themselves by levying surcharges on the land tax, issuing inconvertible paper notes as salaries for their troops, and absconding with carts and animals owned by the peasantry. They were also responsible for the increased use of the *t'an-k'uan.* Many peasants fled their villages for Manchuria rather than remain and farm under these conditions. In 1923, the peasants migrating to the northeast through north China ports tallied around 340,000 a year, and their number rapidly climbed until in 1927 it exceeded the one million mark.[21] Peasants could cope with poor harvests and floods by fleeing with their belongings to other areas, waiting until the disaster passed, and then return. But the ravages of these troops was something else. It usually meant both loss of property and life, and so one of the largest internal migrations of this century took place during the 1920s.

The flight to Manchuria eased after 1931, partly because Japan had occupied Manchuria, partly because the new Nationalist government restored peace and order in north China. For six years north China enjoyed a brief respite from war, and by 1936 agriculture had recovered from the effects of the depression. The government launched many projects for internal improvement. The yearly harvests were good, and food imports were cut drastically. The outbreak of war in 1937 altered everything.

The Impact of War upon the Rural Economy

After invading north China the Japanese military realized the area would have to supply enough for its own needs and export food, fibers, and fuel to Manchuria and Japan. The army was anxious to assess the damage of the war to the countryside so that appropriate steps could be taken to increase the food supply. It requested the South Manchurian Railway Company research offices in north China to study the impact of the war on the village economy. The village and county studies which survived give a vivid picture of what took place between 1937 and 1939.

The rural markets suffered dislocation and began to collapse. Merchants and local financiers fled the market towns, and there were few remaining to carry on commodity exchange and provide credit. Grain and industrial crops were not shipped in the same quantities as in the past, and fewer consumer articles such as yarn, cloth, sugar, matches, tobacco, fuel, and salt were imported from the cities. Villages lost pigs, labor animals, carts, and able-bodied young men. Troops took pigs as food, labor animals and carts to haul supplies and munitions, and labor to cart goods or be conscripted for military service.

Households were unable to fertilize the same amount of land for spring sowing, and the cultivated area declined. Villages formerly specializing in cash crops could not buy enough grain because commodity exchange between market towns and cities had been disrupted. The peasants began to grow food crops instead of continuing to specialize in cash crops. As a result the area under cash crop cultivation declined, and in areas where villages had lost much labor and capital, food crop cultivation also declined.

Food became very scarce in cities, and its price rose. Stocks of raw materials for factories dwindled, and spinning mills, oil-milling factories, and other enterprises dependent on raw materials from the countryside operated at only 30 to 50 per cent of their former capacity. Unemployment rose, and workers were forced to become coolie workers, whose ranks had swollen by the efflux of peasants from villages ruined by the war. Cities produced and exported fewer goods to the countryside, and villages produced and marketed less grain and industrial crops to the cities.

The process by which villages, rural market towns, and then cities were affected by the war was later intensified by guerrilla warfare and Japanese forays into the countryside to seize stocks of grain from villages. Although the Japanese managed to keep the major railway lines operating and north China remained an integrated economy in which commodities were still exchanged between cities and the countryside, the flow of goods between the two progressively dwindled. Some examples of what took place in specific villages show vividly the economic decline taking place.

Li ts'un tien village in Ting county of Hopei lay 30 kilometers from the county seat.[22] Fourteen per cent of the households owned 42 per cent of the cultivated land, and only 12 per cent of the households farmed plots over 30 mow. Three fourths of the village output consisted of cotton, followed by potatoes, peanuts, sorghum, and vegetables. Spinning and weaving had been the main handicraft occupations for the past forty years, and cloth was exported to Suiyan and Kansu. When war came to the county, peasants fled or joined the army, and the village's labor supply declined to some 30–50 per cent of the pre-war labor force. Households which lost able-bodied workers mortgaged some land because they were unable to farm all their land. In 1931 only 53 households mortgaged land, but in 1938 there were 125 households mortgaging land. Peasants with more than 30 mow leased their poorer plots and farmed their better plots because they did not have enough labor. The cloth trade had also collapsed, depriving many households of employment and income. Households with little land had to send workers elsewhere. Normally, the village sent many workers to the nearby market towns, but because merchants had closed their doors and fled, these peasants now had to go as far as Chahar and Mukden to find employment.

Many farm tools had been damaged, and a large number of pigs and labor animals had been carried off by Chinese troops retreating from Peking. With fewer mules, peasants had difficulty working the wells, irrigating the fields, and ploughing the land. The loss of pigs meant a big reduction in fertilizer, and the black beans mixed with ashes and grass was a poor substitute. Cotton cultivation declined most rapidly. A wealthy household in 1936 planted 55 mow of cotton, reduced this to 34 mow in 1939, and in 1940 planted only 12 mow. It became increasingly difficult to obtain food in the county's rural markets, and more households began to grow potatoes, millet, and rice. Consumer goods and tools could still be purchased but their prices had risen greatly: the price of tools between 1937 and 1940 rose fourfold and that of fertilizers threefold. "The gradual decline in peasant living standards, the chaos caused by the way, and the rise in commodity prices were mainly responsible for the decline in commodity exchange." [23] The field report ended on the somber note that unless these conditions were quickly reversed, the Chinese Communists would have their way in this village and others like it.

Sun chia miao village in Hui-min county of Shantung lay 3 kilometers from the county seat.[24] Its population of 500 people living in about 100 households cultivated cotton, potatoes, and grain crops. The village had gradually specialized in cotton after the turn of the century. When the war reached the county, between 15 and 20 households or about one fifth of the village had fled. The collapse of handicraft activity forced peasants with little land to work at odd jobs in the county seat. The rural work force leaving the village seeking employment rose greatly overnight. Households short of labor but owning land either mortgaged or leased it to other households. The amount of tenant land increased, and more households were able to farm land than in former times. A few peasants were even able to buy land and become owner-cultivators instead of renting land. The number of pigs and ducks declined considerably, and the area devoted to cotton also declined. Formerly 90 mow of village land grew cotton, but in 1939 only 27 mow grew cotton, a decline of about 70 per cent.

Conditions in Shih-chia village of Paoting county on the Peking-Hankow railway line were similar.[25] The supply of labor had decreased, labor animals and pigs had been taken away, the amount of land devoted to growing cotton had fallen, and consumer goods had become very expensive. Loss of livestock meant less fertilizer for the fields and greater difficulty for peasants in irrigating their fields. In a village outside Tsingtao, much livestock had been carried away by troops,[26] and, as a result, the peasants cultivated less cotton and turned to raising potatoes. In Wang shu chen village of Yen-shang county in Hopei, the labor supply had declined because able-bodied males had been drafted for military service, been conscripted by local police for road work, or simply fled.[27] More households mortgaged land than ever before, and many leased land, insisting that rents be paid in kind rather than money. The Communist Eighth Route Army had been active in the area urging peasants not to sell their food to the market towns. This was one of their main tactics to reduce commodity exchange between the countryside and towns controlled by the Japanese.[28] It is interesting that by 1940, prices in areas held by the Japanese were already one third higher than prices in areas controlled by the Communist guerrillas.[29] Food shortages due to the decline of marketable village surplus caused prices in the towns to be much higher than in the countryside.

Shifting now to developments throughout the region, between 1937 and 1939 the area of cotton cultivation in north China declined from 2.4 million mow producing 6.25 million piculs to 500,000 mow producing 1.5 million piculs.[30] This decline was greater in Hopei than elsewhere in the region. In Shantung the cultivated area for peanuts declined from 3.7 million mow to 841,000 mow between 1933 and 1939, and the output fell from 10.5 million to 3.0 million piculs.[31] By 1943 the cultivated area for tobacco declined 30 per cent below the 1936 level, cotton declined 50 per cent, wheat declined 19 per cent, sorghum 12 per cent, beans 6 per cent, and for a total of 19 crops the crop cultivation index showed a decline of 5 per cent.[32] It is obvious that the reduction in crop area was greatest for industrial crops and that cultivated area for food grains had not declined very much.

Potatoes, corn, and millet received more attention by the peasants, and even the area under rice cultivation increased. In 1940 rice was grown on 73,262 mow in Shantung and on 386,800 mow in Hopei, but by 1942 it had been increased to 85,712 and 550,223 mow respectively.[33] As one would expect from such a large increase in cultivated area, productivity fell. It was also estimated that land productivity for crops such as wheat, sorghum, corn, potatoes, millet, and soybeans also fell after 1940.[34] The process of commercialization which had taken place before the war was now reversed, agricultural productivity had declined, and these developments in turn greatly influenced the use of land for different crops." [35] The switch to food crops by households now possessing less labor and capital than before the war meant a decline in land productivity.

It is impossible to estimate the amount of capital in terms of pigs, labor animals, and carts lost during the early years of the war, and it is also difficult to measure which areas suffered a great decline in labor. The demands of war drained villages of labor all over China. When workers were conscripted into the military or mobilized for building fortifications, air strips, roads or transporting equipment,[36] the villages were left with few able-bodied men to care for and harvest the crops. Women, children, and old men took their place, but their labor power was inadequate to perform these jobs, and output declined.

A study of a large market town and two nearby villages in Te county of the Tientsin-Pukow railway line in 1941 shows how labor conditions changed.[37] In Hsin-chuang village, located outside the county seat, there were 70 households, but 30 of these families had only entered the village in the past few years. The original households owned very little land, and most had divided their land once or twice within the past fifty years. Household farms had become so small they could not support themselves with farm income alone. After 1937 the village population increased greatly because of the influx of families from villages hard hit by poor harvests and the war.[38] Most of the new arrivals crowded into single rooms and worked in the county seat. Those without money begged for a living. Families with a little cash operated food stalls, but most worked as coolie laborers hauling and transporting goods. The number of transport workers alone in the market town had risen from 30,000 in 1937 to 50,000 in 1941.

About 70 per cent of the market town's work force in 1941 came from villages within a few miles' radius. Some of these were coolie laborer-peasants from Ch'i li pao.[39] This village, located some distance from the county seat, had escaped the ravages of war. It produced the conventional grain crops, vegetables, peanuts, and soybeans. Of the village's 240 households, 213 farmed plots less than 20 mow, 19 farmed between 20 to 50 mow size farms, and only 8 managed farms over 50 mow. Households with less than 20 mow shared their tools and livestock with one another or borrowed from households having more land. Before 1937, many households had sent young men to work in the market town, but after 1937 more peasants went there to work because of higher money wages. Peasants with their carts were in great demand. There seems to have been no serious labor shortage in this village.

The crippling of farm production and the breakdown in commodity trade between countryside and town were two important reasons why prices began to rise rapidly in north China after 1941. Yet, the supply of money also increased, and this factor played an important role in causing price increase. Prices had gradually moved upward after 1937, but it was not until late 1941, when the scarcity of goods became acute in the cities and few raw materials were being imported from the countryside, that prices really began to shoot up rapidly.

Wholesale prices in the coastal provinces from Shantung to Kwangtung rose from five to six fold (Shanghai retail prices rose slightly more than sevenfold) between 1937 and 1941.[40] Throughout Hupei, Honan, Kwangsi, and Kiangsi prices rose in the vicinity of seven to nine and ten fold, and when we reach Kweichow, Szechwan, Shensi, and Kansu the increase has become ten to fifteen fold (for Cheng-tu in Szechwan). Armies retreating inland into regions of greater backwardness required food and housing. A rise in the money supply and military expenditures pushed prices higher than in the coastal provinces where transport and markets were better developed and their normal operation had been quickly restored by the Japanese. In nearly all instances, the prices of fuel and clothing exceeded the rise in food prices, indicating that production costs had risen rapidly because of raw material shortages in the industries producing these goods. These materials were obtained from the countryside, and where their production had been influenced by war and the collapse in transportation, marketing, and credit, acute raw material shortage in the cities developed.

In late 1941 Japan was fully at war, and its empire depended upon north China and Manchuria to supply more food and raw materials. Food imports into these two regions fell to zero. Cities became entirely dependent upon the countryside for food at a time when agricultural production had been disrupted. Although 1940 and 1941 were good harvest years, "production in north China had still not recovered its pre-war output level." [41] To remedy the problem the military introduced a plan in 1942 to purchase food at fixed prices, and quotas were set for each district under Japanese control to supply different food crops.

Although the Japanese were unable to control the countryside, they set high quotas at fixed prices for the amount of grain they hoped to purchase below market prices. In 1943 and 1944 the actual quantities of grain purchased fell far short of planned purchases. In 1943 they obtained only 62 per cent of the planned wheat quota.[42] There were ten districts in northwest and central Shantung where local military commanders achieved some success in purchasing grain at fixed prices. Troops were ordered into the villages to make sure the grain was actually collected and paid for, and in 1943 wheat purchases per mow in Chining county were 30 catties instead of the planned amount of 10 catties.[43] Many counties enjoyed a good harvest in 1943, and the percentage of grain purchased at fixed prices of the planned quota ranged from a low of 6 to a high of 31 per cent with 15 per cent being a rough average.[44] Poor harvests in 1944 made it impossible to purchase as much grain as in 1943.

Economic conditions between 1941 and 1945 are a blank, because the only scraps of evidence are prices. The rate of annual price increase in north China was 10 per cent between 1942 and 1943 and 25 per cent between 1943 and 1945.[45] Prices increased twice as rapidly after 1943. Price data for three major cities show that price increase was more rapid the deeper one moved into the interior of the country. This may be seen in Table 56. These indices show that prices leaped upward between 1939 and 1941 and again after 1943. The rapidity of price increase after 1941 suggests that the trends taking place between 1938 and 1941 merely con-

Table 56. Wholesale price indices for three major north China cities, 1936–1944 (base year 1936).

Year	Chinan[a]	Tientsin[b]	Shihmen[c]
1936	100	100	100
1937	–	117	–
1938	–	152	–
1939	–	226	–
1940	–	399	319
1941	366	450	394
1942	578	599	473
1943	1,678	893	774
1944	2,352	1,035	2,639

[a] Chūgoku rengō jumbi ginkō, comp., *Zainan bukka geppō* (Chinan monthly price report, 4.12:2 (November 1944); index for 1944 only covers months of Jan. through November.

[b] Chūgoku rengō jumbi ginkō, comp., *Tenshin bukka geppō* (Tientsin monthly price report), 3.12:2 (December 1944).

[c] Chūgoku rengō jumbi ginkō, comp., *Sekimon bukka geppō* (Shihmen monthly price report), 5.10:2 (October 1944); index for 1944 only includes months of January through October.

tinued with greater intensity. Commodity shortages had obviously become more acute, and trade between countryside and town undoubtedly declined still further.

The Rural Economy and the Civil War, 1945–1949

The defeat of the Japanese was not the beginning of economic recovery. Agricultural and commercial conditions in north China were probably worse than in any other part of the country, because fighting was intense and Communist guerrilla activity had partially succeeded in isolating the towns from the countryside. Prices of food and industrial crops in north China cities were higher than in any other cities of the country. Wheat prices in Shihmen were 479,000 yuan per shih and in Luan-ch'ang of Shantung they were 729,000 yuan per shih, compared to 243,000 yuan per shih in Nanking and 184,000 yuan per shih in Wu-ch'ang of Hupei.[46] If we take 100 as the base price of different commodities in Shanghai as of February 1948, the index for rice prices was 89 per cent and 113 per cent higher in Tsingtao and Peking, for flour 21 per cent higher in Chinan and 89 per cent higher in Peking, and for cotton, higher by 11 per cent in Tsingtao and 45 per cent in Peking.[47] The same regional price disparity between the north and central areas existed for soybeans and other farm products.

Estimates of agricultural output for the postwar period must be regarded as rough and approximate, and these show that output was only three fifths to four fifths of the prewar output. In 1946 soybean output was only 76 per cent of the average 1931–1937 output for Hopei and Shantung; sorghum output was 62 per cent of the same prewar output in Hopei and 87 per cent in Shantung.[48] Rice production in 1947 was only 60 per cent of Shantung's normal rice harvest and 59 per cent for Hopei. Wheat production was only 64 per cent of Shantung's normal harvest and 48 per cent for Hopei.[49] Cotton production stood at 56 per cent of Hopei's prewar output and 81 per cent for Shantung.[50]

Part of this decline in food production can be explained by the fact that little of the harvest reached the market towns and cities. The transport system had nearly collapsed after the defeat of the Japanese, and commodity price exchange between towns and countryside became so unfavorable for the peasants that they had little inducement to market their crops. A price study of agricultural prices in Sian of Shensi showed that between 1937 and 1947 "agricultural prices still have not been able to keep up with the increase in general consumer goods prices." [51] In provinces along the Yangtze river, rural surveys in 1946–47 concluded that "the major reason for village decline is that the price of rice has not kept pace with the prices of other goods; the price of rice and other agricultural goods rise more slowly than do the prices of everyday consumer goods." [52] Peasants willingly sold some of their food for a few consumer necessities but only after making certain their basic needs were first satisfied.

In some villages population had increased, but the breakdown in markets prevented the peasants from purchasing consumer goods and marketing their produce. The cultivated area diminished and the supply of livestock and labor animals was reduced. Production of industrial crops declined, and peasants continued to grow food crops like millet, sorghum, and potatoes. Although cultivating less land meant that a greater proportion of land could be irrigated, the loss of livestock meant that less fertilizer was available and output decreased. These were the conditions observed by a team studying villages in Shantung in 1950.[53] We can only surmise that in villages where the loss of labor had been severe, such conditions were much more serious.

The Japanese had been able to keep railways open by building trenches and blockhouses to protect key centers and using repair crews to repair sections of track damaged by guerrillas. Communist armies repeatedly attacked and damaged transportation lines, destroying sections of track wherever protection was inadequate in order to isolate the towns from the countryside and starve them into submission. A newspaper report on February 10, 1947, claimed that "since January 1 they [Communist troops] have made 24 disturbances, destroyed 99 steel rails, burned 431 cross-ties and 5 bridges" along the Tsingtao–Chinan rail lines.[54] In December of 1947 the railway stations at Chukechuan and Shihmen on the Pei-ning line were demolished with a loss of 100 rails, 15,000 sleepers, and 400 telephone poles.[55] In January of 1948 the Peking–Tientsin railway administration reported that in 1947 there had been 522 incidents in which 131 kilometers of track had been destroyed, 115 bridges damaged, and 425 railway staff captured by Communist troops.[56] The Peking–Paoting rail line had been suspended for long periods, and during the last quarter of 1947 traffic could move for only 16 days.[57]

The conscription of labor for military purposes continued. In February of 1947 a newspaper reported that "Now conscription of soldiers and the collection of taxes in kind are being carried on energetically, with the result that able-bodied men have either turned into bandits or are seeking a refugee life in the cities. As a result, labor wages in farm villages go up by day, while the quality and quantity of agricultural products drop down considerably."[58] Many villages were short of labor hands during the spring and fall harvesting, while the cities were glutted with the unemployed. "According to people coming from far villages as a result of the war during the past year, farm villages have already become devastated. The people have been concentrated in the municipalities with young and aged left in the villages who will not be able to use their farms after their cows and horses have been commandeered and farm implements spoiled. In the municipalities on the other hand, there is a large army of unemployed. The population there is suffering livelihood privations as a result of the abrupt rise in commodity prices, especially in the daily necessities, such as rice, flour, cotton and oil, which are all farm products."[59]

An editorial in the *Shih chieh jih pao* of Peking in July 1948 pointed out that military units northwest of Tientsin drafted labor from poor families and forced them to give up their grain at ridiculously low prices whereas wealthy households were exempted. "Commandeered grain was paid for by the troops at prices which were only one eighteenth those of the market prices."[60] The government also ordered that peasants pay their taxes in grain instead of money. Tax collectors were often unscrupulous in using fraudulent weights and measures to cheat the peasants of their grain.[61] The grain paid as land tax was collected through the village *pao-chia* organizations and handed over to the police, who usually retained a large amount for their own expenses.

The cultivated area for industrial crops such as cotton had decreased greatly by late 1947. In December of that year it was reported that of Hopei's total cultivated area of cotton, less than 10 per cent could supply towns and cities with raw cotton. "Of the total area of cotton planted in Hopei about 712,000 mow has either been laid waste or seized by the communists and cotton growing is being restricted to the remaining 70,000 mow."[62] Kuomintang officials were unable to revive agricultural production with loans and gifts of free seeds because inflation increased production costs as rapidly as farm prices. Further, taxes rose enormously and increased production costs. In the fall of 1947, a report from Luan county in eastern Hopei stated that military tax levies ranged from 25,000 to 40,000 Chinese dollars per mow even after the land tax had been paid. "If the cost of labor and fertilizers are to be taken into consideration, the receipts from the crops would not be able to meet the expenditures." [63]

While the civil war raged, villages marketed less and hid what they produced from the police, officials, and military troops. As it became increasingly difficult for the towns and cities to obtain commodities from the countryside, the urban economy rapidly came to a stand-still. The crippling of transport reduced the amount of coal for factories. Because Tsingtao could not obtain coal from Kailan her textile mills "had to burn foodstuffs to make up for the coal insufficiency." [64] The process of industrial decline was perhaps best described by the *Ta kung pao* weekly economic review. "Enterprises relying upon agricultural produce were the first to fall to be followed by the closure of factories using imported raw materials. It has now come to the turn of industries depending on natural resources to close down and already drastic declines in production have been reported. It is unthinkable that an agricultural country such as China is, should have allowed her productive industries to fall on account of the inavailability of agricultural produce. In the past year, flour milling and oil refining enterprises have come to a near stand-still." [65]

The money supply was expanded in order to pay the wages and salaries of military personnel and civil servants. The velocity of money in circulation rose rapidly as this money income was quickly spent. The expectation that urban commodity prices would continue to rise rapidly motivated city people to spend their incomes as rapidly as they received them. These expenditures and the worsening food and consumer goods shortages caused commodity prices between 1945 and 1948 to skyrocket. By the spring of 1947 prices quoted in principal market towns were equivalent to those of large cities because the scarcity of goods had become severe in these centers too. Now, even the market towns were cut off from the countryside. The high price of grain in the market towns discouraged city merchants from buying there. Manchuria had also been cut off from north China and could not provide grain and fuel.[66] By the spring of 1948 conditions in the towns and cities had become so bad that businessmen began to transfer their capital to Szechwan and Shanghai. In March a great flight of capital took place with 20 billion Chinese dollars remitted from Peking and Tientsin to Chungking.[67] In May another 7 billion went to Shanghai and Hong Kong.[68] The collapse of both urban and rural economy in north China was now complete.

18. Village and Market Town: Summary

There is scarcely any evidence that exploitation of one group by another was either severe or a consistent practice commensurate with the operation of a rural market. Various economic groups acted in their own best interests through the market, and the highly competitive nature of the market reduced to a minimum the monopoly power any group could exert over another. The price of land, cost of credit, and value of commodity exchange involved the peasant in a continual series of economic transactions with other households or the market towns.

In every village some households leased land to other households each year. There does not seem to have been a case of a household living solely from rental income without farming some land. The land tenure system functioned to equalize land use between households which did not have land and those which did. It did not ensure that new technology was transmitted from one household to another. Tenants were given some incentive to produce more when landowners switched from collecting rents as a percentage to a fixed amount of the harvest. During bad harvests, however, many households returned to the old percentage rent system. This was more common on poorer quality land.

The land farmed by tenants was a small percentage of village land, usually less than 15 per cent. Wealthy households acquired their land by hard work and good fortune, earning income from outside agriculture, or on rare occasion by a windfall gain. The village land tenure system was exceptionally fluid, with parties changing nearly every other year. Land was an asset which continually changed hands and was used to obtain credit and settle debts. This is one important reason why tenure arrangements between parties did not evolve into a more permanent relationship.

Contrary to the assertions made by many that village land distribution became more unequal over time, the evidence for this region suggests that land distribution either remained unchanged or became more equal. Land distribution in the late nineteenth century was already very unequal. Where data for this period could be obtained and compared with that of the 1930s there is every indication that land distribution did not change. The reason for this was the custom of dividing land equally among male heirs at inheritance time. This practice broke up large farms and prevented land from accumulating in the same household every other generation. Although population expansion slowly reduced the average size farm, the inheritance system prevented land distribution from becoming more unequal than it already was. Inequality existed because some households with greater capability and luck than others earned the income to acquire more land. However, in some villages land distribution became more unequal because natural calamities reduced the harvest and village income.

Summary

Absentee landlords resided in market towns or treaty ports. They acquired their land through the credit system. They were unable to farm this land and merely leased it to peasants willing to rent. As claims to land shifted between households of the same village or between villages over the course of a generation, so too did claims to land shift between villages and market towns. When a large number of households became indebted to moneylenders, much land fell into their possession when households could not repay their loans. Many peasants then became tenants on what had been their own land. Whether or not this posed a serious problem for villages depended greatly upon the trend in farm and land prices. Rapidly rising prices like those after 1938 enabled many to repay their loans and redeem their land. The region experienced little serious price deflation except between 1931 and 1934. For this reason, claims to land had not steadily passed into the hands of the wealthy classes in the market towns.

Although the village land tenure system rationed land, the leasing of land by absentee landlords in market towns to peasants was a by-product of the rural credit system. Peasants used their land as security to obtain credit from the market towns. Urban savings were transferred to villages when demand for credit increased. In the absence of any alternative credit system, mortgaging land was an indispensable means by which towns supplied loanable funds to villages. Peasants unable to repay their loans became tenants on their mortgaged land, but they still could redeem their land by repaying their loan. It is significant that absentee landlords probably owned only 5 or 10 per cent of the village land.

Most rural credit was supplied within the village by wealthy households. When more money was required, peasants went to the market towns and borrowed. Credit flowed seasonally from market towns to villages during the spring months, and villages repaid the market towns during the late fall months. Poor harvests sometimes affected this flow, thus forcing households to borrow more than normally. Bumper harvests enabled households to repay long-standing debts and even buy land from absentee landlords.

Interest rates of 2 and 3 per cent per month reflected not just a shortage of loanable funds but the high risk of moneylending. Lenders could never be sure their customers would repay their loans. They could not easily refer the matter to the county seat law court. Lawsuits were costly and long-drawn-out affairs, and if the matter could be settled privately, both parties usually agreed. Monthly interest rates had remained constant for over a century. This stability can only mean that the supply and demand for loanable funds increased at the same rate because urban and rural commercial expansion slowly took place. When new villages formed, new market towns also arose with the same lending institutions and practices that existed in older established towns. With the growth of the treaty port economy, credit became slightly cheaper to obtain from merchants, a development that occurred in the port centers themselves, not in cities of the interior.

Commodities were exchanged in market towns under very competitive market conditions. After 1900 new staple trades developed, and centers that had formerly been small towns became large collection points for grain and industrial crops. The old nineteenth-century guilds declined in importance and were replaced by new merchant groups. Historically, rural markets were designated by local officials as open places for the exchange of goods as long as fees and taxes were collected. Numerous middlemen competed with one another for the goods peasants brought to market. Evidence of the competitiveness of these markets can be seen by the seasonal regularity of price change, aggravated only by poor or bumper harvests, and the large entry of middlemen into rural markets which made it difficult for merchants to restrict trade or corner supply.

The price differential for commodities between their origin of supply and the final market of distribution was considerable. The absence of standardized measurement units and codified marketing procedures made it necessary for city merchants to depend on numerous brokers to handle their transactions in the interior for them. Peasants experienced marketing difficulties only when prices declined sharply or rose abruptly. Their dependency on the market for cash and necessities naturally made them vulnerable to price fluctuations and forced them to adjust their household budget accordingly. This was the price paid for commercial progress without corresponding improvements in credit institutions to provide enough loanable funds to protect the peasants against such hardships. Peasants were very fortunate that prices continually moved upward and that periods of declining prices were few and short-lived.

Local officials, under persistent pressures to raise more taxes, were not assisted or advised in how to reform the tax collection system, and they therefore had to use a system which had long outlived its usefulness. Peasants successfully evaded paying the entire amount of the increased taxes on land because local officials had not measured the amount of cultivated land and valued it according to its real worth. Local officials raised additional taxes mainly by expanding the local constabulary to levy and collect taxes on villages. The task of apportioning the tax burden within villages was left to the headmen and village councils. The new method worked well to garner additional revenue but unfortunately resulted in the creation of a larger bureaucracy which in turn had to be financed from these very same funds.

The local administration was hopelessly understaffed and its officials poorly trained. This delayed the introduction of rural reforms, and forced the administration to depend entirely on the Ch'ing tax collection system and methods of village control. This system consisted of unpaid individuals receiving informal salaries from the villagers. Some of these positions were even hereditary. However, between 1928 and 1937 officials began to move slowly in the direction of a satisfactory solution of how to establish official control more firmly in the villages. They ordered villages below a certain size to amalgamate, created a new administrative unit, the *hsiang,* between the villages and the county sea, and instructed village headmen to work more closely with local officials. Rural projects such as roads and wells were begun. More funds were spent to train schoolteachers and establish village schools. Efforts were gradually being made to revitalize the countryside, but before very much progress could be achieved the Japanese invaded north China.

Under Japanese military administration, land surveys were launched in some counties, and when completed, the old tax collection system was disbanded and tax collection centralized. Taxes were increased, but after an initial increase in tax burden, peasants probably did not continue to pay a higher proportion of income for tax because of inflation. The tax burden on villages may have increased only during the mid 1920s and in 1937 and 1938 when farm production was disrupted and declined and taxes were increased at the same time. The fall in real income coupled with increased taxes undoubtedly raised the peasants' tax burden. However, throughout the remainder of our period, rising farm prices and nonfarm income enabled peasants to pay their taxes with little increase in real burden.

The rural economy was subjected to violent shocks in the 1920s and after 1938. These disturbances destroyed farm capital and diverted farm labor from the villages. The reduction of village capital and manpower forced households to reduce the land they could efficiently farm. Peasants adjusted as best they could by reducing the cultivation of industrial crops and growing crops necessary for consumption. The combined effects of commodity shortages and increased military spending by the Japanese forced prices to rise rapidly between 1939 and 1941 and after 1943. The Japanese successfully kept transportation open and maintained village and town commodity exchange, although on a greatly reduced level, in their sphere of military control. Economic conditions deteriorated rapidly after 1945, and the countryside was soon virtually cut off from the major towns.

19. Conclusion

The numerous studies written about Chinese agriculture before 1949 have an almost doctrinal ring in their explanations of how agriculture developed and what was fundamentally wrong in the countryside. The propositions served up most frequently assert that village land distribution became more unequal, peasant living standards deteriorated steadily after China began to trade with the West, and peasants were cruelly exploited by the wealthy classes of the market towns. For these reasons the peasants lost their land, rural debt increased, and the number of tenants rose. It was also argued that agriculture failed to progress because farms were too small, the rural population was too large, and the peasantry were too conservative and backward to learn new farming methods. The attitudes toward the peasantry ranged from one of sympathy engendered by a justifiable feeling they had been exploited to one of scorn based on the presumption peasants were too ignorant and poor to improve their conditions.

Precisely when village field work was being undertaken, these views and propositions assumed myth-like proportions. As a result, few were encouraged to submit the great body of rural data to thorough examination and critical analysis. Consequently, our understanding of agrarian development in modern Chinese history is a hodgepodge of different beliefs of how peasants were supposed to behave and organize farming. Central to our vision of the growth process is the contention that socioeconomic relations determined the production of rural wealth and its distribution, and these relationships had changed in ways to produce a distinctive trend of rural disintegration moving China inexorably closer to an agrarian crisis.

This study has been undertaken to verify the validity of this model. The findings strongly indicate that it must be rejected. The results of my study are closer to those of J. L. Buck than to those of any other student of the Chinese rural economy. Buck advanced a number of explanations which rested on incontrovertible evidence that the fundamental problems of agriculture had nothing to do with rural socioeconomic relationships. He contended that China's rural problem was rooted firmly in improving farming technology and in the government undertaking various forms of assistance to permit farmers to manage their land more efficiently. Buck's findings are identical with many reached in this study. Yet his conclusions have not influenced our understanding of Chinese peasant agriculture in the way one would expect. Perhaps one reason is the overemphasis given to matters of farm management and land use and his failure to consider institutions and market structure. Another reason may be the absence of a set of organizing principles or theory to explain how agriculture developed within the context of the economy's growth. There is little need to speculate further on this except to conclude by stressing several fundamental themes.

Conclusion

First, the peasant economy of north China performed remarkably well in supporting a population expansion without a reduction of living standards (except during wartime), providing labor for the expanding urban economy, and exporting food and industrial crops to the cities. This agrarian system contributed as well as can be expected to this region's development, considering the half century of political instability, war, and poor government its people had to endure. The notion that the treaty port economy could not develop rapidly because the rural economy was a drag on progress is simply false. If anything is closer to the truth it is that agriculture could not develop more rapidly than it did because the treaty port economy failed to industrialize rapidly and introduce technological change to the peasant economy.

Second, the key problem was the absence of any system generating rapid technological progress in agriculture. Trial and error methods of selecting better seeds and eliminating inappropriate farming methods enabled peasants to utilize their land more intensively and efficiently only in a very gradual way. This approach could not compare with what could be achieved by an organizational system conducting research on new high yield seed varieties and a wide range of related farming problems and an extension system to pass these findings along to the farmer. Local government in China did not possess the interest or the ability to transform traditional farming technology in this way. Nor did it have the resources at its disposal to stabilize farm production by flood control, construction of irrigation facilities, and building of roads.

Chinese officials and scholars had always regarded agriculture as important for the welfare of society but as an industry of inferior status and undeserving of fiscal support except at times of great natural disasters. This leadership really had very little understanding of what made agriculture prosper. Exceptional cases do exist to the contrary. An official or scholar occasionally took an interest in agricultural technology and wrote a treatise on the subject. Such a work might be published in several editions, but its value for farmers was determined solely by how vigorously local officials introduced this knowledge to their administered areas. It may still be premature to generalize on this point, but the available historical evidence so far suggests that official efforts to popularize such texts were simply too feeble and erratic to produce a revolution in the art of farming.

With peace and modest farming improvements taking place, villages multiplied and some even increased in size. Production rose, cities received additional food and industrial crops, and urban commerce and handicraft production expanded throughout the country. The technological and managerial limitations to farming larger size farms efficiently, encouraged wealthy farmers to shift their wealth and energies to urban commercial pursuits. For these reasons the growth of agriculture determined the rate and character of urban growth and the size of the nonfarm population that could be supported. Instead of cities developing new industries and promoting transport to absorb a larger share of the rural population on a permanent basis, instead of cities determining the character and progress of agriculture, agriculture was not influenced by cities in any fundamental way until after the 1890s. We must not infer, however, that the characteristics of China's modern economic growth are to be found in the development of her urban sector. The missing element was and remains that of the absence of technological change in agriculture.

Peasants organized farm production and exchange to meet the requirements cities imposed on the countryside. Agrarian conditions and peasant distress only became acute when severe climatic disturbances and wars occurred. When peace prevailed for long periods traditional technological change still progressed too slowly to increase yield significantly. Backward farming practices, particularly where related to the development of better seed varieties, made it impossible for peasants to increase production at a rate of two or three times that of population growth. Even so, the gradual improvement of traditional technology seems to have enabled this countryside to support a gradually expanding nonfarm share of the region's population at living standards which were equivalent to standards of the past half century. However, without a technological breakthrough, this rural society could not capitalize on the positive attributes its peasantry possessed: a capacity for hard work; ready response to innovation; frugality; rational planning; an ability to calculate gain against loss. Although some new seeds and chemical fertilizers began to find their way into villages after 1890, it was not enough to accelerate the rate of output growth. The income gains derived by peasants producing cash crops and earning nonfarm incomes were lost when the government failed to stabilize the harvest and war damaged the region.

The natural consequences of war upon the village economy were great loss of peasant land, mass migrations to other areas, the destruction of farm capital, and even famine. This rural economy was capable of reviving quickly from such setbacks and could continue to grow thereafter. Measuring peasant living standard trends throughout this period, however, is exceedingly difficult because so little reliable information was systematically collected. As urban living standards rose slightly faster than those in the villages, the rural living style stood out in sharp relief to that of the city dweller. For this reason it was easy for outsiders to infer mistakenly that the countryside was in a state of decline.

A study of Chinese agriculture on a global basis will always be complex and intractable. The huge size and diversity of China must make us cautious in theorizing about agriculture elsewhere in the country. In the famine-ridden northwest great masses of peasants were perpetually on the verge of starvation; the human spirit frequently broke under these conditions, and the family disintegrated. On the other hand, commerce was more developed and rural conditions were more prosperous and stable in the central provinces. If my study will stimulate other scholars to conduct further research on agriculture, the time will soon be at hand when a general theory of the Chinese peasant economy can be advanced.

Appendixes
Notes
Bibliography
Glossary
Index

Appendix A: Statistical Tables

Table A-1. Amount of land necessary to support a peasant family of five persons in ten villages of North China.

County and village	Amount of land necessary to support an owner cultivator and his family: Mow per person	Mow per household	Amount of land necessary to support a tenant and his family (mow per person)	Average size of peasant farm of sample village: Mow per person	Mow per household
Shun-i, Sha-ching[a]	5	25		2.5	14
Luan-ch'eng, Ssu pei ch'ai[b]	5	25	10	2.6	less than 10
			50		
Ch'ang-li, Hou chia ying[c]	10	50		4.7	28
Ch'ang-li, Hou chia ying[d]	6	30		4.7	28
Liang-hsiang, Wu-tien[e]	5	25		3.1	less than 10
I-tu, Wu li pao[f]	15	75		1.3	5.5
Sheng-tu county,[g] 1905, for Pei kao ling, Yeh-yang, Hou-t'ou, Nan t'ao ch'iu, Shih li p'u	6	30		less than 2	less than 10
En, Hou hsia chai[h]	5	25 (with handicraft and side income) 44 (without handicraft or side income)		less than 2	less than 10
Li-ch'eng, Lin shui kou[i]	5	25		2.3	11.4
Cheng-ting, Lo hsin chuang[j]	3	10		1.5	9.6

Sources: [a] *CN*, I, 67; [b] *CN*, III, 6; [c] *CN*, V, 150; [d] *CN*, V, 5; [e] *CN*, V, 6; [f] Kokuritsu, *Santō no ichi shūshichin no shakai teki kōzō* (The social structure of a market town in Shantung, 1942), p. 5; [g] *CC*, I, 196; [h] *CN*, IV, 10; [i] *CN*, IV, 2; [j] *Sagara Norio*, p. 144.

Note: I have not indicated the different square measurement units which existed in villages. The Shantung mow was larger than the Hopei mow.

Table A-2. Relevant data on the earnings of north China railways for selected years.

Year	Number of passengers	Quantity of freight (tons)	Revenue (Chinese dollars)	Expenditures (Chinese dollars)	Revenue per kilometer (Chinese dollars)	Expenditure per kilometer (Chinese dollars)
A. Tsingtao-Chinan Railway (469 kilometers)						
1905	–	–	1,912,298	–	4,807	–
1911	908,900	705,083	3,216,636	1,008,134	8,082	2,533
1912	1,230,043	852,001	4,239,661	1,175,755	10,652	2,954
1915	1,117,760	595,287	3,651,400	3,243,227	7,785	6,915
1920	2,945,132	1,074,672	12,937,402	16,081,691	27,585	34,289
1925	3,640,300	2,284,935	9,447,529	6,310,162	20,143	13,454
1930	3,734,731	2,052,206	12,573,688	7,718,228	26,809	16,456
1935	3,025,709	3,253,973	13,928,203	11,631,209	29,697	24,800
B. Peking-South Manchuria Railway (466 kilometers)						
1915	3,505,475	5,349,223	15,277,931	7,579,599	32,785	16,265
1920	5,076,032	6,827,283	23,146,505	8,528,765	49,670	18,302
1925	6,317,217	7,720,141	24,047,676	13,218,204	51,604	28,365
1931	7,349,544	10,123,122	42,758,750	20,107,283	91,756	47,440
1935	4,438,169	7,185,359	23,906,044	15,250,858	51,300	32,727
C. Tientsin-Pukow Railway (1,105 kilometers)						
1915	1,271,140	1,345,461	4,186,507	–	3,788	–
1920	3,210,240	2,941,371	15,358,368	–	13,899	–
1925	3,658,832	1,985,677	15,747,329	10,985,003	14,250	9,941
1930	2,109,239	1,212,055	13,377,823	11,202,295	12,106	10,137
1935	3,328,080	4,124,983	26,793,032	16,815,437	27,247	15,217
D. Peking-Hankow Railway (1,338 kilometers)						
1926	3,146,962	2,400,520	14,739,137	11,974,787	11,015	8,949
1930	2,063,160	2,321,850	20,138,647	14,799,986	15,051	11,061
1933	3,546,935	4,350,002	31,009,019	20,589,836	23,175	15,388
1935	4,141,804	5,912,786	36,706,225	19,485,413	27,433	14,563

Sources: A. Data for 1905–1911, IMC, *Decennial Reports, 1902–1911*, p. 253; for 1912, IMC, *Decennial Reports, 1912–1921*, p. 244. B. Mantetsu sangyōbu, *Kita Shina keizai sōran* (A general survey of the North China economy; Tokyo, 1938), pp. 71–72, appendix. C. *Ibid.*, pp. 67–68, appendix. D. *Ibid.*, p. 66, appendix.

Table A-3. Correlations to determine the influence of specific variables on rising food imports.

Dependent variable	Independent variable	Regression coefficient	Standard error of regression coefficient	Significance level of regression coefficient	Correlation coefficient between the two variables
Per cent value of food of total imports	Harvest results (6 points scale)	− 1.924	1.641	Not significant	−.30
Quantity of food imports to North China (1,000 piculs)	Food Price Index for North China	+89.858	12.262	Very highly significant (0.1 per cent)	−.87
Quantity of wheat imports (1,000 metric tons)	World wheat prices in gold value	− 2.307	760	Highly significant (1 per cent)	−.63
1 kg (quantity of wheat imports)	World wheat prices in gold value	− .878	.126	Very highly significant (0.1 per cent)	−.88
Quantity of rice imports (1,000 metric tons)	Burma boat paddy price (Rupees per 4,600 lb)[a]	− .874	2.425	Not significant	−.10

[a] Price was not converted to gold value per metric ton because the conversion factor cannot be obtained. Although this difference in units affects the value of regression coefficient by a constant multiple, the significance level and the value of correlation coefficient remains the same.

Table A-4. Types of land tenure systems in Hopei and Shantung (in per cent).

	(1)		(2)	
Type of system	Hopei	Shantung	Hopei	Shantung
Fixed amount of money	62.62	22.14	52.3	30.4
Fixed rent in kind	17.62	36.58	21.6	30.5
Payment in kind as a per cent of the harvest	16.71	40.27	26.1	39.1
Rent payable in labor time	3.0	1.01	–	–
Other	0.05	–	–	–

Sources: (1) T'u-ti wei-yuan hui, p. 43; (2) *Nung-ch'ing pao-kao* (Crop reports) of 1935.

Table A-5. Distribution of land ownership in Hopei and Shantung by farm size (in per cent).

Ranges of land ownership (mow)	(1) Hopei	(1) Shantung	(2) Hopei	(3) Hopei	Range of land ownership (mow)	(4) Shantung
0–10	40.00	49.65	–	–	0–10	38
10–20	28.20	27.29	71.9	67.58	10–50	47
20–50	24.04	19.12	14.2	21.11	–	–
over 50	7.76	3.94	13.9	11.31	over 50	15

Sources: (1) T'u-ti wei-yuan hui, p. 26. (2) Mantetsu research survey of rural Hopei and presented in Kashiwa Yūken, *Hoku-Shi no nōson keizai shakai* (The rural economy and society of North China; Tokyo, 1944), p. 39. (3) From a survey of 43 counties, 242 villages, and 133,696 households in Hopei in 1934; data contained in Feng Ho-fa, ed., *Chung-kuo nung-ts'un ching-chi tzu-liao* (Materials on the Chinese village economy; Shanghai, 1935), II, 145–146. (4) From the sixth agricultural statistical report (1920 by the Agriculture and Commerce Department as presented in Amano, *Santō nōgyō keizai ron*, pp. 319–325.

Table A-6. Land tenure in Hopei and Shantung, 1930s (in per cent).

Categories of ownership	(1)		(2)		(3)		(4)	
	Hopei	Shantung	Hopei	Shantung	Hopei	Shantung	Hopei	Shantung
Landlord	1.89	1.46	–	–	–	–	–	–
Landlord-owner cultivator	1.86	1.37	–	–	–	–	–	–
Landlord-cultivator-tenant	0.02	0.04	–	–	–	–	–	–
Landlord-tenant	–	0.01	–	–	–	–	–	–
Owner-cultivator	71.35	74.73	67	74	68	72	79.8	77.5
Owner-cultivator and tenant	10.95	10.38	20	16	21	19	15.6	18.1
Tenant	5.48	4.61	13	10	11	9	4.6	4.4
Tenant-agricultural worker	–	0.01	–	–	–	–	–	–
Agricultural worker	4.41	2.26	–	–	–	–	–	–
Other	4.04	5.13	–	–	–	–	–	–
	100.00	100.00	100	100	100	100	100	100

Sources: (1) T'u-ti wei-yuan hui, p. 34, of 23 counties and 176,339 households in Hopei and 18 counties and 255,692 households in Shantung. The detailed breakdown of ownership categories for table 1 was obtained from this survey. (2) From surveys by the Central Government Agricultural Experimental Station in 1935 of 117 counties in Hopei and 89 counties in Shantung. Only three categories of ownership were used, and the category of owner-cultivator include those who owned land but did not farm it. (3) From surveys during the 1930s by the research offices of the South Manchurian Railway Company. Three ownership categories were used. It is assumed that the counties surveyed represent land tenure conditions in the province. (4) Buck, *Land Utilization in China*, for data of 13 counties in Hopei and 23 counties of Shantung; also, see his *Statistics*, pp. 57–58.

Table A-7. Factors promoting or retarding village tenancy, 1930s.

County and village	Conditions of tenancy: (a) Tenancy	(b) Part-owner	Factors influencing peasant income: (c) Population density	(d) Village debt	(e) Location	(f) Cash crops	(g) Handicraft, etc.	(h) Off-farm employment
Shantung								
A. 1. I-tu, Tu chia chuang	+	+	+	+	−	−	−	−
B. 1. I-tu, Hsiao tien chia	−	+	+	−	+	+	−	+
2. Tsingtao area, Hsi han k'o	−	+	+	−	+	+	−	+
3. T'ai-an, Yung-wa	−	+	+	−	+	+	+	+
4. An-ch'iu, Chai-shan	−	−	+	−	+	+	+	+
5. I-tu, Wu li pao	−	−	+	−	+	−	+	+
6. Li-ch'eng, Ling shui kou	−	−	+	−	+	+	+	+
7. En, Hou hsia chai	−	−	−	−	+	+	+	+
8. Li-ch'eng, Lu-chia	−	−	+	−	+	+	+	+
9. Hu-min, Sun chia miao	−	+	+	−	+	+	+	+
10. I-tu, Meng chia lu	−	+	+	−	+	+	+	+
11. Chiao, Tai-t'ou	−	+	+	−	+	+	+	+
12. Lin-ch'ing, Tai san li	−	+	+	−	+	+	−	+
Hopei								
A. 1. Luan-ch'eng, Ssu pei ch'ai	+	+	+	+	+	+	+	+
2. Liang-hsiang, Wu-tien	+	+	+	+	−	−	−	+
3. Pao-ting, Hsi ma ch'ih	+	+	+	+	+	−	−	+
4. Twenty-four counties in north Hopei	+	+	+	+	−	−	−	+
5. Four counties in south Hopei	+	+	+	+	−	−	−	+
6. T'ung, Hsiao-chieh	+	+	+	+	+	+	−	+
B. 1. Ch'ang-li, Hou chia ying	−	+	−	−	+	−	+	+
2. Shun-i, Sha-ching	−	+	+	−	+	−	−	+
3. Chou, Hsin-chuang	−	−	+	−	+	+	+	+
4. Wang-tu, Wang-ching	−	+	+	−	+	+	+	+
5. Ting, Kao-t'ou	−	−	+	−	+	+	+	+
6. Cheng-ting, Fang lo hsin	−	−	+	−	+	+	+	+
7. Ting county	−	+	+	−	+	+	+	+
8. Chin county	−	−	+	−	+	+	+	+

Sources: Shantung. A.1 and B.1. Kokuritsu, *Santōsho Kō-Zai ensen chihō nōson no ichi kenkyū.* B.2. Mantetsu chōsabu, *Chintō kinkō ni okeru nōson jittai chōsa hōkoku* (A report of a survey of village conditions in the suburbs of Tsingtao; Peking, 1939). B.3. Hoku-Shi keizai chōsashi, "Taianken ichi buraku no nōgyō jijō" (Agricultural conditions of a village in T'ai-an County) in *Mantetsu chōsa geppō*, 20.3:1–32 (March 1940). B.4. Kahoku kōtsu kabushiki kaisha, *Tetsuro aigoson jittai chōsa hōkokusho.* B.5. Kokuritsu, *Santō no ichi shūshichin no shakai teki kōzō.* B.6. *CN*, IV, 147–190. B.7. *CN*, IV, 459–475. B.8. *CN*, IV, 353–384. B.9. Ishii Toshiyuki, "Hoku-Shi ni okeru jisakunō" (The owner-cultivator in North China) in *Mantetsu chōsa geppō*, 20.12:1–65 (December 1940). B.10. Hattori Mitsue, "Hoku-Shi ni okeru na tabako saibai fukyū irai no nōgyō keiei no henka" (The transformation of farm management since the spread of tobacco cultivation in North China), *Mantetsu chōsa geppō*, 21.20:81–108 (December 1941). B.11. Martin C. Yang, *A Chinese Village: Taito, Shantung Province* (London, 1947), chap. 3. B.12. Kishimoto Mitsuo, "Santōshō Rinshinken nōson jittai chōsa hōkoku" (A report of a survey of village conditions), *Mantetsu chōsa geppō*, 23.6:131–157 (June 1943); see also Pt. 2 of same study in *ibid.*, 23.7:135–165 (July 1943).

Hopei. A.1. *CN*, III, 161–242. A.2. *CN*, V, 509–539. A.3. Cheng Fu-kang, "Kyō-Kan ensen nōson zaki" (Miscellaneous notes on villages along the Peking-Hankow Railway Line), *Mantetsu chōsa geppō*, 19.5 (Pt. 1):140–141 (May 1939). A.4. Chang P'ei-kang, "Chi-pei Ch'a-tung san-shih-san hsien nung-ts'un kai-k'uan tiao-ch'a" (A rural survey of Northern Hopei and Chahar), *She-hui k'o-hsüeh tsa-chih*, 4.2:268–304 (June 1935). A.5. Ch'i Wu, ed., *I-ko ke-ming ken-chu-ti ti ch'eng-ch'ang* (The development of a revolutionary base; Peking, 1957), pp. 101–116. A.6. Tenshin jimusho chōsaka, *Kita Shina ni okeru mensakuchi nōson jijō* (Rural conditions in cotton-producing areas of north China; Tientsin, 1936), pp. 1–250. This village was formerly a grain growing village, but in 1921 the T'ung-chou Cotton Experimental Farm encouraged 15 villages in the vicinity of T'ung-chou to grow cotton. By 1936 roughly one-third of Hsiao-chieh village grew cotton. Peasant incomes had risen and many had acquired land. However, the number of tenants and part-owners still remained high and it has been classified as a village with high tenancy. But the continued emphasis on cotton specialization would probably have eliminated much tenancy if war had not taken place. B.1. *CN*, V, 143–198. B.2. *CN*, Vols. 1 and 2. B.3. Cheng Fu-kang, pp. 132–133. B.4. *Ibid.*, pp. 143–145. B.5. *Ibid.*, pp. 147–149. B.6. Sagara Norio, "Shokuryō seisan chitai," pp. 134–158. Article is continued in *Mantetsu chōsa geppō*, 23.11:1–73 (November 1943). B.7. Li Ching-han, "Ting-hsien t'u-ti tiao-ch'a," *She-hui k'o-hsüeh*, 1.2:435–467 and 1.3:803–872. B.8. Chūgoku nōson keizai kenkyūjo, *Kahokushō Shinken shisatsu hōkoku* (A report of Chin County in Hopei province; Peking, 1933), pp. 1–23.

Note: A plus sign indicates that: (a) More than 5 per cent of village households are tenants. (b) More than 10 per cent of village households are part-owners. (c) High population density exists where more than 50 per cent of village households own and farm less than 10 mow of land. (d) High village indebtedness was caused by a series of poor harvests, etc. (e) Village is located more than 10 kilometers away from the county seat or has no transport facility such as road, canal, or rail-road. (f) More than 10 per cent of village land area consists of a cash crop entirely marketed; cash crops are cotton, tobacco, soy beans, and groundnuts. Wheat could be regarded a cash crop, but for the villages included here it is not considered so. (g) Handicraft and village side work exists or has been on the increase. (h) Considerable off-farm employment opportunity exists.

A minus sign indicates the opposite of the above.

Appendix B. North China Crop Statistics

Crop statistics are essential for testing analytic models to explain important relationships in agriculture. Although incomplete data can be used to indicate the direction of change and more extensive data can be used to record the magnitude of the change and the reasons for it, we still need to know how reliable the crop statistics are in order to determine the purposes to which they can be used. The purpose of this appendix is to compare the various crop statistics collected before the war to show some of the difficulties involved in using these data to estimate farm production. The statistical tests used to appraise these data raise certain questions, unanswered here, as to which set of crop data is most dependable.

Crop Statistics in Imperial and Republican China

The Ch'ing court had always been interested in obtaining certain farm statistics for tax purposes. The tax revenue depended upon an accurate count of population and the area of cultivated land. After the poll tax and land tax were combined in the early eighteenth century, measuring the increase in cultivated land area became more important for fiscal reasons because the tax rate was not to change. In the Manchu administrative system crop statistics were produced in the following way. Information about the number of households, their size, and the amount of cultivated land they farmed was supplied by village headmen to the county magistrate and his assistants. The magistrate then reported to the provincial governor the conditions in his district, and the governor in turn made this information available to the Board of Revenue in Peking. This system was without a means of checking periodically whether various informants were telling the truth. Unless the county magistrate made a vigorous effort to check villages himself, it seems highly unlikely his office had a true picture of countryside conditions.

In 1905 the Ch'ing government finally became interested in taking an inventory of the country's wealth, recognizing that collecting agricultural statistics in a systematic and careful way was a necessary first step toward this goal. It created the Nung-kung shang-pu or Department of Agriculture, Industry, and Commerce, which took over the provincial governors' duties of receiving data from the district magistrates. This department occasionally sent investigators to specific counties to report and check on the data collected, but its staff was too small to do this thoroughly. The main innovation introduced by the department was that magistrates arrange the data to show the amount of land, number of rural households, types of crops, area of crop cultivation, output, area and output of cash crops, area of noncultivated land, and the area damaged by natural disasters.[1] More crop statistics were now collected, but magistrates still relied upon village headmen to supply them with farm statistics.

The principal defect in these statistics was the degree of error engendered by peasant distrust of corrupt officials. Corruption had spread to all strata of officials by the late Ch'ing period. District magistrates were paid a fixed salary, which scarcely changed as prices and administrative duties increased.[2] Clerical assistance had to be paid for out of the magistrates' pockets and, over time, as clerks demanded higher wages, local officials were compelled to supplement their own salaries from any means at hand. Their power was enormous at the county level, and they resorted to bribes and diverting funds from tax revenue, a practice soon followed by the clerks and tax collectors.[3] Corruption tended to snowball and the burden, inevitably, fell on the peasantry.

The peasantry resisted as best they could: they hid their wealth from the tax collectors and falsified reports of the true conditions of farming. We have some indication from county surveys in the 1930s of how drastic the difference was between the reported area of cultivated land in the magistrate's office and the true area of farm land. In 1934–35 the provincial governor of Kiangsu ordered a land survey of Chen-kiang and I-hsing counties for the purpose of putting land cadastres in order. The surveys showed from 20 to 30 per cent more land than was formerly registered for taxation purposes.[4] In 1933 Feng Hua-te gathered data from 100 peasant households in several villages of Hopei. He found a two to three fold difference between recorded taxable land and privately farmed land.[5] In September of 1940, the Japanese surveyed several districts in northeast Hopei and found that the registered land was 8,732,419 mow but that land the peasants farmed was 15,913,738 mow, nearly twice that amount.[6] Because conditions varied throughout the country and changed over time when magistrates were replaced, it is impossible to estimate the difference between registered and unreported farm land. The range may have been as much as 20 to 30 per cent or more and there seems little doubt that officially reported cultivated land was grossly understated.

The Department of Agriculture, Industry, and Commerce issued its first publication in 1911, followed by another in 1915, a third in 1916 and six more to follow, with the last appearing in 1926.[7] Civil war disrupted the department's activities in many areas in 1927–28. The new Nationalist government in Nanking wanted a better collection of crop statistics, and in early 1929 a pilot project to survey 269 villages in Kiangsu was undertaken to work out the methods to apply on a countrywide basis.[8] The national survey was conducted between 1929 and 1933 under the direction of the Legislative Yuan with the assistance of the postal authorities. County officials were asked to report their estimates of the total cultivated area, number of farm households, the percentage share of each crop in the total area, and the yield per mow for each crop in the *average* year. Out of

1,935 counties in 22 provinces, 1,781 were surveyed in this fashion. The task of sorting and processing the county reports was done by the government's newly formed Statistical Bureau. The data was then checked against materials of the old Department of Agriculture, Industry, and Commerce (now the Ministry of Agriculture and Commerce), provincial surveys, and county surveys made by the Ministry of Railroads. The results were published in the government journal, the *Statistical Monthly*.[9]

The government continued to collect data from these 1,781 counties in the same way until 1937. The data processing was done by clerks in the county tax office, and the results were sent to the Statistical Bureau to be assembled and published. The government was unable to carry out a national land survey to eliminate the discrepancies between registered land reports and the true area of farm land.

It is worthwhile digressing at this point to mention how important it is to have a land survey to establish the true amount of land under cultivation and private ownership. The Japanese found that after completing their land survey in the early 1870s the amount of newly registered farm land greatly exceeded the former amount recorded for tax purposes. The new land registers provided the basic statistics for the Ministry of Agriculture to estimate cultivated area and production. Even so, it seems the peasants had successfully withheld information pertaining to the amount of land they farmed during this land survey,[10] and their reticence indicates how deeply rooted were peasant fears of official attempts to obtain reliable farm statistics.

After occupying Taiwan the Japanese carried out a land survey between 1898 and 1902 and found that the amount of cultivated land surveyed exceeded the amount formerly registered by nearly two thirds.[11] Taiwan was small, officials were well aware of peasant resistance to a land survey, and the need for land tax revenue was great, and so it is quite probable the Japanese missed little land in their survey. Cultivated area and yield data made it possible to measure agricultural output from as early as 1910.[12]

An Evaluation of Hopei and Shantung Crop Statistics

A comparison of government crop data of 1930 with those collected by J. L. Buck at the same time will determine whether there is some yield correspondence between the two sets of data. Buck's statistical data have been largely regarded as very reliable. After he completed his first rural survey in 1924 covering seven provinces in north and east-central China, he cautiously concluded that the "number of farms, while large enough to be considered representative of the localities, must yet fall short of the detail and the number necessary for laying down wide assertions for the whole country." [13] It was to overcome this defect that Buck began a second, more comprehensive survey, in which the results were published in 1937. *Land*

Utilization in China was immediately hailed as a milestone in the arduous work of collecting reliable farm statistics in China. This study still commands tremendous respect and is used to this day as an indispensable reference source for Chinese peasant agriculture. The country was divided into farming regions, and "for each type of farming area, a representative village was selected, and 100 farms were studied in detail." [14] Data were collected by the questionnaire method, and trained personnel from the locale under investigation were used. But lack of funds and shortage of staff made it impossible to select for study more than 14 localities per province.[15]

How good are Buck's crop statistics for yield? Like the yield data of the *Statistical Monthly,* Buck's crop statistics have never been subjected to a careful statistical test, but they have been accepted as a basis for estimating food and fiber production. Three scholars recently used the *Statistical Monthly* and Buck's data to estimate food supply for the early 1930s. After making some adjustments they arrived at food production estimates which fall midway between the high estimate derived from Buck's data and the low estimate based on the *Statistical Monthly.*[16] They then compared their estimate with food production estimates published by the Chinese People's Republic for the early 1950s. It is useful to make these estimates and comparisons, and to aid others in this sort of work, I have submitted the data of Buck and of the *Statistical Monthly* for Shantung and Hopei to certain tests to determine which set of data can be used with greater or less assurance of dependability.

Some comment should first be made about the use of the term "representative." A "representative" sample of a population can have two different meanings: the sample may have been chosen at random, in which case a reasonably sized sample would give similar mean and variance to the population it was chosen from and the distribution of sample mean and population mean would be the same; the sample may have been chosen non-randomly to provide coverage of different conditions known to exist in the population. In this case if the population from which it was chosen is normally distributed, then the sample mean should be roughly the same as that of the population, but the variance of the sample may be larger. But if the distribution of the population is skewed, then the mean and variance of the sample may both be different.

In the analysis below, "representative" has the first meaning. In order to test the variances of the samples against the variances of the population, it has been assumed that Buck's selection of villages was random in order to represent the conditions of those counties and the region including Hopei and Shantung.[17] It has also been necessary to assume that the data obtained from these villages in each county were correct. If the sample was not random, the results of a test of homogeneity of variances would not be meaningful because the assumptions on which the tests were based would not hold. In comparing the productivity data for Buck's counties in Hopei and

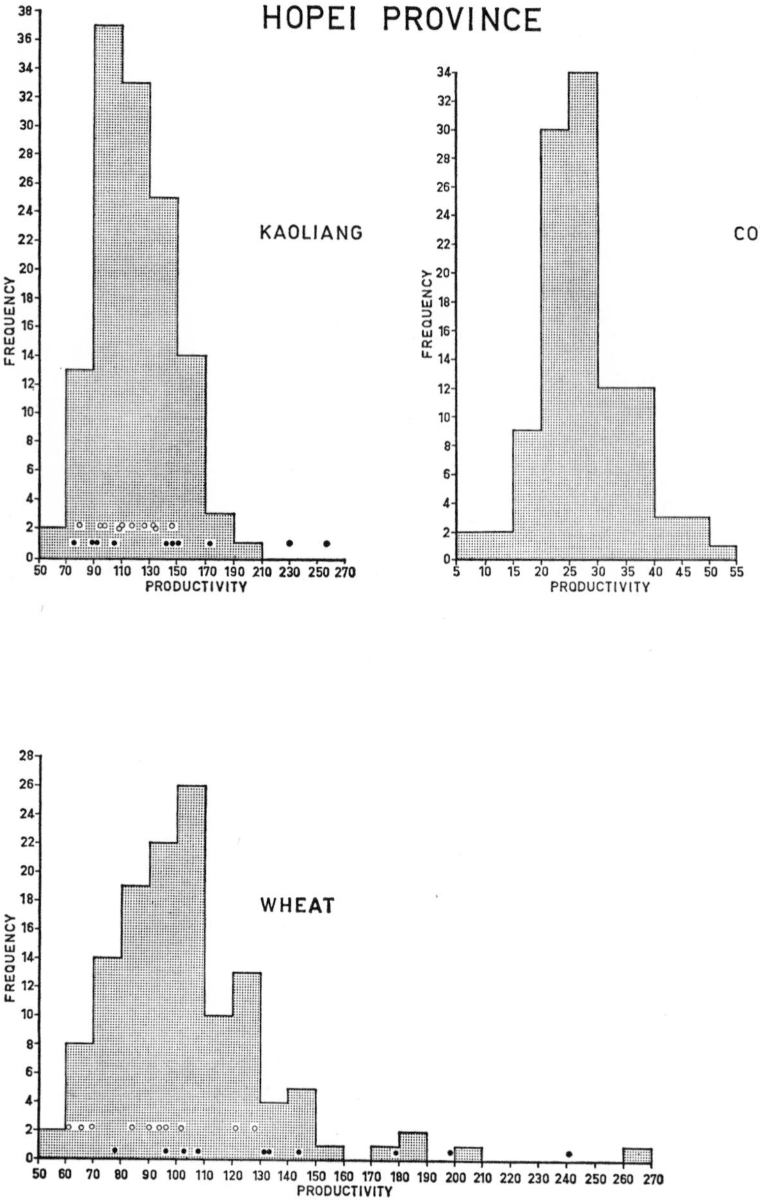

Fig. B-1 Frequency and range of productivity for selected crops in Hopei province, 1930.

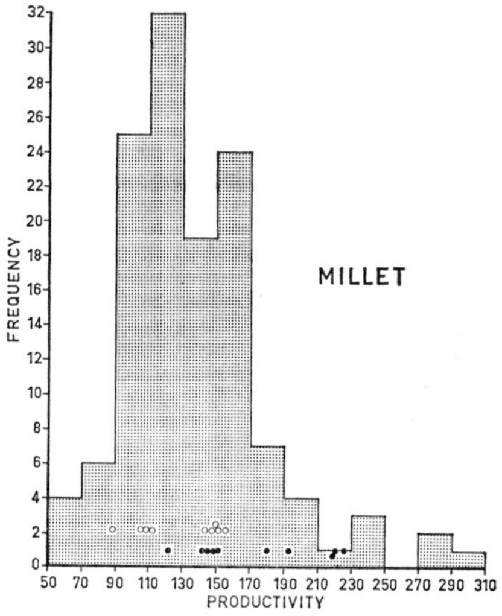
MILLET
FREQUENCY
PRODUCTIVITY
0
2
4
6
8
10
12
14
16
18
20
22
24
26
28
30
32
50 70 90 110 130 150 170 190 210 230 250 270 290 310

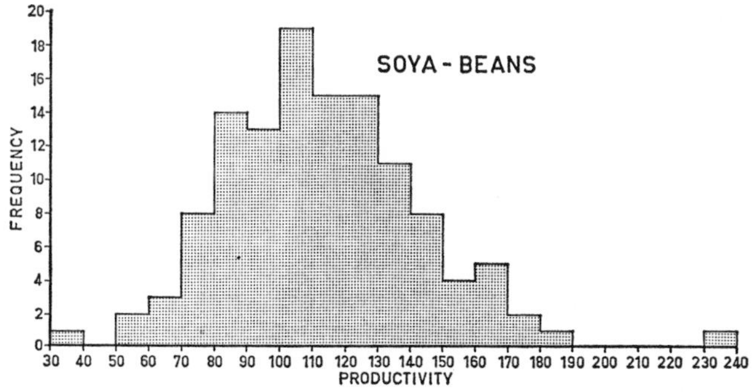
SOYA - BEANS
FREQUENCY
PRODUCTIVITY
0
2
4
6
8
10
12
14
16
18
20
30 40 50 60 70 80 90 100 110 120 130 140 150 160 170 180 190 200 210 220 230 240

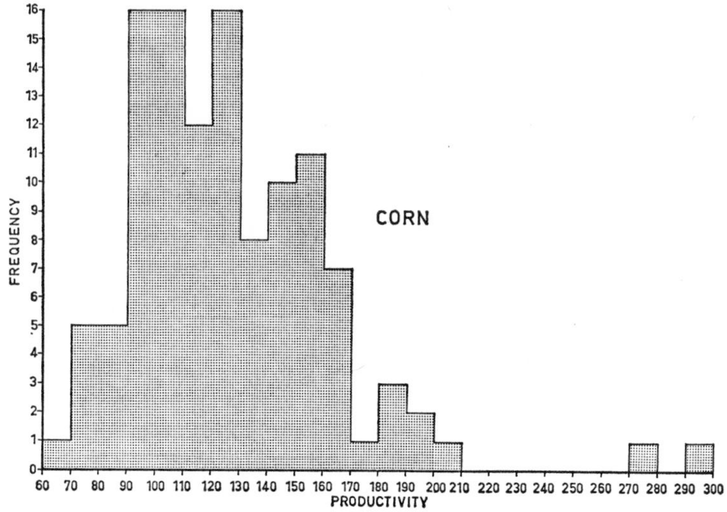
CORN
FREQUENCY
PRODUCTIVITY
0
1
2
3
4
5
6
7
8
9
10
11
12
13
14
15
16
60 70 80 90 100 110 120 130 140 150 160 170 180 190 200 210 220 230 240 250 260 270 280 290 300

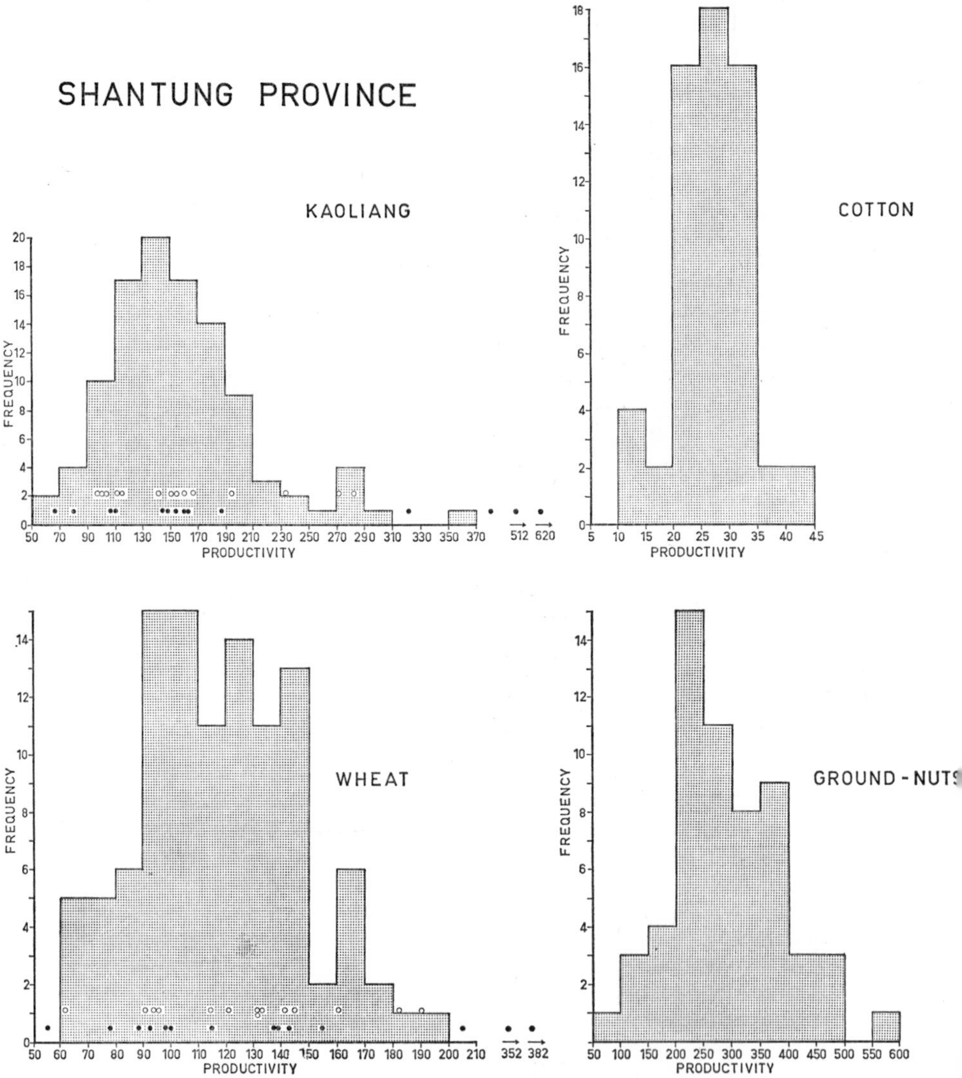

Fig. B-2 Frequency and range of productivity for selected crops in Shantung province, 1930.

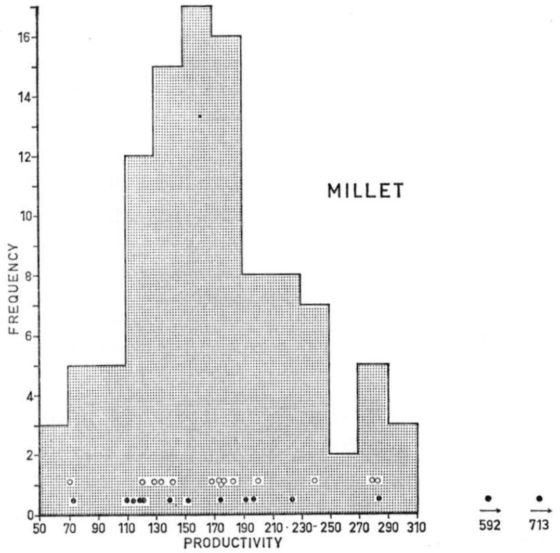
MILLET
FREQUENCY
PRODUCTIVITY
50 70 90 110 130 150 170 190 210 230 250 270 290 310
592 713

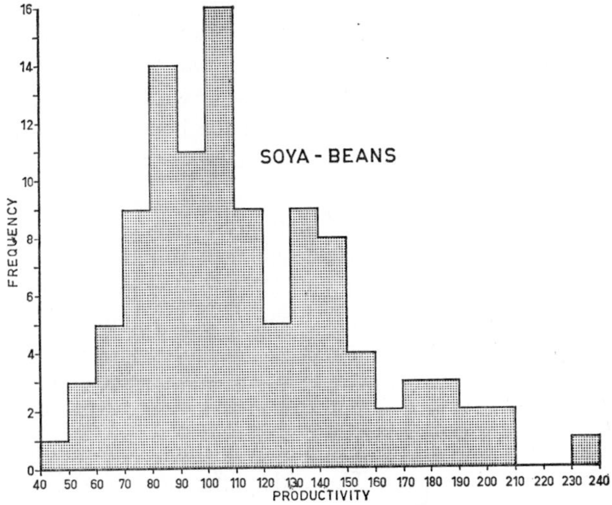
SOYA - BEANS
FREQUENCY
PRODUCTIVITY
40 50 60 70 80 90 100 110 120 130 140 150 160 170 180 190 200 210 220 230 240

Shantung, 10 and 14 respectively, with data for the same counties in the *Statistical Monthly,* we must recognize that in both cases cultivated area and crop output data were obtained from village headmen. Although this reporting can be said to be biased for reasons already stated, we would expect to see some similarities in our two sets of data.

The problem is to find the mean and distribution of productivity values for the localities Buck surveyed and counties reported in the *Statistical Monthly.* Although data were taken from village samples in both cases, I will refer to the unit from which productivity data were collected as the county. First, I compared the two samples in histograms showing different frequency ranges for different levels of yield for six main crops (see Figures B-1 and B-2).

Buck's counties were too few to make independent histograms so they were superimposed upon the *Statistical Monthly* data for the total number of provincial counties to show the range of yield values.[18] It can be seen that for wheat in Shantung Buck's data give a fairly good coverage of the range of productivity values, as indicated by the *Statistical Monthly.* But there were two cases which were of very high value and well outside the established range. Buck's data for kaoliang in Shantung showed a clustering about the mean as determined by the histogram, with a fairly even spread around the other values except again for two extremely high values. These productivity values are indeed erratic, and the histogram method does not provide a sure and easy test of which source gives a more reliable estimate of the mean.

Next, I compared the mean and standard deviation from the yield data for kaoliang, millet, and wheat to determine if similarities or discrepancies existed. When this was done we note a discrepancy in average productivity and standard deviation for Shantung when Buck's 14 counties are compared with the same counties of the *Statistical Monthly.* The same is true when ten counties in Hopei are compared. If the standard deviation readings of data of both Buck and the *Statistical Monthly* were similar, we could be more confident that the villages examined by Buck showed conditions truly representative of each county. The wide differences in standard deviation shown in Table B-1 indicate that the range of yield values varied greatly as do the means. These results beg the question of which set of data provides a true estimate by which the mean (for productivity) can be determined. Our statistical comparison gives no evidence which set of data is more reliable, nor can it be demonstrated that a true estimate of the mean lies between the higher figure of Buck and the lower figure of the *Statistical Monthly.*

We can also measure variance from the data in Table 64. The results show the variances to be homogeneous when *Statistical Monthly* data for Buck's counties are compared with the data for all counties. Buck's counties are a small fraction of the total counties of our two provinces, and when the variance for Buck's data is calculated and compared with the variance for the *Statistical Monthly's* total counties, the results show Buck's variances to be much higher. Hopei millet is the only exception to the case. This is a curious finding because this test should show the variances for the same counties of two different statistical sources when compared to the variances for the population to be similar if the smaller statistical coverage, Buck's counties, are representative of the province.

Ignoring these findings for a moment, suppose we test to determine if the means for Buck's data differ from the data for the same counties in the *Statistical Monthly*. In the case of Shantung, we can compare the data of both sources with data from the *Shantung Gazetteer*. A glance at Table 64 shows the means differ markedly. The explanation may lie in an error in the measurement units. When Buck's unit measures were converted to the units used in the *Statistical Monthly,* an error in the conversion factor may have accounted for the difference in means. In order to rule out such an error, productivity data from Buck's counties were correlated against data of the *Statistical Monthly* to determine if the correlation coefficients were high or low. The expectation was that if the conversion factor did account for the difference in means, correlation analysis should show high correlation for the sample counties even if the actual readings were different. With the exception of Shantung wheat, the results in Table B-2 showed very low correlation coefficients.

It can be seen in Table B-2 that the highest value obtained, .736 for Shantung wheat, explained only 54 per cent of the total variations of wheat productivity in each county. Even though the significance level is high in this case, the question remains, is it high enough to satisfy the purposes for which we want to use the data? Probably not. A single high correlation does not seem sufficient proof, because we expected, on all counts, near perfect correlation. Therefore, error in the conversion factor must be ruled out to explain the difference in means between our sources.

It is now necessary to compare county by county the results of Buck and the *Statistical Monthly*. Because each source gave only one productivity value for a crop for a county, I could not test the difference of productivity values for a single county except by casual observation. But because there are data for two sources for 10 and 14 counties respectively, we can test whether the means of the two sources are different. It is natural that some areas will give higher productivity values than others because of differences in soil conditions, farming methods, and technology. Some information on this question may be presented by analysis of variance.

In the analysis of variance each productivity value (Y_{ij}) was determined by a general mean (v), a particular county (C_i), a particular source (S_j), and a random variation variable (E). The problem is to find out whether the two statistical sources (samples from Buck and similar counties from the *Statistical Monthly*) give different answers for productivity. For well-

Table B-1. Comparison of average productivity and standard deviation from different sources for Shantung and Hopei.

A. Three sources for 14 counties in Shantung.

(1) Buck's counties

	Kaoliang	Millet	Wheat
Average productivity (catty/mow)	225.4	228.7	153.0
Standard deviation of county productivity	169.1	188.9	98.3

(2) Counties from *Statistical Monthly* equivalent to Buck's

	Kaoliang	Millet	Wheat
Average productivity (catty/mow)	163.0	176.4	129.6
Standard deviation of county productivity	62.0	59.8	35.5

(3) Counties from *Shantung Provincial Report* covering same counties as Buck

	Wheat (1933)	Wheat (average for 1931/32/33)
Average productivity (catty/mow)	161.4	141.9
Standard deviation of county productivity	81.5	61.2

B. Three sources for 107 counties in Shantung.

(1) Productivity from *Statistical Monthly* for all available counties

	Kaoliang (105 counties)	Millet (106 counties)	Wheat (107 counties)
Average productivity (catty/mow)	156.7	171.8	117.9
Standard deviation of county productivity	52.6	56.6	28.4

(2) Counties from *Shantung Provincial Report* covering same counties as Buck

	Wheat (1933)	Wheat (average for 1931/32/33)
Average productivity (catty/mow)	132.8	125.5
Standard deviation of county productivity	60.1	60.1

C. Two sources for 10 counties in Hopei.

(1)

	Buck's counties		
	Kaoliang	Millet	Wheat
Average productivity (catty/mow)	146.4	174.7	141.2
Standard deviation of county productivity	60.5	37.9	50.9

(2)

	Counties from *Statistical Monthly* equivalent to Buck's		
	Kaoliang	Millet	Wheat
Average productivity (catty/mow)	115.7	129.5	91.1
Standard deviation of county productivity	20.3	25.3	22.3

D. *Statistical Monthly* for all counties in Hopei.

	Kaoliang (128 counties)	Millet (128 counties)	Wheat (129 counties)
Average productivity (catty/mow)	119.8	135.8	103.3
Standard deviation of county productivity	26.5	42.6	29.1

Source: Buck, *Statistics*, p. 209; Tōa kenkyūjo, *Shina nōgyō kiso tōkei shiryō*, I, 41, 43, and *Chung-kuo shih-yeh chih*, Shantung, chap. 2, pp. 13–20 for wheat, chap. 1, pp. 1–17 for kaoliang and millet.

Table B-2. Correlation coefficients between data of Buck's counties and similar counties of the *Statistical Monthly* and *Shantung Gazetteer*.

A. Comparison of Buck's data with that of *Statistical Monthly*

	Correlation coefficients		
Province	Kaoliang	Millet	Wheat
Shantung	.573	.138	.736
Hopei	.146	.166	.687

B. Comparison of data of *Shantung Gazetteer* with the data of Buck and the *Statistical Monthly*

	Correlation coefficient[a]
1. Buck's data against 1933 Shantung wheat data	.051
2. *Statistical Monthly* data against 1933 Shantung wheat data	.264
3. Buck's data against three-year average (1931/32/33) data	.026
4. *Statistical Monthly* data against three-year average data	.300

[a] None of the correlation coefficients in B are significant.

conducted experiments two sources should give very similar answers for each county if the year the data were collected is the same. The problem is similar to that of multiple regression analysis. We can write our model as $Y_{ij} = v + C_i + S_j + E$. We wish to learn whether C_i and S_j are different from zero. In testing the effect of different county conditions (C_i) we ask whether, on an average, both sources agree in citing differences between counties. In testing the effect of difference of source (S_j), we ask whether one source gives higher values than the other. This effect may be present whether or not the differences between counties are meaningful or vice versa. Table B-3 shows this test to yield three possible results obtainable from comparing data on a county-by-county basis from two different statistical sources.

In Case 1 we observe a strong county effect but no significant source effect. In Case 2 neither effect is present and no regularities in the data can be observed. In Case 3 we have a strong county *and* a strong source effect. The results derived from random sampling should show that the means for each county from the two sources differed and that the means for all counties of the two sources are almost identical. This would be Case 1. If our actual test results were analogous to Case 1 we would have assurance that the data from both sources had been properly collected and

Table B-3. Three possible results obtainable from comparing two sets of data on a county-by-county basis.

Case 1			Case 2			Case 3		
County	Source A	Source B	County	Source A	Source B	County	Source A	Source B
1	4	3	1	4	10	1	4	2
2	8	6	2	8	6	2	8	4
3	16	18	3	16	4	3	16	9
4	12	10	4	12	3	4	12	5
5	3	4	5	3	18	5	3	2
Mean of 10 readings	=	8.4	Mean of 10 readings	=	8.4	Mean of 10 readings	=	6.5
Mean of source A	=	8.6	Mean of source A	=	8.6	Mean of source A	=	8.6
Mean of source B	=	8.2	Mean of source B	=	8.2	Mean of source B	=	4.4
Mean of county 1	=	3.5	Mean of county 1	=	7.0	Mean of county 1	=	3.0
2	=	7.0	2	=	7.0	2	=	6.0
3	=	17.0	3	=	10.0	3	=	12.5
4	=	11.0	4	=	7.5	4	=	8.5
5	=	3.5	5	=	10.5	5	=	2.5

truly represented the area. Cases 2 and 3 show the opposite and indicate that the data were improperly collected and the influences of county conditions and the method of data collection played an important and determining role. The analysis of variance of data from Buck and the *Statistical Monthly* shows results (see Table B-4) strikingly similar to Case 2.

The results of Table B-4 show that neither source nor county effects were significant, and all observations could just as well have been allotted by random numbers. There were no significant variations between counties that were comparable from both sources and no significant differences between sources that were held in common for all counties. The few exceptional cases have to be interpreted correspondingly. The absence of a significant county effect confirms the lack of good correlation found in Table B-2.

From these statistical tests we can conclude that both Buck's and the *Statistical Monthly* data show little correspondence with each other. There is some question, too, whether there exists any statistical basis for asserting that the true yield lies somewhere between Buck's high-yield data and the *Statistical Monthly*'s lower-yield data. Buck's data may be more accurate because he used personnel from the area, who might have established closer bonds of trust with village headmen and therefore could have collected more complete data than that which the headmen normally supplied district officials. It is difficult to know if this was the case or not, and furthermore, Buck's sample counties are still too few and only represent a small fraction of the total number in each province. The defects that characterized the *Statistical Monthly* data stem from the lack of trained personnel and the inability of investigators to check the results obtained from village headmen.

The analysis of the above is open to the same objection as the tests for difference of means in Table B-4: the variances of the two sources are

Table B-4. Analysis of variance for Buck's and *Statistical Monthly* data for the same counties.

Crop	Source of variation	Sum of squares	Degrees of freedom	Mean squares	F	Significance level
			Shantung			
Kaoliang	Between counties	288,840.1	13	22,218.5	2.18	N.S.
	Between sources	27,293.8	1	27,293.8	2.67	N.S.
	Error	132,726.4	13	10,209.7		
	Total	448,860.2	27			
Millet	Between counties	275,255.4	13	21,173.5	1.17	N.S.
	Between sources	19,126.1	1	19,126.1	1.06	N.S.
	Error	234,886.3	13	18,068.2		
	Total	529,267.9	27			
Wheat	Between counties	104,506.8	13	8,039.0	2.78	+
	Between sources	3,830.6	1	3,830.6	1.32	N.S.
	Error	37,621.5	13	2,894.0		
	Total	145,958.8	27			
			Hopei			
Kaoliang	Between counties	19,960.9	9	2,217.9	1.19	N.S.
	Between sources	4,700.2	1	4,700.2	2.53	N.S.
	Error	16,735.0	9	1,859.4		
	Total	41,396.1	19			
Millet	Between counties	9,983.0	8	1,247.9	1.36	N.S.
	Between sources	10,348.8	1	10,348.8	11.24	+
	Error	7,363.7	8	920.5		
	Total	27,695.5	17			
Wheat	Between counties	20,908.2	9	2,323.1	3.04	N.S.
	Between sources	12,565.1	1	12,565.1	16.42	++
	Error	6,885.3	9	765.0		
	Total	40,358.6	19			

N.S. = not significant.
\+ = significance level at 5 per cent.
++ = significance level at 1 per cent.

not the same. Neither set of data contains discernible internal evidence of being unsatisfactory in itself. The data are suspect because they differ greatly. The reason that Buck's data give higher variance than those of the *Statistical Monthly* may be because Buck's counties were chosen to give a picture of the full range of values of all counties in the province rather than being randomly selected. Or it may be that Buck used different data-collecting techniques than those used for the *Statistical Monthly*. The data of both sources for the same counties are widely different, irregular, and a very unsatisfactory low correlation exists between them.

Conclusion

We began our discussion by pointing out that a reliable crop-reporting machinery had never been established in China before the war. The system of relying on village headmen to supply crop statistics very likely produced data which greatly underreported the farming conditions that actually existed. Peasants' fear that officials would extract more tax revenue from them is the main reason for their falsification of corp statistical reports. Therefore, statistics of yield and cultivated area are perhaps the most undependable of all farm statistics. The range of underreporting can never be known or even estimated, but in many districts it was extremely high.

I compared the 1930 data of the *Statistical Monthly* with those gathered by Buck from localities in Hopei and Shantung to show that there was no similarity in the means and standard deviations between these two sets of yield data. The lack of any correspondence raised the question of which source was more reliable. Further tests questioned whether the true yield lay closer to any one set of data and whether there was enough dependable evidence to assume that it could be considered to lie midway between these two sets of data. The inescapable conclusion is that it is exceedingly difficult to know which source is more accurate for the estimation of pre-1937 food supply in north China. It is quite possible that repeating these same tests on the data for other provinces would yield similar findings.

Notes

ABBREVIATIONS USED IN THE NOTES

CC	*Chung-kuo chin-tai nung-yeh shih tzu-liao*
CN	*Chūgoku nōson kankō chōsa*
IMC	China, Imperial Maritime Customs
"KCSK"	Hatada Takashi, "Kyū Chūgoku sonraku no kyōdōtai teki seikaku ni tsuite no kentō: mura no tochi to mura no hito"
Mantetsu chōsabu	Minami Manshū tetsudō kabushiki kaisha chōsabu
NCH	*North China Herald*
PT	*Pei-ning t'ieh-lu yen-hsien ching-chi tiao-ch'a*

1. *Introduction*

1. Hou, Chi-ming, "Economic Dualism: The Case of China, 1840–1937," *The Journal of Economic History,* 23. 3:277–298 (September 1963).

2. John K. Chang, "Industrial Development of Mainland China, 1912–1949," *The Journal of Economic History,* 27.1:79 (March 1967). This argument has been repeatedly stressed and may be found in such standard works on the development of the Chinese economy as Cheng, Yu-kwei, *Foreign Trade and Industrial Development of China* (Washington D.C., 1956), chap. 3; Meng Hsien-chang, *Chung-kuo chin-tai ching-chi shih chiao-ch'eng* (A study of modern Chinese economic history; Shanghai, 1951), pp. 126–133.

3. *CN.*

4. I am indebted to Professor Amano Motonosuke for supplying me with local weights and measures data from his village surveys and research on agrarian conditions in Shantung and Hopei in the 1930s.

5. Before 1928 Hopei was referred to by its Ch'ing dynasty territorial name, Chihli. I used Hopei throughout this study to refer to this province prior to 1928 to maintain consistency in place name usage. This is not strictly correct because the area denoted as Chihli differed from that set by boundary lines and referred to as Hopei. However, I do not think the territorial differences are great enough to cause confusion or inaccuracy in the analysis and discussion.

6. John Lossing Buck, *Land Utilization in China: Atlas* (Chicago, 1937), p. 9.

7. The term sorghum will be used to refer to kaoliang, the large grain crop which grew to a height of eight and ten feet.

8. John H. Borchert, "A New Map of the Climates of China," *Annals of the Association of American Geographers,* 37:175 (1947). Rainfall per growing season is only half what it is in Szechwan. See Liang Ching-chun. "Chung-kuo jan yu kan-tsai chih fen-hsi" (An analysis of droughts and drought disasters in

China) in *She-hui k'o-hsüeh tsa-chih* (Quarterly review of social sciences), 6.1:16 (March 1935).

9. Yao Shan-yu, "The Chronological and Seasonal Distribution of Floods and Droughts in Chinese History," *Harvard Journal of Asiatic Studies,* 6:299 (1941). In Hopei during the summer of 1924, roughly 23 inches of rain fell in 33 hours.

10. William Lockhard, "The Yang-tse-keang and the Hwang-ho, or Yellow River," *The Journal of the Royal Geographical Society,* 28:294 (1858).

11. F. B. Turner, "Flood and Famine in North China," *Journal of the North-China Branch of the Royal Asiatic Society,* 57:2 (1926). The solution to this problem was the construction of additional channels to the sea where the many rivers in Hopei converged. Proposals of this sort were suggested in the 1920s, but to my knowledge there were no channels dug. Sheet erosion has also been most serious in north China, but soil experts feel it can be controlled and reduced because "reafforestation is practicable over much of the Shantung highlands and western Hopei." James Thorp, "Soil Erosion in China," *Journal of the Association of Chinese and American Engineers,* 17.4:189 (July–August 1936). See also Kikuta Tarō, "Hoku-Shi keizai shakai ni tai suru shizen no seisaku" (The influence of natural conditions on the economy and society of north China) in *Tōa jimbun gakuhō,* 1.3:5 (December 1941).

12. Mantetsu chōsabu, *Kita Shina no nōgyō to keizai* (The agriculture and economy of north China; Tokyo, 1942), I, 23–24.

13. J. L. Buck, *Atlas,* p. 33.

14. Yih Chih-yun, "Agricultural Conditions in China," *Chinese Economic Journal,* 7.3:977 (September 1930).

15. *Dispatches from United States Consulate in Tientsin, 1868–1906* (The National Archives, Washington, D.C.), vol. 2, item 101, p. 4.

16. Charles F. Shaw, "The Soils of China," *Soil Bulletin,* no. 1:27 (December 1930).

2. *Theories of China's Agrarian Problem*

1. For a good review of some of these early rural community studies in China see Morton H. Fried, "Community Studies in China," *Far Eastern Quarterly,* 14.1:11–14 (November 1954).

2. *NCH* (Aug. 3, 1878), p. 101. In the same vein the *Herald* asserted "There really exists in China no obstacles except the jealousy of the ruling class to the formation of private mercantile associations."

3. Chao Feng-t'ien, *Wan-ch'ing wu-shih-nien ching-chi ssu-hsiang shih* (Economic thought during the last fifty years of the Ch'ing period; Peiping, 1939), p. 41.

4. An excerpt from a report by the Board of Revenue in 1886 reads: "This office reckons that the true amount of provincial revenue from various taxes totals at least ten million silver taels. The revenue each province stores and submits each year in kind and tax amounts to one million silver taels. Such is

the great disparity between taxes and actual payments. Both the government and the people are denied their wealth because the greatest share is filched by greedy and corrupt officials." *Chao Feng-t'ien,* p. 17.

5. One finds no reference to the need to adopt Western methods to improve agriculture during the 1870s and 1880s. See Chung-kuo shih-hsüeh hui, comp., *Yang-wu yün-tung* (The movement concerning foreign affairs; Peking, 1959). In Japan statesmen like Matsukata Massayoshi urged that Japan borrow Western technology to improve its agriculture.

6. Sun Yat-sen, *The Principle of Livelihood* (Taipei, 1953), p. 50.

7. Mao Tse-tung, *Selected Works of Mao Tse-tung* (London, 1954), I, 21.

8. Fang Hsien-t'ing, "Chung-kuo t'u-ti wen-t'i wen-hsien shu-p'ing" (A commentary on scholarly publications relating to China's land problems) in *Cheng-chih ching-chi hsüeh-pao* (July 1935), pp. 888–889; Much of the large pre-revolutionary literature on Chinese agriculture did not survive the war and has been lost or destroyed. For an excellent bibliography of some of the better literature available at the time these scholars wrote see Amano Motonosuke, *Chūgoku nōgyō no shomondai* (Problems of Chinese Agriculture; Tokyo, 1952), II, 7–16.

9. Knight Biggerstaff, "Modernization — and Early Modern China," *The Journal of Asian Studies,* 24.4:607–621 (August 1966). Biggerstaff argues that by 1919 China already had eight normative characteristics which set a society off from its traditional base.

10. H. O. Kung, "The Growth of Population of Six Large Chinese Cities," *Chinese Economic Journal and Bulletin,* 20.3:301–314 (March 1937). From Kung's raw data it is possible to show that the rate of growth of city population ranged from a low of 3.5 to 9.8 per cent per annum.

11. C. T. Hsia, *A History of Modern Chinese Fiction 1917–1957* (New Haven, 1961), Chap. 2. A listing of the new schools, newspapers, and higher institutions of education can be found in the maritime custom reports which describe cultural development in the treaty ports. For the 1920s see IMC, *Decennial Reports, 1912–1921 and 1922–1931* (Shanghai, 1922 and 1932).

12. Ch'en Han-seng, *The Present Agrarian Problem in China* (Shanghai, 1933), pp. 2–10.

13. *Ibid.,* p. 19.

14. *Ibid.,* p. 32.

15. Heh Shan and Hsü Cheng-hsüeh, *Nung-ts'un wen-t'i* (The village problem; Nanking, 1936). This study stresses that imperialism and warlordism were responsible for village bankruptcy. Ting Ta, *Chūgoku nōson keizai no hōkai* (The disintegration of the Chinese village economy; Dairen 1930), a Japanese translation of a Chinese work, the author's name in Chinese. In this study is examined the effect of burdensome taxes and levies on villages. Ch'ien Chia-chu, ed., *Chung-kuo nung-ts'un ching-chi lun-wen chi* (Collected essays on the Chinese village economy; Shanghai, 1936) contains essays on the effect of natural calamities, high rents, and high taxes on the pageantry. Taiwan sōtoku kambō chōsaka (Research Department of the Taiwan Governor General Secretariat), *Shina nōmin no keizai jōtai* (Economic conditions of the Chinese peasantry; Taipei, 1930) is a translation of an essay in *Tung-fang tsa-chih.* The essay is a discussion of the disruptive affect foreign trade had on Chinese agriculture and how the unequal terms of exchange between agri-

cultural products and consumer goods affected peasant incomes. Feng Ho-fa, comp., *Chung-kuo nung-ts'un ching-chi lun* (Essays on the Chinese rural economy; Shanghai, 1934) discusses similar factors which were harmful to the rural economy and mentions that unequal land ownership distribution was a major cause of China's rural problem. T'i K'o-chu, *Chung-kuo nung-ts'un wen-t'i chih yen-chiu* (Studies and problems of the Chinese village economy; Canton 1933), p. 49, emphasizes land scarcity, excess rural population, defective credit institutions, heavy rural debt, and increasing tenancy as factors responsible for the agrarian problem. Chin Lun-hai, ed., *Chung-kuo nung-ts'un ching-chi yen-chiu* (Studies of the Chinese Village Economy; Shanghai, 1937) explains the agrarian problem in terms of rural social class relationships. Lu P'ing-teng, *Ssu-ch'uan nung-ts'un ching-chi* (Village economy of Szechwan; Shanghai, 1936) contains the model used by a postwar publication from mainland China to organize the data and information on agriculture from 1912 to 1937 (see *CC*). Ozaki Shōtarō, "Chūgoku nōson shakai no kindaika katei" (The modernization process of Chinese rural society) in *Shakai kōseishi taikei* (A comprehensive and systematic corpus of histories of social structure; Tokyo, 1950), pp. 1–84, shows the process of land transfer to private hands, increased differentiation of the peasantry, rebellion. Jack Belden, *China Shakes the World* (New York, 1949), pp. 135–158, also provides a concise, clear statement of this theory.

16. Mantetsu sangyōbu shiryōshi, *Chūgoku nōson keizai no komponteki shomondai* (Basic problems of the Chinese village economy; Dairen, 1937), p. 6. This pamphlet is a Japanese translation of an article from the periodical *Chung-kuo nung-ts'un* (Chinese villages), 2:1. I have been unable to identify the author.

17. *Ibid.*, p. 9.

18. Ch'en Han-seng, *Industrial Capital and Chinese Peasants: A Study of the Livelihood of Chinese Tobacco Cultivators* (Shanghai, 1939).

19. *Ibid.*, pp. 52–53.

20. *Ibid.*, pp. 78–79.

21. L. Magyar, *Majyāru Shina nōgyō keizai ron* (An essay on the Chinese rural economy), tr. Inoue Terumaru (Tokyo, 1935).

22. *Ibid.*, chap. 2.

23. *Ibid.*, pp. 79–86.

24. *Ibid.*, pp. 324, 327.

25. *Ibid.*, chap. 28.

26. *Ibid.*, chap. 29.

27. Fei Hsiao-tung, *China's Gentry: Essays in Rural-Urban Relations,* rev. and ed. Margaret Park Redfield with six life-histories of Chinese gentry families collected by Yung-teh Chow and an introduction by Robert Redfield (Chicago, 1953), p. 36.

28. *Ibid.*, p. 70.

29. Fei Hsiao-tung, "Peasantry and Gentry, An Interpretation of Chinese Social Structure and Its Changes" *The American Journal of Sociology,* 52.1:6 (July 1946).

30. Fei Hsiao-tung, *China's Gentry,* p. 117.

31. Fei's village studies of Kaihsienkung in Kiangsu and Yu ts'un in Yunnan

led him to believe that the average peasant landholder with 8.5 mow or 1.29 acres near Lake Tai or 3 mow near Kunming could not produce enough to live. See Fei Hsiao-tung, *Peasant Life in China* (London, 1962), pp. 202–203; Fei Hsiao-tung and Chang Chih-i, *Earthbound China* (Chicago, 1945), chap. 25. C. K. Yang's study of Nanching village near Canton shows similar results. See C. K. Yang, *A Chinese Village in Early Communist Transition* (Cambridge, 1959), p. 55. Careful methodical budget surveys of sample households in Sha-ching village of Shun-i county in Hopei in 1940–41 by Japanese field researchers also showed similar findings. See *CN,* II, 270–291.

32. Fei Hsiao-tung, "Problems of Rural Industrialization," *China Economist* (April 26, 1948), p. 102.

33. Fei Hsiao-tung, "Financial Rural Industrialization," *China Economist* (Aug. 2, 1948), p. 112.

34. *Ibid.,* p. 113.

35. John Lossing Buck, *Chinese Farm Economy* (Chicago, 1930), p. 5.

36. John Lossing Buck, *Land Utilization in China* (Shanghai, 1937). See also *Land Utilization in China: Atlas* (Chicago, 1937) and *Land Utilization in China: Statistics* (Chicago, 1937) for maps and statistical data.

37. *Ibid.,* p. 1.

38. John Lossing Buck, *Some Basic Agricultural Problems of China* (New York, 1947).

39. John Lossing Buck, "Fact and Theory About China's Land," *Foreign Affairs,* 28.1:94 (October 1949).

40. John Lossing Buck, *Some Basic Agricultural Problems of China* (New York, 1947), pp. 10–11, 19–20, 17.

41. *Ibid.,* p. 59.

42. R. H. Tawney, *Land and Labour in China* (London, 1932), p. 78.

43. *Ibid.,* p. 67.

44. Wilhelm Wagner, *Chūgoku nōsho* (Chinese agriculture), tr. Takeyama Yōkichi (Tokyo, 1942).

45. *Ibid.,* vol. I, pp. 212–213.

46. *Ibid.,* vol. II, pp. 88–89

47. *Ibid.,* vol. II, pp. 612–631.

48. Hsiao Kung-ch'uan, *Rural China: Imperial Control in the Nineteenth Century* (Seattle, 1960), chap. 9.

49. This view differs in substance from that of a recent model, but there are points of similarity. The most sophisticated framework to be offered yet for analyzing modern Chinese economic history rests on one assumption that the self-generating process of economic growth remained largely bottled up in the treaty port segment of the economy and that the multiplier effect of this "investment was thus largely confined to that segment." John K. Fairbank, Alexander Eckstein, and L. S. Yang, "Economic Change in Early Modern China: An Analytic Framework," *Economic Development and Cultural Change,* vol. 9, no. 1, pt. 1, p. 24 (October 1960).

3. Japanese Village Studies in North China

1. These village surveys were carried out by the North China Economic Research Office of the South Manchurian Railway Company and subsequently published as *Chūgoku nōson kankō chōsa,* see *CN.*

2. Chang Han-yu and Ramon H. Myers, "Japanese Colonial Development Policy in Taiwan, 1895–1906: A Case of Bureaucratic Entrepreneurship," *The Journal of Asian Studies,* 22.4:433–449 (August 1963).

3. Amagai Kenzaburō, *Chūgoku tochi bunsho no kenkyū* (Studies of Chinese land documents; Tokyo, 1966), pp. 784–798.

4. Mantetsu chōsabu, *Manshū kyūkan chōsa hōkoku* (Reports on investigations into the old customs of Manchuria; 3rd printing, Shinkyō, 1936).

5. For a good commentary on the history of the Chōsabu see Andō Hikotarō, *Mantetsu: Nihon teikokushugi to Chūgoku* (The South Manchurian Railway Company: China and Japanese imperialism; Tokyo, 1965), pp. 225–239; also John Young, *The Research Activities of the South Manchurian Railway Company, 1907–1945: A History and Bibliography* (New York, 1965).

6. Fukushima Masao, "Okamatsu Santarō hakushi no Taiwan kyūkan chōsa to Kahoku nōson kankō ni okeru Suehiro Itsutarō hakushi" (Dr. S. Okamatsu's survey of old customs in Formosa and the role of Dr. I. Suehiro in the investigation of rural customs in north China); *Tōyō bunka,* no. 25:40 (March 1958). Much of the background information concerning the surveys was taken from this informative essay.

7. Professor Suehiro (1888–1951) was born in Ōita prefecture, the son of an eminent jurist. He was graduated from the Department of Law of Tokyo Imperial University and became an assistant professor there in 1914. He studied abroad in Switzerland, France, and Italy in 1918. He was eventually promoted to a professorship and held the chair of civil law, served as dean of the Faculty of Law between 1935 and 1946, and played a prominent role in drafting labor law as well as serving as chairman of the central labor commission. He was depurged in 1951 and died the same year at the age of 63. Professor Tanaka, born in 1890 in Saga prefecture, graduated in 1915 from the Department of Law at Tokyo Imperial University. He toured Europe in 1919 and 1922 and eventually was promoted to a full professorship at Tokyo University. He published extensively in the field of international law and at the end of the war was appointed education minister in the Shidehara cabinet.

8. *CN,* VI, 547–554.

9. Suginohara Shunichi was born in 1897 in Kumamoto prefecture. He graduated from the Department of Law of Kyoto Imperial University where he specialized in civil and labor law. He taught for a period as assistant professor at Kyushu University, and then he was employed in the Mantetsu chōsabu. After the war he was appointed professor of law at Hokkaidō University and also served as chairman of the Hokkaidō District Labour Relations Board.

10. Tōa kenkyūjo dairoku chōsa iinkai, gakujutsu iinkai, *Shina kankō chōsa ihō* (Miscellaneous reports concerning the survey of Chinese customs; Tokyo, 1942), pp 3–5.

11. *CN*, I, 18.

12. *Ibid.*, p. 22.

13. *CN*, VI, 542.

14. See *CN*, VI, 454–540. For remarks of the participants concerning how the original research outline was compiled see pp. 487–489. The general opinion was that although the research outline was incomplete and failed to anticipate many new topics and questions, the interviews brought forth new data, which when integrated with the earlier outline produced a comprehensive field research outline. The outline topics were assigned accordingly: land ownership — Sugiura Kanichi; land sales and transactions — Hayakawa Tamotsu; tenancy — Yamamoto Akira; water control and rights — Sugiura Kanichi; land deeds and land rights — Shiomi Kingarō; taxes and their collection — Konuma Tadashi and Sano Riichi; credit — Andō Shizumasa; family and clan — Niida Noboru and Hayakawa Tamotsu; village — Murata Kyūichi and Hatada Takashi. See *CN*, I, 13.

15. *Ibid.* See the research outline at the end of vol. VI, pp. 9–52.

16. It is not surprising that the outline received a cold shoulder from many members of the Mantetsu chōsabu. Judging from the type of village field surveys that had been conducted in north China in the 1930s, it had become axiomatic that the basic departure point was an understanding of land distribution. Once the social and economic classes of a village were defined, to be determined by land ownership and renting land, it was believed that rural conditions would be better understood. Suginohara's outline was simply a means to gather information and group it. This inductive approach must have disturbed and annoyed the majority of researchers, who were convinced that land distribution was the key to understanding village society. Suehiro's legalist approach won out, probably because of the unusual administrative power he held in Tōa kenkyūjo. The various group rivalries in the Mantetsu chōsabu have never been discussed, but they most certainly existed.

17. Ohima Riichi, "Kahokushō Jungiken ni Mantetsu chōsashi o tou no ki" (A report on a visit to the Mantetsu Investigation Group in Shun-i county of Hopei province); *Tōhō gakuhō* 4.12:115–129 (March 1942).

18. Many of these studies are cited in J. K. Fairbank and M. Banno, *Japanese Studies of Modern China* (Tokyo, 1955), section 7.6.

19. *CN*, VI, 512.

20. *Ibid.*, I, pp. 14–15.

21. *Ibid.*, pp. 63–65.

4. Shun-i County: Sha-ching Village

1. *Shun-i hsien-chih* (The Gazetteer for Shun-i county; Shun-i, 1933), 6:1–26. These data yield an annual population growth rate of 1.45 per cent. In 1935 population density was 516 people per sq. kilometer, and males greatly exceeded females.

2. According to the first agricultural ministry's survey carried out in 1909–10, the major crops were sorghum, wheat, and corn in that order, in terms of sown area. See the Nihonjin-sho shōgyō kaigisho, comp., *Shina seisan jigyō*

tōkeihyō (Statistical tables of China's products and enterprises; Tientsin, 1912), I, 24.

3. *Ibid.*, 6:19.
4. *PT*, II, 7.
5. *CN*, II, 58.
6. Thirty-three villages in Shun-i were briefly examined by survey teams, and I have collected their demographic information and arranged it according to number of households in a village. There is some indication that in larger villages the sex ratio rises and number per household declines, but this cannot be said to be typical. The village usually comprised about 100 households. In 1928 the Nationalist government ordered villages of less than 100 households to merge with their neighbors in order to improve central government control and village leadership. The mergers rarely occurred.

Sex ratio and number per household according to village size in Shun-i 1941.

Size of village by number of households	Number of villages	Sex ratio (M/F)	Number of persons per household
0–100	29	1.013	5.68
100–200	10	1.027	5.52
200–1000	3	1.048	5.43

Source: *CN*, I, 1, 3, 4, 5, 9, 10, 20–21, 29, 30, 31–32, 36, 39, 40–41, 43–44, 46–47, 60–72.

7. *CN*, I. Data on pp. 35, 39, 41 were used to calculate the share of Shaching's population in these three age groups.
8. *CN*, II, 61.
9. *Ibid.*, pp. 66–68.
10. See data on *CN*, II, 69 and Buck, *Statistics*, pp. 223, 225.

Comparisons with Buck's data for average winter wheat land productivity show the following:

Product	Quintal/hectare for winter wheat area	Quintal/hectare for Sha-ching
Corn	10.76	8.6 (lower)
Sorghum	11.62	8.6 (lower)
Proso Millet	7.93	8.6 (higher)
Wheat	8.77	5.5 (lower)
Soy Beans	7.68	7.2 (lower)
Peanuts	15.82	18.10 (higher)
Irish Potatoes	55.17	86.10 (higher)

Source: Buck, *Statistics*, pp. 223, 225. Data for Sha-ching was derived by converting *tou* to *shih* and then to pounds; areas in mow were converted to hectares. This was then divided by the pounds per quintal (220.46 lb).

11. *CN*, II, 69.

12. *Ibid.*, p. 69. Chinese villages were heavily dependent upon markets and sold a high share of their crop there. Buck has reported that his survey of seven provinces showed that the per cent of total output sold was: Hopei — 54 per cent, Honan — 38 per cent, Shensi — 50 per cent, Anhwei — 35 per cent, Kiangsu — 73 per cent, Chekiang — 83 per cent, south Anhwei — 55 per cent. The overall average was 52.6 per cent. See Amano, *Chūgoku nōgyō no shomondai,* I, 29.

13. *CN*, II, 70.

14. *CN*, I, 102.

15. Before 1920 no white corn had been grown in the area; these new seeds appeared on the market in Shun-i sometime in the early 1920s and villagers thought they had come from Tientsin. *CN*, II, 89.

16. *CN*, II, 61. Informants were the village elders Yang Yuan, Tu Hsiang, Yang Che, Chang Yung-jen, Chang Shui, Yang Jun, Chao Ting-k'uei and Chang Shou-jen. See *CN*, II, 88–89, where further interviewing confirmed that the type of crop and cropping practices had not changed. Villagers explained this on the basis the land was too poor, and they used the argument to account for Sha-ching's poverty.

17. *CN*, II, 62–63.

18. *CN*, II, 63–65. Rising prices in the late 1930s definitely made their purchase nearly impossible for the average peasant. In 1941 a plough cost $20.00 Chinese, while the year before it could be obtained for $6.00 or $7.00.

19. *CN*, II, 214. *T'ao* originally meant tying a rope to hold a donkey and horse together. *Ta* means mutual exchange. The two terms combined carry the meaning of joint sharing of livestock. See *CN*, I, 121.

20 *CN*, II, 1–24, from household survey.

21. *CN*, I, 118. There was the case of two peasants, Chang Tien and Chang Lin-ying who had practiced *ta-t'ao* for over ten years.

22. *CN*, II, 1–24, for household data on land owned and managed, off-farm work, and joint leasing of land and livestock.

23. *CN*, II, 72–86.

24. *CN*, II, 74. For lack of a better term, I use mortgage to mean the exchange of an asset, usually land, for credit in which the lender uses the asset and the borrower does not pay interest on the loan. When the loan is repaid, the asset reverts to the original owner. This is a slightly different meaning than that in the Western commercial dictionary.

25. *CN*, II, 94.

26. *CN*, II, 81.

27. *CN*, II, 106.

28. *CN*, I, 104–105.

29. I have calculated household labor power on the basis of the age distribution of villagers from the following data collected in 1941.

Labor power available according to age distribution in Sha-ching, 1941.

Age category	Number of workers available	
	Maximum	Minimum
16–20 years	22	16
21–25	12	1
26–30	14	10
31–35	17	10
36–40	10	6
41–45	12	8
46–50	6	2
Total	93	67

Source: *CN*, II, 58. These data were used to calculate the amount of labor available per household.

30. The labor requirements for planting in Sha-ching in 1941 were as follows:

Size of farm (mow)	Laborers required per day
1	2
2	2
3	2
4	3
5	3
6	4
7	4
8	5
9	5
10	6
15	7
20	8

Source: *CN*, II, 87.

31. *CN*, II, 193–194.
32. *Ibid.*, p. 194.
33. *Ibid.*, p. 209.
34. *Ibid.*, p. 211.
35. *Ibid.*, p. 169. The person who mortgaged the land was called the *ch'u-tien-chu* and the recipient of the land or lender was called the *tien-chu*.

36. Village land was classified into three grades for taxation purposes. *Shang-ti* was regarded as high-grade land of high value; *chung-ti* was middle-grade land of average price; and *hsia-ti* was low-grade land of low value.

37. *Ibid.*, p. 220.

38. *Ibid.*, p. 182.

39. *Ibid.*, p. 187.

40. *CN*, II, 252. When the peasant borrowed money and pledged his land as collateral, he paid fees to the village crop association and assessments for the village *t'an-k'uan* or periodic levy. When the land was mortgaged, the lender or recipient of the land paid these fees. Thus, the user of the land was assessed village fees, not the landowner. Previously, when most peasants owned more land, this had not been the case.

41. *Ibid.*, p. 181.

42. *Ibid.*, p. 193.

43. *Ibid.*, pp. 270–291.

44. For example, see the chapter describing Ling shui kou village in Shantung.

45. *CN*, I, 236–237.

46. The number of clans is indicated below:

Clan name	Number of clans	Number of clan households	Clan head
Yang	1	11	Yang Yung-ts'ai
Li	1	5	Li Shu-lin
Li	1	9	Li Juh-yuan
Sun	1	3	Sun Yu-jang
Chang	1	11	Chang Wen-t'ung
Chao	1	3	Chao Ting-k'uei
Chao	1	1	Chao Shao-ting
Chao	1	1	Chao Wen-yu
Wang	1	2	Wang Ch'un-lin
Tsung	1	1	Tsung Wen-ch'i
Wu	1	1	Wu Tien-chen
Tu	1	7	Tu Ch'un
Chou	1	1	Chou Shu-tang
Shih	1	1	Shih Chen-wang
Liu	1	3	Liu Fu
Liu	1	2	Liu Chang-ch'un
Liu	1	1	Liu Chen-t'ing
Hsing	1	1	Hsing Juh-chi
Chiang	1	1	Chiang Ch'ing-fu
Fu	1	1	Fu Chu
Pai	1	1	Pai Ch'eng-chih
Kuan	1	1	(woman)
Ching	1	1	Ching Te-fu

It is apparent that the Li, Yang, Ch'ang family surnames were most numerous. Their number dominated in the village council. These three clans owned the largest share of village land. *CN,* I appendix on household survey.

47. *CN,* I, 229.
48. *Ibid.,* p. 242.
49. *Ibid.,* p. 241.
50. *Ibid.,* p. 241.
51. *Ibid.,* pp. 97–98.
52. *Ibid.,* p. 97.
53. *Ibid.,* p. 174.
54. *Ibid.,* p. 180.
55. I am indebted to a long essay on the character of village boundaries in north China by Hatada Takashi. See Hatada, "KCSK," p. 23. The author advances an explanation of the emergence of crop watching associations, and he shows that in the nineteenth century villages were amorphous and did not take on a definite shape until the twentieth century. Many of my ideas on changes in village organization were derived from this brilliant work.
56. *CN,* I, 174–175.
57. *Ibid.,* pp. 134, 152.
58. *Ibid.,* p. 133.
59. *Ibid.,* p. 185. Peasants reported that before 1900 there was no formal village boundary.
60. Hatada, "KCSK," pp. 64–70.
61. *CN,* I, 212.
62. Hatada, "KCSK," p. 70.
63. *CN,* I, 101. No. 1 *chia* was headed by Li Juh-yuan, no. 2 by Yang Yuan no. 3 by Chang Yung-jen, no. 4 by Tu Hsiang, no. 5 by Chao Ting-k'uei, and no. 6 by Chang Shui.
64. *Ibid.,* p. 107, shows a list of the seven peasants selected for night guard each night for a patrol period of one month. It should also be noted that each *chia* head was responsible for arbitrating quarrels and managing various affairs involving the households of his *chia.* The creation of the *pao-chia* gave council members more effective control over the village than in the past.
65. *Ibid.,* p. 144.
66. *Ibid.,* p. 224, tells of a case where Sha-ching had to supply a certain amount of peasant labor to work on dike repairs along the White river. See *CN,* II, 345.
67. *Shun-i hsien-chih,* 6:2–3.
68. *CN,* II, 297, 438–439.
69. *Ibid.,* pp. 364, 439.
70. *Ibid.,* pp. 372–373.
71. *Ibid.,* p. 439.
72. *Ibid.,* p. 440.
73. *Ibid.,* p. 324. It is quite likely this surcharge was first levied in the late 1920s. In 1928–29 it was 2 *ch'ien* per mow, and it was increased to 3 *ch'ien* per mow after 1934.
74. *Ibid.,* p. 323.

75. *Ibid.*, pp. 338–339. In district 1 there were 41 villages. On p. 339 there are data showing the apportionment of a levy among 41 villages. The average amount each village would have paid had the levy been apportioned equally to each village would have been 16.7 yuan. Sha-ching was a small, poor village, and the basis for allocating the levy burden was on an ability to pay basis. Thus, Sha-ching only paid 11.5 yuan.

76. *Ibid.*, pp. 350–351. The levy on merchants in 1939 was apportioned by the merchant's association among 68 firms.

77. *Ibid.*, pp. 336–337.

78. *Ibid.*, pp. 296, 298.

79. *Ibid.*, p. 304.

5. *Luan-Ch'eng County: Ssu pei ch'ai Village*

1. *CN*, III, 346.

2. According to a statistical study of 35 hsien in Hopei province made in 1936, the total cultivated land area for Luan-ch'eng between 1931 and 1933 was 456,000 mow. This is considerably below the 1930 estimate in Table 9, but even then cultivated area still declined. See "Chin-nien Ho-pei sheng san-shih-wu hsien chih jen-k'ou chuan-t'ai" (Population conditions in 35 counties of Hopei during the last few years), *Chi-ch'a tiao-ch'a t'ung-chi ts'ui-k'an* (Statistical bulletin for surveys of north China; September, 1936), p. 19.

3. *CN*, III, 5.

4. *Luan-ch'eng hsien-chih* (The gazetteer of Luan-ch'eng county; Hopei, 1873), 4:2–26, for population data in 1840.

5. *CN*, III, 27.

6. *Ibid.*, p. 38. Males exceeded females at the ratio of 1.08. This figure was based upon calculations from household data in the appendix, pp. 525–533.

7. *Ibid.*, p. 257, provides household budget data for the wealthy peasant Liu.

8. *Ibid.*, p. 27.

9. *Ibid.*, p. 365.

10. *Ibid.*, pp. 2, 36.

11. *Ibid.*, p. 163.

12. *Ibid.*, p. 295. The landlord Wang Tsan-chou had opened a grain shop in the 1920s and had successfully prevented the family property from being divided between his sons. Wang's father had also been a moneylender and absentee landlord. This is an unusual case of a family's fortune steadily improving over three generations.

13. *CN*, III, 5–6.

14. *Ibid.*, p. 197.

15. *Ibid.*, pp. 9, 161.

16. *Ibid.*, pp. 235–237.

17. *Ibid.*, pp. 162–163.

18. *Ibid.*, p. 172.

19. *Ibid.*, p. 164.

20. *Ibid.*, p. 162.

21. *Ibid.*, p. 185.

22. *Ibid.*, p. 283. It also became possible to mortgage one mow of land to redeem two mow after 1938 because the price of mortgaged land rose so rapidly (see p. 300). After 1911 rising land prices enabled all peasants who had mortgaged land in this period to redeem their land by 1926 (see p. 299). In 1937 many peasants also began to redeem land which had been mortgaged in the early 1930s but bad harvests in 1938 and 1939 forced many peasants to mortgage land again (see p. 291).

23. *Ibid.*, p. 174. When Lin Feng-hsi was asked if it was really wrong for the landlords to change custom he replied: "I cannot speak for the others, but if I did so it would make no difference for it would only benefit one tenant. But I am sure the other landlords would be furious with me. In China *custom* is tradition, and if someone departs from the time-honored rules, a few may agree but the majority will vigorously object."

24. *Ibid.*, p. 37. Sometimes cotton was planted two years in a row on the same plot of land, but unless large amounts of fertilizers were used the harvest was very poor (see p. 213).

25. *Ibid.*, pp. 130–132.

26. *Ibid.*, p. 65.

27. *Ibid.*, p. 194.

28. *Ibid.*, p. 194.

29. *Ibid.*, p. 37.

30. *Ibid.*, p. 37.

31. *Ibid.*, p. 38.

32. *Ibid.*, p. 189.

33. *Ibid.*, p. 309.

34. *Ibid.*, p. 307. This was called *ch'un-chieh ch'iu-huan* or borrowing in the spring to repay in the fall. See p. 308.

35. *Ibid.*, p. 352.

36. *Ibid.*, p. 319.

37. *Ibid.*, p. 316.

38. *Ibid.*, p. 260.

39. *Ibid.*, p. 243.

40. *Ibid.*, p. 244.

41. *Ibid.*, pp. 280–281, 299.

42. *Ibid.*, pp. 286–287.

43. *Ibid.*, p. 260.

44. *Ibid.*, p. 170.

45. *Ibid.*, p. 325. I have been able to locate five markets, and they are distributed in the form of a pentagonal (assuming the sixth market town fits this pattern) with the largest market of Pei-kuan located outside the county seat at the center of the other five. Tung-kuan, the largest market, had four scheduled market days, per lunar week (*hsün*) and the other five meshed in such a way that one or more markets were always open. One hsün equals ten days.

46. *Ibid.*, p. 326.

47. *Ibid.*, p. 323.

48. *Ibid.*, p. 347.

49. *Ibid.*, p. 70.

50. *Ibid.*, p. 79.

51. *Ibid.*, p. 21. There appears to be a discrepancy here for on p. 89 it is reported the Ho clan only had 42 households.

52. *Ibid.*, p. 5.

53. *Ibid.*, p. 90 for a list of the five Ho household heads.

54. *Ibid.*, p. 41.

55. *Ibid.*, p. 49. The names of peasants who were *chia* heads are also listed.

56. *Ibid.*, p. 29.

57. *Ibid.*, p. 48.

58. *Ibid.*, p. 59. Ssu pei ch'ai's headman reported that the most difficult task for him was to collect the *t'an-k'uan* demanded by the police.

59. *Ibid.*, p. 64. When the peasant Li Lo-kao was interviewed (he owned 2 mow and rented 8 as a tenant), he claimed that he went to the fields at night because it was cool and the children were noisy. But when questioned further that someone might steal crops if the fields were not watched, he admitted that having a guard did keep thieves away. He reported no cases of theft.

60. *Ibid.*, p. 66.

61. *Ibid.*, p. 41.

62. *Ibid.*, p. 41.

63. *Ibid.*, p. 41.

64. *Ibid.*, p. 30.

65. *Ibid.*, p. 36.

66. *Ibid.*, p. 39.

67. *Ibid.*, p. 60 provides a table showing that 25 villages in Luan-ch'eng contributed 2,191 workers for forced labor to satisfy one county corvee demand.

68. *Ibid.*, p. 30.

69. *Ibid.*, p. 557.

70. *Ibid.*, p. 29.

71. *Ibid.*, pp. 51, 27, 29.

72. *Ibid.*, p. 417.

73. *Ibid.*, p. 403.

74. These figures were obtained from Muramatsu Yūji, "Ranjōken to Jihokusai son" (Luan-ch'eng hsien and Ssu pei ch'ai village) *Hitotsubashi ronsō,* 22.1:183 (July 1949). Professor Muramatsu used the original 123 draft copies of village surveys compiled by investigators of the North China Economic office. He has informed me personally that there is little difference between the original draft copies and the six volumes printed by Iwanami Shoten.

75. *Ibid.*, p. 431.

76. *Ibid.*, p. 371.

77. *Ibid.*, p. 372.

78. *Ibid.*, p. 367.

79. *Ibid.*, pp. 411–413, shows a list of 28 villages which had not paid their land taxes. Frequently police came to such a village and seized the village headman announcing that he would only be released when the village paid its taxes (see p. 372).

80. The land tax was set at one silver tael for every 28 mow, which, when converted to currency used during the 1930s, was 2 yuan 30 ch'ien (see p. 420). If one yuan equals 100 ch'ien, this meant that one mow was taxed about 8 ch'ien, which was a very low amount. Nevertheless, when surcharges were added

to this, the tax could be very heavy for the peasant, particularly when he had only harvested a small crop.

81. *Ibid.*, pp. 405–406.

82. *Ibid.*, p. 406.

83. *Ibid.*, p. 432.

84. *Ibid.*, p. 367.

85. *Ibid.*, p. 504.

86. *Ibid.*, pp. 492–499 for the amounts of various commodity turnover taxes paid and the means of collecting these taxes.

6. Li-ch'eng County: Ling shui kou Village

1. *CN,* IV, 9. When Chinese resistance to the Japanese military stiffened after 1941 and the Japanese were forced onto the defensive, the attitude of Ling shui kou villagers changed abruptly. Peasants became more evasive and less co-operative in answering questions put to them by Japanese investigation teams. For this reason, study of this village was discontinued and Lu chia chuang village in the same county was selected for survey. However, only a small section of this volume deals with Lu chia chuang, whereas half of the volume is devoted to Ling shui kou. Although quantitative evidence is lacking, the rich material on institutions and village life invites examination.

2. Data on the 1924 population were obtained from *Li-ch'eng hsien-chih* (The gazetteer of Li-ch'eng county; Shantung, 1924), 10:1–2b. Data for 1931 were obtained from Amano Motonosuke, *Santōshō keizai chōsa shiryō: Santō nōgyō keizai ron* (Economic research materials relating to Shantung province: An essay on the Shantung agricultural economy; Dairen, 1936), p. 309.

3. *Ibid.*, p. 319.

4. See Appendix 1 for crop area and output for 107 hsien in 1931, Amano, *Santō nōgyō keizai ron.*

5. *CN,* IV, 1.

6. *Ibid.*, pp. 1, 48.

7. For data on village households in 1928 see *Ibid.*, p. 25, and for data in 1941 see p. 325. The latter figure was provided by the Hsiang administrative unit containing four villages.

8. *Ibid.*, p. 327.

9. The difference may be seen from the following figures.

Crop	Ling shui kou, 1941 output per mow	Li-Ch'eng county, 1931 output per mow
Rice	150 catties	–
Sorghum	100 catties	169 catties
Millet	90 catties	194 catties
Soy beans	100 catties	114 catties
Wheat	120 catties	169 catties

Source: CN, IV, 2, for data on Ling shui kou; see Appendix 1 for data on Li-ch'eng county in 1931 from Amano *Santō nōgyō keizai ron.*

10. *Ibid.*, pp. 250, 4.

11. I have estimated land ownership distribution from a list of villagers' names in the village temple copied in 1940 (*CN*, IV, 386–389). The total amount of land recorded from this list is 4,063, just short of the 4,200 mow reported by the village headman. I have made a frequency distribution table with this data which confirms the comments of all informants that few villagers had no land. There is a discrepancy between the list of village names and the total number of village households. It is possible peasants from other villages were also included on this temple list.

Land ownership according to amount of land owned for Ling shui kou, 1940

Amount of land owned (mow)	Number of names listed	Per cent
No land	20	4
0–10	302	61
10–20	135	27
20–50	42	8
Total	499	100

12. *CN*, IV, 14.
13. *Ibid.*, p. 284.
14. *Ibid.*, p. 30.
15. *CN*, IV, 240.
16. *Ibid.*, p. 61.
17. *Ibid.*, p. 2.
18. *Ibid.*, p. 188.
19. *Ibid.*, p. 178.
20. *Ibid.*, p. 4.
21. *Ibid.*, p. 152.
22. *Ibid.*, p. 188.
23. *Ibid.*, p. 189.
24. *Ibid.*, pp. 232, 4.
25. *Ibid.*, p. 3.
26. *Ibid.*, p. 232.
27. *Ibid.*, p. 26.
28. *Ibid.*, p. 26.
29. *Ibid.*, p. 26.
30. *Ibid.*, p. 176. The absentee landlord Jen Fu-tseng owned 50 mow, of which 22 were located in Ling shui kou and leased out.

31. *Ibid.*, p. 3. There is the interesting case of a widow, named Yu Wang-shih, who owned 12 mow in Ling shui kou. She lived in Chinan. Her husband's brother owned the land originally, and when her husband's family divided the wealth among the sons, the brother-in-law sold his share to her husband. When her husband died, the land reverted to her. Because her brother-in-law resided in Ling shui kou, Lady Yu was able to keep the land in his name and only pay

taxes of that village. If the land had been registered in her name, she would have had to pay city taxes which were considerably higher.

32. *Ibid.,* pp. 154, 176, 181.
33. *Ibid.,* p. 165. In nearby Yang chia tun, a village of 210 households, there were roughly 30 households renting land. Owner cultivators predominated there as they did in Ling shui kou.
34. *Ibid.,* p. 158.
35. *Ibid.,* p. 160.
36. *Ibid.,* pp. 177, 170–173. Fifteen households are listed showing amount of land farmed and rented. Rents and crop yields differed greatly.
37. *Ibid.,* p. 158.
38. *Ibid.,* p. 158.
39. *Ibid.,* p. 159.
40. *Ibid.,* p. 161.
41. *Ibid.,* p. 147.
42. *Ibid.,* p. 206. In 1921 a bad drought caused an increase in land sales amounting to about 40 mow. In 1937 floods damaged the harvest and again more land was sold. In the last few years the village had good harvests and was able to purchase additional land.
43. *Ibid.,* p. 217.
44. *Ibid.,* p. 217. It was impossible for peasants to borrow more than 50 yuan from another villager for the majority of peasants had insufficient land to offer as collateral to secure such a loan.
45. *Ibid.,* p. 221.
46. *Ibid.,* pp. 244, 251.
47. *Ibid.,* p. 238.
48. *Ibid.,* p. 204.
49. *Ibid.,* p. 260.
50. *Ibid.,* p. 205.
51. *Ibid.,* p. 246.
52. *Ibid.,* p. 253.
53. *Ibid.,* p. 200. Most land was sold after it had been mortgaged or if the borrower was unable to repay his debt on time to redeem his land.
54. *Ibid.,* p. 191. This draft, called *ts'ao-ch'i,* was used by the go-between to seek a prospective buyer.
55. *Ibid.,* p. 193.
56. *Ibid.,* p. 200.
57. *Ibid.,* p. 201.
58. *Ibid.,* pp. 198–199. The form of land transfer deeds drawn up in the Republican period did not differ from those during the reign of the Ch'ien-lung Emperor of the mid-eighteenth century.
59. *Ibid.,* p. 219.
60. *Ibid.,* p. 218.
61. *Ibid.,* p. 217. Nor had there been any tendency for the number of debtors and money lenders to increase in recent years (see p. 217).
62. *Ibid.,* p. 230. All markets were located about 3 to 6 miles from Ling shui kou. Wang she jen was the closest market. See p. 227.
63. *Ibid.,* p. 227.

64. *Ibid.*, p. 228.
65. *Ibid.*, p. 105.
66. *Ibid.*, p. 110.
67. *Ibid.*, pp. 68–69.
68. *Ibid.*, p. 49.
69. *Ibid.*, p. 25.
70. *Ibid.*, p. 9.
71. *Ibid.*, p. 24.
72. *Ibid.*, p. 288.
73. *Ibid.*, p. 24.
74. *Ibid.*, p. 29.
75. *Ibid.*, pp. 28–29.
76. *Ibid.*, p. 13.
77. *Ibid.*, p. 13.
78. *Ibid.*, p. 35.
79. *Ibid.*, p. 22.
80. *Ibid.*, p. 51.
81. *Ibid.*, pp. 325–326.
82. *Ibid.*, p. 53.
83. *Ibid.*, p. 52.
84. *Ibid.*, p. 52.
85. *Ibid.*, p. 34.
86. *Ibid.*, p. 15.
87. *Ibid.*, p. 16.
88. *Ibid.*, p. 310.
89. *Ibid.*, pp. 274, 302.
90. *Ibid.*, p. 275.
91. *Ibid.*, pp. 287–288.
92. *Ibid.*, p. 288. The headman and *chia* heads collected grain from households who owned land and presented this to the *li-shu* as a gift from the village.
93. *Ibid.*, p. 274.
94. *Ibid.*, pp. 278–279.
95. *Ibid.*, p. 280. For an interesting comment on the introduction of this deed's tax in Hopei and the attempts by the peasants to evade paying it see "The Land Tax in Chihli," *NCH* (Jan. 30, 1915), pp. 307–308.
96. *CN*, IV, 273.
97. *Ibid.*, p. 274.
98. *Ibid.*, p. 328.
99. *Ibid.*, pp. 343, 330. Thirty *ch'ien* were paid for each pig slaughtered.
100. *Ibid.*, p. 272. For the amount of tax collected on sale of livestock in markets near Ling shui kou for December 1940, see p. 349.
101. *Ibid.*, p. 315.
102. Roughly the same percentage of total revenue went for administrative salaries in the mid 1920s compared with percentage of revenue spent in 1940 for official salaries. See *Li-ch'eng hsien-chih,* 4:1–4b (1924).

7. En County: Hou hsia chai Village

1. Amano, *Santō nōgyō keizai ron,* p. 305.
2. *Ibid.*, p. 323.
3. *Ibid.*, p. 316.
4. *Ibid.*, chart 1 in Appendix.
5. *CN*, IV, 397.
6. *Ibid.*, p. 397.
7. *Ibid.*, p. 398.
8. This condition may be seen in the following statistics comparing village and county yields.

Productivity in Hou hsia chai and En county (catties per mow)

Crop	Average yield in En county, 1931	Yield on good land in Hou hsia chai, 1941	Yield on poor land in Hou hsia chai, 1941
Sorghum	98	120	100
Millet	132	160	150
Cotton	30	100	60
Corn	99	100	40
Soybean	73	80	50
Wheat	62	80	150
Groundnut	218	200	150

Source: Data for 1931 obtained from Amano, *Santō nōgyō keizai ron*, chart 1; data for 1941 obtained in *CN*, IV, 460.

9. *Ibid.*, p. 459.
10. *Ibid.*, p. 398.
11. *Ibid.*, p. 401.
12. *Ibid.*, p. 10.
13. *Ibid.*, pp. 416, 463.
14. *Ibid.*, p. 475 has a table listing the 13 tenants; see also p. 402.
15. *Ibid.*, pp. 461–462.
16. *Ibid.*, p. 468.
17. *Ibid.*, p. 463.
18. *Ibid.*, p. 402.
19. *Ibid.*, p. 462.
20. *Ibid.*, p. 469.
21. *Ibid.*, pp. 399, 401. These peasants owned over 100 mow of land.
22. *Ibid.*, p. 460.
23. *Ibid.*, p. 460.

24. *Ibid.*, p. 460.
25. *Ibid.*, p. 461.
26. *Ibid.*, p. 411.
27. *Ibid.*, p. 403.
28. *Ibid.*, p. 401.
29. *Ibid.*, p. 403.
30. *Ibid.*, p. 403.
31. *Ibid.*, p. 403.
32. *Ibid.*, p. 400.
33. *Ibid.*, p. 510.
34. *Ibid.*, p. 485.
35. *Ibid.*, p. 479. See the example of a peasant who sold 8 mow to another peasant in neighboring Ch'ien hsien chai village for 240 yuan to pay for the burial expenses of his father and mother.
36. *Ibid.*, p. 506. If a loan was between 100 and 200 yuan, the interest was 50 to 60 yuan if repaid within a year after the harvest. Such loans did run for as long as 3 years, but one year was the usual period.
37. *Ibid.*, p. 478.
38. *Ibid.*, p. 479.
39. *Ibid.*, pp. 478, 488.
40. *Ibid.*, p. 485.
41. *Ibid.*, p. 485.
42. *Ibid.*, p. 485. In some parts of Shantung, for example, Weihaiwei, land was mortgaged over many generations, and a family's descendants had the right to redeem land mortgaged by a great-grandfather. For such an illustration, see the case described in R. F. Johnston, *Lion and Dragon in Northern China* (London, 1910), pp. 140–141.
43. *CN,* n. 511.
44. *Ibid.*, p. 511. About 60 to 70 per cent of the villagers borrowing credit did so by mortgaging their land rather than using it as security.
45. *Ibid.*, pp. 481.
46. *Ibid.*, pp. 414–415.
47. *Ibid.*, p. 424.
48. *Ibid.*, p. 445.
49. *Ibid.*, pp. 424, 432.
50. It should be pointed out that prior to 1937 the three *p'ai-ch'ang* of Hou hsia chai had considerable wealth and land, but by the late 1930s they owned little land. See *ibid.*, p. 408. This case illustrates how rapidly family fortunes could change.
51. *Ibid.*, p. 419.
52. *Ibid.*, p. 420.
53. *Ibid.*, p. 410.
54. *Ibid.*, pp. 422–423, 411.
55. *Ibid.*, p. 412.
56. *Ibid.*, p. 412.
57. *Ibid.*, pp. 420–421.
58. *Ibid.*, p. 477.
59. *Ibid.*, p. 478.

60. *Ibid.*, p. 524.
61. Calculated from tax data in the *En hsien-chih* (The gazetteer of En County; chüan 10, Shantung, 1908).
62. *CN*, IV, 548–553.
63. *Ibid.*, p. 523.
64. *Ibid.*, p. 523.
65. *Ibid.*, p. 517.
66. *Ibid.*, p. 515.
67. *Ibid.*, p. 515.
68. *Ibid.*, p. 537.
69. *Ibid.*, p. 516.
70. *Ibid.*, p. 515.

9. Peasant Farm Organization: Labor

1. Fei Hsiao-tung, *Peasant Life in China*, p. 1.
2. See data presented in Feng Ho-fa, comp., *Chung-kuo nung-ts'un ching-chi tzu-liao* (Materials on the Chinese village economy; Shanghai, 1935), I, 639.
3. *Ibid.*, p. 12. Ch'iao Ch'i-ming, "Chung-kuo nung-ts'un jen-k'ou chih chieh-kou chi ch'i hsiao-ch'ang" (The structure and change in China's rural population) in *Tung-fang tsa-chih*, 32:1 (January 1935), p. 29; J. L. Buck, *Land Utilization in China*, p. 370; Sydney D. Gamble, *North China Villages: Social, Political, and Economic Activities before 1933* (Berkeley and Los Angeles, 1963), p. 17; Amano, *Chūgoku nōgyō no shomondai*, I, 150; Li Ching-han, *Pei-p'ing chiao-wai chih liang-ts'un chia-t'ing* (The village family in the outskirts of Peking; Shanghai, 1929), pp. 15–16.
4. A good example may be seen in the narrative account of the peasant family of Wang Lung and O-Lan in Pearl Buck's *The Good Earth* (New York, 1931), Chaps. 3–4.
5. Niida Noboru, *Chūgoku no nōson kazoku* (The Chinese rural family; Tokyo, 1952), p. 145.
6. Martin C. Yang, *A Chinese Village: Taitou, Shantung Province* (New York, 1945), p. 72.
7. *Ibid.*, p. 73.
8. This assertion is contrary to the statements made by some anthropologists recently in their studies of peasant societies in Latin America and the Mediterranean areas. For example see George M. Foster, "Peasant Society and the Image of Limited Good," *American Anthropologist*, 67.2:293–316 (April 1965). Foster advances the paradigm that peasants view their environment in such a way that the good things in life are always in short supply and awareness of such scarcity produces certain observable patterns of behavior, both personal and social. For example, "Wealth is seen by villagers in the same light as land: present, circumscribed by absolute limits and having no relationship to work" (p. 298). The case may very well be that peasant societies pass through two decisive stages; the first stage is one where land scarcity is not viewed as acute or critical by the peasant, and its acquisition is related directly to frugality and

hard work; the second stage is one where resource scarcity has become embarrassingly pervasive and the peasant has had to adapt accordingly in the manner described by Foster.

9. Kokuritsu Pekin daigaku fusetsu nōson keizai kenkyūjo, *Santōshō Zainei kenjō o chūshin to seru nōsanbutsu ryūtsu ni kansuru ichi kōsatsu* (A study of agricultural commodity circulation in the county seat of Chi-ning County of Shantung Province; Peking, 1942).

10. T'u-ti wei-yuan hui, *Ch'üan-kuo t'u-ti tiao-ch'a pao-kao kang-yao* (A summary report of the land survey in China; Nanking, 1937), p. 23.

11. Amano Motonosuke, "Shindai no nōgyō to sono kōzō" (Agriculture during the Ch'ing period and its structure) in *Ajia kenkyū* (Asiatic studies), 3.2:50 (1957).

12. "Peasant Proprietorship in North China," *NCH* (Aug. 3, 1883), p. 136.

13. Alexander Williamson, *Journeys in North China, Manchuria and Eastern Mongolia; With Some Account of Corea* (London, 1870), I, 168.

14. Ch'iao Ch'i-ming, "Chung-kuo nung-ts'un jen-k'ou chih chieh-kou chi-ch'i hsiao-chang" (The structure and transformation of China's rural population) in *Chung-kuo li-tai jen-k'ou wen-t'i lun-chi* (Collected essays on the population problem in China's history), ed. Ya-tung hsüeh-she (Hong Kong, 1965), p. 203. See also my estimates of rural population increase for Szechwan province between 1710 and 1930 based upon household registration data in local gazetteers in "The Usefulness of Local Gazetteers for the Study of Modern Chinese Economic History: Szechwan Provinces during the Ch'ing and Republican Periods," *Ts'ing-hua Journal of Chinese Studies,* new ser. 6, no. 1.

15. See the discussion on village and household increase as observed from maps in local gazettes by Momose Hiromu, "Shin-matsu Chokureishō no sonzu sanshu ni tsuite" (On three village maps of Chihli province in the Late Ch'ing period) in *Katō hakushi kanreki kinen Tōyōshi shūsetsu* (Studies of Oriental history collected to commemorate the 60th birthday of Dr. Katō Shigeshi; Tokyo, 1941), pp. 841–860. The average village in Hopei in the 1880s contained around 100 households (see p. 858).

16. Kokuritsu Pekin daigaku fusetsu nōson keizai kenkyūjo, *Santō no ichi shūshichin no shakai teki kōzō* (The social structure of a market town in Shantung; Peking, 1942), p. 47.

17. Amano, *Santō nōgyō keizai ron,* pp. 61–65.

18. Hsiao Hung-lin, "Kahoku nōgyō rōdō ni kan suru kenkyū" (A study of agricultural labor in north China) in *Nōgyō keizai kenkyū* 18.3:65–107 (December 1942). Wang Ching-t'ing, "Nōgyō keiei teki soshiki oyobi rōdōryoku no bumpei ni tsuite" (The allocation of labor power and the organization of agricultural management) in *Nōgyō keizai kenkyū* 19.2:54–55 (September 1943). This particular study compares demand for labor in districts where different crops are grown. The yearly pattern of labor allocation for areas of different land utilization are graphed. Where two harvests per year occur, demand for labor is greatest in spring and fall. Where vegetables are the main crop, labor demand tends to be more uniform throughout the year with only a mild hump appearing in the fall.

19. Buck, *Chinese Farm Economy,* p. 274. See *ibid.,* pp. 252–253, for several graphs showing two periods of intense labor demand. Buck reports that "a

greater shortage occurred for harvesting, and to a less extent for cultivation in the Wheat Region where farms" were larger than in the rice region. Labor shortages were prominent in rice growing areas because of transplanting seedlings and irrigating of paddies. See Buck, *Land Utilization in China,* p. 299. Other observers also noted that agricultural laborers' wages fluctuated with the harvest. The following is an excerpt from a customs official's report of Lungkow (Shantung): "It will be noted that the wage of an unskilled labourer varies greatly. The explanation is that at harvest time he may earn (for a few days only when the demand for labor is greatest) the relatively large pay of 1.10 and food per day; but in the winter months he will be fortunate if he finds someone to hire him, for there are no large factories here to keep the demand for labor level throughout the year. In such times of slackness his wage will fall to the minimum now ruling for an unskilled labourer, and as a healthy manual worker is said to require 30 coppers' worth of food a day, a minimum wage of 40 coppers/cents cannot be said to be excessive. The scale of living in the district is low, probably kept down by the high price of food more than anything else." See IMC, *Decennial Reports, 1912–1921,* I, 190 (1924).

20. Kita Shina kaihatsu kabushiki kaisha chōsa kyoku, *Ro-Sei mensaku chitai no ichi nōson ni okeru rōdōryoku chōsa hōkoku* (A survey report of labor in the cotton-growing area of western Shantung; Peking, 1942), pp. 1–135.

21. *Ibid.,* p. 111.

22. *Ibid.,* p. 116.

23. Buck, *Statistics,* p. 306.

24. *Ibid.,* statistical appendix I, table 57.

25. In the case of Sha-ching village, farms had become so small that most households were unable to support themselves from farm income alone and about one quarter of the village income was obtained from outside the village. The same can be said of Chai-shan village in An-ch'iu county where roughly half the village income was earned outside the village. These same conditions undoubtedly held true for many villages where the size of farm had dwindled to less than two acres or 13 mow.

26. IMC, *Decennial Reports, 1912–1921,* p. 165.

27. *Ibid., IMC, Decennial Reports, 1902–1911,* p. 232; also IMC, *Decennial Reports, 1922–1931,* p. 446.

28. *Chiao-ao chih,* (Gazetteer of Tsingtao and its environs) 3:82, 85, 87. (Tsingtao, 1928).

10. Peasant Farm Organization: Capital and Technology

1. Martin C. Yang, p. 84.

2. Fujita Keiichi, "Shindai Santō keiei jinushitei shakai seishitsu" (The social characteristics of managerial landlords in Shantung during the Ch'ing period) in *Atarashii rekishigaku no tame* (For a new historical science), 111:14–15 (February 1966).

3. Isoda Susumu, "Hoku-Shi no kosaku: sono seikaku to sono hōritsu kankei" (North China tenancy: Its nature and its legal relationships) in *Hōgaku kyōkai zasshi,* 61.7:39 (1943).

4. Martin C. Yang, p. 132.

5. Sagara Norio, "Shokuryō seisan chitai nōson ni okeru nōgyō seisan kankei narabi ni nōsanbutsu shōhinka" (Commercialization of agricultural products and rural production relationships in villages of food producing areas) in *Mantetsu chōsa geppō,* 23.10:137 (October 1943).

6. *Ibid.,* p. 142.

7. Mantetsu Hoku-Shi jimmukyoku chōsabu, *Seitō kinkō ni okeru nōson jittai chōsa hōkokusho* (Survey report of village conditions in the suburbs of Tsingtao; Peking, 1939), p. 121.

8. Uchida Tomō, *Chūgoku nōson no bunke seido* (The system of household division in Chinese villages; Tokyo, 1956), p. 36. Also Maurice Freedman, *Chinese Lineage and Society: Fukien and Kwangtung* (London, 1966), pp. 53–54.

9. A good example may be found in Pearl S. Buck's *The Good Earth* where the eldest son of Wang Lung urges his father to divide the household's wealth and upon the death of Wang Lung, plots with his younger brother to sell the land.

10. *Niida,* pp. 88–90.

11. *Ibid.,* p. 106.

12. Arthur Henderson Smith, *Village Life in China: A Study in Sociology* (New York, 1899), p. 321.

13. Kokuritsu, *Santō no ichi shūshichin no shakai teki kōzō,* p. 47. The Chinese scholar, Martin C. Yang, also strongly stressed the importance of this institution. See Martin C. Yang, *A Chinese Village,* Chap. 2.

14. Gamble, *North China Villages,* pp. 26–27.

15. Momose, p. 859. Between 1790 and 1890 the gazetteer for Ch'ing county in Hopei showed a population change of 60,063 households to 27,363 households and a population decline from 260,017 to 145,810. This decline in county population was due to the war and devastation of the 1860s and 1870s.

16. Tōa kenkyūjo, *Keizai ni kansuru Shina kankō chōsa hōkokusho: toku ni Hoku-Shi ni okeru kosaku seido* (A report of investigations of old customs in China with special attention to the tenant system; Tokyo, 1943), pp. 31–35.

17. *Ibid.,* p. 39.

18. *Ibid.,* pp. 40–42.

19. *Ibid.,* pp. 26–29.

20. Kishimoto Mitsuo, "Santōshō Rinshinken nōson jittai chōsa hōkoku" (A survey report of village conditions in Lin-ch'ing county of Shantung province) in *Mantetsu chōsa geppō,* 23.6:153 (June 1943); and *ibid.,* 23.8:146 (August 1943).

21. Buck, *Chinese Farm Economy,* p. 106.

22. *Ibid.,* p. 182.

23. *Ibid.,* pp. 119–124.

24. For similar supporting evidence see Alfred Kaiming Chiu, "Recent Statistical Surveys of Chinese Rural Economy, 1912–1932: A Study of the Sources of Chinese Agricultural Statistics, Their Methods of Collecting Data and Their Findings about Rural Economic Conditions," Ph.D. diss. (Harvard University, 1933), p. 430. Chiu noted that "animal labor efficiency falls off the larger the farm becomes."

25. For similar supporting evidence see Chao Ts'ai-piao, "A Statistical Study of Crop Yields in 12 Provinces in China," Ph.D. diss. (Cornell University, 1933), p. 210.

26. See the remarks to this effect by the American soil expert, F. H. King, who visited China in 1910: "Not only are these people extremely careful and painstaking in fitting their fields and gardens to receive the crop, but they are even more scrupulous in their care to make everything that can possibly do so serve as fertilizer for the soil, or food for the crop: ashes, liquid manure, compost with dirt, straw, etc." F. H. King, *Farmers of Forty Centuries or Permanent Agriculture in China, Korea and Japan* (New York, 1927), p. 67.

27. Ching Su and Lo Lun, *Ch'ing-tai Shan-tung ching-ying ti-chu ti she-hui hsing-chih* (The social characteristics of managerial landlords in Shantung during the Ch'ing period; Shantung, 1957), appendix, pp. 106–110. Calculated from data in statistical appendix.

28. *Ibid.*, part 2 of the statistical appendix shows the type of nonfarm enterprises managed by these 131 wealthy peasant households.

29. Kahoku sangyō kagaku kenkyūjo, *Hoku-Shi no nōgu ni kansuru chōsa* (A survey of agricultural implements of north China; Peking, 1941), p. 1. For the development of the plough see Amano Motonosuke, *Chūgoku nōgyōshi kenkyū* (A study of Chinese agricultural history; Tokyo, 1962), pp. 756–810.

30. Kahoku sangyō kagaku kenkyūjo, *Hoku-Shi no nōgu ni kansuru chōsa,* pp. 2–22. A good discussion of the many reasons why the supply of livestock did not increase in China may be found in Mantetsu chōsabu, *Kita Shina no nōgyō to keizai,* II, 771–806. See also Chū-Shi kensetsu shiryō seibu iinkai, *Shina no kōgu mondai* (The problem of plough animals in China; Shanghai, 1940), p. 62.

31. Amano Motonosuke, "Dry Farming and the Ch'i-min Yao-shu," *Tōhō gakuhō* (Journal of Oriental Studies), 25:456 (1956). This article was translated by Leon Hurvitz for the special issue of the *Tōhō gakuhō* commemorating the Silver Jubilee Conference of Kyoto University.

32. *Ibid.*, p. 457.

33. *Ibid.*, p. 460.

34. Yonada Kenjirō, "Seimin Yōjutsu to ninen sanmosaku" (The Ch'i-min yao-shu: A guide to agriculture and animal husbandry and the system of three crops in two years) in *Tōyōshi kenkyū,* 16.4:1–25 (March 1959).

35. Nishijima Sadao, *Chūgoku keizaishi kenkyū* (Studies in Chinese economic history; Tokyo, 1966), pp. 235–253.

36. *Ibid.*, pp. 250–253.

37. *Ibid.*, pp. 753–804.

38. Amano, *Chūgoku nōgyōshi kenkyū,* pp. 510–513.

39. *Ibid.*, p. 539.

40. *Ibid.*, p. 544.

41. *Ibid.*, pp. 631–642.

42. *Ibid.*, pp. 651–657.

43. Murakami Sutemi, "Hoku-Shi nōgyō keiei ni okeru sakubutsu hensei to sono shōhinka: toku ni Santōshō Keiminken Sonkabyō a chūshin to shite" (Commercialization and changing land utilization in agricultural management in north China: Sun Chia Miao village of Hui-min county of Shantung province)

in *Mantetsu chōsa geppō,* 21.6:20–22 (June 1941). The same argument is repeated in Murakami's collection of essays, *Hoku-Shi nōgyō keizairon* (Essays in agricultural economics of north China; Tokyo, 1942), also Mantetsu chōsabu, *Kita Shina no nōgyō to keizai,* II, 824.

44. E. L. Jones, "Agriculture and Economic Growth in England, 1660–1750: Agricultural Change," *The Journal of Economic History,* 5.1:4–8 (March 1965).

45. Ch'uan Han-sheng and Wang Yeh-chien, "Ch'ing-ch'ao ti jen-k'ou pien-tung" (Population changes in China during the Ch'ing period), *Bulletin of the Institute of History and Philology* 32, (1961). Also Ho Ping-ti, "Early Ripening Rice in Chinese History," *Economic History Review* 9.2:206–207 (December 1956).

46. The first agricultural associations in China were established in 1916. By 1936 membership was only 72,911 and the largest number of technicians, about one third, was stationed in Kiangsu, Chekiang, and Anhwei. Shantung and Hopei had only 66 and 44 respectively (although Peking city did have 72 members). See Chen Shan-yung, "Chung-hua nung-hsüeh-hui ch'eng-li ehr-shih chou-nien kai-k'uan" (A report on China's agricultural associations twenty years after their establishment) in *Chung-hua nung-hsüeh hui-pao,* 155:1–22 (December 1936).

47. For Japan see Ronald Dore, "Agricultural Improvement in Japan: 1870–1900," *Economic Development and Cultural Change,* vol. 9, no. 1, pt. 2 (October 1960), pp. 69–93. For the case of Taiwan see Ramon H. Myers and Adrienne Ching, "Agricultural Development in Taiwan under Japanese Colonial Rule," *The Journal of Asian Studies,* 23.4:555–570 (August 1964).

11. Peasant Farm Organization: Land Utilization and Commercial Development

1. Examples of this may be found in Amano Motonosuke, *Chūgoku nōgyō no shomondai,* II, 31–47. However, some field studies show that small household farms of less than 10 to 20 mow often had a higher percentage of farm land devoted to cash crops than larger farms. For an example of this see evidence cited by Kashiwa Yūken, "Kita Shina ni okeru nōgyōsha no seikaku" (The characteristics of farmers in north China), *Tōa jimbun gakuhō,* 1.1:18 (March 1941).

2. IMC, *Decennial Reports, 1882–1891,* p. 83.

3. *NCH* (June 7, 1872), p. 494.

4. "Letter to James Porter," June 14, 1886, *Dispatches from United States Consuls in Chefoo, 1863–1906.*

5. *NCH* (July 13, 1880), p. 31.

6. *NCH* (Apr. 27, 1878), p. 422.

7. *Ibid.,* for translation of an imperial edict blaming the Shansi famine on the cultivation of the poppy.

8. IMC, *Decennial Reports, 1922–1931,* p. 112. Imperial edicts prohibiting the extension of poppy cultivation "broke down in the end in face of the inexorable economic urge — farmers to more profitable crops, landlords to higher rentals, and officials to increased taxation" (see p. 112).

9. IMC, *Decennial Reports, 1882–1891*, p. 83.

10. *Ibid.*

11. *CC*, II, 202. In 1913 there were only 39 acres under tobacco, but by 1920 the area had increased to 23,272 or 153,506 mow. This area was reduced slightly by civil war, but after 1930 more tobacco continued to be grown. Higher tariff schedules in 1928–1929 reduced the import of foreign tobacco and cultivated area increased to 84,370 acres in 1937. See Hoku-Shi jimmukyoku chōsashitsu, *Kō-Zai ensen ni okeru kōshoku ha-tabako seisan jōkyō chōsa* (Investigation of the production of the yellow tobacco on the Tsingtao-Chinan Railway; Tientsin, 1938), pp. 29–30.

12. Kōain seimubu, *Hoku-Shi ni okeru rakkasei, rakkaseiyū oyobi chōsa* (An investigation of peanuts, their oil and cake in north China; Tientsin, 1940), p. 89.

13. Buck, *Land Utilization in China*, p. 217. See also Amano, *Chūgoku nōgyō no shomondai*, II, 3–28; Amano, *Santō nōgyō keizairon*.

14. Tang, Chih-yu, *An Economic Study of Chinese Agriculture* (Ithaca, 1924), p. 114.

15. T. W. Kingsmill, James Scott and Reverend Geo. W. Clarke, "Inland Communications in China," *Journal of the China Branch of the Royal Asiatic Society*, 28:145 (1893–94).

16. Great Britain Foreign Office, "Report by Mr. Garnett on Journeys in the Mountains of North China," *Confidential Prints*, no. 9235:2.

17. *Dispatches from United States Consulate in Tientsin*, item 101.

18. John Markham, "Notes on the Shantung Province, Being a Journey from Chefoo to Tsiuhsien, the City of Mencious," *Journal of the North-China Branch of the Royal Asiatic Society for 1869–70*, p. 7.

19. IMC, *Decennial Reports, 1892–1901*, p. 85.

20. *NCH* (July 22, 1876), p. 69. See also the article in June 22, 1878, edition, p. 62, reporting that great quantities of grain spoiled on the docks because of the lack of facilities and roads to move it inland.

21. Yen Chung-p'ing, *Chung-kuo chin-tai shih t'ung-chi tzu-liao suan-chi* (Selected materials on the economic history of modern China) (Peking, 1955), pp. 184–185. (In 1912 the Tientsin to Pukow line was completed and joined the Tsingtao-Chinan line at Chinan, putting Tsingtao within 24 hours of Tientsin and 36 hours of Pukow). For an excellent description of early railroad construction, distances between stations, goods hauled, and revenue earned see Tōa dōbunkai, *Shina shōbetsu zenshi* (Comprehensive gazetteer of the various provinces of China; Tokyo, 1917–1920), Chihli, XVIII, 329–400.

22. IMC, *Decennial Reports, 1911–1921*, Tientsin, p. 161.

23. *Ibid.*, p. 199.

24. *Ibid.*, p. 225.

25. IMC, *Decennial Reports, 1912–1921*, p. 129.

26. Percy H. Kent, *Railway Enterprise in China: An Account of its Origin and Development* (London, 1907), p. 71. See table 58 in statistical appendix for additional data,

27. *PTYS*, p. 3.

28. Great Britain Foreign Office, *Confidential Prints*, no. 8517:3.

29. IMC, *Decennial Reports, 1911–1921*, p. 160.

30. IMC, *Decennial Reports, 1902–1911,* p. 242.

31. IMC, *Decennial Reports, 1922–1931,* pp. 101–102.

32. National Research Institute of Social Sciences of Academia Sinica, *Statistics of China's Foreign Trade during the Last Sixty-five Years,* monograph no. IV (Shanghai, 1931). See charts 1, 2, 3 in the introductory chapter.

33. IMC, *Decennial Reports, 1922–1931,* p. 171.

34. This was the conclusion reached by C. F. Remer, "International Trade Between Gold and Silver Countries: China, 1885–1915," *Quarterly Journal of Economics,* 40:597–643 (August 1926). Remer contends that devaluation of the exchange rate did not affect internal prices because of the obstruction and defects of the price mechanism.

35. IMC, *Decennial Reports, 1892–1910,* p. 96.

36. *Ibid.*

37. IMC, *Decennial Reports, 1902–1911,* p. 242.

38. *Ibid.,* p. 200.

39. IMC, *Decennial Reports, 1921–1931,* p. 325.

40. *Ibid.,* p. 337.

41. *Ibid.,* p. 425.

42. Friedrich Otto, "Correlation of Harvests with Importation of Cereals in China," *The Chinese Economic Journal,* 15.4:391 (October 1934).

43. Jean Chesneaux, *Le Mouvement ouvrier chinois de 1919 à 1927* (Paris, 1962), pp. 86–87. See chap. 3, which deals with the social origins of industrial workers.

44. IMC, *Decennial Reports, 1912–1921,* p. 133.

45. She-hui tiao-ch'a suo pien-chih, *Pei-p'ing she-hui kai-k'uan t'ung-chi t'u* (Statistical maps of social conditions in Peking; Peking, 1931), p. 5. Urban population of various north China cities shows that males occupied about three-fifths of a city's population. In 1932 males accounted for 61 per cent of Peking's population, 61 per cent of Tientsin's population, 61 per cent of Tsingtao's population, and 59 per cent of Chinan's population. See *Hoku-Shi keizai tōkei kihō* (Statistical report of north China's economy; July 1939), p. 90.

46. Buck, *Statistics,* p. 227.

47. Harold C. Hinton, *The Grain Tribute System of China, 1845–1911.* (Cambridge, Mass., 1956), p. 2.

48. Abe Takeo, "Beikoku jukyū no kenkyū" (A study of supply and demand for staple food in the reign of Emperor Yung-cheng) in *Tōyōshi kenkyū,* 15.4:157–175 (March 1957).

49. Sudō Yoshiyuki, "Shindai no Manshū ni okeru ryōmai no sōun ni tsuite" (On the water transport of government grain in Manchuria under the Ch'ing) in *Tōa ronsō* (September 1945), pp. 143–167.

50. Imports of food can be correlated against regional food prices between 1913 and 1931 by the simple regression equation $Y = a + bX$, where Y is food imports and X is price of food. When food imports and price data are fitted to this equation by the method of least squares, a correlation coefficient of .8715, significant at the 5 per cent level, and a coefficient of determination of .76 were obtained. These results indicate that variations in food imports were explained chiefly by variations in domestic food price fluctuations. The economist Wu

Pao-san did the first thorough study of food imports into China and found that in 1930 and 1931 "it took nearly half the value of the country's exports . . . to cover the transactions" for importing, rice, wheat, and wheat flour. See Wu Pao-san, *Chung-kuo liang-shih tui-wai mao-i ch'i ti-wei ch'ü-shih chi pien-ch'ien chih yuan-yin.* (The causes of fluctuations and trends of food and grain in China's foreign trade; Shanghai, 1934). See particularly the tables in the statistical index from which my table 43 was compiled.

51. Data obtained from IMC, *Report on the Trade of China* for years 1932, 1933, 1934, 1935 and 1936, compiled by the Customs Department.

52. IMC, *Report on the Trade of China,* 1940, vol. 1, pt. 1, p. 79.

53. V. D. Wickizer and M. K. Bennett, *The Rice Economy of Monsoon Asia* (Stanford, 1941), p. 156.

54. T. S. Chu and T. Chin, *Marketing of Cotton in Hopei Province* (Peking, 1929), p. 3.

55. IMC, *Decennial Reports, 1912–1921,* p. 154. In 1926 the U.S. Tientsin consulate commented that "cotton cultivation has received considerable impetus in recent years owing to the development of the spinning industry in north China and the demand for raw cotton in Japan. As the profit from cotton growing is nearly double that realized from kaoliang or wheat, cotton cultivation has substantially increased and experimental stations have been established." Julean Arnold, ed., *China: A Commercial and Industrial Handbook* (Department of Commerce, Washington, 1926), p. 524.

56. C. C. Chang, "China's Food Problem," *Data Papers on China, 1931* (Shanghai, 1931), p. 29.

57. Kokuritsu Pekin daigaku fusetsu nōson keizai kenkyūjo, *Kyō-Kan ensen shuyō toshi o chūshin to seru ryōkoku shijō kōzō* (The structure of grain markets centered in the major cities along the Peking-Hankow Railway line; Peking, 1942), chap. 1.

58. Takasu Toraroku, "Hoku-Shi shokuryō mondai" (The food problem in North China) in *Nōgyō keizai kenkyū,* 16.2:261 (June 1940); see also "Agricultural Practices in Kiaochow," *The Chinese Economic Journal,* 1:993 (November 1937), which emphasizes that peasants tended to specialize more in potato production because their farms were only garden size. This trend toward cultivating crops, which demanded more intensive exploitation of the soil, was also pointed out by Buck, *Land Utilization in China,* p. 217.

12. Changes in Peasant Living Standards

1. Buck, *Statistics,* pp. 100–101.
2. *Ibid.,* pp. 96–98.
3. *Ibid.,* pp. 380–386.
4. *Ibid.,* pp. 390–392.
5. *Ibid.,* pp. 413–414.

14. Landlord and Peasant

1. *CC,* I, 32. In 1937 the government owned only 604,000 mow in Hopei and 4.7 million mow in Shantung. See T'u-ti wei-yuan hui, p. 38.

2. *CC,* I, 32. Shantung only had 4,000 mow under school in 1937.

3. Sudō Yoshiyuki, "Shinchō ni okeru Kiho no Happochi ni tsuite" (The land given to persons displaced from the area around Peking in the Early Ch'ing period) in *Shakai keizai shigaku* 14.4:23–24 (July 1944); also Ma Feng-ch'en, "Ch'ing-chu Man-Han she-hui ching-chi ch'ung-t'u chih i-pan" (Social and economic conflict between the Manchus and Chinese in the Early Ching period) in *Shih-huo,* 4.6:262–269 (August 1936), 4.8:349–356 (September 1936), 4.9:384–402 (October 1936). Sudō Yoshiyuki, *Shindai Manshū tochi seisaku no kenkyū* (A study of the land policy in Manchuria during the Ch'ing period; Tokyo, 1944), pp. 30–79, pp. 225–235; Ishida Kōhei, *Manshū ni okeru shokuminchi keizai no shiteki tenkai* (Historical development of Manchuria's colonial economy; Tokyo, 1964), pp. 187–198; Liu Chia-chü, *Ch'ing-ch'ao ch'u-ch'i ti pa-ch'i ch'üan-ti* (Land policy concerning the Eight Banners in the Early Ch'ing period; Taipei, 1964); *CC,* I, 24–27.

4. Ishibashi Hideo, "Shinchō chūki no Kiho Kichi seisaku" (Policy toward banner land in the region around Peking during the mid Ch'ing period) in *Tōyō gakuhō,* 39.2:28 (September 1956). This article is continued in the same journal, 39.3:67–99 (December 1956); see also *CC,* I, 197–198.

5. Muramatsu Yūji, "Kichi no 'Ch'u-tsu ts'e-tang' oyobi 'Ch'a-yin ts'e-tang' ni tsuite" (Banner land rent books) in *Tōyō gakuhō,* 45.2:57 (September 1962).

6. *Ibid.,* p. 57.

7. Saeki Tomi, "Shindai Yōseichō ni okeru tsuka mondai" (The currency problem during the Yung-cheng period of the Ch'ing period) in *Tōyōshi kenkyū,* 28.3:142–212 (December 1959).

8. "Kichi ni tsuite," Muramatsu, 45.3:53 (December 1962).

9. Liu Chia-chü, p. 147.

10. Ishibashi, 39.2:55 (September 1956); Amano, *Shina nōgyō keizai ron* (A treatise on the Chinese farm economy; Tokyo, 1940), I, 20.

11. Nakamura Jihei, "Shindai Santō no gakuden" (School land in Shantung during the Ch'ing period) in *Shien,* 64:53 (February 1955).

12. Nakamura Jihei, "Shindai Santō no gakuden no kosaku" (The tenant on school land in Shantung Province during the Ch'ing period) in *Shien,* 71:65–71 (December 1956).

13. Li Ching-han, "Ting-hsien t'u-ti tiao-ch'a" (A land survey of Ting County) in *She-hui k'o-hsüeh,* 1.2:435 (June 1930).

14. *NCH* (Aug. 3, 1883), p. 136. The *Herald* goes on to say that "a very large number have only ten or twenty mow. Although the people appear poor few suffer from actual want, except in bad season they are often reduced to eating garbage; and when that fails, they die in crowds, as was the case in 1878 and 1879."

15. *Dispatches from United States Consulate in Tientsin, 1868–1906,* item 101.

16. Gamble, *North China Villages,* p. 336.

17. Ching Su and Lo Lun, appendix I, pp. 1–4. This excellent survey of late nineteenth-century rural conditions examines to what extent a rural capitalist class developed before Western enterprise and trade penetrated China. For a concise summary of this study see Fujita, pp. 11–22.

18. T'u-ti wei-yuan hui, p. 43.

19. Ken Yō, "Kahokushō no tochi seido ni tsuite" (The land system of Hopei province) in *Tōa ronsō,* 1:198 (July 1939). A similar view is stressed by Chen Cheng-mu, *Chung-kuo ko-sheng ti ti-tsu* (Land rents in various provinces of China; Shanghai, 1936), p. 29.

20. Tōa kenkyūjo, *Toku ni Hoku-Shi ni okeru kosaku seido,* pp. 63–127; also Yagi Yoshinosuke, "Hoku-Shi no kosaku seido" (The tenant system of North China), *Tōa keizai ronsō,* 2.3:63–84 (September 1944).

21. Tōa kenkyūjo, *Toku ni Hoku-Shi ni okeru kosaku seido,* p. 97.

22. *Ibid.,* p. 129.

23. See Franklin L. Ho, *Wholesale Prices and Price Index Number in North China, 1913 to 1928* (Tientsin, 1929), p. 7 and also my statistical appendix; also *CC,* I, 562–563.

24. "Kahoku ni okeru tsuka nami ni bukka no genkyō" (Current conditions of currency and prices in North China), *Chōsa geppō,* 2.5:37–38 (May 1941), which shows price increase in Peking, Tientsin, Tsingtao, and Shihmen cities.

25. Tōa kenkyūjo, *Toku ni Hoku-Shi ni okeru kosaku seido,* p. 155.

26. This argument has been stressed in an excellent study of the north China land tenure system. See Hatada Takashi, "Chūgoku tochi kaikaku no rekishi teki seikaku" (The historical traits of land reform in China) in *Tōyō bunka,* 4:33–60 (November 1950). Hatada also believes that the emergence of money rents on former banner land should not be associated with commercial development of that land but with the money needs of banner men who leased their land, pp. 55–56. The same argument is made in Tōa kenkyūjo, *Shina nōson kankō chōsa hōkokusho: Hoku-Shi ni okeru kosaku no hōritsu kankei* (A report on the survey of Chinese village customs: The institutional aspects of tenancy in North China; Tokyo, 1944).

27. This point is made by Professor Amano Motonosuke in his study of the Shantung rural economy. The following table was arranged by Professor Amano.

Types of rent payment according to county for Shantung, 1933

Types of rent payment	Number of counties
Rent paid in kind as a per cent of harvest	10
Fixed rent in kind	17
Money rent	23
Percentage and fixed rent	2
Percentage rent and money rent	12
Percentage, fixed, and money rent	28
Fixed and money rent	14
Total	106

Source: Amano, *Santō nōgyō keizai ron,* p. 198.

28. Kawano Shigetō, "Kosaku kankei yori mitaru Hoku-Shi nōson no tokushitsu" (Characteristics of north China villages with special reference to tenancy) in Tōa kenkyūjo, *Shina nōson kankō chōsa hōkokusho,* ser. I, p. 303 (Tokyo, November 1943).

29. Tōa kenkyūjo, *Toku ni Hoku-Shi ni okeru kosaku seido,* p. 97.

30. Isoda, 61.5:670–672 (1943).

31. See the example in Pearl Buck's *Good Earth* where Wang Lung and his wife discover hoarded silver in a southern coastal city and then return to their village and buy land.

32. *CN,* V, 1–58.

33. Kokuritsu, *Santōshō Zainei kenjō,* p. 9. For a similar discussion of absentee Landlords see Amano, *Shina nōgyō keizairon,* I, 165–166.

34. *CN,* V, 410, 520.

35. *Ibid.,* p. 515.

36. *Ibid.,* p. 526.

37. *Ibid.,* p. 515.

38. Hoku-Shi keizai chōsajo, "Shōtoku kenjō ni okeru gunshō fuson jinushi ni tsuite" (Small absentee landlords in P'eng-te county seat) in *Mantetsu chōsa geppō,* 20.4:171–191 (April 1940).

39. *CC,* I, 177–178, 199.

40. Li Wen-chih, "Lun Ch'ing-tai ch'ien-ch'i ti t'u-ti chan-yu kuan-hsi" (An essay on landowner relationships in the Early Ch'ing period) in *Li-shih yen-chiu,* 5:98 (1963).

41. Chung-kung Ch'i-hsia hsien-wei hsüan-ch'uan pu-p'ien, "Mou Jen-heh hsueh-hsing fa-chia lu" (A history of the rise of the land-grasping landlord, Mou Jen-heh) in *Li-shih yen-chiu,* 2:43–59 (1965).

42. T'u-ti wei-yuan hui, p. 34. See statistical appendix, table 60.

43. *Ibid.,* p. 26. See statistical appendix, tables 61 and 62.

44. Kokuritsu Pekin daigaku fusetsu nōson keizai kenkyūjo, *Santōshō Ko-Zai ensen chihō nōson no ichi kenkyū* (A study of agricultural villages along the Tsingtao–Chinan Railroad in Shantung province; Peking, 1942).

45. Hattori Mitsue, "Hoku-Shi ni okeru na tabako saibai fukyū irai no nōgyō

keiei no henka" (The transformation of farm management since the spread of tobacco cultivation in north China), *Mantetsu chōsa geppō,* 21.20:82 (December 1941).

46. Fang Hsien-t'ing, "Rural Weaving and the Merchant Employers in a North China District," *Nankai Social and Economic Quarterly,* 8.1:75–120 (April 1935); *ibid.,* 8.2:274–308 (July 1935). These two essays analyze the handicraft weaving industry of Kao-yang in Hopei. Gotō Bunji, "I-ken ni okeru mensōgyō" (The cotton weavers of Wei County) in *Mantetsu chōsa geppō,* 23.6:90–107 (June 1942). See the map showing the statistical expansion of this industry, *ibid.,* p. 129. This study was continued in the same journal, pt. 2, vol. 23, no. 7, pp. 25–67 (July 1942) and pt. 3, vol. 23, no. 8, pp. 35–83 (August 1942).

47. Ozaki Shōtarō, "Hokū-Shi nōson kōgyō no shomondai" (Problems of rural industries in north China) *Mantetsu chōsa geppō,* pt. 1, vol. 19, no. 3, p. 29 (March 1939); also pt. 2, vol. 19, no. 5, pp. 81–115 (May 1939); Sidney D. Gamble, *Ting Hsien: A North China Rural Community* (New York, 1954), chap. 15.

48. *Chung-kuo shih-yeh chih: Shantung* (Investigations of Chinese enterprises; Shanghai, 1933), vol. 3, pt. 1, pp. 53–61.

49. Buck, *Statistics,* pp. 57–58.

50. Ch'ü Chih-sheng, "Ho-pei sheng pa-hsien ho tso-she nung-min keng-tien chuang-k'uang chih i-pu-fen" (One aspect of peasant farming conditions in eight counties of Hopei Province) in *She-hui k'o-hsüeh,* 4.1:54–56 (March 1933).

51. Chang P'ei-kang, "Ch'ing-yuan ti nung-chia ching-chi" (The Peasant Economy of Ch'ing-yuan County) in *She-hui k'o-hsüeh,* 7.1:114 (March 1936).

52. Chang P'ei-kang, "Chi-pei Chi-tung san-shih-san hsien nung-ts'un kai-k'uan tiao-ch'a" (A rural survey of northern Hopei and Chahar) in *She-hui k'o-hsüeh,* 6.2:308 (June 1935).

15. *Moneylender, Merchant, and Peasant*

1. See, for example, how rapidly land values rose in Li-shu county of Liaoning province in Manchuria, Yang-yuan county in Chahar, and K'un-shan, Nan-t'ung, and Su counties in Kiangsu between 1855 and 1926 in *CC,* II, 58–61.

2. T'u-ti wei-yuan hui, p. 52.

3. Chung-yang yin-hang ts'ung-k'an, *Chung-kuo nung-yeh chin-yung kai-yao* (A survey of agricultural credit in China; Shanghai, 1936), pp. 91–92. Tōa kenkyūjo, *Hoku-Shi nōson ni okeru kankō gaisetsu* (A general account of the customs in north China villages; Tokyo, 1944), p. 86; Tōa kenkyūjo, *Toku ni Hoku-Shi ni okeru kosaku seido,* pp. 167–189; Tōa kenkyūjo, *Keizai ni kansuru Shina kankō chōsa hōkokusho: Hoku-Shi ni okeru tochi shoyu no idō to bumpu narabi ni tochi no kaikon* (A report of the survey of old customs in China concerning the economy: The transfer and distribution of land ownership and reclamation of land in north China; Tokyo, 1944), pp. 167–189. Gamble, *Ting hsien,* p. 252.

4. Andō Shizumasa, "Kahoku nōson no kinyū kikō" (The credit structure

of a north China village) in *Gendai Ajia no kakumei to hō: Niida Noboru hakushi tsuitō rombunshū* (Revolution and law in contemporary Asia: A collection of essays mourning Dr. Niida Noboru; Tokyo, 1966), I, 67–70.

5. Shimizu Kenjirō, "Hoku-Shi no ten kankō" (The practice of Tien in north China) in *Tōa jimbun gakuhō,* 3.2:25 (October 1941).

6. Andō Shizumasa, I, 70–75.

7. Shiomi Kingarō, "Hoku-Shi ni okeru fudōson kenri hendō ni kan suru kōshō seido" (The notarization system with respect to the transfer of immovable property rights in north China) in *Mantetsu chōsa geppō* 22.12:21–29 (December 1942).

8. *CC,* I, 96. Also "Kahoku ni okeru shunki kosaku taifukin no sōgō teki kansatsu" (A comprehensive survey of spring loans to cultivators in north China) in *Chōsa geppō,* 1.2:1–24 (February 1943).

9. T'u-ti wei-yuan hui, p. 49

10. Amano, *Shina nōgyō keizai ron,* p. 253. Amano presents data for Shen-che county of Hopei of various amounts of loans borrowed at different interest rates. Over three fifths of the loans were borrowed at 24 per cent per year, and the average amount of these loans was around 100 yuan.

11. T'u-ti wei-yuan hui, p. 50.

12. *Ibid.,* p. 50.

13. *CC,* I, 98.

14. *CC,* I, 565.

15. T'u-ti wei-yuan hui, p. 51.

16. Tōa kenkyūjo, *Toku ni Hoku-Shi ni okeru kosaku seido,* pp. 94–117. In Ting county, Li Ching-han reported that 41 per cent of peasants who mortgaged land did so to obtain funds for immediate consumption; 19 per cent did so to repay old debts; 29 per cent mortgaged for purposes of weddings and funerals and the remainder to make up for a commercial loss or to keep a child in school (see p. 111). For further discussion of the custom of *tien* see Tōa kenkyūjo, *Hoku-Shi noson ni okeru kankō gaisetu,* pp. 91–98.

17. Amano, *Santō nōgyō keizai ron,* p. 251.

18. Buck, *Land Utilization in China,* p. 465.

19. Amano, *Santō nōgyō keizai ron,* p. 252.

20. Mi Kung-kan, *Tien tang lun* (An essay on pawn shops; Shanghai, 1936), pp. 246–249 for Hopei and p. 244 for Shantung pawn shop capital.

21. Watanabe Yasumasa, "Tenshin no gingō" (The yin-hao or native banks of Tientsin), *Mantetsu chōsa geppō,* 22.3:158 (March 1942). For additional information about this institution see Lien-sheng Yang, *Money and Credit in China: A Short History* (Cambridge, Mass., 1942), chap. 9; Tōa kenkyūjo, *Keizai ni kansuru Shina kankō chōsa hōkokusho: kyūshiki kinyū ni okeru kankō* (A report of investigations of economic customs in China with special attention to traditional types of credit; Tokyo, 1944), pp. 1–8 for a survey of north China credit institutions.

22. Watanabe, 22.3:168 (March 1942).

23. *Ibid.,* 22.4:143–163 (April 1942).

24. Andrew James Nathan, *A History of the China International Famine Relief Commission* (Cambridge, Mass., 1965), p. 33.

25. Mi Kung-kan, pp. 102–103.

26. William G. Skinner, "Marketing and Social Structure in Rural China," pt. 1, *The Journal of Asian Studies,* 24.1:3–45 (November 1964). Part 2 appeared in the same journal, 24.2:195–299 (February 1965). Part 3 which dealt with rural marketing after 1949 appeared in a later issue of the same journal but since this period and theme is of no relevance to the pre-1949 scene, it is not cited.

27. Skinner, I, 17.

28. *Ibid.,* p. 34. Skinner argues further that the peasant's social horizons may be limited by the environment of the standard market center rather than the confines of his village. Although it is true that periodic markets were important meeting places and information of the outside world flowed in freely (albeit distorted), there is no firm evidence that a peasant's social relationship with market town groups determined or greatly influenced his values and attitudes. Peasants of Sha-ching, for example, lived only a few kilometers from the county seat, but there is no tangible evidence this large town influenced their thinking and behavior.

29. *Ibid.,* II, 197.

30. Morton R. Solomon, "The Market in Underdeveloped Economies" *Quarterly Journal of Economics,* 62.3:519–541 (August 1948).

31. *Ibid.,* p. 526.

32. *Ibid.,* p. 527.

33. Peng Chang, "The Distribution and Relative Strength of the Provincial Merchant Groups in China, 1842–1911," Ph.D. diss. (University of Washington, 1957), p. 29.

34. R. Montgomery Martin, *China: Political, Commercial, and Social* (London, 1847), II, 107–108.

35. An excellent map showing the canal route, major cities, and markets on the Grand Canal and embankments to control the canal's water flow can be found in Baba Kuwatarō, *Shina keizai chirishi* (An economic geography of China; Shanghai, 1922), I, 466–467.

36. Fujita, p. 13.

37. *Records of the Board of Foreign Missions of the Presbyterian Church* (Aug. 14, 1957). See roll no. 204, item 24, where mention is made that Wei county seat surpasses Chi-nan-fu in commercial activities. Wei city "probably is not surpassed by any inland city in this part of China." Quoted from a letter "Three Years That I Have Spent in China," Nov. 16, 1881.

38. *Ibid.,* p. 109.

39. Peng Chang, p. 102. I would like to comment briefly on Peng Chang's analysis of why certain provinces produced more merchants with great power while others did not. Peng considers the inability to supply necessities like rice and cotton as evidence a province must depend upon trade. Second, he points out that the top ranking provinces of mercantile influences, Kiangsi, Fukien, Shansi, Kwangtung, Hunan, and Anhwei also exported a number of important commodities. What he fails to stress is that the principal commodities the top six exported were non-bulky articles characterized by high income elasticity of demand. Further, these provinces were far removed from the country's capital and had a better opportunity to develop their commercial ties independent of court control.

40. See in particular, Hosea B. Morse, *The Guilds of China* (Taipei, 1966), pp. 18–24; IMC, *Decennial Reports, 1882–1891,* pp. 46–47, 77–78; IMC, *Decennial Reports, 1902–1911,* p. 55. D. J. Macgowan, "Chinese Guilds, or Chambers of Commerce and Trades Unions," *Journal of North-China Branch of the Royal Asiatic Society* (1888–1889), pp. 133–192.

41. Tōa dōbunkai, *Shina keizai zensho* (China economic series; Tokyo, 1908), VII, 211–214, VII, 241–246.

42. Shinkoku chūtongun shireibu, *Tenshin shi* (A gazetteer of Tientsin; Tokyo, 1909), p. 427.

43. Even before Shihmen became an important railroad junction in Huo-lu county of Hopei, it had become a famous center providing cart services by the mid-nineteenth century. Wealthy peasants pooled their savings and invested in carts which they hired out to merchants eager to ship their goods overland. Merchants shops soon congregated in this area, and before long it was an important trans-shipment center. See Tominaga Kazuo, "Sekimonshi nai kasangyō chōsa hōkoku" (A report of a survey of merchant wholesalers in Shihmen market) in *Mantetsu chōsa geppō,* 23.6:158–160 (June 1943).

44. Gaimusho tsūshōkyoku, *Shinkoku jijō* (Conditions in the Ch'ing empire; Tokyo, 1907), I, 463. This two-volume study consists of a series of reports by Japanese consuls in the treaty ports. It is an indispensable primary reference source for conditions of the late Ch'ing dynasty.

45. Calculated from data in Table 53.

46. H. D. Fong, "Terminal Marketing of Tientsin Cotton," *Monthly Bulletin on Economic China,* vol. 7, no. 7 (July 1934), maps on pp. 278 and 281; also T. S. Chu and T. Chin, pp. 1–10.

47. Wu Chih-i, "Shan-tung sheng mien-hua chih sheng-ch'an yu yün-hsiao," (Production and circulation of cotton in Shantung province) in *Cheng-chih ching-chi hsüeh-pao* (The quarterly journal of economics and political science), 5.1:26 (October 1936).

48. Wang Ting-hsien, *A Research on Raw Cotton and Its Trade in Tientsin* (Tientsin, 1935), pp. 50–62; Mantetsu chōsabu, *Hoku-Shi menka sōran* (A comprehensive survey of cotton in north China; Tokyo, 1940), pp. 297–305.

49. Wu Chih-i, pp. 40–41.

50. Mantetsu chōsabu, *Kita Shina nōgyō chōsa shiryō* (Survey materials on North China agriculture; Dairen, 1937). See section "Zainan no kinyū jijō" (Credit conditions in Chinan), pp. 494–496.

51. "Santōshō mensaku jijō chōsa" (a survey of cotton cultivation conditions in Shantung province) in *Chōsa geppō,* 2.10:72–74 (October 1941) for data on the quantity of cotton supplied monthly to the Chinan market between 1936 and 1940. For data on monthly cotton prices over a ten year period see Mantetsu chōsabu, *Hoku-Shi menka sōran,* statistical index, tables 2, 3.

52. Fong, p. 275; also Mantetsu Hoku-Shi chōsajo, "Hoku-Shi jūyō nōson shigen no ryūtsū jijō" (The circulation of major agricultural products in North China) in *Mantetsu chōsa geppō,* 19.11:151–160 (November 1939).

53. Wu Chih-i, p. 68.

54. Fong, p. 300.

55. Yeh Ch'ien-chi, "Hsi-ho mien-hua chih sheng-ch'an chi ch'i yun-hsiao kai-k'ung" (The production of cotton in the Hsi-ho Area and transportation

conditions) in Fang Hsien-T'ing, ed., *Chung-kuo ching-chi yen-chiu,* I, 214–222. Yeh's estimates of marketing costs are similar. He attributes the high marketing costs to the proliferation of brokers, taxes, delays in transport, and the lack of a systematic weights and measures system.

56. "T'ien-chin mien-hua hsu-chiu i chia-ke hsiang-kuan chih yen-chiu" (A study of price elasticity of demand for Tientsin cotton) in *Cheng-chih ching-chi hsüeh-pao* 4.1:26–32 (October 1935).

57. Huang Ting-hsien, "China's Cotton Trade," *Chinese Economic Journal,* 10.4:30 (April 1932). According to Huang the excess amount of water in the cotton fibers and the short staple cotton were the two major factors limiting domestic manufacturing demand for cotton.

58. Mai Shu-tu, "Ho-pei sheng hsiao-mo chih fan-yün (The marketing of wheat in Hopei province) in *She-hui k'o-hsüeh tsa-chih,* 1.1:77 (March 1930).

59. Sun Ching-chih, ed., *Hua-pei ching-chi ti-li* (An economic geography of north China; Peking, 1957), p. 31, map 7.

60. Kokuritsu, *Santōshō Zainei kenjō,* p. 3.

61. *Ibid.,* p. 9.

62. Kokuritsu, *Kyō-Kan ensen,* chap. 2.

63. Pao Hung-hsiang, *Wheat Problems in China* (Tientsin, 1937), p. 45.

64. Kokuritsu, *Kyō-Kan ensen,* p. 58.

65. *Ibid.,* p. 39.

66. "Kahoku kakuchi in okeru ryōkoku torihiki kikō no chōsa" (An investigation of the grain exchange mechanism in various markets of north China) in *Chōsa geppō,* 2.7:38 (July 1941).

67. Nakamura Shōzō, "Zainan ni okeru ryōsan" (Grain storehouses in Chinan) in *Mantetsu chōsa geppō,* 23.1:50–53 (January 1943).

68. *Ibid.,* pp. 50–53.

69. Moritsugu Isao, "Tenshin ni okeru kasangyō" (Merchant wholesalers of Tientsin) in *Mantetsu chōsa geppō,* 22.1:62–78 (January 1942).

70. Moritsugu Isao, "Tenshin o chūshin to suru Hoku-Shi kokumotsu shijō — Beisō ni kansuru chōsa hōkokusho" (The grain markets of Tientsin: An investigation report of rice brokerage firms) in *Mantetsu chōsa geppō,* 23.6:36–38 (June 1943).

71. Hoku-Shi keizai chōsajo Tenshin chōsa bunshitsu (Tientsin Investigating Office of the North China Economic Bureau), "Tenshin o chūsin to suru Hoku-Shi kokumotsu shijō" (Grain markets of Tientsin) in *Mantetsu chōsa geppō,* 22.11:1–67 (November 1942). This article is continued in pt. 2, vol. 2, no. 12, pp. 33–67 (December 1942). These two excellent reports provide a brief history of the *tou-tien,* their number, size of business operations, managerial functions, profits, and expenditures.

72. Kabayama Yukio, "Pekin ni okeru shūryō shijō no gaikon" (Conditions of the Peking grain market) in *Mantetsu chōsa geppō,* 21.8:166 (August 1941).

73. Chang T'ieh-cheng, "Pei-p'ing liang-shih kai-k'uang" (Conditions of the Peking grain market) in *Sheh-hui k'o-hsüeh tsa-chih,* 8.1:156–158 (March 1937).

74. Mai Shu-tu, p. 87.

75. *Kita Shina nōgyō chōsa shiryō,* pp. 671–676.

76. *Ibid.,* p. 679.

77. Kōain seimubu, *Hoku-Shi ni okeru rakkasei, rakkaseiyū oyobi rakkasei-haku chōsa* (An investigation of peanuts, their oil and care in north China; Tientsin, 1940), p. 36.

78. "China's Production and Export of Groundnuts," *Chinese Economic Journal,* 10.2:133 (February 1932).

79. Kabayama Yukio, "Santōshō Rinshinken fugyō gaikon" (The general conditions in the cotton cloth industry in Lin-ch'ing County of Shantung Province) in *Mantetsu chōsa geppō,* 23.7:15–16 (July 1943).

80. Pi Hsiang-hui, "Ho-pei sheng Pao-chih hsien chin-jung liu-t'ung fang-shih" (The method of credit circulation in Pao-ti county of Hopei province) in Fang Hsien-t'ing, ed., *Chung-kuo ching-chi yen-chiu* (Economic studies of China; Shanghai, 1938), II, 840.

81. Gamble, *Ting Hsien,* p. 307.

16. *Bureaucrat and Peasant*

1. Hsiao Kung-ch'uan; Chang Chung-li, *The Chinese Gentry: Studies on Their Role in Nineteenth-Century Chinese Society* (Seattle, 1955); Ch'u T'ung-tsu, *Local Government in China Under the Ch'ing* (Cambridge, Mass., 1962).

2. Chang Chung-li, *Chinese Gentry,* p. 52.

3. Hsiao Kung-ch'uan, p. 322.

4. Gamble, *North China Villages,* p. 45; *CN,* I, 96.

5. Hatada Takashi, "Hoku-Shi ni okeru sonraku jichi no ichi keitai—tokuni sonkōkai no kōsei ni tsuite" (A form of village self-government in north China with special reference to the structure of village public meetings) in *Katō hakushi kanreki kinen Tōyōshi shūsetsu* (Studies of Oriental History collected to commemorate the 60th birthday of Dr. Kato; Tokyo, 1941), p. 623.

6. Gamble, *North China Villages,* p. 62.

7. *Ibid.,* pp. 49–52; Martin C. Yang, p. 176. Yang gives an example of this speaking through a native villager: "Brother Heng Chun is right . . . We must ask Uncle P'an Chi to continue as our Chwang-chang (village head). He has the ability and the experience. Who else can deal with those tricky government servants as he can? I know I couldn't."

8. Evidence may be obtained from *CN,* VI, 97–115. These data were obtained from surveys of Tung wang ts'un of Hsing-t'ai county of Hopei.

9. Maeda Katsutarō, "Kahoku nōson ni okeru suiri kikō" (The irrigation system in north China villages) in *Gendai Ajia no kakumei to hō: Niida Noboru hakushi tsuitō rombunshū,* p. 44.

10. *Ibid.,* p. 44.

11. *CN,* VI, 97, 99–106. See the article by Maeda Katsutarō, "Kyū Chūgoku ni okeru suiri dantai no kyōdōtai teki seikaku ni tsuite" (The characteristics of the cooperative system of group water usage in Old China) in *Rekishigaku kenkyū,* no. 271:50–55 (December 1962), which summarizes two earlier Japanese studies of the water control system in north China villages.

12. Maeda Katsutarō, "Kahoku nōson ni okeru suiri kikō," p. 58.

13. *Ibid.*

14. Hatada, "KCSK," p. 59.

15. See pt. 2 for a discussion of village organizations in the four village studies.

16. Hatada, "KCSK," p. 18.

17. *Ibid.*, p. 62.

18. *Ibid.*

19. Smith, p. 166.

20. Hatada Takashi, "Kahoku no nōson ni okeru 'kai yōshi' no kankō—sonraku kyōdōtai teki kankei (The custom of "K'ai yeh tzu" in villages of north China) in *Shigaku zasshi,* 58.4:49 (October 1949).

21. Hatada, "KCSK," pp. 64–70.

22. *Ibid.*, pp. 71–74; *Gamble, North China Villages,* pp. 41–44.

23. Edwin George Beal, Jr., *The Origin of Likin (1853–1864)*, Cambridge, Mass., 1958), p. 7.

24. *CC,* III, 2, 4.

25. *Ibid.*, p. 13.

26. Amano Motonosuke, "Shina ni okeru denfu no ichi kōsatsu" (An examination of the land tax in China) in *Mantetsu chōsa geppō,* 14.2:3 (February 1934).

27. *CC,* III, 14. See also Chen Teng-yuan, *Chung-kuo t'ien-fu shih* (A history of China's land tax; Taipei, 1967), pp. 235–247.

28. Amano, *shina nōgyō keizairon,* II, 22.

29. *CC,* III, 17. The land tax was increased throughout southern Hopei between 1912 and 1927 (*CC,* II, 566) and heavy surcharges on the land tax were levied in the Chinan area occupied by the warlord Chang Tsung-ch'ang in 1925 (*ibid.*, p. 574).

30. *CC,* III, 32.

31. P'eng Yu-hsin, "Ch'ing-mo chung-yang yu ko-sheng tsai-cheng kuan-hsi" (The fiscal relationship between central and local government at the end of the Ch'ing period) in *She-hui k'o-hsüeh tsa-chih,* 4.1:92–100 (June 1947).

32. Wang Yin-sheng, *Chung-kuo pei-pu ti ping-ch'ai yu nung-min* (Military levies and farmers in north China; Shanghai, 1931), p. 1.

33. *Ibid.*, p. 3.

34. Li Ling, "Ho-pei sheng Ch'ing-hai hsien chih t'ien-fu chi ch'i cheng-shou chih-tu" (The system of land tax and its collection in Ch'ing-hai county of Hopei) in *Chung-kuo ching-chi yen-chih,* 2:997.

35. Feng Hua-te and Li Ling, "Hopei Ting-hsien chih t'ien-fang c'hi-shui" (Land and household deeds' taxes in Ting county of Hopei province) in *Cheng-chih ching-chi hsüeh-pao* (1936), p. 774.

36. Wang Chih-hsin, "Ho-pei sheng chih pao-shui chih-tu" (The miscellaneous excise tax system of Hopei province) in *Cheng-chih ching-chi hsüeh-pao,* 3.3:545 (1935).

37. Feng Hua-te, "Ho-pei sheng Ting-hsien ti ya-shui" (Brokerage taxes in Ting county of Hopei province) in *Cheng-chih ching-chi hsüeh-pao,* 5.2:305 (1937).

38. *Ibid.*, p. 320.

39. Tōa kyōkai, *Kita Shina sōran* (A general survey of North China; Tokyo, 1938), pp. 342, 345.

40. Tōa kenkyūjo, *Shina nōson kankō chōsa hōkokusho: tochi kōso-kōka no kenkyū* (Reports of investigations of rural customs in China. A study of taxes and other public charges, Tokyo, 1944), III, 12. This report is probably the clearest presentation of the local government tax system in north China. The evidence used includes materials in the *CN,* vols. 1, 2, 3, and 4.

41. Lo Yung-ching, "Ho-pei sheng shih-i hsien fu-shui kai-k'uan" (Hsien taxes in Hopei province: A sample study of eleven counties) in *Ching-chi t'ung-chi ch'i-kan,* 2.3:631 (1933). There are data showing the average land tax per mow for 11 counties in Hopei. The variation between each is enormous; see also Li Ling and Feng Hua-te, "Ho-pei sheng Ting-hsien chih t'ien-fu" (The land tax in Ting County of Hopei) in *Cheng-chih ching-chi hsüeh-pao,* 4.3:509–511 (1936), which shows that there was no uniformity in land tax and no relationship between households supposed to pay this tax and the amount actually collected. The land tax paid in Ting (0.12 yuan per mow) was far less than the same tax paid in Wu-chin and Nan-t'ung counties of Kiangsu (1.2 yuan per mow).

42. Tōa kenkyūjo, *shina nōson kankō chōsa hōkokusho,* III, 42.

43. Konuma Tadashi, "Kahoku nōson ni okeru denfu chōshu kikō ni tsuite no ichi kōsatsu" (An examination of the state tax collection mechanism in north China villages) in *Gendai Ajia no kakumei to hō: Niida Noboru hakushi tsuitō rombunshū,* II, 21–39; Yagi Yoshinosuke, "Shina nōson no hōzei seido ni tsuite" (On the tax-farming in the Chinese village) in *Tōa keizai ronsō,* 1.1:1–25 (February 1941).

44. Konuma, p. 28.

45. *Ibid.,* p. 29.

46. *Ibid.,* p. 31.

47. *Ibid.,* p. 32.

48. *Ibid.,* p. 35.

49. Tōa kenkyūjo, *Tochi kōso-kōka no kenkyū,* III, 46.

50. *Ibid.,* p. 48.

51. Frank Ki Chun Yee, "Police in Modern China," Ph.D. diss. (University of California, Berkeley, May 1942), p. 187.

52. Tōa kenkyūjo, *Tochi kōsō-kōka no kenkyū,* III, p. 51.

53. *CC,* II, 608. Between 1922 and 1930 an average of 10 major armed conflicts broke out in China on annual basis. See *ibid.,* p. 609.

54. C. M. Chang, "Local Government Expenditures in China," *Monthly Bulletin on Economic China,* 7.6:245 (June 1934).

55. H. T. Feng, "Local Government Expenditures in Hopei," *Monthly Bulletin on Economic China,* 7.12:511 (December 1934). See also the survey of a number of counties in northern Hopei reviewing county expenditures in the early 1930s (*PT*). There are budget expenditure data for Peking city, Mi-yun county, P'ing-ku, Shun-i, T'ung, Ku-an, Yung-ch'ing, Wu-ch'ing, Luan, Yu-t'ien, and Wan-p'ing counties which support the proposition that administrative, education, and police expenditures were the principal items of county expenditures. Feng Hua-te, "Ho-pei sheng hsien ts'ai-cheng chih-chi chih fen-hsi" (An Analy-

sis of Fiscal Outlays of Hopei Province and its Counties) in *Chung-kuo ching-chi yen-chiu,* II, 1051.

56. H. T. Feng, "Local Government," p. 510.

57. Feng Hua-te, "Hsien ti-fang hsing-cheng chih ts'ai-cheng chi-ch'u" (Fiscal basis of county administration) in *Cheng-chih ching-chi hsüeh-pao,* 3.4:747 (July 1935).

58. C. M. Chang, "Local Government Expenditures in China," *Monthly Bulletin on Economic China,* 7.6:246 (June 1934).

59. H. T. Feng, "Tax Burden of Peasants in a Hopei Village," *Monthly Bulletin on Economic China,* 7.3:107–108 (March 1934).

60. *CC,* III, 57.

61. Tōa kenkyūjo, *Tochi kōso-kōka no kenkyū,* III, 64.

17. *Random Disturbances to the Rural Economy*

1. Williamson, I, 199–200.

2. Great Britain Foreign Office, "Report on the Coast of the Gulf of Pecheli," *Confidential Prints,* no. 831:9 (1859).

3. John Markham, "Notes on the Shantung Province, Being a Journey from Chefoo to Tsiuhsien, the City of Mencious," *Journal of the North-China Branch of the Royal Asiatic Society for 1869–1870,* pp. 25–26.

4. "Report by Mr. Garnett on a Journey in the Mountains of North China," Great Britain Foreign Office, *Confidential Prints,* no. 9235:13 (1908).

5. "Report by Mr. Campbell of a Journey in Outer Chih-li," Great Britain Foreign Office, *Confidential Prints,* no. 6512:3.

6. Great Britain Foreign Office, *Confidential Prints,* no. 8903:7.

7. *Dispatches from United States Consulate in Tientsin, 1868–1906,* item 242.

8. Buck, *Atlas,* pp. 30–31.

9. Amano, "Shindai no nōgyō to sono kōzō," no. 1:240.

10. *CC,* I, 667–668.

11. Yao Shan-yu, "The Chronological and Seasonal Distribution of Floods and Droughts in Chinese History, 206 B.C.–A.D. 1911," *The Far Eastern Quarterly* (1943), p. 365.

12. Ch'ang-tu Hu, "The Yellow River Administration in the Ch'ing Dynasty," *The Far Eastern Quarterly,* 14.4:508 (August 1955).

13. *Ibid.,* p. 512.

14. Lockhard, p. 288.

15. "Repairing the Yellow River," *NCH* (June 18, 1886), p. 639.

16. Report of the Peking United International Famine Relief Committee, *The Famine of 1920–1921 in North China* (Peking, October 1922). This study is perhaps the best account of the causes, extent of damage, and remedial steps to alleviate the disaster.

17. Mantetsu chōsabu, *Minkoku jūnananen no Manshū dekasegisha* (Transient labor in Manchuria in 1928; Dairen, 1929), pp. 120–21; also Kuo-li

chung-yan yen-chiu yuan, *Nan-min ti tung-pei liu-wang* (The flight of refugees to the northeast); Shanghai, 1930), p. 14, indicates over 70,000 fled from northeast Shantung between 1927 and 1929. Over half came from Chinan and Chinchou.

18. Chinto Nihon shōgyō kaigisho, *Shashi heiran no Zainan oyobi Shin-Ho sen nandan chihō no keizai ni oyabaseru eikyō* (The mounting military conflict and its influence on the regional economy south of Chinan along the Tientsin-Pukow Railroad; Tsingtao, 1926), p. 2.

19. *Ibid.*, pp. 76–96.

20. Mantetsu chōsabu, *Shina no dōran to Santō nōson* (Shantung villages and the upheaval in China; Dairen, 1930), pp. 20, 27.

21. Franklin L. Ho, "Population Movement to the Northwestern Frontier in China," *Data Papers on China, 1931* (Shanghai, 1931), p. 1.

22. Mantetsu chōsabu, *Jihenka no Hoku-Shi nōson* (A North China village after the outbreak of the Sino-Japanese War; Tientsin, March 1942).

23. *Ibid.*, p. 93.

24. Chūgoku nōson keizai kenkyūjo, *Nōson chōsa hōkoku: Ni-Shi jihen no nōson keizai ni oyoboshitaru eikyō* (A report of a village survey: The influence of the Sino-Japanese Incident on the village economy; August 1939), pp. 1–50. This report was based on a survey by a team from the National Peking University Agricultural Science Institute.

25. Mantetsu Hoku-Shi jimmukyoku chōsashitsu, *Kyō-Kan ensen chitai ni okeru nōson no genjō* (Present conditions in rural villages in the region along the Peking-Hankow Railroad; February 1938), pp. 1–31.

26. Mantetsu Hoku-Shi jimmukyoku chōsashitsu, *Kō-Zai ensen ni okeru jihengo no nōgyō chōsa hōkoku* (Investigation report of agriculture after 1937 along the Tsingtao-Chinan Railroad; March 1938), pp. 1–80.

27. Hoku-Shi keizai chōsajo, *Kahokushō Enzanken dai-san-ku Bōjuchin nōson gaikyō chōsa hōkoku* (Investigation report of Wang shu chen village of the third section of Yen-shan hsien of Hopei province; September 1941), pp. 1–94.

28. After February of 1938 many Communist guerrilla-held bases embarked on the policy of limiting cotton cultivation to the barest needs for local consumption. "In central Hopei, where the Japanese [had] the highest control, it was reported in 1942 that only one tenth of the area actually suitable for cotton was in fact producing that crop." See Claire and William Band, *Two Years with the Chinese Communists* (New Haven, 1948), pp. 141–142.

29. See Research Section, Central Committee for the Extermination of Communism, "Kichū-ku chūbu chihō ni okeru Chūkyō no minshū kakutoku kōsaku jitsujō chōsa hōkoku" (Field survey report of Chinese Communist efforts to win support of the people in central Hopei), *Riku-Shi mitsu dai nikki* (The secret grand records of the Japanese military), 40:38 (1940).

30. *The Chinese Economic and Statistical Review*, 7.11:275 (November 1940).

31. Kōain, p. 24.

32. Ma Li-yuan, "Chan-shih Hua-pei nung-tso-wu sheng-ch'an chi ti-wei tui shih-liang chih lioh-two" (Agricultural production in North China during the

war and the seizure of food stuffs by the enemy) in *She-hui k'o-hsüeh tsa-chih* (Quarterly review of social sciences), 7.1:69 (June 1948).

33. Unryōjō seikoku kabushiki kaisha chōsabu (Investigation section of the food transport's White Rice Co. Ltd.), *Shōwa jūnananendo Kahoku Mōkyō beikoku seisan shukkai gaikyō chōsa* (Investigation concerning the conditions of rice production and transport in North China and Mongolia in 1942; Tientsin, 1942), p. 3.

34. *Ma Li-yuan,* p. 65.

35. *Ibid.* For further evidence of the shift in land use from cash crops to food see Kashiwa Yūken, "Hoku-Shi nōgyō ni okeru shōhin seisan no kichō" (The basis of commercial production in North China agriculture) in *Tōa jimbu gakuhō,* 1.4:159 (February 1942).

36. For examples of this in other parts of China at this time see Hsiao-tung Fei, "Agricultural Labor in Yunnan Village," *Nankai Social and Economic Quarterly,* 12.1–2:146–168 (January 1941); Wang Yin-yuan, "Ssu-ch'uan chan-shih nung-kung wen-t'i (The problem of the agricultural laborer in wartime Szechwan), *Ssu-ch'uan ching-chi li-k'an,* 2.3:105–109 (July 1945). Wang mentions that the use of peasant labor to assist the military and to construct projects in wartime Szechwan greatly reduced the supply of farm labor. Rural households offered higher wages to hire agricultural workers, and this caused their production cost to rise. As a result, the peasants tried to reduce these costs by restricting the area of cultivation and output. This merely caused food prices to rise higher. In other parts of China there is frequent mention of the part village labor played in the war effort, and these examples, easily multiplied many times, suggest the great drain of manpower from the countryside for the war effort. For example, see Gerald F. Winfield, *China: The Land and the People* (New York, 1947), p. 195, where 450,000 workmen were recruited in Szechwan to construct new airfields; T. H. White and A. Jacoby, *Thunder Out of China* (London, 1947), p. 67, for an account of Chinese laborers serving in the military; and *Claire and William Band,* p. 165, for a discussion of Japanese conscription of peasants to build block houses in north China.

37. Kokuritsu Pekin daigaku fusetsu nōson keizai kenkyūjo, *Santōshō ni okeru nōson jinkō idō* (Rural population mobility in Shantung province; Peking, 1942); for another study of the mobility of labor to shift between village and city factory see Yoshida Yoshiyuki, "Seitō bōseki rōdō jijō" (Labor conditions in Tsingtao's spinning industries) in *Mantetsu chōsa geppō,* 20.6:47–88 (June 1940). Many of the Tsingtao factory workers came from Chiao, Chi-mei, Lai-yang, Ping-tu, I-tu, and Kao-mi counties of Shangtung.

38. Kokuritsu, *Santōshō ni okeru nōson jinkō idō,* pp. 23–24.

39. *Ibid.,* pp. 89–90.

40. Nihon sōryōjikan tokubetsu chōsahan, *Senji Shina keizai tōkei ihen* (Collected statistics of China at war; Shanghai, 1942). These prices were collected by banks which used 1937 as the base period. Indices for the years 1937–1942 were compiled from retail prices of 25 consumer commodities, 11 food commodities, 5 fuel commodities, and 5 miscellaneous commodities. For a discussion of the cause for the sudden price rise in 1940 see Tokunaga Seikō, "Hoku-Shi kinkyū bukka taisaku no ichi dammen" (One aspect of price

controls to counter the sudden rise in prices in north China) in *Tōa keizai ronsō* 2.4:38–39 (1942); also, "Indices of Rural Prices of Agricultural Products and Farm Expenses in Changchow Kiangsu," *The Chinese Economic and Statistical Review,* 8.7:164 (July 1941), which shows that the great jump in prices came in 1940. The index for farm and household expenses gradually inched upward above the price index for rice, wheat and dry cocoons, products sold by farmers. This price disparity indicates that as the inflation became more severe, the terms of price exchange no longer benefitted the peasants. Production costs had risen rapidly, and the prices offered by market towns were below production costs and far below the prices farmers had to pay for goods in the market towns.

41. Ma Li-yuan, p. 75.

42. *Ibid.,* p. 76.

43. *Ibid.,* p. 79.

44. *Ibid.,* p. 81.

45. Lin Mao-mei, "K'ang-chan sheng-li hou Kuo-min-tang t'ung-chih ch'i-chien Hua-pei wu-chia chih fen-hsi" (An analysis of prices in north China during the period of Kuomintang control after the victory over Japan) in *Yen-ching she-hui k'o-hsüeh,* 2:167 (October 1949).

46. Lin Sung-nien, "I-nien lai ch'uan-kuo nung-ch'ing chih hui-ku" (A review of agricultural conditions in China over the last year) in *Chung-nung yüeh-k'an* 9.6:45 (March 1947).

47. Ch'ien Ying-nan, "Ko-ti wu-chia tung-t'ai" (Commodity prices in various localities) in *Chung-nung yüeh-k'an,* 9.5:71–72 (May 1948).

48. Data taken from Chan Tsung-han and Mei Chieh-fang, "Chung-kuo liang-shih wen-t'i yu mo-liang ch'an-shao" (Production and distribution of grain and the food problem in China) in *Chung-nung yüeh-k'an,* 9.5:25,30 (May 1948).

49. T'ai-p'ing yang ching-chi yen-chiu she ch'u-pan, *Chung-kuo ching-chi nien-chien* (China economic yearbook) comp., (Shanghai, 1947), p. 48.

50. "China's Demand and Supply of Raw Cotton," *China Economist* (July 12, 1948), p. 39.

51. Wang Tien-chün, "Chin shih-nien lai Hsi-an nung-ch'an p'in chia-ko chih yen-chiu" (A study of agricultural commodity prices in Sian over the last ten years) in *Chung-nung yüeh-k'an,* 8.10:43 (October 1947). The decline of peasant purchasing power due to the failure of agricultural prices to keep pace with urban consumer goods was also stressed by Shih Hua, "Sheng-li i-lai wo-kuo nung-ts'un ching-chi kai-k'uan" (Conditions in our village economy since victory over Japan) in *Chung-nung yüeh-k'an,* 9.4:37 (April 1948). Shih Hua concluded his study saying that "peasant real income has declined daily, their purchasing power is now lower, and the village economy has fallen into greater misery."

52. *Chung-kuo ching-chi nien-chien,* p. 60.

53. Chung-yang nung-yeh pu chi-hua ssu-pien, *Liang-nien lai ti Chung-kuo nung-ts'un ching-chi tiao-ch'a hui-pien* (Collected survey materials of the Chinese rural economy for the past two years; Shanghai, 1952), pp. 224–236.

54. U.S. Consulate General, Tientsin, *Chinese Press Review,* microfilm series, no. 6 (Feb. 10, 1947), no. 1 (Feb. 3, 1947) to no. 347 (July 19, 1948).

55. *Ibid.,* no. 208 (Dec. 22, 1947).

56. *Ibid.*, no. 215 (Jan. 5, 1948).
57. *Ibid.*, no. 518 (Jan. 22, 1948).
58. *Ibid.*, no. 268 (Feb. 14, 1947).
59. *Ibid.*, no. 641 (June 18, 1948).
60. *Ibid.*, no. 658 (July 9, 1948).
61. *Ibid.*, no. 260 (Feb. 5, 1947).
62. *Ibid.*, no. 209 (Dec. 23, 1947).
63. *Ibid.*, no. 245 (Feb. 18, 1947).
64. *Ibid.*, no. 229 (Jan. 23, 1948).
65. *Ibid.*, no. 225 (Jan. 19, 1948).
66. *Ibid.*, no. 339 (May 9, 1947).
67. *Ibid.*, no. 570 (March 26, 1948).
68. *Ibid.*, no. 610 (May 12, 1948).

Appendix B. North China Crop Statistics

1. Ch'ü Chih-sheng, "Chung-kuo chung-yang cheng-fu ti nung-yeh t'ung-chi" (Agricultural statistics of the central government of China) in *She-hui k'o-hsüeh tsa-chih,* (Quarterly review of social sciences), 4.2:257 (June 1933).

2. From the following data we can see that official salaries according to rank did not change during the Ch'ing dynasty.

Rank	1794	1838	1871	1906
First	180 taels	180	180	180
Second	150 taels	150	150	150
Third	130 taels	130	130	130
Fourth	105 taels	105	105	105
Fifth	80 taels	80	80	80
Sixth	60 taels	60	60	60
Seventh	45 taels	45	45	45
Eighth	40 taels	40	40	40
Ninth	30 taels	30	30	30

Source: Ta Ching ching-shen ch'üan-shu (A compendium of gentry scholar officials of the Ch'ing dynasty), 1:1–4. See also Chang Chung-li, *The Income of the Chinese Gentry* (Seattle, 1962), pp. 11–15.

3. Etienne Balazs, *Political Theory and Administrative Reality in Traditional China* (London, 1965), pp. 69–73. Hsiao Kung-chuan, chap. 4; Ch'u, T'ung-tsu, pp. 28–32.

4. Chao Tu-hua, *Kiang-su sheng t'u-ti chen-pao* (A report of the land cultivation in Kiangsu Province; Kiangsu, 1935), p. 10.

5. H. T. Feng, "Notes on Peasants' Tax Burden in a Hopei Village," *Monthly Bulletin on Economic China,* 73:106 (March 1934).

6. *CN,* VI, 1.

7. The first issue of data may be found in the Shinkoku nōkō shōbu (Department of Agriculture, Industry, and Commerce of China), *Shina seisan jigyō tōkeihyō* (Statistical tables of Chinese enterprises), vols. 1, 2 (Tientsin, 1912).

8. Ch'ü Chih-sheng, p. 265.

9. Alfred Kaiming Chiu, "Recent Statistical Surveys of Chinese Rural Economy, 1912–1932: A Study of the Sources of Chinese Agricultural Statistics, Their Methods of Collecting Data and Their Findings about Rural Economic Conditions," Ph.D. diss. (Harvard University, 1933), pp. 89–106.

10. James Nakamura, *Agricultural Production and the Economic Development of Japan, 1873–1922* (Princeton, 1965), chap. 1. When a noted Chinese scholar wrote about the correct procedures to adopt for studying Chinese villages, he warned that "the greatest difficulty with respect to land surveys is that they are likely to arouse the suspicion of the peasants that the government wants to increase land taxes." Chang Shih-wen, *Nung-ts'un she-hui tiao-ch'a fang-fa* (Methods for investigating rural society; Szechwan, 1943), p. 124.

11. Taiwan sōtokufu minseibu zaimu kyoku zeimuka, *Taiwan zeimu shi* (A history of Taiwan's financial affairs; Tokyo, 1907), I, 104–110; Ramon H. Myers and Adrienne Ching, "Agricultural Development in Taiwan under Japanese Colonial Rule," *The Journal of Asian Studies,* 23.4:560–562 (August 1964).

12. S. C. Hsieh and T. H. Lee, *An Analytic Review of Agricultural Development in Taiwan — An Input-Output and Productivity Approach* (Taipei, 1958), pp. 3–4.

13. Buck, *Chinese Farm Economy,* p. 422.

14. Buck, *Land Utilization in China,* p. viii. Also see Liu Ta-chung, Chong Twanmo, and Yeh Kung-chia, *Production of Food Crops on the Chinese Mainland: Prewar and Postwar* (Santa Monica, 1964), pp. 43–54.

15. *Ibid.* Buck, *Statistics,* pp. 209–227, indicates that crop data were obtained from 14 counties of Shantung, 10 counties of Hopei, 10 counties of Kiangsu, and 8 counties of Chekiang. Shantung and Hopei contained the largest number of counties sampled.

16. *Liu, Twanmo, and Yeh,* p. 15.

17. Buck, in the Preface (pp. xi-xii) to his 1937 land utilization study, suggests that despite the difficulty of acquiring trained personnel, he tried to select areas for their representativeness.

18. Most statistical tests apply only for data that are reasonably normally distributed. If the distribution is not normal, then often the mean estimated from the transformed data is more meaningful than the mean of the raw data, and analysis should be based on transformed data. Fortunately, many of the distributions in Figures B-1 and B-2 are not too far from normal, and in any case the conclusions reached by analyzing transformed data were not essentially different.

Bibliography

Abe Takeo 安部健夫. "Beikoku jukyū no kenkyū" 米穀需給の研究 (A study of supply and demand for staple food in the reign of Emperor Yung-cheng) in *Tōyōshi kenkyū* 東洋史研究 (The Journal of Oriental research), 15.4: 120–213 (March 1957).

"Agricultural Practices in Kiaochow," *The Chinese Economic Journal*, 1.11: 991 993 (November 1927).

Allen, George Cyril, and Audrey G. Donnithorne. *Western Enterprise in Far Eastern Economic Development: China and Japan*. New York, 1954.

Amagai Kenzaburō 天海謙三郎. *Chūgoku tochi bunsho no kenkyū* 中國土地文書の研究 (A study of Chinese land documents). Tokyo, 1966.

Amano Motonosuke 天野元之助. "Shina ni okeru denfu no ichi kōsatsu" 支那に於ける [田賦] の一考察 (An examination of the land tax in China) in *Mantetsu chōsa geppō* 滿鐵調査月報 (South Manchurian Railway Company Research Department monthly), 14.2: 1–35 (February 1934).

——— *Santōshō keizai chōsa shiryō: Santō nōgyō keizairon* 山東省經濟調査資料：山東農業經濟論 (Economic research materials relating to Shantung Province: An essay on the Shantung agricultural economy). Dairen, 1936.

——— *Shina nōgyō keizai ron* 支那農業經濟論 (A treatise on the Chinese farm economy). Tokyo; vol. 1, 1940; vol. 2, 1942.

——— *Chūgoku nōgyō no shomondai* 中國農業の諸問題 (Problems of Chinese agriculture). Tokyo, vol. 1, 1952; vol. 2, 1953.

——— "Dry Farming and the Ch'i-min Yao-shu," *Tōhō gakuhō* 東方學報 (Journal of Oriental studies), 25: 451–465 (1956).

——— "Shindai no nōgyō to sono kōzō" 清代の農業とその構造 (Agriculture during the Ch'ing period and its structure) in *Ajia kenkyū* アジア研究 (Asiatic studies), 3.1: 230–257 (October 1956), 3.2: 49–91 (February 1957).

——— *Chūgoku nōgyōshi kenkyū* 中國農業史研究 (A study of Chinese agricultural history). Tokyo, 1962.

Andō Hikotarō 安藤彥太郎. *Mantetsu: Nihon teikokushugi to Chūgoku* 滿鐵—日本帝國主義と中國— (The South Manchurian Railway Company: Japanese imperialism and China). Tokyo, 1965.

Andō Shizumasa 安藤鎭正. "Kahoku nōson no kinyū kikō" 華北農村の金融機構 (The credit structure of a north China village) in *Gendai Ajia no kakumei to hō: Niida Noboru hakushi tsuitō rombunshū* 現代アジアの革命と法：仁井田陞博士追悼論文集 (Revolution and law in contemporary Asia: A collection of essays mourning Dr. Niida Noboru), I, 61–80. Tokyo, 1966.

Arnold, Julean, et al. *China: A Commercial and Industrial Handbook*, no. 38. Washington, D.C., 1926.

Baba Kuwatarō 馬場鍬太郎. *Shina keizai chirishi, seido zempen* 支那經濟地理誌制度全編 (Gazetteer of Chinese economics and geography, volume on institutions, complete). Tokyo, 1928.

Balazs, Etienne. *Political Theory and Administrative Reality in Traditional China*. London, 1965.

Bibliography

Band, William, and Claire. *Two Years With the Chinese Communists*. New Haven, 1948.

Biggerstaff, Knight. "Modernization—and Early Modern China," *The Journal of Asian Studies*, 24.4: 607–621 (August 1966).

Borchert, John "A New Map of the Climates of China," *Annals of the Association of American Geographers*, 37: 169–176 (1947).

Buck, John Lossing. *Chinese Farm Economy: A Study of 2866 Farms in Seventeen Localities and Seven Provinces in China*. Chicago, 1930.

——— *Land Utilization in China: A Study of 16,786 Farms in 168 Localities and 38,256 Farm Families in Twenty-two Provinces in China, 1929–1933*. Shanghai, 1937.

——— *Land Utilization in China: Atlas*. Chicago, 1937.

——— *Land Utilization in China: Statistics*. Chicago, 1937.

——— *Some Basic Agricultural Problems of China*. New York, 1947.

——— "Fact and Theory About China's Land," *Foreign Affairs*, 28.1: 92–101 (October 1949).

Buck, Pearl. *The Good Earth*. New York, 1931.

CC: Chung-kuo chin-tai nung-yeh shih tzu-liao 中國近代農業史資料 (Historical materials on modern China's agriculture). 3 vols., vol. 1, ed. Li Wen-chih, vols. 2 and 3, ed. Chang Yu-i. Peking, 1957.

Chai K'o 翟克. *Chung-kuo nung-ts'un wen-t'i chih yen-chiu* 中國農村問題之研究 (A study of problems of the Chinese village economy). Canton, 1933.

Chang, C. C. "China's Food Problem," *Data Papers on China, 1931*. Shanghai, 1931, pp. 1–29.

Chang, C. M. "Local Government Expenditures in China," *Monthly Bulletin on Economic China*, 7.1: 233–247 (June 1934).

Chang Chung-li. *The Chinese Gentry: Studies on Their Role in Nineteenth-Century Chinese Society*. Seattle, 1955.

——— *The Income of the Chinese Gentry*. Seattle, 1962.

Chang, John. "Industrial Development of Mainland China, 1912–1949," *The Journal of Economic History*, 27.1: 56–82 (March 1967).

Chang P'ei-kang 張培剛. "Chi-pei Ch'a-tung san-shih-san hsien nung-ts'un kai-k'uang tiao-ch'a" 冀北察東三十三縣農村概況調查 (A rural survey of thirty-three counties in northern Hopei and eastern Chahar) in *She-hui k'o-hsüeh tsa-chih*, 社會科學雜誌 (Quarterly review of social sciences), 6.2: 267–312 (June 1935).

——— "Ch'ing-yüan ti nung-chia ching-chi" 清苑的農家經濟 (The farm economy of Ch'ing yuan in Hopei) in *She-hu k'o-hsüeh tsa-chih*, pt. 1, 7.1: 1–65 (March 1936), pt. 2, 7.2: 187–266 (June 1936), pt. 3, 8.1: 53–120 (March 1937).

Chang Shih-wen 張世文. *Nung-ts'un she-hui tiao-ch'a fang-fa* 農村社會調查方法 (Methods for investigating rural society). Szechwan, 1947.

Chang T'ieh-cheng 張鐵錚. "Pei-p'ing liang-shih kai-k'uang" 北平糧市概況 (Conditions of the Peking grain market) in *She-hui k'o-hsüeh tsa-chih*, 8.1: 121–158 (March 1937).

Chao Feng-t'ien 趙豐田. *Wan-Ch'ing wu-shih-nien ching-chi ssu-hsiang shih* 晚清五十年經濟思想史 (Economic thought during the last fifty years of the Ch'ing period), *Yen-ching hsüeh-pao* 燕京學報 (Yenching journal of Chinese studies), monograph series, no. 18. Peiping 1939.

Chao Ts'ai-piao. "A Statistical Study of Crop Yields in 12 Provinces in China." Ph. D. diss., Cornell University, 1933.

Ch'en Cheng-mo 陳正謨. *Chung-kuo ko-sheng ti ti-tsu* 中國各省的地租 (Land rents in various provinces of China). Shanghai, 1936.

Ch'en Shan-yung 陳山榮. "Chung-hua nung-hsüeh-hui ch'eng-li erh-shih chou-nien kai-k'uang" 中華農學會成立二十週年概況 (A report on China's agricultural associations twenty years after their establishment) in *Chung-hua nung-hsüeh-hui pao* 中華農學會報 (Report of China's agricultural associations), 155: 1–22 (December 1936).

Ch'en Han-seng. *The Present Agrarian Problem in China*. Shanghai, 1933.

——— *Industrial Capital and Chinese Peasants: A Study of the Livelihood of Chinese Tobacco Cultivators*. Shanghai, 1939.

Cheng Yu-kwei. *Foreign Trade and Industrial Development of China: An Historical and Integrated Analysis through 1948*. Washington, D.C., 1956.

Chesneaux, Jean. *Le Mouvement ouvrier chinois de 1919 à 1927*. Paris, 1962.

Ch'i Wu 齊武, ed. *I-ko ke-ming ken-chü-ti ti ch'eng-chang* 一个革命根据地的成長 (The development of a revolutionary base). Peking, 1957.

Chiao-ao chih 膠澳誌. (Gazetteer of Tsingtao and its environs). 3 vols. Tsingtao, 1928.

Ch'iao ch'i-ming 喬啓明. "Chung-kuo nung-ts'un jen-k'ou chih chieh-kou chi ch'i hsiao-chang" 中國農村人口之結構及其消長 (The structure and change in China's rural population) in *Tung-fang tsa-chih* 東方雜誌 (The Eastern miscellany), 32: 25–45 (January 1935).

Ch'ien Chia-chü 千家駒. *Chung-kuo nung-ts'un ching-chi lun-wen chi* 中國農村經濟論文集 (Collected essays on the Chinese village economy). Shanghai, 1936.

Ch'ien Ying-nan 錢英男. "Ko-ti wu-chia tung-t'ai" 各地物價動態 (Commodity prices in various localities) in *Chung-nung yüeh-k'an* 中農月刊 (The Chinese farmer's monthly), 9.5: 71–79 (May 1948).

Chin Lun-hai 金輪海. *Chung-kuo nung-ts'un ching-chi yen-chiu* 中國農村經濟研究 (Studies of the Chinese village economy). Shanghai, 1937.

"Chin-nien Ho-pei sheng san-shih-wu hsien chih jen-k'ou chuang-t'ai" 近年河北省三十五縣之人口狀態 (Population conditions in 35 counties of Hopei during the last few years) in *Chi-Ch'a tiao-ch'a t'ung-chi ts'ung-k'an* 冀察調查統計叢刊 (Statistical bulletin for surveys of north China), 1.1: 1–25 (September 1936).

China, Imperial Maritime Customs, see IMC.

"China's Demand and Supply of Raw Cotton," *China Economist*, pp. 39–40 (July 12, 1948).

"China's Production and Export of Groundnuts," *Chinese Economic Journal*, 10.2: 127–140 (February 1932).

Ching Su and Lo Lun 景甦，羅崙. *Ch'ing-tai Shan-tung ching-ying ti-chu ti shè-hui hsing-chih* 清代山東經營地主底社會性質 (The social characteristics of managerial landlords in Shantung during the Ch'ing period). Shantung, 1957.

Chiu, Alfred Kaiming. "Recent Statistical Surveys of Chinese Rural Economy, 1912–1932: A Study of the Sources of Chinese Agricultural Statistics, Their Methods of Collecting Data and Their Findings about Rural Economic Conditions." Ph. D. diss., Harvard University, 1933.

Chōsabu 調查部. *Shina no dōran to Santō nōson* 支那の動亂と山東農村 (Chinese rebellion and Shantung villages). Dairen, 1930.

Ch'ü Chih-sheng 曲直生. "Ho-pei sheng pa-hsien ho-tso-she nung-min keng-tien chuang-k'uang chih i-pu-fen" 河北省八縣合作社農民耕田狀況之一部分 (One aspect of peasant farming conditions in eight counties of Hopei province) in *She-hui k'o-hsüeh*, 4.1: 54–67 (March 1933).

——— "Chung-kuo chung-yang cheng-fu ti nung-yeh t'ung-chi" 中國中央政府的農業統計 (Agricultural statistics of the central government of China) in *She-hui k'o-hsüeh tsa-chih*, 4.2: 256–268 (June 1933).

Chū-Shi kensetsu shiryō seibi iinkai 中支建設資料整備委員會. *Shina no kōgu mondai* 支那の工具問題 (The problem of plough animals in China). Shanghai, 1940.

Chu, T. S., and T. Chin. *Marketing of Cotton in Hopei Province*. Peking, 1929.

Ch'u T'ung-tsu. *Local Government in China under the Ch'ing*. Cambridge, Mass., 1962.

Chūgoku nōson kankō chōsa, see *CN*.

Chūgoku nōson keizai kenkyūjo 中國農村經濟研究所. *Kahokushō Shinken shisatsu no hōkoku* 河北省晉縣視察の報告 (A survey report of Chin county in Hopei province). Peking, 1939.

Chūgoku rengō jumbi ginkō 中國聯合準備銀行, comp. *Zainan bukka geppō* 濟南物價月報 (Chinan monthly price report), vol. 1, no. 1, vol. 4, no. 12 (June 1941–November 1944).

——— *Sekimon bukka geppō* 石門物價月報 (Shihmen monthly price report), vol. 1, no. 5–vol. 5, no. 10 (May 1940 to August–October 1944).

——— *Tenshin bukka geppō* 天津物價月報 (Tientsin monthly price report), vol. 1, no. 1–vol. 3, no. 12 (July 1942–December 1944).

Chung-kuo chin-tai nung-yeh shih tzu-liao, see *CC*.

Chung-kuo ching-chi nien-chien 中國經濟年鑑 (China economic yearbook). T'ai-p'ing yang ching-chi yen chiu she ch'u-pan, comp. Shanghai, 1947.

Chung-kuo k'o-hsüeh yüan Shang-hai ching-chi yen-chiu so 中國科學院上海經濟研究所, ed. *Shang-hai chieh-fang ch'ien-hou wu-chia tzu-liao hui-pien, 1921–1957* 上海解放前后物价資料滙編 (A collection of Shanghai price data before and after the liberation, 1921–1957). Shanghai, 1958.

Chung-kuo shih-hsüeh hui 中國史學會, comp. *Yang-wu yün-tung* 洋務運動 (The movement concerning foreign affairs). 8 vols. Peking, 1961.

Chung-kuo shih-yeh chih: Shantung 中國實業誌：山東 (Investigations of Chinese enterprises: Shantung). Shanghai, 1934.

Chung-yang nung-yeh pu chi-hua ssu-pien 中央農業部計劃司編. *Liang-nien lai ti Chung-kuo nung-ts'un ching-chi tiao-ch'a hui-pien* 兩年來的中國農村經濟調查彙編 (Collected survey materials of the Chinese rural economy for the past two years). Shanghai, 1952.

Chung-yang yin-hang ching-chi yen-chiu ch'u 中央銀行經濟研究處. *Chung-kuo nung-yeh chin-yung kai-yao* 中國農業金融概要 (A survey of agricultural credit in China). Shanghai, 1936.

CN: Chūgoku nōson kankō chōsa 中國農村慣行調查 (Investigations of rural customs in China), vol. 1, 1952, vol. 2, 1954, vol. 3, 1955, vol. 4, 1955, vol. 5, 1957, vol. vol. 6, 1958. Tokyo.

Dispatches from United States Consulate in Tientsin; 1868–1906. The National Archives, Washington, D.C.

Dore, Ronald. "Agricultural Improvement in Japan, 1870–1900," *Economic Development and Cultural Change*, pt. 2, 9.1: 69–93 (October 1960).

En-hsien chih 恩縣志 (The Gazetteer of En county). 10 chüan. Shantung, 1908.

Famine of 1920–1921 in North China. The Report of the Peking United International Famine Relief Committee on Relief Work in the West Chihli Area. Peking, 1922.

Fang Hsien-t'ing 方顯廷. "Chung-kuo t'u-ti wen-t'i wen-hsien shu-p'ing" 中國土地問題文獻述評 (A detailed bibliography of China's land problem) in *Cheng-chih ching-chi hsüeh-pao* 政治經濟學報 (Quarterly journal of economics and political science), 3.4: 887–941 (July 1935).

——— *Chung-kuo ching-chi yen-chiu* 中國經濟研究 (Studies of the Chinese economy). 2 vols. Shanghai, 1938.

"Farms and Orchards at Chefoo, Shantung," *The Chinese Economic Journal*, 3.1: 612–615 (July 1928).

Fei Hsiao-tung. *Peasant Life in China*. London, 1939. Reprinted 1962.

——— "Agricultural Labor in a Yunnan Village," *Nankai Social and Economic Quarterly*, 12.1–2: 146–168 (January 1941).

——— "Peasantry and Gentry: An Interpretation of Chinese Social Structure and Its Changes," *The American Journal of Sociology*, 52.1: 1–17 (July 1946).

——— "Problems of Rural Industrialization," *China Economist*, pp. 102–104 (April 26, 1948).

——— "Financial Rural Industrialization," *China Economist*, pp. 110–112 (Aug. 2, 1948).

——— *China's Gentry: Essays in Rural-Urban Relations*. Rev. and ed. Margaret Park Redfield, with six life-histories of Chinese gentry families collected by Yung-teh Chow and an introduction by Robert Redfield. Chicago, 1953

——— and Chang Chih-i. *Earthbound China*. Chicago, 1945.

Feng Ho-fa 馮和法, comp. *Chung-kuo nung-ts'un ching-chi lun: nung-ts'un ching-chi lun-wen hsüan-chi* 中國農村經濟論：農村經濟論文選集 (Essays on the Chinese rural economy: Collected essays on the rural economy). Shanghai, 1934.

——— *Chung-kuo nung-ts'un ching-chi tzu-liao* 中國農村經濟資料 (Materials on the Chinese village economy). 2 vols. Shanghai, 1935.

Feng, H. T. "Local Government Expenditures in Hopei," *Monthly Bulletin on Economic China*, 7.12: 507–512 (December 1934).

Feng Hua-te 馮華德. "Hsien ti-fang hsing-cheng chih ts'ai-cheng chi-ch'u" 縣地方行政之財政基礎 (Fiscal basis of county administration) in *Cheng-chih ching-chi hsüeh pao*, 3.4: 697–749 (July 1935).

——— *Ho-pei sheng Ting-hsien ti ya-shui* 河北省定縣的牙稅 (Brokerage taxes in Ting hsien of Hopei province) in *Cheng-chih ching-chi hsüeh-pao*, 5.2: 285–323 (1937).

Fong, H. D. "Terminal Marketing of Tientsin Cotton," *Monthly Bulletin on Economic China*, 7.7: 275–321 (July 1934).

Foster, George M. "Peasant Society and the Image of Limited Good," *American Anthropologist*, 67.2: 293–316 (April 1965).

Freedman, Maurice. *Chinese Lineage and Society: Fukien and Kwangtung*. London, 1966.

Fried, Morton H. "Community Studies in China," *The Far Eastern Quarterly*, 14.1: 11–36 (November 1954).

Fujita Keiichi 藤田敬一. "Shindai Santō keiei jinushitei shakai seishitsu" 清代山東經營地主底社會性質 (The social characteristics of managerial landlords in

Shantung during the Ch'ing period) in *Atarashii rekishigaku no tame* あたらしい歴史學のため (For a new historical science), 111: 11–22 (February 1966).

Fukushima Masao 福島正夫. "Okamatsu Santarō hakushi no Taiwan kyūkan chōsa to Kahoku nōson kankō chōsa ni okeru Suehiro Itsutarō hakushi" 岡松参太郎博士の臺灣舊慣調査と華北農村慣行調査における末弘嚴太郎博士 (Dr. S. Okamatsu's survey of old customs in Formosa and the role of Dr. I. Suehiro in the investigation of rural customs in north China) in *Tōyō bunka* 東洋文化 (Oriental culture), no. 25: 22–49 (March 1958).

Fukushima Yōichi 福島要一. "Kahoku nōgyō no gijutsu suijun" 華北農業の技術水準 (The level of agricultural technology in north China); *Tōyō bunka*, no. 4: 61–93 (November 1950).

Gaimushō tsūshō kyoku 外務省通商局 (Foreign office, bureau of commercial affairs), comp. *Shinkoku jijō* 清國事情 (Conditions in the Ch'ing empire). 2 vols. Tokyo, 1907.

Gakujutsubu iinkai 學術部委員會. Tōa kenkyūjo dairoku chōsakai 東亜研究所第六調査會 in *Shina tochihō kankō josetsu* 支那土地法慣行序說 (Introductory remarks on the customs surrounding land laws in China). Tokyo, 1942.

Gamble, Sidney D. "A Chinese Mutual Savings Society," *The Far Eastern Quarterly*, 4.1: 41–52 (November 1944).

——— *Ting-Hsien: A North China Rural Community*. New York, 1954.

——— *North China Villages: Social, Political, and Economic Activities before 1933*. Berkeley and Los Angeles, 1963.

Gotō Bunji 後藤文治. "I-ken ni okeru mensōgyō" 濰縣に於ける綿莊業 (The cotton weavers of Wei county) in *Mantetsu chōsa geppō*, 23.6: 90–107 (June 1942), pt. 2, 23.7: 25–67 (July 1942), pt. 3, 23.8: 35–83 (August 1942).

Great Britain Foreign Office. *Confidential Prints*, no. 6512: 1–4, no. 9235: 2, no. 8517: 3.

Habakkuk, H. J. "Family Structure and Economic Change in Nineteenth-Century Europe," *The Journal of Economic History*, 15.1: 1–12 (1955).

Han te-chang 韓德章. *Ho-pei sheng Shen-che hsien nung-ch'ang ching-ying tiao-ch'a* 河北省深澤縣農場經營調査 (Farm management survey of Shen-che county in Hopei) in *She-hui k'o-hsüeh tsa-chih*, 5.2: 212–259 (June 1934).

Hatada Takashi 旗田巍. "Hoku-Shi ni okeru sonraku jichi no ichi keitai—tokuni sonkōkai no kōsei ni tsuite" 北支における村落自治の一形態—とくに村公會の構成について (A form of village self-government in north China, with special reference to the structure of village public meetings) in *Katō hakushi kanreki kinen Tōyōshi: Shūsetsu* 加藤博士還曆紀念東洋史: 集說 (Studies of Oriental history collected to commemorate the 60th birthday of Dr. Katō), pp. 615–635. Tokyo, 1941.

——— "Kahoku sonraku ni okeru kyōdō kankei no rekishiteki seikaku, 'Kansei' no hatten katei" 華北村落における協同關係の歴史的性格—[看青] の發展過程 (The historical nature of cooperative relations in north China villages, the process of development of crop-watching [*K'an-ch'ing*]) in *Rekishigaku kenkyū* 歴史學硏究 (The journal of historical studies), 139: 1–23 (May 1949).

——— "Kahoku no nōson ni okeru 'Kaiyōshi' no kankō sonraku kyōdōtai teki kankei eno saikentō" 華北の農村における開葉子の慣行—村落共同體的關係への再檢討 (The custom of k'ai-yeh-tzu in rural communities of northern China: Re-examination into circumstances of village community) in *Shigaku zasshi*,

史學雜誌 (The journal of historical science), 58.4: 43–54 (October 1949).

——— "Chūgoku tochi kaikaku no rekishiteki seikaku" 中國土地改革の歷史的性格 (The historical traits of land reform in China) in *Tōyō bunka*, 4: 33–60 (November 1950).

——— "Kyū Chūgoku sonraku no kyōdōtai teki seikaku ni tsuite no kentō: Mura no tochi to mura no hito," see "KCSK."

Hattori Mitsue 服部満江. "Hoku-Shi ni okeru hatabako saibai fukyū irai no nōgyō keiei no henka" 北支に於ける葉煙草栽培普及以來の農業經營の變化 (The transformation of farm management since the spread of tobacco cultivation in north China) in *Mantetsu chōsa geppō*, 21.20: 81–106 (December 1941).

Hei Shan 黑山 and Hsü Cheng-shüeh 徐正學. *Nung-ts'un wen-t'i* 農村問題 (The village problem). Nanking, 1936.

Hinton, Harold C. *The Grain Tribute System of China, 1845–1911*. Cambridge, Mass., 1956.

Ho, Franklin L. *Wholesale Prices and Price Index Number in North China, 1913 to 1928*. Tientsin, 1929.

——— "Population Movement to the Northeastern Frontier in China," *The Chinese Social and Political Science Review*, 15.3: 346–401 (October 1931).

Ho Ping-ti. "Early Ripening Rice in Chinese History," *Economic History Review*, 9.2: 200–219 (December 1956).

Hoku-Shi jimukyoku chōsashitsu 北支事務局調査室. *Kō-Zai ensen ni okeru kōshoku hatabako seisan jōkyō chōsa* 膠濟沿線ニ於ケル黃色葉煙草生產狀況調查 (A survey of the production conditions for yellow leaf tobacco along the Chinan-Tsingtao Railway). Tientsin, 1938.

Hoku-Shi keizai chōsa shitsu daiyonhan 北支經濟調查室第四班. "Shōtoku kenjō fukin ni okeru gunshō fuzai jinushi ni tsuite" 彰德縣城附近に於ける郡小不在地主に就いて (Small absentee landlords in P'eng-te county seat) in *Mantetsu chōsa geppō*, 20.4: 171–191 (April 1940).

Hoku-Shi keizai chōsabu 北支經濟調查部. *Jihen-ka no Hoku-Shi nōson: Kahoku-shō Tei-ken nai nōson jittai chōsa hōkoku* 事變下の北支農村—華北省定縣內農村實體調查報告 (Rural villages in north China under the impact of the Sino-Japanese Incident: A survey report of general conditions in a village of Ting county in Hopei). Dairen, 1942.

Hoku-Shi keizai chōsajo 北支經濟調查所. "Tenshin o chūshin to suru Hoku-Shi kokumotsu shijō" 天津を中心とする北支穀物市場 (The North China grain markets as centered in Tientsin) in *Mantetsu chōsa geppō*, 22.11: 1–67 (November 1942), 22.12: 33–67 (December 1942).

Hoku-Shi keizai tōkei kihō 北支經濟統計季報 (Statistical quarterly report of north China's economy). Tientsin, October 1939.

Hoku-Shi keizai chōsajo 北支經濟調查所. "Hoku-Shi jūyō nōsan shigen no ryūtsū jijō 北支重要農產資源の流通事情 (The circulation of major agricultural products in North China) in *Mantetsu chōsa geppō*, 19.11: 151–185 (November 1939).

"Hoku-Shi mensaku keiei chōsa" 北支棉作經營調查 (Survey of farm management in cotton production in north China) in *Mantetsu chōsa geppō*, 2.12: 240–390 (December 1941).

Hsia, C. T. *A History of Modern Chinese Fiction, 1917–1957*. New Haven, 1961.

Hsiao Hung-lin 蕭鴻麟. "Kahoku nōgyō rōdō ni kansuru kenkyū" 華北農業勞働に

關する研究 (A study of agricultural labor in north China) in *Nōgyō keizai kenkyū* 農業經濟研究 (Studies in farm economics), 18.3: 65–107 (December 1942).

Hsiao Kung-ch'uan. *Rural China: Imperial Control in the Nineteenth Century*. Seattle, 1960.

Hu Ch'ang-tu. "The Yellow River Administration in the Ch'ing Dynasty," *The Far Eastern Quarterly*, 14.4: 503–513 (August 1955).

Huang Ting-hsien. "China's Cotton Trade," *Chinese Economic Journal*, 10.4: 287–304 (April 1932).

IMC: Imperial Maritime Customs. Decennial Reports, 1882–1891, vol. 1, 1892–1901, vol. 2, 1892–1901, vols. 3–5, 1902–1911, 1912–1921, 1922–1931. Shanghai: Inspector General of Customs.

——— *Report on the Trade of China*. Shanghai: Inspector General of Customs, 1932–1940. 9 vols.

"Indices of Rural Prices of Agricultural Products and Farm Expenses in Changchow, Kiangsu," *The Chinese Economic and Statistical Review*, 8.7: 164 (July 1941).

Ishibashi Hideo 石橋秀雄. "Shinchō chūki no Kiho Kichi seisaku" 清朝中期の畿輔旗地政策 (Policy toward banner land in the region around Peking) in *Tōyō gakuhō*, 39.2: 23–73 (September 1956), 39.3: 67–99 (December 1956).

Ishida Kōhei 石田興平. *Manshū ni okeru shokuminchi keizai no shiteki tenkai* 滿洲における植民地經濟の史的展開 (Historical development of Manchuria's colonial economy). Tokyo, 1964.

Isoda Susumu 磯田進. "Hoku-Shi no kosaku: Sono seikaku to sono hōritsu kankei" 北支の小作—その性格とその法律關係 (North China tenancy: Its nature and its legal relationships) in *Hōgaku kyōkai zasshi* 法學協會雜誌 (The journal of the Jurisprudence Society), 61.5: 635–672 (May 1943), 61.7: 939–980 (July 1943).

Jamieson, G. "Tenure of Land in China and the Condition of the Rural Population," *Journal of the North China Branch of the Royal Asiatic Society*, 23.59: 59–174 (1888).

Johnston, Reginald Fleming. *Lion and Dragon in Northern China*. London, 1910.

Jones, E. L. "Agriculture and Economic Growth in England, 1660–1750: Agricultural Change," *The Journal of Economic History*, 5.1: 1–18 (March 1965).

Kabayama Yukio 樺山幸雄. "Pekin ni okeru shokuryō shijō no gaikyō" 北京に於ける食糧市場の概況 (The general conditions of the Peking grain markets) in *Mantetsu chōsa geppō*, 21.8: 163–192 (August 1941).

——— "Santōshō Rinshinken fugyō gaikyō" 山東省臨清縣布業概況 (General conditions in the cotton cloth industry of Lin-ch'ing county of Shantung) in *Mantetsu chōsa geppō*, 23.7: 1–25 (July 1943).

"Kahoku kakuchi ni okeru ryōkoku torihiki kikō no chōsa" 華北各地に於ける糧穀取引機構の調査 (A survey of the organization of grain exchange in various areas of north China) in *Chōsa geppō*, 2.7: 1–136 (July 1941).

Kahoku kōtsū kabushiki kaisha sōsaishitsu shigyō kyoku 華北交通株式會社總裁室資業局. *Tetsuro Aigoson jittai chōsa hōkokusho* 鐵路愛護村實態調查報告書 (A survey report of conditions in Ai-huo village along the Chinan-Kiaochow railroad line). 1940.

"Kahoku ni okeru tsūka narabi bukka no genkyō" 華北に於ける通貨竝物價の現況 (The present condition of currency and prices in north China) in *Chōsa geppō*, 2.5: 1–40 (May 1941).

"Kahoku ni okeru shunki kōsaku kashitsuke kin no sōgōteki kansatsu" 華北に於ける春期耕作貸付金の總合的觀察 (A comprehensive survey of spring loans to cultivators in north China) in *Chōsa geppō*, 1.2: 1–23 (February 1943).

Kahoku sangyō kagaku kenkyūjo 華北產業科學研究所. *Hoku-Shi no nōgu ni kansuru chōsa* 北支の農具に關する調查 (A survey of agricultural implements of north China). Peking, 1941.

"Kahokushō Kyō-Kan ensen menka jijō chōsa" 河北省京漢沿線棉花事情調查 (Survey of cotton cultivation conditions along the Peking-Hankow Railroad) in *Chōsa geppō*, 3.8: 1–51 (August 1942).

Kashiwa Yūken 柏祐賢. "Kita Shina ni okeru nōgyōsha no seikaku" 北支那に於ける農業者の性格 (The characteristics of farmers in north China) in *Tōa jimbun gakuhō* 東亜人文學報 (East Asian journal of humanistic science), 1.1: 1–39 (March 1941).

——— "Hoku-Shi nōgyō ni okeru shōhin seisan no kichō" 北支農業に於ける商品生產の基調 (The basis of commercial production in north China agriculture) in *Tōa jimbun gakuhō*, 1.4: 156–175 (February 1942).

——— *Hoku-Shi no nōson keizai shakai: Sono kōzō to tenkai* 北支の農村經濟社會: その構造と展開 (The rural economy and society of north China: Its structure and development). Tokyo, 1944.

Kawano Shigetō 川野重任. "Kosaku kankei yori mitaru Hoku-Shi nōson no tokushitsu" 小作關係より見たる北支農村の特質 (Characteristics of north China villages with special reference to tenancy), pp. 285–329, in Toa Kenkyūjo, ed., *Shina nōson kankō chōsa hōkokusho* 支那農村慣行調查報告書 (Reports of investigations of rural customs in China). Ser. 1, Tokyo, 1943.

"KCSK" Hatada Takashi, 旗田巍. "Kyū chūgoku sonraku no kyōdōtai teki seikaku ni tsuite no kentō: mura no tochi to mura no hito" 舊中國村落の共同體的性格についての檢討—村の土地と村の人— (An examination of the communal character of old Chinese villages: Village boundaries and villagers) in *Jimbun gakuhō* (Journal of humanistic studies), no. 51: 1–152 (February 1966).

Keizai chōsajo 經濟調查所. *Kahokushō futsū nōson jittai chōsa hōkokusho* 華北省普通農村實體調查報告書 (Survey report of two farm villages in Hopei provinces). Dairen, 1942.

Keizai chōsakai 經濟調查會. *Santōshō ichi nōson ni okeru shakai keizai jijō* 山東省一農村に於ける社會經濟事情 (Social and economic conditions in one village of Shantung province). Dairen, 1935.

Kent, Percy Horace. *Railway Enterprise in China: An Account of Its Origin and Development*. London, 1907.

"Kichūku chūbu chihō ni okeru chūkyō no minshū kakutoku kōsaku no jitsujō chōsa hōkoku" 冀中區中部地方に於ける中共の民衆獲得工作の實情調查報告 (A field survey report of Chinese Communist efforts to win support of the people in central Hopei) in *Riku-Shi mitsu dai nikki* 陸支密大日記 (The secret grand records of the Japanese military in China), Tokyo, 1940.

Kikuta Tarō 菊田太郎. "Hoku-Shi keizai shakai ni taisuru shizen no seiyaku" 北支經濟社會に對する自然の制約 (Natural limitations on the economy and society of north China) in *Tōa jimbun gakuhō*, 1.3: 599–626 (December 1941).

King, F. H. *Farmers of Forty Centuries or Permanent Agriculture in China, Korea and Japan*. New York, 1927.

Kishimoto Mitsuo 岸本光男. "Hoku-Shi ni okeru daizu gaikyō 北支に於ける大豆概況 (The conditions of soy beans in north China) in *Mantetsu chōsa geppō*, 20.11: 131–139 (November 1940).

——— "Santōshō Rinshinken nōson jittai chōsa hōkoku" 山東省臨淸縣農村實態調査報告 (A survey report of village conditions in Lin-ch'ing county of Shantung province) in *Mantetsu chōsa geppō*, 23.6: 131–157 (June 1943), 23.8: 119–192 (August 1943).

Kita Shina kaihatsu kabushiki kaisha chōsa kyoku 北支那開發株式會社調査局. *Rosei mensaku chitai no ichi nōson ni okeru rōdōryoku chōsa hōkoku* 魯西棉作地帶の一農村に於ける勞働力調査報告 (A survey report of labor use in one village in the cotton growing zone of northwest Shantung). Peking, 1942.

Kōain seimubu 興亜院政務部. *Hoku-Shi ni okeru rakkasei, rakkaseiyu oyobi rakkasei-haku chōsa* 北支に於ける落花生，落花生油及落花生粕調査 (An investigation of peanuts, their oil and cake in north China). Tientsin, 1940.

Kokuritsu Pekin daigaku fusetsu nōson keizai kenkyūjo 國立北京大學附設農村經濟硏究所. *Kyō-Kan ensen shuyō toshi o chūshin to seru ryōkoku shijō kōzō* 京漢沿線主要都市を中心とせる糧穀市場構造 (The structure of grain markets centered in the major cities along the Peking-Hankow railway line). Peking, 1942.

——— *Santō no ichi shūshichin no shakai teki kōzō* 山東の一集市鎮の社會的構造 (The social structure of a market town in Shantung). Peking, 1942.

——— *Santōshō ni okeru nōson jinkō idō* 山東省に於ける農村人口移動 (Rural population mobility in Shantung province). Peking, 1942.

——— *Santōshō Zainei kenjō o chūshin to seru nōsanbutsu ryūtsū ni kansuru ichi kōsatsu* 山東省濟寧縣城を中心とせる農產物流通に關する一考察 (A study of agricultural commodity circulation in the county seat of Chi-ning county of Shantung province). Peking, 1942.

——— *Santōshō Kō-Zai ensen chihō nōson no ichi kenkyū* 山東省膠濟沿線地方農村の一硏究 (A study of agricultural villages along the Tsingtao–Chinan Railroad in Shantung province). Peking, 1942.

Konuma Tadashi 小沼正. "Kahoku nōson ni okeru denfu chōshū kikō ni tsuite no ichi kōsatsu" 華北農村における田賦徵收機構についての一考察 (An examination of the state tax collection mechanism in north China villages) in *Gendai Ajia no kakumei to hō: Niida Noboru hakushi tsuitō rombunshū* 現代アジアの革命と法: 仁井田陞博士追悼論文集 (Revolution and law in contemporary Asia: A collection of essays mourning Dr. Niida Noboru), II, 19–39. Tokyo 1966.

Kung, H. O. "The Growth of Population of Six Chinese Cities," *Chinese Economic Journal and Bulletin*, 20.3: 301–314 (March 1937).

Kuo-li chung-yang yen-chiu yüan 國立中央硏究院. *Mou ti ch'a-i* 畝的差異 (The difference in size of the mow). Shanghai, 1929.

Kuo-li chung-yang yen-chiu yüan she-hui k'o-hsüeh yen-chiu so 國立中央硏究院社會科學硏究所. *Nan-min ti tung-pei liu-wang* 難民的東北流亡 (The flight of refugees to the northeast). Shanghai, 1930.

"Land Tax in Chihli, The." *The North China Daily Herald*, pp. 307–308 (Jan. 30, 1915).

Li-ch'eng hsien-chih 歷城縣志 (The gazetteer of Li-ch'eng county). 54 chüan. Shantung, 1924.

Li Ching-han 李景漢. *Pei-p'ing chiao-wai chih liang-ts'un chia-t'ing* 北平郊外之良村

家庭 (The village family in the outskirts of Peking). Shanghai, 1929.

——— "Ting-hsien t'u-ti tiao-ch'a" 定縣土地調查 (A land survey of Ting county) in *She-hui k'o-hsüeh* 社會科學 (The social sciences), 1.2: 435–467 (June 1930), 1.3: 803–887 (September 1930).

Li Ling 李陵 and Feng Hua-te 馮華德. "Ho-pei sheng Ting-hsien chih t'ien-fu" 河北省定縣之田賦 (The land tax in Ting hsien of Hopei province) in *Cheng-chih ching-chi hsüeh-pao*, 4.3: 443–520 (1936).

——— "Ho-pei sheng Ting-hsien chih t'ien-fang ch'i-shui" 河北省定縣之田房契稅 (Deed tax on land and household in Ting-hsien of Hopei) in *Cheng-chih ching-chi hsüeh-pao*, 4.4: 751–800 (1936).

Li Wen-chih 李文治. "Lun Ch'ing-tai ch'ien-ch'i ti t'u-ti chan-yu kuan-hsi" 論淸代前期的土地占有關係 (An essay on landowner relationships in the early Ch'ing period) in *Li-shih yen-chiu*, 5: 75–108 (1963).

Liang Ch'ing-ch'un 梁慶椿. "Chung-kuo han yü han-tsai chih fen-hsi" 中國旱與旱災之分析 (An analysis of droughts and drought disasters in China) in *She-hui k'o-hsüeh tsa-chih*, 6.1: 1–64 (March 1935).

Lin Mao-mei 林懋美. "K'ang-chan sheng-li hou Kuo-min-tang t'ung-chih ch'i-chien Hua-pei wu-chia chih fen-hsi" 抗戰勝利後國民黨統治期間華北物價之分析 (An analysis of prices in north China during the period of Kuomintang control after the victory over Japan) in *Yen-ching she-hui k'o-hsüeh* 燕京社會科學 (Social science review of Yenching University), 2: 165–198 (October 1949).

Lin Sung-nien 林松年. "I nien-lai ch'üan-kuo nung-ch'ing chih hui-ku" 一年來全國農情之回顧 (A review of agricultural conditions in China over the last year) in *Chung-nung yüeh-k'an*, 9.6: 31–49 (March 1947).

Liu Chia-chü 劉家駒. *Ch'ing-ch'ao ch'u-ch'i ti Pa-ch'i ch'üan-ti* 淸朝初期的八旗圈地 (Land policy concerning the eight banners in the early Ch'ing period). Taipei, 1964.

Liu Ta-chung, Chong Twanmo, and Yeh Kung-chia. *Production of Food Crops on the Chinese Mainland: Prewar and Postwar*, Santa Monica, 1964.

Lo Yung-ch'ing 樂永慶. "Ho-pei sheng shih-i-hsien fu-shui kai-k'uang 河北省十一縣賦稅概況 (Tax conditions in eleven counties of Hopei province) in *Ching-chi t'ung-chi chi-k'an* 經濟統計季刊 (Quarterly journal of economics and statistics), 2.3: 623–692 (1933).

Lockhard, William. "The Yang-tse-keang and the Hwang-ho, or Yellow River," *The Journal of the Royal Geographical Society*, 28: 288–297 (1858).

Lü P'ing-teng 呂平登. *Ssu-ch'uan nung-ts'un ching-chi* 四川農村經濟 (The village economy of Szechwan). Shanghai, 1936.

Luan-ch'eng hsien-chih 欒城縣志. The gazetteer of Luan-ch'eng county). 15 chüan. Hopei, 1873.

MacGowan, D. J. "Chinese Guilds or Chambers of Commerce and Trades Unions," *Journal of the China Branch of the Royal Asiatic Society*, 21.3 and 4: 133–192 (1886).

Maeda Katsutarō 前田勝太郞. "Kyū Chūgoku ni okeru suiri dantai no kyōdōtai teki seikaku ni tsuite" 舊中國における水利團體の共同體的性格について (The characteristics of the cooperative system of group water usage in Old China) in *Rekishigaku kenkyū*, 271: 50–56 (December 1962).

——— "Kahoku nōson ni okeru suiri kikō" 華北農村における水利機構 (The irrigation system in north China villages) in *Gendai Ajia no kakumei to hō:*

Niida Noboru hakushi tsuitō ronbunshū, II, 41–60. Tokyo, 1966.

Magyar, L. *Majyāru Shina nōgyō keizai ron* マヂャール支那農業經濟論 (Magyar's essay on the Chinese rural economy), tr. Inoue Terumaru 井上照丸. Tokyo, 1935.

Mai Shu-tu 麥叔度. "Hopei sheng hsiao-mo chih fan-yün" 河北省小麥之販運 (The marketing of wheat in Hopei province) in *She-hui k'o-hsüeh tsa-chih*, 1.1: 73–107 (March 1930).

Mantetsu chōsabu 滿鐵調査部. Minami Manshū tetsudō kabushiki kaisha chōsabu 南滿洲鐵道株式會社調査部. *Kita Shina nōgyō chōsa shiryō* 北支那農業調査資料 (Survey materials on north China agriculture). Dairen, 1937.

——— *Kita Shina menka chōsa shiryō* 北支那棉花調査資料 (Survey materials on north China cotton). Dairen, 1939.

——— *Chintō kinkō ni okeru nōson jittai chōsa hōkoku* 靑島近郊に於ける農村實態調査報告 (A report of a survey of village conditions in the suburbs of Tsingtao). Peking, 1939.

——— *Jihenka no Hoku-Shi nōson* 事變下の北支農村 (A north China village after the outbreak of the Sino-Japanese war). Tientsin, 1942.

——— *Kita Shina no nōgyō to keizai* 北支那の農業と經濟 (The agriculture and economy of north China). 2 vols. Tokyo, 1942.

Mantetsu Hoku-Shi jimmukyoku chōsa shitsu 滿鐵北支事務局調査室. *Kyō-Kan ensen chitai ni okeru nōson no genjō* 京漢沿線地體における農村の現狀 (Present conditions in rural villages in the region along the Peking-Hankow Railroad). Peking, 1938.

Mantetsu Hoku-Shi keizai chōsajo 滿鐵北支經濟調査所. "Hoku-Shi jūyō nōsan shigen no ryūtsū jijō 北支重要農產資源の流通事情 (The circulation of major agricultural products in north China) in *Mantetsu chōsa geppō*, 19.11: 151–185 (November 1939).

Mantetsu Hoku-Shi keizai: Keizaibu 滿鐵北支經濟: 經濟部. *Shōwa jūsan nendo nōka keizai chōsa hōkoku* 昭和13年度農家經濟調査報告 (A survey report of the farm household economy in 1937). Tientsin, 1940.

Mantetsu sangyōbu 滿鐵產業部. *Kita Shina keizai sōran* 北支那經濟綜覽 (A general survey of the north China economy). Tokyo, 1938.

Mantetsu sangyōbu shiryōshi 滿鐵產業部資料史. *Chūgoku nōson keizai no kompon-teki shomondai* 中國農村經濟の根本的諸問題 (Basic problems of the Chinese village economy). Dairen, 1937.

Mao Tse-tung. *Selected Works*. 4 vols. London, 1954.

Markham, John. "Notes on the Shantung Province: Being a Journey from Chefoo to Tsiuhsien, the City of Mencius," *Journal of the North-China Branch of the Royal Asiatic Society for 1869 and 1870*, no. 6: 1–29 (1871).

Martin, R. Montgomery. *China: Political, Commercial and Social*. 2 vols. London, 1847.

Meng Hsien-chang 孟憲章. *Chung-kuo chin-tai ching-chi shih chiao-ch'eng* 中國近代經濟史教程 (A study of modern Chinese economic history). Shanghai, 1951.

Mi Kung-kan 宓公幹. *Tien tang lun* 典當論 (An essay on pawn shops). Shanghai, 1936.

Minami Manshū tetsudō kabushiki kaisha 南滿洲鐵道株式會社. *Manshū kyūkan chōsa hōkoku* 滿洲舊慣調査報告 (Reports on investigations into the old customs of Manchuria). 9 vols. Dairen, 1913–1915.

——— *Kita Shina nōgyō chōsa shiryō* 北支那農業調査資料 (Investigation report materials on north China agriculture). Dairen, 1937.

Minami Manshū tetsudō kabushiki kaisha chōsabu, *see* Mantetsu chōsabu.

Minami Manshū tetsudō kabushiki kaisha Tenshin jimmusho chōsaka 南滿洲鐵道株式會社天津事務所調査課. *Kahokushō nōson jittai chōsa shiryō: Bōtoken, Tōyōkyū mura hoka jū-hachi ka son* 河北省農村實態調査資料: 望都縣, 東陽邱村外18個村 (Survey materials of village conditions in Hopei province: Wang-tu county, Tung yang ch'iu village and eighteen additional villages). Tientsin, 1937.

Momose Hiromu 百瀨弘. "Shin-matsu Chokureishō no sonzu sanshu ni tsuite" 清末直隸省の村圖三種について (On three village maps of Chihli province in the late Ch'ing period) in *Katō hakushi kanreki kinen Tōyōshi shūsetsu* 加藤博士還暦記念東洋史集說 (Studies of Oriental history collected to commemorate the 60th birthday of Dr. Katō Shigeshi), pp. 841–860. Tokyo, 1941.

——— "Shin-matsu Chokureishō sonchin kokō shōkō" 清末直隸省村鎭戶口小考 (A brief statement of the household number and population of villages in Chihli province toward the end of the Ch'ing dynasty) in *Tohō gakuhō*, 12.3: 99–112 (December 1941).

Moritsugu Isao 森次勳. "Tenshin ni okeru kasangyō" 天津に於ける貨棧業 (Merchant wholesalers of Tientsin) in *Mantetsu chōsa geppō*, 22.1: 62–78 (January 1942).

Morse, Hosea B. *The Guilds of China*. Taipei, 1966.

Moyer, Raymond T. "The Aridity of North China," *Journal of the North China Branch of the Royal Asiatic Society*, 58: 65–80 (1932).

Moritsugu Isao 森次勳. "Tenshin o chūshin to suru Hoku-Shi kokumotsu shijō: Beisō ni kansuru chōsa hōkokusho" 天津を中心とする北支穀物市場—米莊に關する調査報告書 (The grain markets of Tientsin: An investigation report of rice brokerage firms) in *Mantetsu chōsa geppō*, 23.6: 1–87 (June 1943).

Myers, Ramon, and Adrienne Ching, "Agricultural Development in Taiwan under Japanese Colonial Rule," *The Journal of Asian Studies*, 23.4: 555–570 (August 1964).

Murakami Sutemi 村上拾己. "Hoku-Shi nōgyō keiei ni okeru sakumotsu no hensei to sono shōhinka: Toku ni Santōshō Keiminken Sonkabyō o chūshin to shite" 北支農業經營に於ける作物の編成とその商品化: 特に山東省惠民縣孫家廟を中心として (Commercialization and changing land utilization in agricultural management in north China: Sun chia miao village of Hui-min county of Shantung province) in *Mantetsu chōsa geppō*, 21.6: 44–120 (June 1941).

——— *Hoku-Shi nōgyō keizai ron* (Essays on the north China farm economy). Tokyo, 1942.

Muramatsu Yūji 村松祐次. *Chūgoku keizai no shakai taisei* 中國經濟の社會態制 (The social structure of the Chinese economy). Tokyo, 1949.

——— "Ranjōken to Jihokusaison" 欒城縣と寺北柴村 (Luan-ch'eng hsien and Ssu pei ch'ai village) in *Hitotsubashi ronsō* 一橋論叢 (The Hitotsubashi review), 22.1: 180–207 (July 1949).

——— "Kichi no 'ch'u-tsu ts'e-tang' oyobi 'ch'a-yin ts'e-tang' ni tsuite" 旗地の [取租册檔] 及び [差銀册檔] に就いて (Banner land rent books) in *Tōyō gakuhō*, 45.2: 39–71 (September 1962).

Nakamura Jihei 中村治兵衛. "Shindai Santō no gakuden" 清代山東の學田 (School land in Shantung province during the Ch'ing dynasty) in *Shien* 史淵 (The shien or journal of history), 64: 43–64 (February 1955).

——— "Shindai Santō no gakuden no kosaku" 清代山東の學田の小作 (The tenant on school lands in Shantung province during the Ch'ing period) in *Shien*, **71**: 55–77 (December 1956).

Nakamura Shōzō 中村正三. "Zainan ni okeru ryōsan" 濟南に於ける粮棧 (Grain storehouses in Chinan) in *Mantetsu chōsa geppō*, 23.1: 43–83 (January 1943).

Nathan, Andrew James. *A History of the China International Famine Relief Commission.* Cambridge, Mass., 1965.

National Research Institute of Social Sciences of Academia Sinica, *Statistics of China's Foreign Trade during the Last Sixty-five Years*. Shanghai, 1931.

NCH: North-China Herald (Shanghai, 1850–1870), or *North-China Herald and Supreme Court and Consular Gazette* (Shanghai, 1870–1941).

Nihonjin-shō shōgyō kaigisho 日本人商商業會議所, comp. *Shina seisan jitsugyō tōkeihyō* 支那生產實業統計表 (Statistical tables of China's products and enterprises). 2 vols. Tientsin, 1912.

Nihon sōryōjikan tokubetsu chōsahan 日本總領事館特別調查班. *Senji Shina keizai tōkei ihen* 戰時支那經濟統計彙編 (Collected statistics of China at war). Shanghai, 1942.

Niida Noboru 仁井田陞. *Chūgoku no nōson kazoku* 中國の農村家族 (The Chinese rural family). Tokyo, 1952.

Nishijima Sadao 西嶋定生. *Chūgoku keizaishi kenkyū* 中國經濟史研究 (Studies in Chinese economic history). Tokyo, 1966.

Nishimura Kōichi 西村甲一. "Kahoku ni okeru daikeiei nōka no genkin shūshi" 華北に於ける大經營農家の現金收支 (Cash income and expenditures of a large scale farm in north China) in *Nōgyō keizai kenkyū*, 20.1 (December 1948), pp. 27–40.

"North China Cotton Production," *The Chinese Economic and Statistical Review*, 7.11: 245 (November 1940).

Nung-ch'ing pao-kao 農情報告 (Crop reports), 4.1: 1–40 (January 1936).

North China Herald and Supreme Court and Consular Gazette, see *NCH*.

Ōshima Riichi 大島利一. "Kahokushō Jungiken ni Mantetsu chōsahan o otonau no ki" 河北省順義縣に滿鐵調查班を訪ふの記 (A report on a visit to the Mantetsu Investigation Group in Shun-i county of Hopei province) in *Tōhō gakuhō*, 4.12: 115–129 (March 1942).

Otte, Friedrich. "Correlation of Harvests with Importation of Cereals in China," *The Chinese Economic Journal*, 15.4: 388–414 (October 1934).

Ozaki Shōtarō 尾崎庄太郎. "Hoku-Shi nōson kōgyō no shomondai" 北支農村工業の諸問題 (Problems of rural industrials in north China) in *Mantetsu chōsa geppō*, 19.3: 25–46 (March 1939), 19.5: 81–115 (May 1939).

——— "Chūgoku nōson shakai no kindaika katei" 中國農村社會の近代化過程 (The modernization process of Chinese rural society) in *Shakai kōseishi taikei* 社會構成史體系 (A comprehensive and systematic corpus of histories of social structure). Tokyo, 1950.

"Peasant Proprietorship in North China," *North China Daily Herald*, no. 136 (Aug. 3, 1883).

Pei-ning t'ieh-lu yen-hsien ching-chi tiao-ch'a pao-kao, see *PT*.

"Pei-p'ing shih chin-nien jen-k'ou nien-ling chih fen-p'ei" 北平市近年人口年齡之分配 (The population of Peking in recent years according to age distribution) in *Chi-ch'a tiao-ch'a t'ung-chi ts'ung-k'an*, 6.1: 1–20.

Peng Chang. "The Distribution and Relative Strength of the Provincial Merchant Groups in China, 1842–1911." Ph. D. diss., University of Washington, 1957.

P'eng Yü-hsin 彭雨新. "Ch'ing-mo chung-yang yü ko-sheng ts'ai-cheng kuan-hsi" 清末中央與各省財政關係 (Fiscal relations between central and local government at the end of the Ch'ing period) in *She-hui k'o-hsüeh tsa-chih*, 4.1: 83–110 (June 1947).

PT: Pei-ning t'ieh-lu yen-hsien ching-chi tiao-ch'a pao-kao 北寧鐵路沿線經濟調查報告 (Report of an economic survey along the Pei-ning railway line). 6 vols. Peking, 1936.

Remer, C. F. "International Trade Between Gold and Silver Countries: China, 1885–1913," *The Quarterly Journal of Economics*, 40.4: 594–643 (August 1926).

"Repairing the Yellow River," *North China Herald*, no. 639 (June 18, 1886).

Saeki Tomi 佐伯富. "Shindai Yōseichō ni okeru tsūka mondai" 清代雍正朝における通貨問題 (The currency problem during the Yung-cheng period of the Ch'ing period) in *Tōyōshi kenkyū*, 18.3: 142–212 (December 1959).

Sagara Norio 相良典夫. "Shokuryō seisan chitai nōson ni okeru nōgyō seisan kankei narabi ni nōsanbutsu shōhinka" 食糧生產地帶農村に於ける農業生產關係竝に農產物商品化 (Commercialization of agricultural products and rural production relationships in villages of food producing areas) in *Mantetsu chōsa geppō*, 23.10: 133–154 (October 1943).

"Santōshō mensaku jijō chōsa" 山東省棉作事情調查 (Survey of cotton cultivation conditions in Shantung province) in *Chōsa geppō*, 2.10: 43–110 (October 1941).

Shaw, Charles. "The Soils of China," *Soil Bulletin*, 1: 24–29 (December 1930).

She-hui tiao-ch'a so pien-chih 社會調查所編製. *Pei-p'ing she-hui kai-k'uang t'ung-chi t'u* 北平社會概況統計圖 (Statistical tables of social conditions in Peking). Peking, 1931.

Shen Tsung-han 沈宗瀚 and Mei Chieh-fang 梅藉芳. "Chung-kuo liang-shih wen-t'i yü mo-liang ch'an-hsiao 中國糧食問題與麥糧產銷 (Production and marketing of wheat and the food problem); *Chung-nung yüeh-k'an*, 8.11: 13–20 (November 1947).

Shih Hua 石樺. "Sheng-li i-lai wo-kuo nung-ts'un ching-chi kai-k'uang" 勝利以來我國農村經濟概況 (Conditions in our village economy since victory over Japan); *Chung-nung yüeh-k'an*, 9.4: 31–41 (April 1948).

Shimazu Tadao 島津忠男, comp., *Shashi heiran no Zainan oyobi Shin-Ho sen nandan chihō no keizai ni oyoboseru eikyō* 這次兵亂の濟南及津浦線南段地方の經濟に及ぼせる影響 (Mounting military conflict and its influence on the regional economy south of Chinan along the Tientsin-Pukow railroad). Tsingtao, 1926.

Shimizu Kinjirō 清水金太郎. "Hoku-Shi no ten kankō" 北支の典慣行 (The custom of *tien* or mortgaging property); *Tōa jimbun gakuhō*, 3.2: 1–34 (October 1941).

Shinkoku nōkō shōbu 清國農工商部. *Shina seisan jigyō tōkeihyō* 支那生產事業統計表 (Statistical tables of Chinese enterprises). 2 vols. Tientsin, 1912.

Shiomi Kingorō 鹽見金五郎. "Hoku-Shi nōson ni okeru fudōsan kenri hendō ni kansuru kōshō seido" 北支農村に於ける不動產權利變動に關する公證制度 (The notarization system with respect to the transfer of immovable property rights in north China Chinese villages) in *Mantetsu chōsa geppō*, 22.12: 1–33 (December 1942).

Shun-i hsien-chih 順義縣志. (The gazetteer for Shun-i county). 16 chüan. Shun-i, 1933.

Skinner, William G. "Marketing and Social Structure in Rural China," *The Journal of Asian Studies*, 24.1: 3–45 (November 1964), 24.2: 195–292 (February 1965).

Smith, Arthur Henderson. *Village Life in China: A Study in Sociology*. New York, 1899.

Solomon, Morton R. "The Market in Underdeveloped Economies," *Quarterly Journal of Economics*, **62.3:** 519–541 (August 1948).

Statistical monthly, see *T'ung-chi yüeh-pao*.

Sudō Yoshiyuki 周藤吉之. "Shindai no Manshū ni okeru ryōmai no sōun ni tsuite" 清代の滿洲に於ける糧米の漕運に就いて (On the water transport of government grain in Manchuria under the Ch'ing) in *Tōa ronsō* 東亞論叢 (The East Asian review), 3: 141–165 (September 1940).

——— *Shindai Manshū tochi seisaku no kenkyū* 清代滿洲土地政策の研究 (A study of the land policy in Manchuria during the Ch'ing period). Tokyo, 1944.

——— "Shinchō ni okeru Kiho no Happochi ni tsuite" 清初に於ける畿輔の撥補地に就いて (The land given to persons displaced from the area around Peking in the early Ch'ing period) in *Shakai keizai shigaku* 社會經濟史學 (Studies in social and economic history), 14.4: 13–53 (July 1944).

Sun Ching-chih 孫敬之, ed. *Hua-pei ching-chi ti-li* 華北經濟地理 (An economic geography of north China). Peking, 1957.

Sun Yat-sen. *The Principle of Livelihood.* Taipei, 1953.

Swen, W. Y. "Types of Farming, Costs of Production and Annual Labor Distribution in Wei hsien county, Shantung, China," *Chinese Economic Journal*, 3.2: 642–680 (August 1928).

Ta Ch'ing ching-shen ch'üan-shu 大清搢紳全書 (A compendium of gentry scholar officials of the Ch'ing dynasty). Peking; chüan 1–4, 1794, chüan 1–4, 1838, chüan 1–4, 1871, chüan 1–4, 1–6, 1–4, 1906.

Taiwan sōtokufu kambō chōsaka 臺灣總督府官房調查課. *Shina nōmin no keizai jōtai* 支那農民の經濟狀態 (Economic conditions of the Chinese peasantry). Taipei, 1930.

Taiwan sōtokufu minseibu zaimukyoku zeimuka 臺灣總督府民政部財務局稅務課. *Taiwan zeimu shi* 臺灣稅務史 (A history of Taiwan's financial affairs). 3 vols. Tokyo, 1907.

Takasu Toraroku 高須虎六. "Hoku-Shi shokuryō mondai.' 北支食料問題 (The north China food problem) in *Nōgyō keizai kenkyū*, 16.2: 83–92 (June 1940).

Tanaka Seijirō 田中清次郎, tr. *Chūgoku nōsho* 中國農書 (A study of Chinese agriculture). 2 vols. Tokyo, 1940.

Tang Chi-yu. "An Economic Study of Chinese Agriculture," Ph. D. diss., Cornell University, 1924.

Tawney, Richard Henry. *Land and Labor in China*. London, 1932.

"Teiken ni okeru nōson keizai" 定縣に於ける農村經濟 (Agarian economy in Ting-hsien) in *Mantetsu chōsa geppō*, 16.1: 107–145 (January 1936).

Tenshin jimusho 天津事務所. *Kita Shina nōson jittai chōsa hōkokusho* 北支那農村實態調查報告書 (Survey reports on rural communities in north China). 3 vols. Tientsin, 1936.

Tenshin jimusho chōsaka 天津事務所調查課. *Kita Shina ni okeru mensakuchi nōson jijō* 北支那に於ける棉作地農村事情 (Rural conditions in cotton-producing areas of north China). Tientsin, 1936.

——— *Kahokushō nōson jittai chōsa shiryō* 河北省農村實態調査資料 (Survey materials regarding conditions of villages in Hopei province). Tientsin, 1937.

Tenshin shi 天津誌 (A gazetteer of Tientsin). Shinkoku chūtongun shireibu 清國駐屯軍司令部 (Headquarters of the army stationed in China), comp. Tokyo, 1909.

"Three Years that I Have Spent in China," Nov. 16, 1881, *Records of the Board of Foreign Missions of the Presbyterian Church*, microfilm roll 204, item 24.

Ting ta 丁達. *Chūgoku nōson keizai no hōkai* 中國農村經濟の崩壞 (The disintegration of the Chinese village economy). Dairen, 1930.

Tōa dōbunkai 東亞同文會. *Shina keizai zensho* 支那經濟全書 (China economic series). Vols. 1–4, Osaka, 1907, vols. 5–12, Tokyo, 1908.

——— *Shina shōbetsu zenshi* 支那省別全誌 (Comprehensive gazetteer of the various provinces of China), 18 vols. Tokyo, 1917–1920.

Tōa kenkyūjo 東亞研究所. *Shina nōgyō kiso tōkei shiryō* 支那農業基礎統計資料 (Statistical materials concerning the foundations of Chinese agriculture). 2 vols. Tokyo, 1940.

——— *Keizai ni kansuru Shina kankō chōsa hōkokusho: Toku ni Hoku-Shi ni okeru kosaku seido* 經濟に關する支那慣行調査報告書: 特に北支に於ける小作制度 (A report of investigations of economic customs in China with special attention to the tenant system). Tokyo, 1943.

——— *Hoku-Shi nōson ni okeru kankō gaisetsu* 北支農村に於ける慣行概説 (A general account of the customs in north China villages). Tokyo, 1944.

——— *Keizai ni kansuru Shina kankō chōsa hōkokusho: Hoku-Shi ni okeru tochi shoyū no idō to bumpu narabini tochi no kaikon* 經濟に關する支那慣行調査報告書: 北支に於ける土地所有の移動と分布竝に土地の開墾 (A report of investigations of economic customs in China, with special attention to the transfer and distribution of landownership and opening to cultivation of land in north China). Tokyo, 1944.

——— *Shina nōson kankō chōsa hōkokusho: Hoku-Shi ni okeru kosaku no hōritsu kankei* 支那農村慣行調査報告書—北支に於ける小作の法律關係 (A report on the survey of Chinese village customs: The institutional aspects of tenancy in north China). Tokyo, 1944.

——— *Shina nōson kankō chōsa hōkokusho: Tochi kōso-kōka no kenkyū* 支那農村慣行調査報告書: 土地公租公課の研究 (Reports of investigations of rural customs in China: A study of taxes and other public charges). Tokyo, 1944.

Tōa kenkyūjo dairoku chōsakai 東亞研究所第六調査會. *Shina kankō chōsa ihō* 支那慣行調査彙報 (Collection of investigation reports on Chinese customs). Tokyo, 1941.

——— *Keizai ni kansuru Shina kankō chōsa hōkokusho: Kyūshiki kinyū ni okeru kankō* 經濟に關する支那慣行調査報告書: 舊式金融に於ける慣行 (A report of investigations of economic customs in China with special attention to traditional types of credit). Tokyo, 1944.

Tōa kenkyūjo dairoku chōsa iinkai gakujutsubu iinkai 東亞研究所第六調査委員會學術部委員會. *Shina kankō chōsa ihō* 支那慣行調査彙報 (Miscellaneous reports concerning the survey of Chinese customs). Tokyo, 1942.

Tokunaga Seikō 德永清行. "Hoku-Shi kinkyū bukka taisaku no ichi dammen" 北支緊急物價對策の一斷面 (One aspect of price controls to counter the sudden rise of prices in north China) in *Tōa keizai ronsō*, 2.4: 38–53 (December 1942).

Tominaga Kazuo 富永一雄. "Sekimonshi nai kasangyō chōsa hōkoku" 石門市內

貨棧業調査報告 (A survey report of merchant wholesalers in Shihmen city) in *Mantetsu chōsa geppō*, pt. 1, 23.6: 157–188 (June 1943), pt. 2, 23.8: 83–119 (August 1943).

Turner, F. B. "Flood and Famine in North China," *Journal of the North China Branch of the Royal Asiatic Society*, 57: 1–18 (1926).

T'u-ti wei-yüan hui 土地委員會 (National Land Commission). *Ch'üan-kuo t'u-ti tiao-ch'a pao-kao kang-yao* 全國土地調査報告綱要 (A summary report of the land survey in China). Nanking, 1937.

T'ung-chi yüeh-pao 統計月報 (Statistical monthly), no. 1 (March 1929)—no. 27 (January 1937).

Uchida Tomoo 內田智雄. *Chūgoku nōson no bunke seido* 中國農村の分家制度 (The system of household division in Chinese villages). Tokyo, 1956.

Unryōjō seikoku kabushiki kaisha chōsabu 運糧城精穀株式會社調査部 (Investigation section of the Food Transport's White Rice Co. Ltd.). *Shōwa jūnananendo Kahoku Mōkyō beikoku seisan shukkai gaikyō chōsa* 昭和十七年度華北蒙疆米穀生產出廻概況調査 (Investigation concerning the conditions of rice production and transport in north China and Mongolia in 1942). Tientsin, 1942.

U.S. Consulate General, Tientsin, *Chinese Press Review*.
Tientsin, no. 6: 3 (Feb. 10, 1947), no. 208: 1 (Dec. 22, 1947), no. 209: 1 (Dec. 23, 1947), no. 215: 2 (Jan. 5, 1948), no. 225: 1 (Jan. 19, 1948), no. 229: 1 (Jan. 23, 1948), no. 245: 2 (Feb. 18, 1948);
Peking, no. 260: 1 (Feb. 5, 1947), no. 268: 1 (Feb. 14, 1947), no. 339: 1 (May 9, 1947), no. 518: 3 (Jan. 22, 1948), no. 570: 1 (March 26, 1948), no. 610: 1 (May 12, 1948), no. 641: 1–2 (June 18, 1948), no. 658: 1–2 (July 9, 1948).

Wagner, Wilhelm. *Chūgoku nōsho* 中國農書 (A study of Chinese agriculture). Tr. Takayama Yōkichi 高山洋吉. 2 vols. Tokyo, 1942.

Wang Chih-hsin 王志信. "Ho-pei sheng chih pao-shui chih-tu" 河北省之包稅制度 (The miscellaneous excise tax system of Hopei province) in *Cheng-chih ching-chi hsüeh-pao*, 3.3: 530–589 (1935).

Wang Ching-t'ing 王敬亭. "Nōgyō keieiteki soshiki oyobi rōdōryoku no bumpai ni tsuite" 農業經營的組織及び勞働力の分配に就いて (The allocation of labor power and the organization of agricultural management) in *Nōgyō keizai kenkyū*, 19.2: 49–80 (September 1943).

Wang Tien-chün 王殿俊. "Chin shih-nien lai Hsi-an nung-ch'an-p'in chia-ko chih yen-chiu" 近十年來西安農產品價格之硏究 (A study of agricultural commodity prices in Sian over the last years) in *Chung-nung yüeh-k'an*, 8.10: 41–50 (October 1947).

Wang Yin-sheng 王寅生. *Chung-kuo pei-pu ti ping-ch'ai yü nung-min* 中國北部的兵差與農民 (Military levies and farmers in north China). Shanghai, 1931.

Wang Yin-yüan 汪蔭元. "Ssu-ch'uan chan-shih nung-kung wen-t'i" 四川戰時農工問題 (The problem of the agricultural laborer in wartime Szechwan) in *Ssu-ch'uan ching-chi li-k'an* 四川經濟季刋 (The Szechwan economic quarterly), 2.3: 105–109 (July 1945).

Watanabe Yasumasa 渡邊安政. "Tenshin no gingō 天津の銀號 (The *yin-hao* or native banks of Tientsin) in *Mantetsu chōsa geppō*, 22.3: 149–179 (March 1942), 22.4: 143–163 (April 1942).

White, Theodore H., and A. Jacoby. *Thunder out of China*. New York, 1946.

Wickizer, V. D., and M. K. Bennett. *The Rice Economy of Monsoon Asia*. Stanford University, 1941.

Williamson, Alexander. *Journeys in North China, Manchuria, and Eastern Mongolia With Some Account of Corea.* 2 vols. London, 1870.

Winfield, Gerald F. *China: The Land and the People.* New York, 1948.

Wu Chih-i 吳知義. "Shan-tung sheng mien-hua chih sheng-ch'an yü yün-hsiao" 山東省棉花之生產與運銷 (Production and circulation of cotton in Shantung province) in *Cheng-chih ching-chi hsüeh-pao*, 5.1: 1–90 (October 1936).

Wu Pao-san 巫寶三. *Chung-kuo liang-shih tui-wai mao-i ch'i ti-wei ch'ü-shih chi pien-ch'ien chih yüan-yin* 中国糧食對外貿易其地位趨勢及變遷之原因 (The causes of fluctuations and trends of food grains in China's foreign trade). Shanghai, 1934.

Yagi Yoshinosuke 八木芳之助. "Shina nōson no hōzei seido ni tsuite" 支那農村の包税制度に就いて (On the tax-farming system in the Chinese village) in *Tōa keizai ronsō*, 1.1: 1–25 (February 1941).

——— "Hoku-Shi no kosaku seido" 北支の小作制度 (The tenant system of north China) in *Tōa keizai ronsō*, 2.3: 63–84 (September 1942).

——— and Yamazaki Takeo 山崎武雄 for the Tōa kenkyūjo, *Keizai ni kansuru Shina kankō chōsa hōkokusho, Hoku-Shi ni okeru tochi shoyū no idō to bumpu narabini tochi no kaikon* 經濟に關する支那慣行調查報告書—北支に於ける土地所有の移動と分布並に土地の開墾 (A report of investigation of economic customs in China, with special attention to the transfer and distribution of land ownership and opening to cultivation of land in north China). Tokyo, 1944.

Yang Lien-sheng. *Money and Credit in China: A Short History.* Cambridge, Mass., 1942.

Yang, Martin C. *A Chinese Village: Taitou, Shantung Province.* New York, 1945.

Yao Shan-yu. "The Chronological and Seasonal Distribution of Floods and Droughts in Chinese History," *Harvard Journal of Asiatic Studies*, 6.3 and 4: 273–312 (February 1942).

——— "The Geographical Distribution of Floods and Droughts in Chinese History, 206 B.C.–A.D. 1911," *The Far Eastern Quarterly*, 2: 4: 357–378 (August 1943).

Yee, Frank Ki Chun. "Police in Modern China," Ph. D. diss., University of California, Berkeley, 1942.

Yeh Ch'ien-chi 葉謙吉. "T'ien-chin mien-hua hsü-ch'iu i chia-ko hsiang-kuan chih yen-chiu" 天津棉花需求—價格相關之研究 (A study of price elasticity of demand for Tientsin cotton) in *Cheng-chih ching-chi hsüeh-pao*, 4.1: 1–33 (1935).

Yen Chung-p'ing 嚴中平. *Chung-kuo chin-tai ching-chi shih t'ung-chi tzu-liao hsüan-chi* 中國近代經濟史統計資料選輯 (Selected materials on the economic history of modern China). Peking, 1935.

Yih Chih-yun. "Agricultural Conditions in China," *Chinese Economic Journal*, 7.3: 972–983 (September 1930).

Yoneda Kenjirō 米田賢次郎. "Seimin yōjutsu to ninen sanmōsaku" 齊民要術と二年三毛作 (The Ch'i-min yao-shu: A guide to agriculture and animal husbandry and the system of three crops in two years) in *Tōyōshi kenkyū*, 16.4: 1–25 (March 1959).

Yoshida Yoshiyuki 吉田美之. "Chintō bōseki rōdō jijō" 青島紡績勞働事情 (Labor conditions in Tsingtao's spinning industries) in *Mantetsu chōsa geppō*, 20.6: 47–88 (June 1940).

Young, John. *The Research Activities of the South Manchurian Railway Company, 1907–1945: A History and Bibliography.* New York, 1965.

Glossary

cha 閘
ch'ang-kung 長工
cheng-shou-ch'u 徵收處
chi-fu ch'i-ti 畿輔旗地
chia 家
chia-huo 傢伙
chi-ku-hui 積穀會
ch'ien 錢
ch'ien-hui 錢會
chih-ti chieh-ch'ien 指地借錢
ching-cheng-ch'u 經徵處
ch'ing-miao-hui 青苗會
ch'u-tien-chu 出典主
chuang-chang 莊長
ch'un-chieh ch'iu-huan 春借秋還
Chung-kuo yin-hang 中國銀行
chung-ti 中地

En 恩
erh-pa fen-tzu 二八份子

fen 分
fen-chia 分家
fen-chü 分居
fen-chung 分種
fen-i 分益
fen-so 分所
fen-tan 分單

ho-chü 合具
ho-lao 河老
ho-t'ou 河頭
Hou hsia chai 後夏寨
hsiang 鄉
hsia-ti 下地
hsün 旬
hu-chang 戶長
hu-fang 戶房
hung-ch'i 紅契
hung-ch'iang-hui 紅槍會
hung-pu 紅簿
huo-chan 貨棧
huo-chung 夥種
huo-chung 伙種
huo-mai 伙買

i-p'o 義坡

k'ai-yeh-tzu 開葉子
k'an-ch'ing 看青
k'an-p'o 看坡
kuan-mow 官畝
kuei 櫃
kung 弓
kuo-ko 過割
kuo-po 過撥

liang-fang 糧房
Li-ch'eng 歷城
li-shu 里書
lien-chuang-hui 聯莊會
lien-pao 聯保
lin 隣
Ling shui kou 冷水溝
Luan-ch'eng 欒城
lu 閭

mi-chuang 米莊
min-sheng 民生
mow 畝

Nung-cheng ch'üan-shu 農政全書

p'ai 牌
p'ai-chang 牌長
pai-ch'i 白契
pang-mang 幫忙
pao-cheng 保正
pao-chia 保家
pao-chung-jen 保中人
pao-chung-ti 保種地
pao-shui 包稅
ping-ch'ai 兵差
pu-fan 布販
pu-t'an 布攤
pu-tien 布店

Sha-ching 沙井
shang-ti 上地
shao-chung-ti 捎種地
shao-nien-t'uan 少年團
she-shu 社書
sheng 升
shih 石
shih-ch'i 實契
shou-shih 首事
shu-chi 書記
shui-ch'i 稅契
Shun-i 順義
ssu-fang-ti 私放地
Szu pei ch'ai 寺北柴

ta-fen-tzu 大份子
ta-huo-mai 搭伙買
ta-keng 打更
t'an-k'uan 攤款
tang-ti 當地
ta-t'ao 搭套
tao 道
ti-fang 地方
ti-pao 地保
t'ien-fu cheng-shu ch'u 田賦徵收處
tien 典
tien-ch'i 典契
tien-chu 典主
tien-fang 典房
tien-ti 典地
tou 斗
tou-tien 斗店
ts'ao-ch'i 草契
tsu-ti 租地
tsu-ying-ti 租營地
tsung-fang 總房
t'u-tsai-shui 屠宰稅
tuan-kung 短工
t'un 屯
tung-shih 董事
tzu-wei-t'uan 自衞團

wu-na ting-e 物納定額

ya-hang 牙行
ya-tsa-shui 牙雜稅
yang-lao-ti 養老地
ying-yeh-shui 營業稅
Yüan 元

Index

(For cross-references to individual villages see Hou hsia chai, Ling shui kou, Sha-ching, Ssu pei chai.)

Harvard East Asian Series

1. *China's Early Industrialization: Sheng Hsuan-huai (1844–1916) and Mandarin Enterprise.* By Albert Feuerwerker.
2. *Intellectual Trends in the Ch'ing Period.* By Liang Ch'i-ch'ao. Translated by Immanuel C. Y. Hsü.
3. *Reform in Sung China: Wang An-shih (1021–1086) and His New Policies.* By James T. C. Liu.
4. *Studies on the Population of China, 1368–1953.* By Ping-ti Ho.
5. *China's Entrance into the Family of Nations: The Diplomatic Phase, 1858–1880.* By Immanuel C. Y. Hsü.
6. *The May Fourth Movement: Intellectual Revolution in Modern China.* By Chow Tse-tsung.
7. *Ch'ing Administrative Terms: A Translation of the Terminology of the Six Boards with Explanatory Notes.* Translated and edited by E-tu Zen Sun.
8. *Anglo-American Steamship Rivalry in China, 1862–1874.* By Kwang-Ching Liu.
9. *Local Government in China under the Ch'ing.* By T'ung-tsu Ch'ü.
10. *Communist China, 1955–1959: Policy Documents with Analysis.* With a foreword by Robert R. Bowie and John K. Fairbank. (Prepared at Harvard University under the joint auspices of the Center for International Affairs and the East Asian Research Center.)
11. *China and Christianity: The Missionary Movement and the Growth of Chinese Antiforeignism, 1860–1870.* By Paul A. Cohen.
12. *China and the Helping Hand, 1937–1945.* By Arthur N. Young.
13. *Research Guide to the May Fourth Movement: Intellectual Revolution in Modern China, 1915–1924.* By Chow Tse-tsung.
14. *The United States and the Far Eastern Crises of 1933–1938: From the Manchurian Incident through the Initial Stage of the Undeclared Sino-Japanese War.* By Dorothy Borg.
15. *China and the West, 1858–1861: The Origins of the Tsungli Yamen.* By Masataka Banno.
16. *In Search of Wealth and Power: Yen Fu and the West.* By Benjamin Schwartz.
17. *The Origins of Entrepreneurship in Meiji Japan.* By Johannes Hirschmeier, S.V.D.
18. *Commissioner Lin and the Opium War.* By Hsin-pao Chang.
19. *Money and Monetary Policy in China, 1845–1895.* By Frank H. H. King.
20. *China's Wartime Finance and Inflation, 1937–1945.* By Arthur N. Young.
21. *Foreign Investment and Economic Development in China, 1840–1937.* By Chi-ming Hou.
22. *After Imperialism: The Search for a New Order in the Far East, 1921–1931.* By Akira Iriye.
23. *Foundations of Constitutional Government in Modern Japan, 1868–1900.* By George Akita.
24. *Political Thought in Early Meiji Japan, 1868–1889.* By Joseph Pittau, S.J.
25. *China's Struggle for Naval Development, 1839–1895.* By John L. Rawlinson.
26. *The Practice of Buddhism in China, 1900–1950.* By Holmes Welch.
27. *Li Ta-chao and the Origins of Chinese Marxism.* By Maurice Meisner.

28. *Pa Chin and His Writings: Chinese Youth Between the Two Revolutions.* By Olga Lang.
29. *Literary Dissent in Communist China.* By Merle Goldman.
30. *Politics in the Tokugawa Bakufu, 1600–1843.* By Conrad Totman.
31. *Hara Kei in the Politics of Compromise, 1905–1915.* By Tetsuo Najita.
32. *The Chinese World Order: Traditional China's Foreign Relations.* Edited by John K. Fairbank.
33. *The Buddhist Revival in China.* By Holmes Welch.
34. *Traditional Medicine in Modern China: Science, Nationalism, and the Tensions of Cultural Change.* By Ralph C. Croizier.
35. *Party Rivalry and Political Change in Taishō Japan.* By Peter Duus.
36. *The Rhetoric of Empire: American China Policy, 1895–1901.* By Marilyn B. Young.
37. *Radical Nationalist in Japan: Kita Ikki, 1883–1937.* By George M. Wilson.
38. *While China Faced West: American Reformers in Nationalist China, 1928–1937.* By James C. Thomson Jr.
39. *The Failure of Freedom: A Portrait of Modern Japanese Intellectuals.* By Tatsuo Arima.
40. *Asian Ideas of East and West: Tagore and His Critics in Japan, China, and India.* By Stephen N. Hay.
41. *Canton under Communism: Programs and Politics in a Provincial Capital, 1949–1968.* By Ezra F. Vogel.
42. *Ting Wen-chiang: Science and China's New Culture.* By Charlotte Furth.
43. *The Manchurian Frontier in Ch'ing History.* By Robert H. G. Lee.
44. *Motoori Norinaga, 1730–1801.* By Shigeru Matsumoto.
45. *The Comprador in Nineteenth Century China: Bridge between East and West.* By Yen-p'ing Hao.
46. *Hu Shih and the Chinese Renaissance: Liberalism in the Chinese Revolution, 1917–1937.* By Jerome B. Grieder.
47. *The Chinese Peasant Economy: Agricultural Development in Hopei and Shantung, 1890–1949.* By Ramon H. Myers.